LIFE AND DEATH IN A ROMAN C

Excavation of a Roman cemetery with a mass grave
London Road, Gloucester

By *Andrew Simmonds, Nicholas Márquez-Grant and Louise Loe*

with contributions by

Paul Booth, Angela Boyle, Carolyn Chenery, Hilary Cool, Jonny Geber, Tim Haines, Kevin Hayward, Martin Henig, Leif Isaksen, Rebecca Nicholson, Cynthia Poole, Kelly Powell, Ruth Shaffrey, Danielle Schreve, Mike Simms, Alex Smith, Jane Timby, Roger Tomlin, Annsofie Witkin and Fay Worley

Illustrations by

Frances Chaloner, Markus Dylewski, Anna Komas, Sarah Lucas, Lucy Martin, Mary Saunders, Georgina Slater and Magdalena Wachnik

Oxford Archaeology Monograph No. 6
2008

The publication of this volume has been generously funded by McCarthy and Stone (Developments) Ltd.

Designed by Oxford Archaeology Graphics Office

Edited by Alex Smith

This book is part of a series of monographs from Oxford Archaeology which can be bought from all good bookshops and Internet Bookshops. For more information visit thehumanjourney.net

Figures 1.1, 1.3, 1.5, 6.1 are reproduced from the Ordnance Survey on behalf of the controller of Her Majesty's Stationery Office, © Crown Copyright, AL 100005569

ISBN 978-0-904220-49-0

Typeset and printed in Europe by the Alden Group, Oxfordshire

Contents

Contents

List of Figures

List of Plates

CHAPTER 6

APPENDICES

List of Tables

Summary

Between August 2004 and January 2006 Oxford Archaeology undertook a programme of archaeological excavation and watching brief in advance of construction of sheltered apartments on a site formerly occupied by a disused service station at 120–122 London Road, Gloucester (NGR SO 843 189). These investigations, commissioned by CgMs Consulting on behalf of McCarthy and Stone (Developments) Ltd, recorded burials forming part of the Wotton Roman cemetery, including a rare mass grave, along with an assemblage of Pleistocene vertebrate remains (detailed in Appendix 6).

The part of the Roman cemetery within the area of the excavation comprised the remains of at least ten individuals recovered from nine cremation burials and 64 inhumation graves. The cemetery was established during the Neronian period as the burial ground for the fortress at nearby Kingsholm, and subsequently became one of the main cemeteries of the *colonia* that was established at Gloucester following the departure of the military. Four crouched burials dating from the late 1st–early 2nd century are interpreted as being the remains of members of the native population who had integrated into the community at the *colonia*. Inhumation superseded cremation as the dominant funerary rite during the 2nd century, after which no further cremation burials were made. The cemetery continued to be used until some time in the 4th century.

The evidence for funerary rites is described and the possible beliefs informing them considered. The demographic make-up of the population and evidence for status based on age and sex have also been examined. Strontium and oxygen isotope analysis demonstrated that the population had a range of origins, deriving both from the local area and also from elsewhere in the province of Britannia, as well as a small group probably from the Mediterranean area and two individuals from another, unidentified non-UK source.

The mass grave contained the remains of at least 91 individuals, thrown haphazardly into a pit during the second half of the 2nd century AD. The bodies showed no evidence of violence and are believed to have been the victims of an epidemic. It is tentatively suggested that this may have been the Antonine Plague, an outbreak of smallpox that swept across the Roman Empire between AD 165 and 189.

After the disuse of the cemetery at the end of the Roman period the site appears to have been abandoned, with no further activity being recorded until the area was cultivated during the 11th–15th centuries. Boundary ditches were dug across the site during the 16th–17th centuries, most likely associated with the rebuilding of the adjacent hospital of St Mary Magdalen at this time. These features remained open until they were levelled when the area was developed during the 19th century.

Acknowledgements

Oxford Archaeology would like to thank McCarthy and Stone (Developments) Ltd for funding the excavations and post-excavation programme, and Greg Pugh, Steve Weaver and Rob Bourne of CgMs Consulting for acting as the archaeological consultant. Richard Sermon, Archaeological Officer for Gloucester City Council, also played an important role in facilitating the project.

The various stages of fieldwork were directed by Jonny Geber, Tim Haines, Gerry Thacker, Mike Simms and Annsofie Witkin, and were managed by Angela Boyle. The post-excavation work was managed by Alex Smith. Support was provided by Leigh Allen (finds management), Rebecca Nicholson (environmental management) and Nicky Scott (archives management). Bob Williams (Director of Operations) and Nick Shepherd (Head of Fieldwork) gave valuable management support and advice. The authors are also grateful to the many other OA and non OA staff who worked on the project, both in the field and at the post-excavation stage. In particular we acknowledge the contribution of Peter Hacking to the osteological analysis.

Oxygen and strontium analysis of tooth enamel from a sample of burials was carried out by Carolyn Chenery at the NERC/BGS Isotope Geoscience Laboratory as part of the University of Reading Archaeology Department's AHRC funded project 'A Long Way from Home: Diaspora Communities in Roman Britain'. Caroline Chenery would like to thank Dr. Jane Evans (NIGL/BGS) for providing consultation on strontium interpretation.

Many thanks are due to Dr. John Pearce and Paul Booth for reading and commenting on the text.

Chapter 1   Introduction

This report describes and analyses the results of a programme of archaeological excavation carried out by Oxford Archaeology between August 2004 and January 2006 at 120–122 London Road, Gloucester (Fig. 1.1). These investigations were designed to mitigate the effects of the construction of sheltered apartments on a site formerly occupied by a disused service station, as the site lies within the area of one of the main cemeteries of Roman Gloucester. The work was commissioned by CgMs Consulting on behalf of McCarthy and Stone (Developments) Ltd in accordance with a condition attached to the planning permission for the development by Gloucester City Council.

LOCATION, GEOLOGY AND TOPOGRAPHY

Gloucester lies on the east bank of the River Severn, c 4 km from the foot of the Cotswolds escarpment. The site is situated 1.2 km east of the city centre in the suburb of Wotton, which occupies the north-western end of a gravel ridge formed by the erosion of parts of the terrace gravel and underlying Lias clay by glacial meltwater flowing westward into the Severn from the Cotswolds (Fig. 1.2). The ridge is recorded by the British Geological Survey as part of the fourth (Kidderminster) terrace of the River Severn. It is aligned NW-SE, the ground falling away sharply on the north-eastern side into a small valley containing the Wotton Brook, a minor tributary of the Severn, and rather more gradually to the south-west toward a second tributary, the Twyver, which has been re-aligned and culverted in modern times. The Severn itself has also changed its course since the Roman period, when its eastern branch is believed to have followed the course of the Old Severn, a channel which passed 130 m to the east of the present course and which had disappeared by the 19th century (Rowbotham 1978). Beyond the Twyver the ground rises again onto a gravel hillock formerly occupied by the Roman city, and now by the modern city centre. London Road lies on the line of a Roman road that exited the former north gate of the Roman city and climbed the gentle gradient to Wotton where it joined Ermin Street (Fig. 1.3), the line of which is now represented at this point by Barnwood Road and Denmark Road. The site itself is located on the south side of London Road, c 80 m south-west of this junction, at NGR SO 8432 1893 (Fig. 1.1). It encompassed an area of c 0.17 ha and was generally fairly level at c 23 m OD, although the modern topography was clearly the result of deliberate levelling as the ground level of the site was substantially higher than that of a lane that ran along its western boundary. A depth of up to 1.5 m of post-medieval and modern deposits was recorded during the excavation. At the time of the excavation, the service station that formerly occupied the site had been demolished and the ground remediated. This included the removal of its underground fuel tanks and the back-filling of the resultant pit.

ARCHAEOLOGICAL BACKGROUND

The development of Roman Gloucester

At the time of the Roman invasion in AD 43, Gloucester is believed to have lain within the territory of a tribal group known as the Dobunni. This group has been equated with the otherwise unattested 'Bodunni', whom the Roman historian Dio Cassius records as having surrendered to the invading force following the defeat of the main resistance at an unnamed river believed to have been the Medway (Dio, 60.20). The Dobunnic territory appears to have passed under Roman rule peacefully (or at least with very little disruption visible in the settlement pattern), and it is possible that parts (southern Cotswolds and Upper Thames Valley) lay initially within a locally governed client kingdom (Miles et al. 2007, 385).

The first direct intervention in the Gloucester area was the establishment of a fortress at Kingsholm, beside a former channel of the River Severn in what is now the northern part of the city (Fig. 1.3). Tacitus records that in AD 49 the Twentieth Legion was moved forward from its former base at Colchester to subdue the Silures of south Wales (Annals XII 32), and this is likely to be the context in which the Kingsholm fortress was built. The precise location of the fortress seems to have been selected due to the likely presence here of a native centre of some size and importance, which has only fairly recently been recognised (Hurst 1999b, 119; Timby 1999, 38). The Kingsholm fortress was the destination of the western end of Ermin Street, which extended across southern Britain from Silchester. A branch road extended south-west from this road along the line of the modern London Road toward the Severn near the modern city centre, where a crossing point was presumably located. The proximity of the fortress to this crossing would have provided easy access into Wales and allowed the army to control traffic moving across and along the river, an additional reason for locating it in this area.

The ceramic and numismatic dating evidence indicates that the Kingsholm fortress was abandoned during the 60s, at around the same time as a new fortress was established on the site of the modern city centre (Hurst 1988, 50). Earlier theories that this

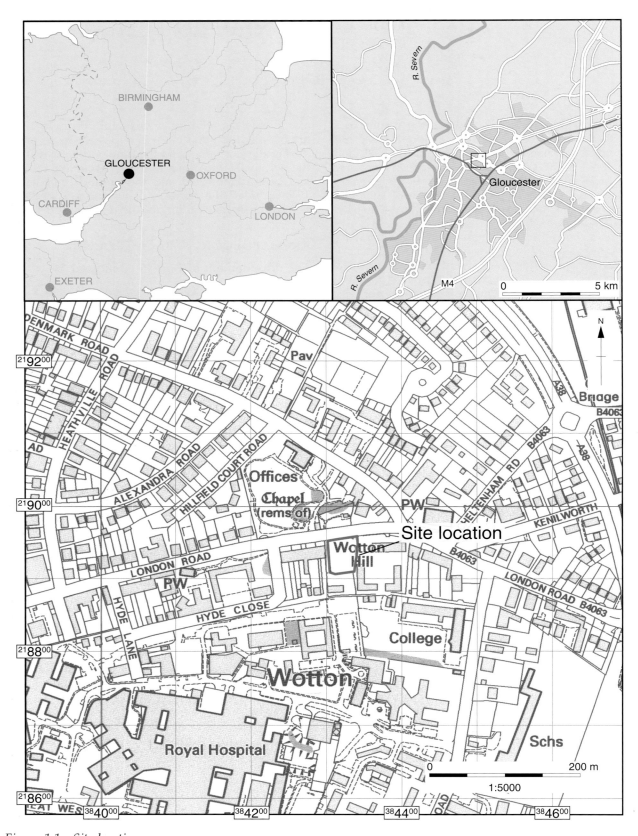

Figure 1.1   Site location map.

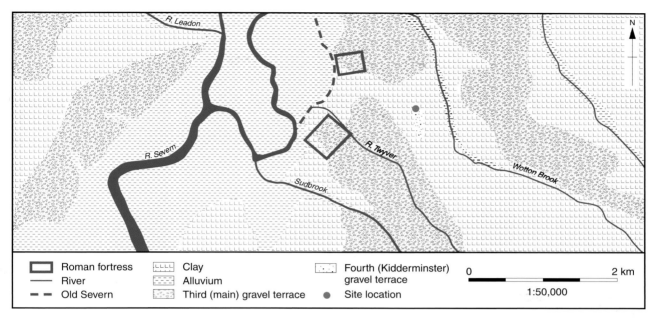

Figure 1.2   The geology and hydrology of the Gloucester area.

relocation was prompted by a need to move to higher ground due to flooding of the original site have been refuted by a closer consideration of the topography of the area and it is now thought more likely that the new location was chosen to give a better command of the crossing over the Severn (Hurst 1985, 2–3). This was a period of frequent alterations to the disposition of the legions in Britain, the details of which are still only poorly understood, and it is uncertain whether the replacement of the Kingsholm fortress with that at the city centre represented a direct relocation or whether there was a period during which the military

was absent from the Gloucester area. The establishment of the city centre fortress formed part of the consolidation of the deployment of the British garrison after the withdrawal from the province of the Fourteenth Legion in AD 66 (Frere 1991a, 81). It has traditionally been supposed (eg Frere 1991a; Webster 1993) that the new Gloucester fortress housed the Second Legion which had moved from Exeter, with the Twentieth having previously moved from Kingsholm to Usk (early 60s?) and then to Wroxeter (*c* AD 66) and Chester (*c* AD 87). However, Hassall (Hassall and Hurst 1999; Hassall 2000, 63) has

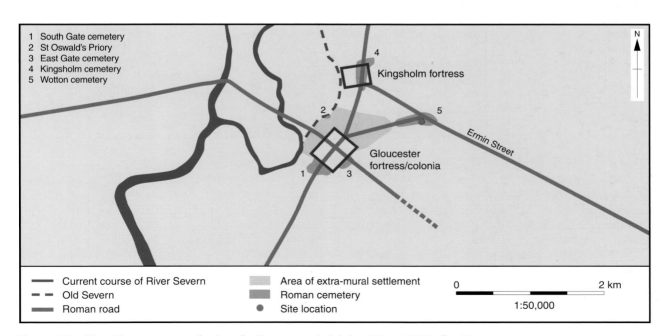

Figure 1.3   The Gloucester area during the Roman period (after Hurst 1999, fig. 5).

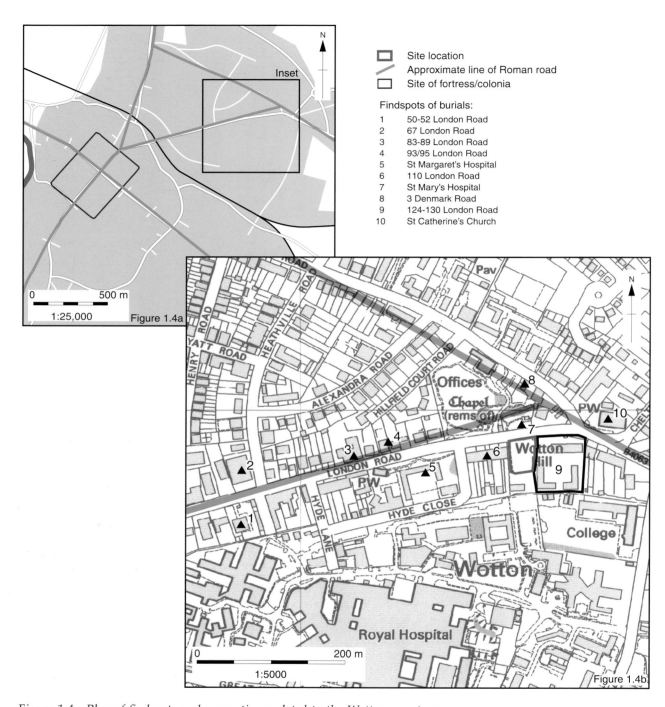

Figure 1.4   Plan of findspots and excavations related to the Wotton cemetery.

suggested that the Second Legion may have moved directly from Exeter to Caerleon, with the Twentieth remaining in Gloucester until *c* AD 75, whereupon it moved to Wroxeter.

The subsequent history of the Gloucester fortress and the date of its conversion into a *colonia*, a settlement for retired soldiers, is still a matter of some debate. A tombstone found at Rome of a soldier of the Sixth Legion who originated from Gloucester indicates that the official name of the *colonia* was *Colonia Nerva* (or *Nerviana*) *Glevensium*

(Wacher 1995, 150), which would suggest that it was founded during the reign of Nerva (AD 96–98). However, an alternative suggestion is that the conversion of the fortress to civilian use is represented by a major programme of rebuilding identified in excavations at a number of locations and dated to shortly after AD 86 (Hurst 1972; 1974). According to this argument the *colonia* would have been founded under Domitian and renamed following his assassination and subsequent *damnatio memoriae* (Hassall and Hurst 1999, 183–4). It is

4

Table 1.1 Known archaeological sites related to the Wotton cemetery (see Fig. 1.4).

No.	Location	Comments	Reference
1	50–52 London Road	Two inhumation burials, sealed by a metalled surface, were found during the digging of service trenches in 1983.	Rawes 1983
2	67 London Road	Disarticulated human remains were found here in 1961.	Heighway 1980, 63
3	83–89 London Road	Two cremation burials and two inhumations were recorded during a watching brief at the street frontage. One of the cremations was contained within an early 2nd century urn.	Sermon 2003, 55
4	93/95 London Road	A large number of cremations in cinerary urns were found in 1876 on the site of a 19th century villa in the vicinity of the current 93/95 London Road. Most of the cinerary urns from these burials have been lost, but the three that remain are now in Gloucester City Museum.	Fullbrook-Leggatt 1933, 87
5	St Margaret's Hospital	Cremation burials contained in glass and ceramic vessels placed in stone cists were found between 1861 and 1864. A watching brief undertaken during the digging of service trenches in 1976 recorded five cremation burials of late 1st – 2nd century date fringing an extensive metalled surface, and six inhumations associated with a wall revetting an area of raised ground that may have been part of a mausoleum. A second watching brief in 1992 uncovered a further seven inhumations, two cremation burials, part of a metalled surface and a stone structure that may be a second mausoleum.	Heighway 1980, 63–4; Rawes 1993, 223–4
6	110 London Road	A group of three inhumations were discovered in 1886 during building work. A further burial was recorded in a watching brief in 1998.	Heighway 1980, 63; Rawes and Wills 1998
7	St Mary's Hospital	Burials were found in 1856 in the graveyard of the leper hospital of St Mary Magdalen	Fullbrook-Leggatt 1933, 88
8	3 Denmark Road	A single adult inhumation was found during building work in 1987. Subsequently, a group of eight inhumations, six cremation burials of 2nd century date, and the stone footing of a possible funerary monument were recorded during a watching brief undertaken on the digging of foundations and service trenches in 1991.	Atkins and Garrod 1988, 216; Rawes 1992, 221
9	124–130 London Road	During the 19th century a grave containing a flanged bowl and coins issued by the emperor Gratian (AD 367–83) was found at 124 London Road. An archaeological evaluation undertaken in 1993 recorded 17 inhumations and a subsequent watching brief to the east of the evaluation area found a further four inhumations. In 1996 four inhumation burials with coffins were recorded during realignment of a sewer on the street frontage. During 2002 an archaeological excavation in advance of redevelopment of the site uncovered a further 39 inhumations and 19 cremations.	Heighway 1980, 63; Gloucester Archaeology 1993; Sermon 1996; Foundations Archaeology 2003
10	St. Catherine's Church, London Road	A cremation within a stone cist was found during the building of the church in 1912. A watching brief here undertaken during the digging of drainage trenches in 1999 recorded a late 1st century cremation burial, the inhumation of a child, a gravel surface, and a possible monument foundation.	Heighway 1980, 64; Wills 2000, 226

possible that the fortress may have been abandoned during the 70s, when the Second Legion moved to Caerleon, and stood empty for some time before being given over to civilian use.

Whichever date is accepted for the foundation of the *colonia*, it is certain that the site, complete with its defensive circuit, had passed wholesale into civilian hands before the end of the 1st century. A large forum was established on the former site of the legionary *principia*, presumably during the reign of Trajan (AD 98–117), and the areas of former barracks were given over to civilian housing (Wacher 1995, 141).

The traditional view of the subsequent development of the *colonia* has been one of relative failure. This opinion was firmly established by Richmond, based on the belief that the town failed to grow beyond the limits of the former fortress defences (Richmond 1946, 83), and has been maintained by unfavourable comparisons of Gloucester with the neighbouring city at Cirencester (eg Wacher 1995, 165). Recent research (eg Hurst 2005), however, has indicated that Gloucester possessed sizeable areas of extramural settlement, particularly to the north and north-east and to the west between the fortress and the river Severn (Hurst 1999b, 120–1), giving it a total area on a par with more successful *civitas* capitals such as Silchester and Verulamium. Clarke (1996) meanwhile has argued from a rank-order analysis of settlements in the area that Gloucester was better integrated with its hinterland than was Cirencester, with a well-developed trading infrastructure. Gloucester is not thought to have had a major administrative role, becoming neither a *civitas* nor a provincial capital, although Reece (1999, 77–8) has argued that Gloucester rather than Cirencester may have become capital of the late Roman province of Britannia Prima. Nevertheless the *colonia* is likely to have been an important node in the trading and communications network of the south-western part of Britannia, on account of its location at the meeting point of waterborne traffic arriving from the Bristol Channel and the main land route between south-eastern England and southern Wales.

The cemeteries of Roman Gloucester

Roman law required burials at urban sites to be located beyond the official limits of the city. Most Roman cities were consequently surrounded by a ring of cemeteries, usually located along the main approach roads. At Gloucester cemeteries have been identified along the roads approaching the south and east gates, to the west near the old course of the River Severn at St Oswald's Priory, and beyond the extramural settlement to the north and north-east at Kingsholm and Wotton (Fig. 1.3, Heighway 1980). The cremation cemeteries at Kingsholm and Wotton appear to have been the earliest, having perhaps been originally established to serve the fortress at Kingsholm, while the discovery of potentially early cremations to the south of the defences during the construction of parts of the Dock basin in the 19th century may indicate that the south gate cemetery was also established during the early part of the Roman period (Hurst 1988, 62). The majority of the burials found at Gloucester are inhumations and are thus likely to date to after the 2nd century, when inhumation replaced cremation as the predominant form of burial in the Roman world (Jones 1987, 815–7), although the London Road excavation has demonstrated that earlier inhumations can occur (see Chapter 2). The absence of cremations from the east gate cemetery suggests that it may not have been established until the later part of the Roman

period, and the group of burials excavated at St Oswald's Priory were likewise all inhumations, and are likely to indicate a similarly late date. During the later part of the Roman period the cemeteries at Kingsholm and Wotton expanded southward toward the north gate of the city, possibly due to a contraction in the area of extramural settlement.

The Wotton cemetery

The present site lies within the Wotton cemetery, which is known to have extended for at least 500 m along the road connecting the *colonia* to Ermin Street, between 50–52 London Road and St Catherine's Church at the junction with Denmark Road. The majority of the cremations known from this cemetery are concentrated at the east end, suggesting that it began as a cremation cemetery located at the junction of the two roads during the 1st century AD. Inhumations extending along the road to the south-west attest to the subsequent expansion of the cemetery toward the city during the later Roman period.

Much of what is known about the cemetery derives from individual finds of burials known from observations made during the development of the area during the 19th century, and from small scale investigations of more recent date (Fig. 1.4 and Table 1.1). The first recorded evidence for the cemetery was the discovery in 1827 of two military tombstones (Fullbrook-Leggatt 1933, 89). One of these, now lost, was dedicated to a soldier of Twentieth Legion (RIB 122) and is one of the main pieces of material evidence associating that legion with the Gloucester area. The other tombstone (RIB 121) commemorates a cavalryman of the Sixth Cohort of Thracians. Other antiquarian discoveries include an unspecified number of burials in the graveyard of the church of the Hospital of St Mary Magdalen, on the opposite side of London Road from the site (Fullbrook-Leggatt 1933, 88), and stone cists containing cremated remains in pottery and glass vessels found at St Margaret's Hospital (Heighway 1980, 63–4). A large group of cremation burials was found in 1876 on the site of a 19th century villa in the vicinity of the current 93/95 London Road, but most of the cinerary urns have been lost, with the exception of three now in Gloucester City Museum.

Many of the early observations were not accurately recorded, and Fullbrook-Leggatt (1933, 88–90) records numerous finds which have now been lost, and for which no precise findspot is known. These include an assemblage of 110 urned cremations found on land belonging to a Mr Niblett at Wotton in 1870, and a 'large quantity' of human bone and finds including a brass handle, part of a surgical instrument, coins, tile and pottery found in a field adjoining London Road in 1827.

During the past three decades a number of more controlled archaeological investigations within the area of the cemetery have added further information. Most of these investigations have taken the form of watching briefs during the digging of foundation or service trenches and have consequently uncovered only a small number of burials. A number of observations relating to the Wotton cemetery have been made at 124–130 London Road, adjacent to the current site. The earliest of these was the discovery during the 19th century of a grave containing a flanged bowl and coins issued by the emperor Gratian (AD 367–83). More recently an archaeological evaluation undertaken in 1993 recorded 17 inhumations (Gloucester Archaeology 1993) and a subsequent watching brief to the east of the evaluation area found a further four inhumations, including an infant and a child. In 1996 four inhumation burials with coffins were recorded during realignment of a sewer on the street frontage, all buried on north-south or east-west alignments (Sermon 1996), and during 2002 an archaeological excavation in advance of construction of new buildings and an access road uncovered an additional 39 inhumations and 19 cremations, as well as a number of ditches, pits and postholes (Foundations Archaeology 2003).

The hospital of St Mary Magdalen and post-medieval development of the site

Gloucester appears to have been more or less abandoned as an urban settlement after the Roman period, although it retained some significance as an administrative and religious centre for the Anglo-Saxon kingdom of the Hwicce (Herbert 1988, 2). It was not until the 10th century that the town emerged again as a commercial centre, and became a prosperous manufacturing and market centre during the medieval period. During this time Wotton would have lain some distance from the built up area, and it is for this reason that it was chosen as the location of the leper hospital of St Mary Magdalen, established by Llanthony Priory in the early 12th century. The site of the excavation lay within the grounds of the hospital, the main buildings of which lay a short distance to the east, where a wall footing and associated drain and boundary ditches were found during a recent excavation at 124–130 London Road (Foundations Archaeology 2003). Following the Dissolution the hospital fell into ruins but it was rebuilt during the 17th century, finally being demolished when the area was developed as residential housing in the mid-19th century. The only part of the hospital to survive was the chancel of the church, which is now known as St Mary Magdalene's Chapel and stands in Hillfield Gardens, across the road from the site of the excavation. Arthur Causton's map of 1843 shows that the Victorian development of the area included the construction of a large rectangular building on the site of the excavation. The building, which was presumably a substantial villa similar to others built along London Road during the mid-19th century, was situated in the north-western part of the site, fronting onto London Road and was surrounded by gardens. It was also at this time that

the north-eastern end of London Road was diverted from its original course to run to the south of the Chapel (Spry 1971, 4). During the 20th century the house was replaced by a service station, which was demolished shortly before the excavation took place.

THE EXCAVATION

Previous evaluation of the site

An archaeological field evaluation of the site, comprising the excavation of three trenches, was carried out during 2004 by Gloucester Archaeology Unit (Cook 2004). A sequence of deposits dating from the Roman, medieval and post-medieval periods was found to survive in the southern and eastern parts of the site, including an urned cremation near the southeast corner. The north-western part of the site and the street frontage had been significantly disturbed by the construction of the service station that formerly occupied the site and the digging of a pit for its fuel tanks, destroying any archaeological remains that may have been located in this area.

The stages of excavation

The excavation strategy originally adopted to mitigate the effects of the development consisted of the full excavation of a limited area measuring 6 × 3 m (Fig. 1.5, Area A) and comprising the part of the footprint of the new building that would impact on the rear of the site, where the previous evaluation had indicated that archaeological remains survived intact. The rest of the rear of the property (Fig. 1.5, Area B) lay outside the intended area of impact and any archaeological remains in this area were to be preserved *in situ*. In the area toward the street frontage, where the impact of the construction of the former service station was greatest, a watching brief was to be maintained during ground reduction and the digging of foundation trenches (Fig. 1.5, Area C).

However, following the excavation of Area A during August 2004, ground reduction within Area B exposed a number of burials and consequently it was decided, in consultation with the Gloucester City Archaeologist, that the whole of this area should be subject to full excavation. The excavation of this area was carried out in two phases, running from October 2004 to March 2005 and May to September 2005. During the latter phase of work part of a substantial square pit containing the remains of a large number of individuals was discovered, the larger part of which was subsequently excavated during an additional phase of excavation in November and December 2005.

Excavation methodology

In Area A the post-medieval and modern overburden was removed by a mechanical excavator

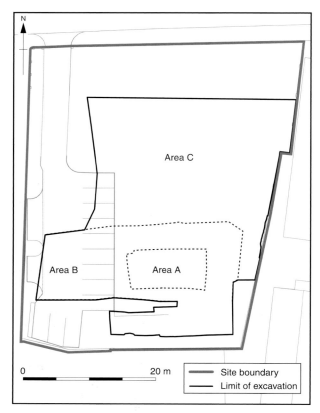

Figure 1.5 Plan of the site showing the phases of excavation.

in the soil. It was therefore necessary to adopt a strategy of excavating the area in spits by hand in order to locate further burials, and consequently it was not possible to establish the height from which grave pits had been cut.

A watching brief was maintained during ground reduction and the digging of foundation trenches in the northern part of the site but only a small number of burials were identified. It is likely that this area had experienced some degree of truncation during the construction of the Victorian villa and 20th century service station that had formerly occupied this part of the site and that this had resulted in the loss of a number of features. In the area toward the London Road frontage the archaeological horizon had been completely removed, and consequently no burials survived here. Similarly no burials were identified in the western part of the site despite this area being subject to careful excavation in spits and detailed cleaning, and this absence is attributed to truncation of the area associated with the lane that bordered the western edge of the site.

Once each inhumation grave had been identified it was fully excavated by hand and recorded in accordance with the recommendations of IFA Technical Paper No. 13 (McKinley and Roberts 1993) and the OA Field Manual (OA 1992). A full graphic and photographic record was made of each burial and any associated artefacts were located three-dimensionally by means of an EDM. In the later phases of work, from October 2004, hand drawing of graves was largely replaced by geo-referenced photography, from which digital plans could be generated.

All cremation deposits were subjected to full recovery for wet sieving and flotation to maximise the retrieval of cremated bone, charred plant remains and small artefacts. The cremation pit, urn and any other contents were planned at a scale of 1:10. The majority of the cremation urns were found to be in a fragmentary condition, but two (1061, 1251) were sufficiently well preserved to be lifted intact with the cremation deposit *in situ* for laboratory excavation by an osteologist. All non-burial discrete features were half-sectioned and planned at a scale of 1:10. Linear features were sampled by excavation of sections regularly spaced along the length of the feature sufficient to characterise it, to establish any stratigraphic relationships with other features, and to retrieve artefactual material.

Location of the archive

The finds, paper records and digital archive are to be deposited at Gloucester City Museum under accession code GLRCM 2004/52.

under archaeological supervision, revealing a medieval soil layer (1025) into which medieval and later features were cut. Following hand excavation of these features the layer was removed by hand to expose a soil layer of Roman date (1020). A number of inhumations and cremations were cut into this layer, as well as a pit containing the fragments of a sculpted tombstone (see Chapter 5). These features were excavated and layer 1020 removed by hand to expose the natural geology beneath, into which further burials were cut.

Across the rest of the site the overburden was removed by machine under watching brief conditions, exposing burials in Area B and resulting in the decision to carry out a full excavation of this area. The exposed surface was cleaned in order to define the archaeological features, and those features that could be identified at this level were excavated. It was found that archaeological features were very difficult to identify due to the similarity of their back-fills to the surrounding geology, and graves and cremations were generally recognised initially only by the presence of coffin nails, skeletal material or grave goods rather than by any visible difference

Chapter 2 Archaeological Description

The total area excavated measured 37 m north-south by 32 m east-west and encompassed an area of 0.1 ha (Fig. 2.1). The northern part of the site, fronting onto London Road, had been completely truncated by the construction of the 19th century villa and 20th century garage that had been sited here, resulting in the loss of any archaeological remains in this area. Similarly no features were identified in the western part of the site, and this is attributed to truncation associated with the lane that ran along this edge of the site. In addition to these areas of significant truncation a number of modern intrusions penetrated into the natural geology and in some instances were dug partly through graves.

GEOLOGY AND PLEISTOCENE FAUNAL REMAINS

The stiff grey Lias clay outcropped along the eastern side of the excavation and sloped down to the west. Across most of the site it was overlain by a layer of orange brown silty gravel that increased in depth westward to a maximum of 0.5 m at the western edge of the excavation.

During the watching brief stage of the investigation poorly preserved faunal remains within the gravel were exposed in a section in the north central part of the site. The section was subsequently reduced by machine to enable the remains to be cleaned, recorded and excavated by hand. Where possible the bones were lifted in blocks of soil for detailed excavation by a Pleistocene specialist (see Schreve Appendix 6). The remains were identified as those of part of a single adult hippopotamus, with additional material from a single individual each of probable bison and elephant. They appeared to lie on the surface of the Lias clay, within the lower part of the gravel, although some of the fragments to the south overlay an area of sub-angular cobbles.

ACTIVITY PRE-DATING THE CEMETERY

A group of plough scars were observed in the eastern part of the site, where the plough had dragged bands of limestone gravel into areas of Lias clay (Fig. 2.1). Parts of at least twelve such plough scars were observed, measuring up to 2.55 m and all lying on the same ENE-WSW orientation. No datable material was recovered from these features, but they were cut by at least one grave (1151) and are likely to represent prehistoric or early Roman cultivation of the area pre-dating the establishment of the cemetery.

THE ROMAN CEMETERY

The excavation revealed part of a cemetery dating from the 1st–4th centuries that contained both cremation and inhumation burials, as well as a mass grave. A buried soil associated with the use of the cemetery was recorded across most of the site, except in the north-western and south-western parts where it had been truncated by medieval ploughing. The soil layer (1020/1106/1440) was 0.15–0.26 m thick and was composed of brownish yellow/orange silty clay, with inclusions of limestone gravel that varied in quantity according to variations in the underlying geology. The similarity of this material to the deposits with which the graves were back-filled made it impossible to establish its stratigraphic relationship with all but a handful of features, which were all dug into the soil layer. These included cremation burial 1767, which was one of the earliest burials, suggesting that this soil layer was the original ground surface into which the graves were dug. The layer yielded an assemblage of pottery spanning the 1st and 2nd centuries, which was presumably introduced into it by disturbance resulting from the use of the cemetery.

The part of the cemetery within the excavation area comprised a total of nine cremation burials and 64 inhumation graves, including three probable graves in which no skeletal remains were present (Fig. 2.1). Three disturbed inhumations for which no grave could be identified were also recorded, resulting in a total of 64 bodies from inhumations (though one was unable to be examined, see Chapter 3). The cremation burials comprised six urned cremations and three deposits of burnt bone placed unaccompanied in shallow pits, and were generally located in the south central part of the excavation. The inhumation graves were more widely, though unevenly, distributed and occurred as both discrete graves and small clusters of intercutting burials.

Ceramic and stratigraphic evidence provided dates for a small number of graves, and radiocarbon determinations were obtained for seven, but the majority could not be ascribed absolute dates. The sequence of the dated graves is discussed in more detail below.

Pre-Flavian burials

The earliest use of the cemetery comprised three cremation burials (1766, 1767, 1770) and three pits (1149, 1074, 1306) containing pottery dating from the Neronian period (AD 54–68, Fig 2.2). Pit 1149 lay toward the eastern edge of the excavation but the other five features were located close together in the central part of the site, the two urned cremations

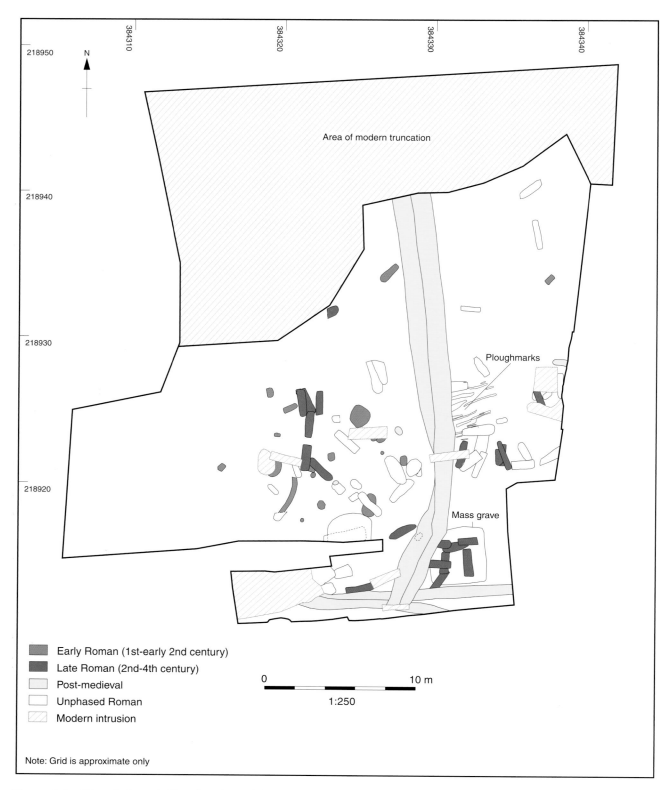

Figure 2.1   Phased plan of all archaeological features.

(1766 and 1767) being only 2.5 m apart. Both these cremation burials had been placed in pits apparently dug for this purpose. In both cases the cremated remains were contained in a grey ware jar. The northern half of cremation burial 1766 had been removed by a modern geotechncal pit, and cremation burial 1767 contained the remains of at least three adults of indeterminate sex and was accompanied by a

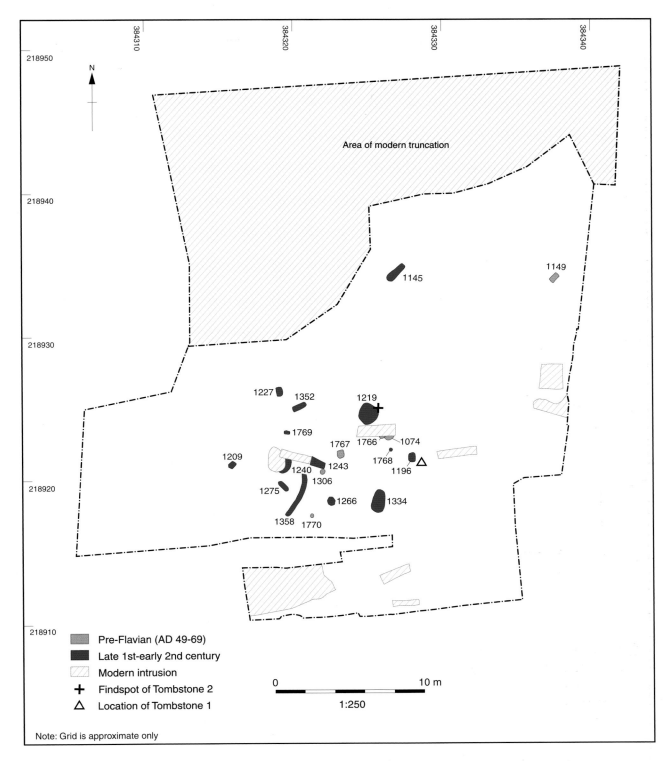

Figure 2.2   The early phase of the cemetery (1st–early 2nd century).

collared rim flagon of Hofheim type (1063) that had toppled onto its side and lay against the eastern side of the cinerary urn. The cremated remains (1324) from un-urned cremation burial 1770 further south yielded a radiocarbon date of 50 BC–AD 70 (OxA-16792 cal 2 sigma).

Pit 1149 (Plate 2.1) was rectangular in plan, measuring 0.6 m x 0.4 m and 0.2 m deep. The upper part of a flagon of Neronian-early Flavian date (1141, see Timby, Chapter 5), which may have been placed deliberately, lay inverted near the centre of the pit, and was accompanied by a small assemblage of

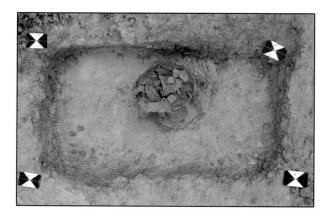

Plate 2.1 Pit 1149, with flagon (1141) placed in an inverted position near its centre.

animal bone including a right forelimb pork joint. A pottery vessel had also been deliberately placed in pit 1306. The pit (Plate 2.2) was circular in plan, measuring 0.5 m in diameter and only 0.1 m deep. A buff ware flagon appeared to have been deliberately placed upright in the bottom of the pit, although only the base of the vessel had survived the subsequent truncation of the feature. Four sherds of a grey ware beaker were also recovered, all the pottery being of Neronian date.

Pit 1074 contained a handful of sherds of 1st century pottery and part of a copper alloy pin (sf 11) and was cut by cremation burial 1766. The pit appeared to be roughly circular and measured *c* 0.65 m in diameter, although its northern half had been removed by the same test pit that had truncated the cremation burial.

Late 1st-early 2nd century burials

A total of four urned cremation burials (1196, 1209, 1227, 1266), at least one (and probably two) un-urned cremation burial (1768, 1769), four crouched inhumations (1145, 1240, 1243, 1334), a possible

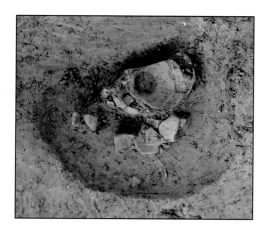

Plate 2.2 Truncated pit 1306, with base of a flagon preserved in situ.

inhumation (1352), and a pit (1196) were dated to the late 1st-early 2nd century (Fig. 2.2).

The cremation burials were located in the same general area of the site as those of the pre-Flavian period. The four urned cremation burials all contained pottery used as cinerary urns or placed as grave goods that was of Flavian-Trajanic date, and burial 1266 was particularly notable for the presence of a gaming set within the cinerary urn (see Cool, Chapter 5). The cremated remains (1187) from burial 1769 produced a radiocarbon determination of AD 60–220 (OxA-16811 cal 2 sigma), and it is likely that cremation burial 1768, which was not dated by radiocarbon, is of similar date.

Inhumation burials 1145, 1243 and 1334 were each accompanied by a vessel of Flavian-Trajanic date. Burial 1334 was placed in a crouched position, burial 1243 was partly crouched, placed on the right side with legs partially flexed, and burial 1145 was a prone burial. The dating of burials 1243 and 1334 were confirmed by radiocarbon determinations from samples of the skeletons, which yielded dates of AD 1–130 (NZA 27005 cal 2 sigma) and AD 50–230 (NZA 27004 cal 2 sigma) respectively. It is likely that two other crouched burials (1219, 1240) that lacked any intrinsic dating evidence also date from this phase.

Pit 1352 (Plate 2.3) contained several items that appeared to have been placed as grave goods and

Plate 2.3 Feature 1352, facing south-west. Two flagons and some animal bone can be seen at the north-eastern end of the pit, with two glass unguent bottles near the north-west edge.

may have been an inhumation grave, although no bone survived. Two flagons and some animal bone had been placed at the north-eastern end of the feature, and a pair of glass unguent bottles lay near its north-western side. An assemblage of seven nails recovered from the grave may be evidence for a wooden box or coffin. A single outlier of this group of nails was located at the north-eastern end of the grave and it is possible that this nail had been disturbed and that the box/coffin occupied the south-western half of the feature, with the other items placed outside it. If this was the case, the box/coffin can have measured no more than 0.6 m x 0.3 m, but this may have been large enough to contain the body of a child.

2nd century or later burials

A few burials within stratigraphic sequences produced radiocarbon dates suggestive of a 2nd/early 3rd century AD date, though later 1st century is also possible (Fig. 2.3). The mass grave is dated to the later 2nd century.

A sample from skeleton 1286, an adult male buried in grave 1288, yielded a radiocarbon determination of AD 60–240 (NZA 27007 cal 2 sigma). This grave was part of a group of three intercutting graves, and was later in this sequence than grave 1243 (see above), which was radiocarbon dated to AD 1–130 (NZA 27005 cal 2 sigma), and earlier than grave 1264, which has been assigned a 3rd–4th century date on the basis of its apparent spatial association with grave 1370. Similarly, a sample from skeleton 1184, which was buried in grave 1228, the earliest in this sequence, produced a radiocarbon determination of AD 70–240 (NZA 27006 cal 2 sigma). The burial was cut by grave 1229 and this was in turn cut by 1230, which produced a late 3rd century coin (see below).

The remains of a young child (1277) aged 2–5 years buried in isolated grave 1275 produced a radiocarbon determination of AD 50–220 (NZA 29423 cal 2 sigma) and so could be either 1st or 2nd/early 3rd century AD in date.

Pottery dating from the 2nd century was recovered from the back-fills of graves 1388, 1403 and 1720, the latter including a fragment of amphora, while a fragment of vessel glass dating from the 2nd–3rd centuries was recovered from grave 1144. Although this material does not provide definite dates for these burials it does enable a *terminus post quem* in the 2nd century to be assigned to each of them.

3rd–4th century burials

A total of five graves contained artefacts dating from the 3rd to 4th century, and a number of further graves with stratigraphic relationships with these burials are also likely to date to this period (Fig. 2.3). Most of these late burials were located within two distinct clusters.

The densest and most complex of the clusters of late burials was a sequence of seven graves dug during the 3rd–4th centuries into the upper part of the back-fill of the mass grave (Fig. 2.4). The earliest of these burials were two graves (1505, 1764) on parallel NE-SW alignments, both of which were truncated by the digging of subsequent graves with the result that only partial skeletons survived in each feature. The burial in grave 1505, an elderly male, was accompanied by a Dorset black burnished ware jar dating from the 3rd–4th century (1489) that provided a *terminus post quem* for the sequence of burials. The north-eastern half of grave 1764 was subsequently truncated by the digging of a grave oriented roughly east-west (1765), which appears to represent the adoption of the practice in this part of the cemetery of aligning graves on more cardinal orientations. Grave 1503 was then dug, cutting slightly into the western end of grave 1765 and also truncating the end of grave 1505. Graves 1501 and 1508, which both lay on the same east-west alignment, were also later than grave 1765, but it is uncertain whether they were contemporary with 1503. If they were, then the final phase of burial in this area is represented by grave 1504, but it is also possible that graves 1501 and 1508 were later than burial 1503 and form part of the final phase with 1504. An eighth grave (1507) was located adjacent to this complex of features and is likely to have been contemporary with it, but where it fitted into the sequence is uncertain as it did not intersect with any of the other graves. The orientation of this grave, however, suggests that it is most likely to be contemporary with either grave 1503 or graves 1501, 1504 and 1508.

The second cluster of 3rd–4th century graves consisted of a group of burials located toward the western edge of the distribution of graves (Fig. 2.3), and included a sequence of intercutting graves (1374, 1369, 1370). Grave 1374 was the earliest grave in this sequence, and contained the burial of an adult of indeterminate sex accompanied by the substantial part of a flared-rim grey ware jar. This grave was cut by two subsequent graves (1369 and 1370) which must therefore also date from this later phase of the cemetery. Graves 1264 and 1353 were located in close proximity to this group and shared a common alignment with grave 1370, possibly indicating that they are contemporary.

Grave 1230 also belongs to this latest phase of burials, as a coin dating from AD 270–95 was recovered from the back-fill. This burial was the latest in a sequence of three graves dug in approximately the same location, albeit with slightly varying orientations (see above).

A single discrete burial was also assigned to the later part of the Roman period. Grave 1362 contained the remains of a young adult of indeterminate sex buried wearing a copper alloy ring (sf 219) and bracelet (sf 216). The ring is of a 3rd–4th century form and the presence of the bracelet also probably indicates a 4th century date for this burial.

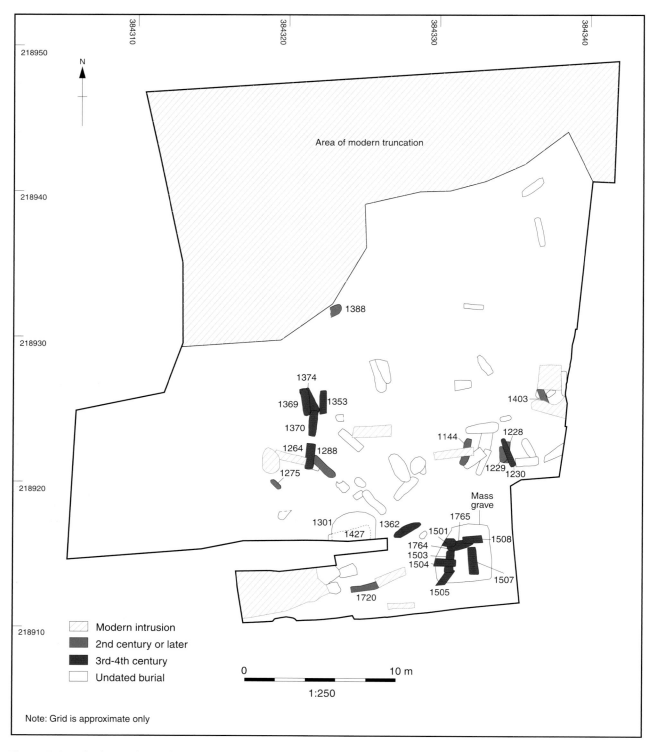

Figure 2.3 The later phase of the cemetery (2nd–4th century).

Mass grave

During the late 2nd or early 3rd century multiple individuals were deposited in a mass grave (1483) in the south-eastern part of the site (Fig. 2.3; Plate 2.4), in an area that does not appear to have previously been used for burials. The grave was roughly square in plan and a little over 3.5 m across, with vertical sides and a depth of *c* 0.85 m. The north-western corner of the grave had been truncated by post-medieval ditch 1055, while a group of burials dating from the later phase of the cemetery had been dug into its back-fill (see above). However, the latter features had only been dug to a relatively shallow depth and did not

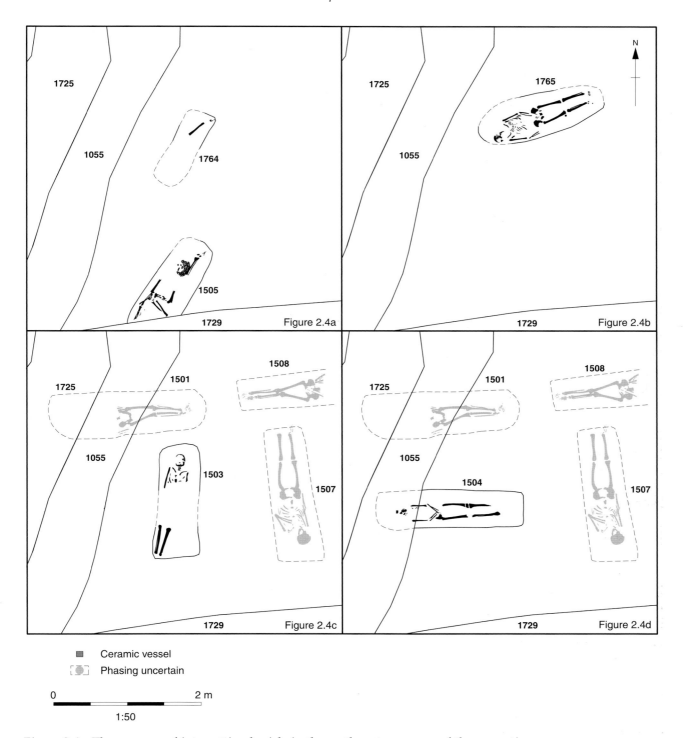

Figure 2.4 The sequence of intercutting burials in the south-eastern corner of the excavation.

penetrate as deep as the mass burial deposit at the base of the grave, although disturbance associated with them has resulted in the introduction of some later pottery into the upper grave fill.

The lower part of the grave contained a deposit of human remains that appeared to have been unceremoniously dumped into it without any degree of care, resulting in a complicated array of entangled skeletal parts (Plates 2.5–2.7). The degree of entanglement certainly suggests that bodies were deposited in a single event rather than individually (see Chapter 6 for full discussion). Skeleton 1558, for example, lay on top of the legs of skeleton 1562 and the skull of skeleton 1564, but the arms of 1558 were beneath the pelvis of 1562 and the left arm of 1564 (Plate 2.8). Such a circumstance would clearly not

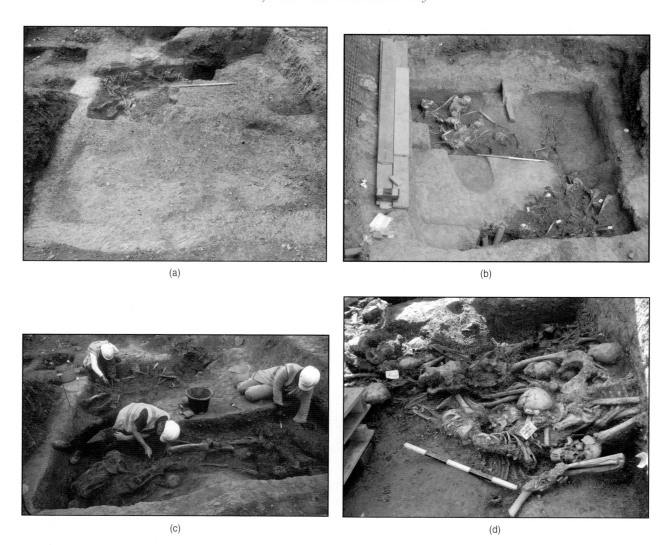

(a)

(b)

(c)

(d)

Plate 2.4a–d   The mass grave. (a) The mass grave as first discovered. (b) General view of the mass grave during excavation. (c) The mass grave under excavation. (d) Detail of the northern part of the mass grave showing its depth and complexity.

Plate 2.5   Skeleton 1520 in mass grave lying in a prone position with the upper body turned slightly to the left and the right arm pinned beneath it.

have arisen had the bodies been deposited one at a time, which would have resulted in a much more clearly stratified deposit, and it suggests bodies were dumped into the pit together, perhaps from a cart or wheelbarrow.

The complexity of the deposit had been exacerbated by the post-depositional movement of elements resulting from the settling of individual bones under the influence of gravity as the soft tissue connecting them and beneath them decomposed, disassociating them from the skeleton to which they belonged (see Chapter 3). In some cases it was clear from the proximity of elements that they had originally been associated, and had presumably been deposited as a complete, articulated corpse (Plate 2.9), but many individual bones or articulating elements could not be confidently associated with a specific skeleton at the time of recovery.

Due to the complexity of the deposit it was not possible to apply normal excavation procedures.

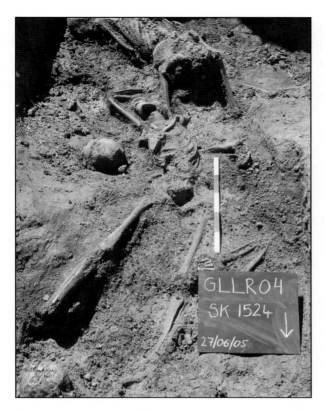

Plate 2.6   Skeleton 1524 in mass grave lying in a supine position with the back arched and twisted to the right, with the right arm thrown back over the head.

Plate 2.7   Skeleton 1564 in mass grave lying on the right side with the head tilted sharply back and the right arm extended behind the body.

Normal practice would be to record and lift complete individual skeletons in their correct stratigraphic sequence, but the nature of the deposit was such that it was often not possible to isolate individual skeletons or to understand the sequence of deposition in the field. It was therefore necessary to adopt a

Skeleton 1558
Skeleton 1564
Skeleton 1562

Plate 2.8   Entangled skeletons 1558, 1562 and 1564 within the mass grave.

more pragmatic approach to the excavation and recording of the deposit: each complete or substantially complete articulated skeleton was allocated a unique skeleton number, prefixed with 'sk', and was recorded on a *pro forma* sheet, including a sketch plan recording its location and posture, and each individual bone or articulating element that could not be associated with a specific skeleton at the time of recording was allocated a small find number, prefixed with 'sf'. Both skeletons and small finds were recorded *in situ* by rectified digital photography, which recorded their exact position so that spatial relationships and associations could be explored during post-excavation analysis. Many of the remains to which skeleton numbers were allocated were partial skeletons and many of those to which small find numbers were allocated were articulated elements, or even complete limbs, and consequently there was a certain amount of subjectivity to the allocation of individual remains to either group, which were not absolute categories. This procedure resulted in the recording of 201 articulated skeletons and 419 elements recorded as small finds, although it was appreciated at the time of recording that the true number of individuals buried in the pit was likely to be smaller than this. As the majority of the remains to which skeleton

Plate 2.9 Skeleton 1553 in mass grave in a prone position with the legs drawn up under the torso. The lumbar vertebrae and pelvis had become disarticulated from the upper part of the body due to settling as the soft tissue decomposed.

numbers were allocated were only partial skeletons it was accepted that in some instances more than one skeleton number may have been allocated to the remains of a single individual, particularly where parts of the skeleton were not recognised as belonging to a single individual due to the entangled nature of the deposit or where they had become disassociated due to post-depositional effects.

There was evidence that at least some of the bodies in the mass grave were clothed at the time of burial (see Cool, Chapter 5). An iron buckle (sf 386) was found beneath the pelvis of skeleton 1544, where it may have fastened a belt. Two fragments of an iron bar (sfs 399, 408) found over the left hip of skeleton 1542 may also be some form of belt equipment. Skeleton 1660 was wearing a pair of shoes or boots with hobnail soles (sfs 676, 677) and four other such items of footwear (sfs 516, 517, 2004, 2018) were recovered from the pit but could not be attributed to specific individuals. Skeleton 1596, a female aged 26–35 years, had a copper alloy bracelet (sf 464) on the right forearm. In addition to these items, the deposit contained three copper alloy rings (sfs 378, 383, 2027), a Wroxeter brooch (sf 406) a copper alloy knee brooch (sf 437), two bone pins (sfs 341, 711) and two unidentified iron objects (sfs 409, 541) that could not be associated with individual skeletons, as well as an

iron penannular brooch (sf 345) that was adhered to a skull (sf 344) but was not necessarily originally associated with that individual.

The remains of a complete chicken and the left hind leg of a sheep or goat also lay among the human remains (Worley, Chapter 5), along with an assemblage of 168 sherds of pottery weighing 1341 g, including the substantially complete remains of at least six south-west black burnished ware jars dating from the late 2nd to 3rd century that provide a *terminus post quem* for the deposit (Timby, Chapter 5). The brooches, bracelets and ring are also types consistent with such a date (Cool, Chapter 5). A radiocarbon determination of AD 70–240 (NZA 27008 cal 2 sigma) was obtained for a sample of bone from skeleton 1630, one of the bodies toward the base of the deposit, but samples from a further three skeletons failed to produce a date due to poor collagen preservation (see below). The pit had been back-filled with a deposit of orange and blue clay that is likely to have been derived from its original excavation.

Other features

The tombstones

Two tombstones were recovered in the course of the excavation, though sadly neither was *in situ* and consequently it was not possible to associate them with specific graves (see Henig and Tomlin, Chapter 5 for full analysis).

Tombstone 1 had been buried in a pit (1003) cut into the soil layer associated with the use of the cemetery (Plate 2.10, Fig. 2.2). The tombstone was of Aalenian Lower Jurassic limestone (see Appendix 5) and survived in three main pieces and a number of smaller fragments. The top and bottom were both incomplete. The tombstone bore an inscription dedicated to a slave boy, 'Martialis, slave of C ..lonus', above which was a recessed panel containing a relief sculpture. The tombstone had clearly been removed from the location at which it had been

Plate 2.10 Tombstone 1 in pit 1003, as initially exposed by machining.

originally set up and so could not be associated with a specific grave. No other material was recovered from the pit that might aid in establishing the date of the disposal of the tombstone, although it is possible that it was buried during the clearing of the site for cultivation during the medieval period.

A second tombstone (Tombstone 2), also of Aalenian Lower Jurassic limestone was uncovered lying face down in the upper surface of the soil layer, *c* 5 m from the first tombstone (Fig. 2.2). This monument was largely complete, albeit in a large number of fragments. It was dedicated to Lucius Octavius Martialis, a soldier of the Twentieth Legion. The lower part of a locally made vessel of Flavianic-Trajanic date (1101) lay crushed beneath the stone, which appears to have toppled over and to have been left where it fell.

Gully 1358 (Fig. 2.2)

Part of a shallow curving gully (1358) recorded toward the western limit of the distribution of graves was dated to the 1st century on the basis of part of the rim of a white ware flask recovered from its fill. The gully was difficult to distinguish as its fill was very similar to the surrounding natural clay, and could be traced for a total length of only 3.4 m from a possible terminus at its southern end. To the north it petered out before reaching a group of later burials, while to the south it was truncated by inhumation grave 1422.

Pit 1301 (Fig. 2.3)

A large circular pit (1301) was recorded in the south-central part of the excavation. It measured *c* 2.9 m in diameter and 0.34 m deep and is likely to have been dug as a quarry pit to extract gravel. Grave 1427 was discovered cut into the natural beneath the base of the pit but it is uncertain which feature was earlier. As the fills were very similar, it was not possible to establish whether the grave had been dug through the fill of the pit or the pit had truncated the upper part of the grave. Two coins dating from the 4th century were recovered from the fill of the pit but it is possible that they are residual and that the feature is later in date.

THE BURIALS

The cremation burials (Fig. 2.5)

Nine cremation burials were identified within the area of the excavation, six of which (1196, 1209, 1227, 1266, 1766, 1767) were placed in ceramic cinerary urns, while three were un-urned (1768, 1769, 1770).

Urned cremation burials

Of the six urned cremation burials, three (1196, 1209, 1227) had been placed in sub-rectangular pits, with dimensions ranging from 0.55 x 0.40 m (1209) to 0.70 x 0.50 m (1196), and one (1767) lay in a square pit 0.45 m wide. The remaining two burials (1266, 1766) were roughly circular in shape, measuring 0.44 m (1766) and 0.60 m (1266) in diameter. All six had been truncated to a greater or lesser degree by the effects of later ploughing, and the northern part of burial 1766 had been removed by a geotechnical investigation pit (Plate 2.11). Only in burials 1266 and possibly 1767 had the cinerary urn and its contents survived intact, although in the latter case the urn was still very fragmented. Burial 1266 comprised a cirucular grave pit (1253) with a grey ware cinerary urn and an ancillary vessel (ring necked flagon), both of which had toppled over presumably during the funeral or back-filling, with the result that they lay below the level to which the feature had been truncated (Plate 2.12). This burial, which contained the cremated remains of two children aged 5–10 years and 10–15 years, was particularly notable for a set of 33 bone and glass gaming counters (sfs 249–252, 256–269, 271–277, 279–286), two bone dice (sfs 253, 254) and a frit melon bead (sf 248), which appeared to have been placed within the urn in a stack against one side. None of these items showed any evidence of having been burnt.

The truncation of the remaining four urned burials had removed the upper parts of the urns, and potentially caused the loss of part of the cremation deposit. Burial 1227 was particularly badly affected, with only the bottom 0.05 m of the feature surviving, along with the base of a flagon that may have been the cinerary urn and a mere 1.5 g of cremated bone. The cinerary urns containing five of the cremations were grey ware jars, four of which were accompanied by ancillary vessels in the form of flagons in oxidised fabrics. Only in burial 1227 was there a variation from this pattern, with an oxidised flagon apparently being used as the cinerary urn, although the disturbance of this feature due to later ploughing was such that it is possible that this was an ancillary vessel and that the cinerary urn had been completely destroyed.

Un-urned cremation burials

The three un-urned cremation burials (1768, 1769, 1770) each comprised a shallow pit in which the cremated remains of a single adult of indeterminate sex had been deposited with no accompanying artefacts. These features had been particularly severely truncated by later ploughing and survived to depths of only 0.03–0.07 m. Burial 1769 comprised a rectangular pit measuring 0.43 m x 0.28 m into which a deposit of charcoal and calcined bone from the pyre had been deposited, while burials 1768 and 1770 had been placed in circular pits measuring *c* 0.25 m in diameter. The deposits in these two burials consisted of re-deposited natural clay containing small quantities of calcined bone and very little charcoal, the latter suggesting that the bone had been picked very carefully out of the pyre debris.

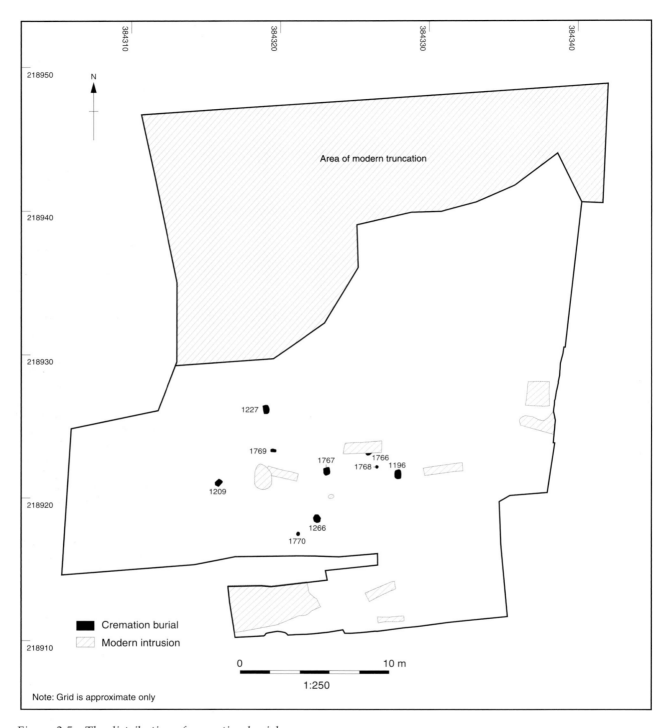

Figure 2.5   The distribution of cremation burials.

The inhumation burials (Fig. 2.6)

The grave pits

Grave pits were generally rectangular or sub-rectangular in plan and of a size to accommodate the body of the deceased. Many burials had been truncated by modern features or the digging of subsequent graves, but those adult graves for which

full dimensions could be measured varied from 1.72–2.17 m in length and 0.38–0.77 m in width. Due to the nature of the excavation, with material being removed in spits until each burial became apparent, it was not possible to establish the level from which each grave was cut and so the depths of the grave pits could not be established. A few smaller graves had been provided for burials of children. These

Plate 2.11   Cremation burial 1766 exposed in section in the side of a modern geo-technical pit. Scale = 0.5 m.

Plate 2.12   Cremation burial 1266, showing cinerary urn and complete ring-necked flagon.

were the same shape as those for adults, but correspondingly smaller. The only graves that varied from this shape were the sub-circular pits dug for crouched burials 1219 and 1234, and a rather oval grave for crouched burial 1344.

Rectangular graves naturally lend themselves to alignment on deliberately chosen orientations. A total of 31 of the 61 rectangular graves with skeletal material present within the area of the excavation had cardinal orientations, divided almost equally between east-west (26.2%) and north-south (24.6%). Of the remainder, 11 (18%) were oriented NE-SW, 10 (16.4%) NW-SE and nine (14.8%) could not be assigned to any of these orientations.

The body

A considerable amount of variation was observed in the details of the laying out of the corpse, although most of the postures were very similar. Of the 51

adult burials that were sufficiently well preserved for the posture to be established 40 were supine, the remainder comprising six prone burials, four crouched burials (Fig. 2.6) and a single individual (1288) who appeared to have been placed in the grave lying on his left side in an extended rather than crouched posture, and to have subsequently slumped somewhat onto his front. Although it is possible that in some instances the position that survived to be recorded in the excavation may have been the result of disturbance during burial or the movement of bones during the course of decomposition, there were no burials in which this was demonstrably the case, and it is assumed that the postures that were recorded preserve the posture chosen for them at the time of burial.

The arrangement of the arms was particularly variable (Plate 2.13). Four principle arrangements were identified: extended beside the body; flexed with the hand lying over the pelvis; bent at a right angle with the hand lying across the stomach; and tightly flexed with the hand on the upper torso or shoulder. A total of 20 adult burials was sufficiently well preserved for the positions of both arms to be established, and among these eight of the 16 possible combinations of arm positions were represented. No single arrangement was dominant, the most frequently encountered being with both hands resting on the pelvis (five instances), both beside the body (four instances) and with the left arm beside the body and the right flexed with the hand lying on the pelvis (four instances). No other combination was represented by more than two examples. Asymmetrical arrangements were slightly more common than symmetrical ones, with 11 instances. Where one arm was placed across the waist or chest the other was usually by the side.

Of the 32 supine burials where both legs survived 22 lay with the legs extended and parallel and eight with the legs together, with two in more irregular positions.

Discrepant burial rites: prone, decapitated and disarticulated burials

The burials of six individuals had been placed face down in a prone position (1143, 1145, 1150, 1230, 1234, 1765). All but one of these burials were distributed in the southern part of the excavation, the only outlier being burial 1145 which was located toward the northern edge of the distribution of burials (Fig. 2.6). The pits dug for these burials did not differ in any way from those containing supine burials. All six were sub-rectangular in shape and the three that had not been truncated by subsequent burials measured 1.88–2.06 m long and 0.41–0.69 m wide. Both sexes were represented, and they ranged in age from an adolescent male (1112, grave 1143) to a mature female (1103, grave 1150). In burial 1145, a flagon had been deposited beside the skull (Plate 2.14). The postures of the bodies themselves varied somewhat. All six appeared to have been placed in

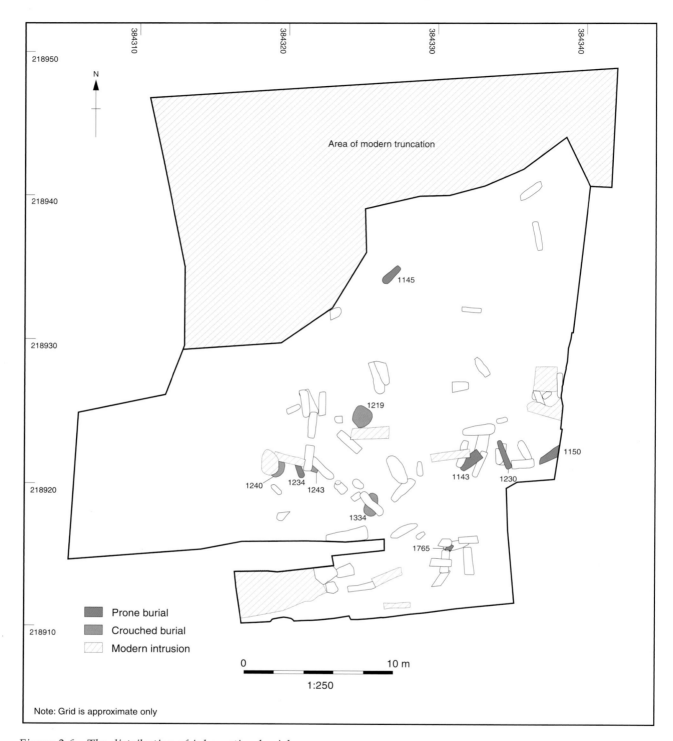

Figure 2.6 The distribution of inhumation burials.

the grave fairly carefully rather than thrown in like the bodies in the mass grave, although body 1127 in grave 1145 was slightly askew. Three burials had arm postures consistent with the range of positions found among the supine burials: in burial 1145 the left arm was straight and the right flexed beneath the chest, in burial 1150 the arms were slightly flexed with the hands beneath the pelvis, and in burial 1230

the left arm was straight beside the body and the right flexed with the hand beneath the pelvis. The bodies in two burials (1143, 1765) were buried with their arms behind their backs, although the lower parts of the arms of the former had been removed by truncation (Plate 2.15). Grave 1234 had been truncated by a modern geotechnical test pit, leaving only the legs, which lay in a prone posture with a

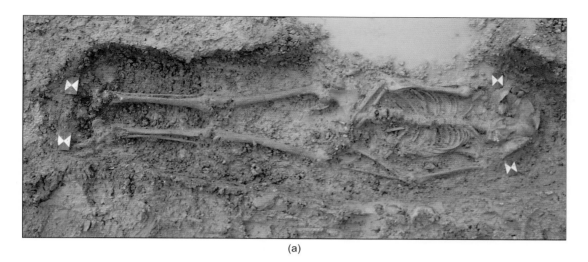

(a)

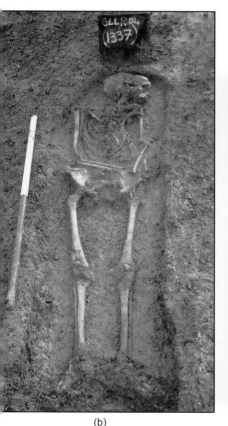

(b)

(c)

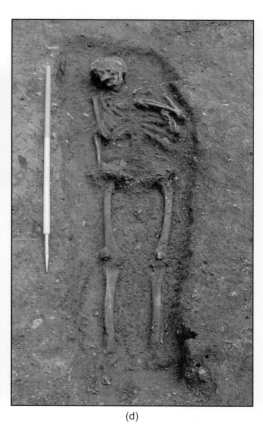

(d)

Plate 2.13a-d   Supine burials, showing some of the variety of arm positions encountered. (a) Skeleton 1165, grave 1167, with both hands resting over the pelvis (b) Skeleton 1337, grave 1353, with left arm lying beside body and right flexed across pelvis (c) Skeleton 1372, grave 1374, with the right arm straight and left flexed across the stomach (d) Skeleton 1496, grave 1507, with right arm straight and left flexed tightly across the chest.

decapitated skull, presumably from the same in-dividual, placed on the back of the knees (Plate 2.16).

Four adult individuals were buried in a crouched position, lying on one side with the arms and knees flexed (Fig. 2.6). These burials comprised the remains of a female aged 18–25 years lying on her right side (1206, grave 1219), and a male aged over 45 years (1238, grave 1240) and two adult individuals of undetermed sex (1211, grave 1243; 1332, grave 1334) lying on their left sides. Burial 1243 was accompa-nied by the upper part of a ring-necked flagon, which had toppled over and lay on the individual's feet, and burial 1334 was accompanied by a grey ware jar, also placed near the feet (Plate 2.17).

Plate 2.14   Prone inhumation burial 1145, with flagon placed by the skull.

Plate 2.15   Prone inhumation burial 1143 with arms positioned behind back.

In addition to the articulated burials, a single deliberate burial of disarticulated remains was found (1757). This comprised a rectangular pit into which the disarticulated bones of an adult male (1089) had been placed, in a tightly packed cluster as though bound or held within an organic container such as a bag or sack that has since decomposed.

Coffins and other containers

No evidence for coffins survived in the form of timber or coffin stains, but groups of nails indicative of the presence of coffins were recorded *in situ* in a total of 19 graves. Smaller numbers of nails that may also indicate the former presence of coffins were recovered from a further 21 burials, but some of these assemblages may comprise material incorporated into the back-fills of graves accidentally and it is thus not possible to establish the exact number of graves that contained coffins. Nevertheless, even if some instances do not represent the remains of coffins, the presence of nails in 40 of the 66 inhumation graves within the area of the excavation indicates that a substantial proportion of the graves contained burials in coffins secured by nails (see Powell, Chapter 5).

The groups of nails from most of the graves were small, and none contained evidence for an upper layer of nails used to secure the lid. This could suggest that some or all of the assemblages represent the remains of biers rather than coffins, or that coffins were buried without lids. However, it could also be explained by a combination of poor survival and the vertical movement of upper nails resulting from the collapse of the coffin under the weight of overburden. The method of excavation, in which soil was removed in spits across the area until evidence for a burial was identified, may also have resulted in upper nails from some graves being lost before the features were recognised. The only coffined burials with grave goods were burial 1374, which was accompanied by a pottery vessel that may have lain within the coffin, and skeleton 1360 in grave 1362, which was wearing a bracelet and ring.

A single burial (1756) had been provided with a stone cist (Plate 2.18). The cist was formed from five slabs of limestone set on edge to form a trapezoidal box (1081) measuring 0.5 m x 0.3 m and 0.2 m. A flat stone at the wider, south-western end of the grave may have been provided for the head to rest on, although this cannot be proven as the only surviving skeletal material was the left femur of a perinatal

Plate 2.16 Skeleton 1232, grave 1234, mostly truncated with just the legs (in prone position) and decapitated skull remaining.

Plate 2.17 Inhumation burial 1334, with crouched skeleton and grey ware jar placed by feet.

individual. No capstones were found, but these may have been removed by subsequent truncation or deliberate robbing for building material.

Grave goods

A total of 17 burials, or 26.6% of the graves within the area of the excavation, were provided with grave goods. The artefacts placed with the burials consisted of ceramic vessels, hobnailed footwear, jewellery and animal remains, although only one burial (1505) was accompanied by more than one item.

Ceramic grave goods

Pottery vessels were placed with six burials (1145, 1243, 1334, 1374, 1352, 1505) including possible burial 1352 which may have been a cenotaph or memorial rather than a grave (see Timby, Chapter 5). This feature contained two vessels, but otherwise no grave contained more than one vessel. The vessels were normally placed near the feet (in burials 1243, 1374, 1505 and 1334). The only exception was prone burial 1145, where the flagon lay beside the head. The black burnished ware jar placed in grave 1505 contained the partial skeleton of a domestic fowl, but no evidence survived for the contents of the vessels in the other burials.

Plate 2.18 Stone cist in inhumation grave 1756.

Footwear

The burials in six graves (1234, 1330, 1344, 1353, 1369, 1764) were recorded as wearing footwear represented by groups of hobnails associated with the feet (see Powell, Chapter 5). Grave 1167 contained a group of hobnails that appear to represent footwear placed at the foot of the grave, and possibly outside the coffin, rather than worn. A further five graves (1283, 1284, 1315, 1508 and 1765) yielded sufficiently large assemblages to indicate the probable presence of footwear, although these were not recorded *in situ* and it is uncertain whether the items were worn or were placed in the grave separately. Variations in the numbers of hobnails recovered from different graves presumably represent different types of footwear. The largest assemblages, comprising 178 hobnails from grave 1344 and 104 hobnails from grave 1369, may represent heavily shod boots, but were not accurately located and may be the remains of more than one pair of shoes. In the burials where it was possible to attribute hobnails to individual feet, the surviving leg of burial 1510 in grave 1764 wore a boot or shoe with 42 hobnails, and in burial 1232 in grave 1234 32 hobnails were associated with the left foot and 37 with the right. Grave 1330 produced a similar total, with 13 hobnails associated with the left foot, 22 with the right foot and 28 unlocated. Four other graves contained between 5 and 11 hobnails, but it is impossible to be certain whether these assemblages represent items of footwear, with the number of hobnails perhaps diminished by truncation or differential preservation, or else accidental inclusions.

Jewellery

Three individuals (1246, 1362, 1505) were buried wearing or accompanied by items of jewellery. Skeleton 1360 in grave 1362 wore a copper alloy bracelet (sf 216) on the left arm. The sex of the individual could not be established from osteological evidence, but the wearing of bracelets is normally associated with female burials (Cool, Chapter 5). This burial also contained a ring or earring (sf 219), although it is uncertain from the excavation records whether this item was worn at the time of burial or simply placed with the corpse. A copper alloy ring (sf 319) was worn on the third or fourth finger of the left hand of the individual buried in grave 1505, and an iron ring (sf 88), minus its intaglio, was recovered

from grave 1246, the burial of a child aged 5–12 years. The latter item was not worn at the time of burial but may have been deliberately placed as a grave good.

Animal remains

In addition to the domestic fowl contained within the jar in burial 1505, parts of similar birds had been placed in burials 1374 and 1759, and some mammal bone had been placed behind the legs of a male aged 18–25 years buried on his left side in grave 1288 (Plate 2.19; see Worley, Chapter 5). The placing of the individual with his legs in a slightly flexed posture may have been deliberate, intended to create a space for placing of the animal. The partial skeleton of a third domestic fowl was recovered from possible cenotaph 1759.

MEDIEVAL AND POST-MEDIEVAL ACTIVITY

The burials of the Roman cemetery were sealed by a soil layer (1025/1047/1052) containing an assemblage of pottery dating from between the 11th and 15th centuries, as well as some residual Romano-British material.

During the early part of the post-medieval period a number of boundary ditches were dug across the area of the excavation and cut through the soil layer (Fig. 2.7). Ditch 1725 defined a boundary extending on a slightly curving north-south orientation through the middle of the site, cutting through graves 1501, 1504 and 1758 and the north-western corner of the mass grave. Pottery from the fill of the ditch indicated that it was probably dug during the 16th–17th centuries, although it also yielded a substantial quantity of residual material of Roman and medieval date. The ditch had a single re-cut (1055) which contained four sherds of earthenware dating from the 17th–19th century.

Boundary ditch 1461 extended on an approximate east-west orientation across the southern edge of the

Plate 2.19   Burial 1286 in grave 1288, a male aged 18-25 buried on his left side with legs tightly flexed. Animal bones had been placed behind the legs.

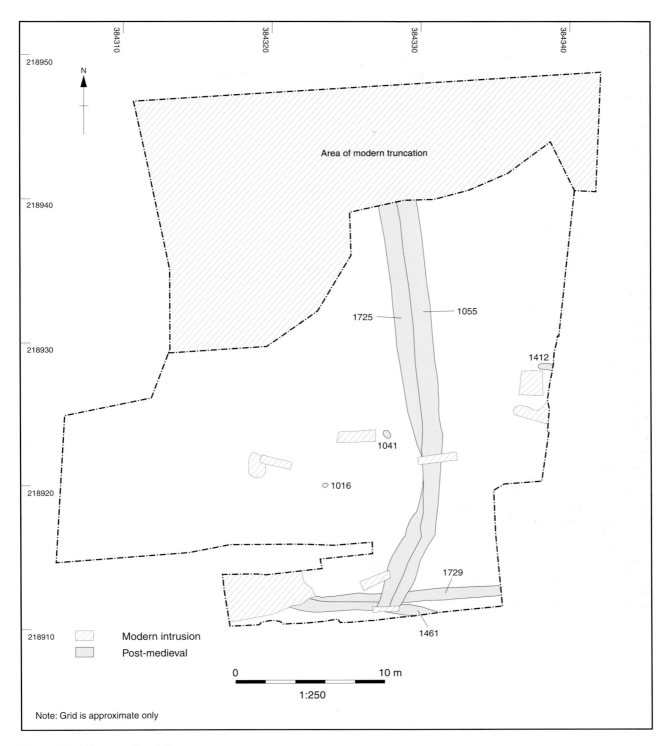

Figure 2.7   Post-medieval features.

site and was subsequently re-cut on a straighter alignment as ditch 1729, which partly truncated graves 1505, 1720 and 1723. No artefactual material was recovered from the earlier phase of the ditch, and the later phase contained only Roman pottery, but its relationship with the burials suggests that it is post-Roman in date. Attempts to clarify the relation-

ship between this boundary and that represented by ditch 1725/1055 were frustrated by the presence of a modern pit at the point where the ditches intersected.

A ditch terminus (1412) extended for 1.0 m into the edge of the excavation from the eastern side. The ditch contained two sherds of 12th–13th century

Table 2.1 Radiocarbon dates from 120–122 London Road, Gloucester.

Lab ID	Sample ID	Grave group	Material	Radiocarbon age (BP)	Calibrated date (95% confidence)
OxA-16792	GLLR04 SK1324 ID10	1770	Cremated human bone	1993 ± 27	50 BC–AD 70
OxA-16811	GLLR04 SK1187 ID11	1769	Cremated human bone	1884 ± 28	AD 60–220
NZA 29423	1277 GLLR04	1275	Left petrous temporal, Occipital crest fragments, parietal fragments	1893 ± 30	AD 50–220
NZA 27004	GLLR04 SK1332	1334	Left femur, mid-shaft	1885 ± 30	AD 50–230
NZA 27005	GLLR04 SK1211	1243	Left femur, proximal shaft	1932 ± 30	AD 1–130
NZA 27006	GLLR04 SK1184	1228	Right femur, mid-shaft	1867 ± 30	AD 70–240
NZA 27007	GLL04 SK1286	1288	Left femur, mid-shaft	1869 ± 30	AD 60–240
NZA 27008	GLLR04 SK 1630	Mass grave	Left femur, shaft fragments	1856 ± 30	AD 70–240

pottery, but as with the medieval pottery recovered from ditch 1729 this may be residual.

Pit 1041 and posthole 1016 both contained small quantities of 16th–17th century pottery, but the function of these apparently isolated features could not be ascertained.

RADIOCARBON DATING

A total of eleven samples was submitted for radiocarbon dating. Human bone from nine burials was submitted to Rafter Radiocarbon Laboratory, New Zealand and two samples of cremated bone were submitted to the Oxford Radiocarbon Accelerator Unit, Oxford University. Three of the samples could not be dated due to the poor preservation of the collagen in the bone, which resulted in no collagen being extracted following the demineralisation and gelatinisation processes.

The samples of human bone were pre-cleaned, crushed and demineralised to obtain collagen, which was gelatinised and combusted to convert the carbon to CO_2. The resultant gas was converted to elemental carbon graphite and the proportion of C^{14} measured using conventional mass spectrometry.

The cremated bone samples were prepared and measured following procedures outlined by Bronk Ramsey *et al.* 2002, Bronk Ramsey *et al.* 2004a and Bronk Ramsey *et al.* 2004b.

The dates of the successful samples are shown in Table 2.1. They are presented as conventional radiocarbon ages (Stuiver and Polach 1977), quoted according to the international standard known as the Trondheim convention (Stuiver and Kra 1986). The calibrations of these results, which relate the radiocarbon measurements directly to the calendrical time scale, were calculated using the atmospheric data published in Reimer *et al.* (2004) and the Oxcal (v3.10) computer program (Bronk Ramsey 1995; 1998; 2001) using the 'INTCAL04' dataset (Reimer *et al.* 2004). The calibrated date ranges cited within the text are those for the 95% confidence level (2 sigma).

Chapter 3   The Human Remains

UNBURNT HUMAN BONE
by Nicholas Márquez-Grant and Louise Loe

Introduction

A total of 63 discrete skeletons and at least 91 commingled skeletons from the 1st to 4th century cemetery were subjected to standard osteological examination. This is in addition to a small quantity of disarticulated bone, recovered from various contexts within the cemetery. A further partial skeleton (1420, grave 1422) was not examined due to its very poor preservation. The remains represented a mixed population of males and females who ranged in age from perinatal to over 45 years. In terms of nutrition, health and lifestyle, biological and pathological indicators suggest that they are broadly similar to other populations that are of similar date and type. These trends did not vary greatly between the discrete inhumations and the commingled inhumations. However, more non-specific infection was indicated among the London Road sample compared to other Romano-British populations and among the discrete skeletons compared to the commingled skeletons.

The assemblage was most notable for the context in which the commingled remains were found, which suggests they had been deposited in a single episode as a result of a catastrophic event. This deposit (the 'mass grave' hereafter) has been dated to around the later 2nd century AD. No such deposits of this date have been osteologically analysed from Britain before. Data for age, sex and pathology were examined to explore what events might have led to the deposition of these individuals in a single grave. In addition, a basic examination of taphonomic changes was also undertaken to explore mode of disposal. A wider discussion of the mass grave can be found in Chapter 6.

Few of the discrete burials could be assigned to finer date ranges other than 1st to 4th centuries AD (Table 3.1). Thus, there has been a limited attempt to examine the remains by phase. Discrete inhumations and the mass grave are reported upon separately here, but compared when relevant.

Table 3.1 Number of discrete burials that could be assigned to finer date ranges.

Date range	Number of inhumations
1st–early 2nd century	4
3rd–4th century	15

Skeletal biology

Osteological methodology

Standard osteological analysis of all remains was undertaken by following the recommendations set out by Brickley and McKinley (2004) and Buikstra and Ubelaker (1994). Human bone identification was facilitated by reference to White and Folkens (1991), Bass (1987), and Scheuer and Black (2000). Tooth identification benefited from White and Folkens (1991) and Hillson (1996b). All data were recorded on a skeletal recording form and entered onto a Microsoft Access database.

Inventory, condition and completeness

A detailed record of bone presence and absence, condition and completeness was made for all remains. Presence or absence was scored according to bone segment. For example, for the long bones, this included the proximal epiphysis, proximal third of the shaft, middle third of the shaft, distal third of the shaft and the distal epiphysis. This allowed calculation of the true prevalence rate (TPR), as based on the number of observable elements or teeth, in addition to the crude prevalence rate (CPR), as based on the number of skeletons, for palaeopathological and dental analyses, described below.

Bone condition was scored by employing the grades set out by McKinley (2004), whereby 0 means excellent and 5 means poor, depending on the level of erosion of the bone surface. The completeness of discrete skeletons was indicated by assigning them to one of the following categories:

1 = >75%
2 = 75–50%
3 = 50–25%
4 = <25%

Estimation of biological age and sex

Subadult age estimation was based primarily on observations relating to the stage of dental development (Moorrees *et al.* 1963; Smith 1991, Ubelaker 1989) and epiphyseal fusion (Scheuer and Black 2000). Diaphyseal long bone lengths were used as the basis for ageing perinates and neonates, as based on the methods developed by Fazekas and Kósa (as adapted in Scheuer and Black 2000) and, for older children, Maresh (1972). Wherever possible, a combination of methods was used to estimate age-at-death for adult individuals, classified here as those over 18 years of age. This involved observations relating to the degeneration of the auricular surface of the pelvis (Buckberry and Chamberlain 2002) and the pubic symphysis (Brooks and Suchey 1990), late fusing epiphyses (Scheuer and Black 2000) and dental attrition (Miles 1962; 2001). General observations relating to cranial suture closure (eg Meindl and Lovejoy 1985) were only used as a complementary aid, since this method is not considered to be very reliable (Cox 2000; Key *et al.* 1994). The spheno-occipital synchondrosis was employed to assign a minimum adult age (Scheuer and Black 2000).

The highly fragmentary nature of the assemblage precluded the application of other methods (for example, observing of sternal rib ends) that may be employed to estimate age. Skeletons were assigned to one of the age categories in Table 3.2.

Sexually dimorphic features of the pelvis and cranium were employed to estimate the sex of skeletons (Buikstra and Ubelaker 1994). Osteometrics were employed as secondary indicators (Brickley and McKinley 2004). Skeletons were assigned to one of the categories listed in Table 3.3. This does not apply to immature (subadult) skeletons for whom there are currently no accepted methods available (ibid.). For the purposes of analysis, all possible females have been treated as females, all possible males have been treated as males, and all ambiguous cases have been categorised as 'sex unknown'. This is unless otherwise stated.

Table 3.2   Age categories employed in this study.

Age category	Age
Fetus	Third month to birth
Perinate	Around the time of birth
Neonate	birth–1 month
Infant	>1 month–2 years
Young child	>2–5 years
Older Child	>5–12 years
Adolescent	13–17 years
Young Adult	18–25 years
Middle Adult	26–35 years
Mature Adult	36–45 years
Older Adult	>45 years
Subadult (age unknown)	<18 years
Adult (age unknown)	>18 years
Unknown	Unknown

Table 3.3   Categories employed in sex determination.

Sex category	Definition
F	Female
F?	Possible female
Ambiguous	Ambiguous traits
M?	Possible male
M	Male
?	Unknown

Metric and non-metric analysis

A standard set of cranial and post-cranial measurements were taken wherever possible, as recommended by Brothwell and Zakrzewski (2004). These were primarily taken as a means of providing data for estimating biological sex and for calculation of stature. Spreading and sliding callipers were used for these measurements and an osteometric board was employed to measure the lengths of the long bones. Where possible, measurements were taken using bones from the left side in keeping with standard osteological practice.

Stature was estimated by taking the maximum lengths of any complete major long bones and applying them to the relevant regression equations devised by Trotter and Gleser (1952; 1958) and modified by Trotter (1970). The maximum length of the femur was used preferentially, as the femur is considered to be the most accurate bone for estimating stature for British populations (Trotter and Gleser 1952; Waldron 1998). If the femur was not available, the tibia was the next bone of choice. The major bones of the upper limb were only used if no lower limb bones were available.

Where appropriate, adult skeletons were examined for non-metric traits by following the guidelines set out by Berry and Berry (1967), Finnegan (1978), Hauser and De Stefano (1989) and Buikstra and Ubelaker (1994). Non-metric traits are minor variants in the skeleton and are of no pathological significance. Early studies of these traits placed great emphasis on examining them to explore relatedness between individuals (Berry and Berry 1967). However, experimental studies have shown that the extent to which they are genetically controlled is far from clear (Mays 1998). Some are believed to be indicative of mechanical or occupational stress (Kennedy 1989; Tyrell 2000). For example, accessory facets on the ilium of the pelvis may be related to weight bearing as a result of carrying heavy loads (Kennedy 1989, 146). Cranial traits may have a stronger genetic component in their manifestation than post-cranial traits (Hauser and De Stefano 1989). However, this was not borne out by a study by Molleson and Cox (1993) on a documented post-medieval assemblage from Spitalfields, London.

Taphonomy

Taphonomy refers here to the processes that are responsible for the organisation, appearance and composition of a burial assemblage from its deposition to recovery and analysis (Haglund and Sorg 1997). It primarily concerns burial position, distribution of elements and alteration to bone surfaces.

Standard taphonomic analysis of the skeletons from the mass grave was undertaken to explore the treatment of the individuals following death, mode of burial and whether burial of the individuals had taken place at once or over several episodes. More specifically, they were examined to explore why disarticulation had occurred, whether the remains were disarticulated prior to their burial (either as a result of natural decomposition or deliberate dismemberment), or whether the disarticulation was a result of natural processes following deposition. These were explored by analysing bone surfaces for ancient modifications and by undertaking element or skeletal part matching exercises, whilst taking into account archaeological context information (see Chapter 2).

Analysis of ancient modifications involved macroscopic observation of bone surfaces for marks that may be indicative of deliberate and/or natural disarticulation. For example, cut marks in areas of muscle attachment and in the region of articulations may indicate deliberate disarticulation (Hurlburt 2000), while animal gnawing and bleaching may suggest exposure (ibid.). All ancient modifications were recorded with reference to published criteria (McKinley 2004; Loe and Cox 2005).

The visual matching of elements or skeletal parts was undertaken based on overall morphology, whilst taking into account articulations, conjoining fragments, biological parameters (eg age and sex), pathology, condition, ancient modifications, bone dimensions and stratigraphic relationships (Adams and Byrd 2006; Duday 2006; Stewart 1979; White 2003; Wright 2003). The three dimensional relationship between elements and/or skeletal parts with each other and articulated skeletons was explored by the application of *Crossbones*, a computer software programme specifically designed for the present analysis (Isaksen *et al.* forthcoming). The background to this methodology is described more fully below.

Time constraints did not allow for anything but minimal examination of the assemblage for modifications and matches. Thus, fragmented elements were not reconstructed. This has precluded the employment of conjoining exercises, except in the most limited manner, as described by White (1992, 67–92). Further, there was no microscopic analysis of bone surfaces to facilitate the identification of ancient modifications. More detailed examination would be beneficial in light of the results of the preliminary observations presented below.

Background to the Crossbones methodology

Crossbones is a software package that was developed to facilitate the visualisation of relationships between the skeletons in the mass grave (Isaksen *et al.* forthcoming). It works in conjunction with the X-Bones survey methodology which creates total station data using ID points that are assigned to locations on each major element of the skeleton. These methods were developed because the 'three-dimensional chaos' (Wright 2003, 1) presented by the mass grave meant that traditional methods, for example, two dimensional plans and photographs, were an inadequate means of recording and interpreting the deposit. During excavation, skeletons and/or bones often had to be removed before a sufficient amount had been excavated to allow full

appreciation of the spatial relationships (from all angles) between them, other than indicated in two dimensional photographs, sketches and plans. Analysis of the deposit from all angles was essential in order to explore whether individuals had been disposed of in a orderly fashion, whether the deposit represented a single event or several burial episodes, and whether complete or incomplete, fully decomposed or partially decomposed bodies had been deposited.

Although several different approaches have been employed to record and analyse previously excavated mass deposits of human remains, these were not considered to be ideal for the present study. Two-dimensional recording was employed during the excavation of mass deposits from the north and south burial chambers at Hazelton North, Somerset, England (Saville 1990). In addition to photography, this involved drawing bones in plan on overlays, assigning each bone a unique number and recording the absolute height of each bone *in situ*, as a vertical control (ibid., 81). This information was used to create a series of plans, in sequence, which were amalgamated to give an overall two dimensional impression of the density of the deposits in plan. Combined with an element matching exercise and creating plots of particular skeletal parts, the distribution of elements, both horizontally and vertically, was analysed to explore patterning. Larger, more recognisable elements were represented naturalistically, while symbols were employed to represent smaller bones.

This approach was time consuming and provided no opportunity for on-site interpretation of the deposit so that excavation strategy could be informed. Some bones were overlain and thus not represented in the overall amalgamated drawing. Further, the drawing, as the authors state, gives a rather false impression of the deposits in that they '…compress the vertical dimension…[and]…record only the bones and not any of the accompanying stones……' Thus, relationships to structures and layers cannot be fully appreciated.

An approach that involved superimposing rectified photographs over surveyed points was employed by Sutherland (2000) to a mass grave of individuals who met their fate at the battle of Towton (1461) in Yorkshire, England. Vertical photographs, copied to scale, were traced, superimposed over the surveyed points of each skeleton and digitally scanned to create a composite of the skeletons superimposed over each other (ibid., 38). This resulted in '… a representation of the original appearance of the grave, as if it were in an x-ray.' (ibid.). This process allowed stratigraphic relationships within the grave to be explored, elements of skeletal parts to be matched, and the calculation of the minimum number of individuals to be clarified (the Harris matrix suggested a different number to that calculated during osteological analysis). Furthermore, hypotheses raised during the excavation could be tested. This included purported evidence for binding based on the posture of one of the skeletons, a hypothesis that was disproved when the rectified images were scrutinised and, combined with osteological analysis, suggested an alternative explanation. Lastly, the images revealed the manner in which the pit had been filled with bodies, in this case by laying (rather than throwing) them down in a way that aimed to fit as many individuals in as possible.

Similar methods that employ digital rectification have been employed elsewhere (for example, see Jacobi *et al.* 2006 on an Iron Age mass grave from Westerhausen, Germany). These provide a more rapid means of representing mass deposits than hand drawing. However, the method is nevertheless still time consuming and relies on good quality photographs taken in a horizontal plane, requirements that may not always be met during some excavations where access is inhibited, time is pressured and the work undertaken in poor weather conditions. Further, the resultant images, which show naturalistic representations of bones superimposed upon one another, are un-necessarily complex for exploring spatial relationships.

A solution to these problems was recently provided by Wright (2003) who produced a three-dimensional program called 'BODROT'. Aimed at mass graves that are encountered in forensic contexts, the program creates three-dimensional stick figures based on survey data taken at certain anatomical landmarks. The figures can be rotated so that they may be viewed from all angles to explore spatial relationships. Primarily designed for a wide audience comprising lawyers, archaeologists, magistrates and courts in general, the program was made freely available and was designed to be very accessible. Unfortunately, the linear representation of bones makes it hard to ascertain bone type or directionality, and the software is not easy to integrate with other data sources.

Crossbones works on the same principle as BODROT: it uses abstraction and schematisation in order to facilitate the visualisation of relationships between skeletons and elements (Isaksen *et al.* forthcoming). However, unlike BODROT, it generates pyramids which allow the direction of the bones, and orientation of the skeletons, to be observed (see Figs 3.2–3 below). When integrated with osteological and archaeological databases skeletons can be sorted visually (by colour or line) according to different variables (for example, sex and location). For the purposes of the present report, data were sorted by colour according to bone type and/or skeletal component (eg cranium, mandible, upper limb or lower limb) and their location within the pit in an attempt to match elements and/or components and analyse spatial relationships between elements and/or components.

Comparative samples

Osteological data were compared with those that have been reported for several Romano-British assemblages, where relevant. This was primarily

undertaken to explore whether the London Road population differed significantly from other Romano-British populations in terms of its health and physical attributes. Selection of the comparative populations was largely determined by availability of data, but prioritised samples from Gloucestershire, as well as a combination of urban and rural populations. The samples that were employed from Gloucestershire were 124–130 London Road (Clough 2003), Cirencester (Wells 1982a and b), and Kingsholm (Roberts and Cox 2003). Other samples are referenced, where appropriate, in the text.

Results

The discrete inhumations

Condition and completeness

Most skeletons were in a very good to fair condition (Table 3.4). This means that most of the assemblage had undergone minimal or moderate surface erosion. However, fragmentation was considerable across all condition categories. Few epiphyses had survived and there were no skulls that had survived completely intact. This has significantly limited metrical analysis and the estimation of age and sex. The fragmentary nature of most pelves has meant that, for the vast majority of skeletons, observations relating to sex have had to rely on traits of the skull and for age, wear patterns on the molar teeth.

Almost half of the skeletons were less than 25% complete (Table 3.5). This is not surprising given the high level of truncation that had occurred across the site caused by the later digging of ditches (five skeletons), modern features (21 skeletons) and Roman graves (nine skeletons).

Biological age and sex

The assemblage comprised 51 adults and nine subadults. Three skeletons were of unknown age, but all had dimensions that indicated that they were probably over 10 years old when they died.

Adult deaths were highest between the ages of 18 and 35 years (Table 3.6; Fig. 3.1). Seven individuals had survived into the older age category, set here as being over the age of 45 years. Subadults comprised

Table 3.4 Condition of the skeletons from the discrete burials.

Condition	Number of skeletons	%
Excellent (grade 0)	0	0
Very good (grade 1)	16	25.3
Good (grade 2)	15	23.8
Fair (grade 3)	20	31.7
Poor (grade 4)	12	19.0
Destroyed (grade 5)	0	0
TOTAL	63	

Table 3.5 Completeness of the skeletons from the discrete burials.

Completeness	Number of skeletons	%
>75% (grade 1)	7	11.1
75–50% (grade 2)	14	22.2
50–25% (grade 3)	12	19.0
<25% (grade 4)	30	47.6
TOTAL	63	

Table 3.6 Age-at-death distribution of the discrete burials.

Age category	Number of skeletons	%
Fetus	0	0
Perinate	1	1.5
Neonate	0	0
Infant	0	0
Young child	2	3.1
Older Child	2	3.1
Adolescent	3	4.7
Subadult (age unknown)	1	1.5
Young adult	12	19.0
Middle Adult	11	17.4
Mature Adult	3	4.7
Older Adult	7	11.1
Adult	18	28.5
Unknown	3	4.7
Total	63	

15% (9/60) of the total aged sample (Table 3.6). Deaths among this group were highest in adolescence, followed by young and old childhood. Subadults, including infants and younger, were under-represented. Only one perinate was identified based on the presence of one right femur (Skeleton 1073).

There were 11 males, 12 possible males, four females and seven possible females (Table 3.7). In addition, one late adolescent skeleton was estimated to have been male (Skeleton 1112), based on cranial and pelvic traits. This skeleton has been included in all calculations involving male skeletons. Sex could not be estimated for 17 skeletons.

There were more females (36.3%; 4/11) below the age of 25 years (young adult age category) compared to males (26%; 6/23). However, more males (21.7%; 5/23) were present than females (9%; 1/11) in the over 45 year age category (Table 3.7). Numbers were too small to observe any pattern in the age and sex distribution of skeletons by phase.

Metrical analysis

As a result of fragmentation, only a limited number of cranial and post-cranial measurements could be taken. Only those relating to stature estimation are presented here. The remainder have been retained for the archive. It was possible to calculate the stature of eight skeletons (Table 3.8), including four females and four males. One of these, Skeleton 1181, dated from the 3rd to 4th centuries AD and was estimated to have been 162 cm (5' 3.1") tall. Four skeletons provided measurements from the most accurate element, the femur. Three skeletons provided measurements from the humerus, the least accurate bone for estimating stature.

The average female height was 160 cm (5' 2.4") and the average male was 169 cm (5' 5.4") (Table 3.9). Although the average male stature is skewed by a height of 156 cm (5' 1.1") for Skeleton 1393, the three remaining males measured 170 cm (5' 5.7") and over.

Non-metric traits

A total of 46 adult individuals provided information on 20 cranial and 18 post-cranial non-metric traits (Tables 3.10 and 3.11). The small sample size has precluded analysing the data by sex or age.

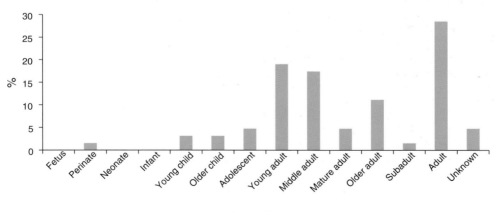

Figure 3.1 Mortality profile (discrete burials).

Table 3.7 Age distribution in the adult sample (N=51) according to biological sex.

Age category	Female	?Female	Unknown	?Male	Male	% Females (n)	% Males (n)
Young adult	0	4	2	5	1	7.8 (4)	11.7 (6)
Middle adult	2	2	2	4	1	7.8 (4)	9.8 (5)
Mature adult	1	0	1	1	0	1.9 (1)	1.9 (1)
Older adult	0	1	1	1	4	1.9 (1)	9.8 (5)
Adult	1	0	11	1	5	1.9 (1)	11.7 (6)
Total	4	7	17	12	11	21.5 (11)	45.0 (23)

Table 3.8 Bones from the discrete burial assemblage employed in the computation of stature*.

Skeleton	Sex	Element employed in Stature calculation	Side	Maximum Length	Stature (Trotter 1970)	Feet/inches
1103	F	Femur	L	41.3 cm	156 cm ± 3.72 cm	5′ 1″
1165	F	Humerus	R	31.4 cm	163 cm ± 4.45 cm	5′ 3″
1181	F	Femur	L	43.9 cm	162 cm ± 3.72	5′ 3″
1390	F	Femur	L	43.5 cm	161 cm ± 3.72	5′ 2″
1109	M	Humerus	L	34.5 cm	176 cm ± 4.05 cm	5′ 7″
1153	M?	Humerus	L	32.4 cm	170 cm ± 4.05	5′ 5″
1313	M	Radius	R	25.4 cm	175 cm ± 4.32	5′ 7″
1393	M?	Femur	L	40.1 cm	156 cm ± 3.27 cm	5′ 1″

*F = female; F? = possibly female; M = Male; M? = possibly male; L = Left; R = Right

The most frequent cranial non-metric trait was the supraorbital notch (93.7%), followed by the mastoid foramen (53.8%). The supraorbital notch is manifested early on in skeletal development and therefore may be under stronger genetic influence than other traits that are not (Hauser and De Stefano 1989). The mastoid foramen on the other hand, is believed to be under a low genetic influence compared to other cranial traits (Sjøvold 1984). In fact, this trait is frequently observed in skeletal remains (Hauser and De Stefano 1989). Preliminary analysis of the present data suggests no obvious association between individuals with the same cranial traits and their location in the cemetery. Cranial non-metric data, therefore, would not seem to indicate any genetic relationships between individuals.

The most frequent post-cranial non-metric traits were atlas double facets and lateral tibial squatting facets (Table 3.11). These were both present on over 66.6% of the skeletons that had these elements available for examination. Traits that involve joint

surfaces in particular may be under greater mechanical influence than genetic influence. For example, Os acromiale, represented as non-fusion of the acromial process of the scapula, has been linked to activity-induced trauma occurring at a young age (Stirland 1998). In the present sample, no such trait was observed and, overall, traits involving joint surfaces were not very frequent.

Comparative analysis of non-metric traits is difficult owing to the varied manner in which data for these have been collected and published for various populations. However, metopism would seem to have been more frequent among the London Road individuals (TPR 25%) compared to those from 124–130 London Road (TPR 5.4%), Kempston, Bedfordshire (TPR 12%) and Cirencester (TPR 8.2%) (Boylston and Roberts 1996). Also more frequent was the septal aperture which had a TPR of 25% at London Road compared to a TPR of 8.4% for Kempston and a TPR of 4.5% for Cirencester, and the vastus notch which had a TPR of 28.5% at London Road, a TPR of 5.7% at Kempston and a TPR of 11.8% at Cirencester.

The mass grave

Condition and completeness

Articulated skeletons within the mass grave were very incomplete (Table 3.12). The majority (65%) were represented by less than 25% and mainly comprised articulated limbs. Only 17 skeletons (8.4%) were over 75% complete. All of the small finds ('sf' number allocated to each individual bone or articulating

Table 3.9 Stature summary data from the discrete burial assemblage*.

Sex	N	Method	Average stature	Minimum	Maximum	S.D.
F	4	Trotter	160 cm	156 cm	163 cm	2.69
M	4	(1970)	169 cm	156 cm	176 cm	7.98

* F = female, M = male; N = number of individuals in the sample; S.D. = standard deviation

Table 3.10   Cranial non-metric trait frequencies in the discrete burial assemblage.

Trait	Left side % (n/N)	Right side % (n/N)	Unilateral traits % (n/N)	Cranial prevalence % (n/N)
Highest nuchal line	–	–	14.2 (2/14)	14.2 (2/14)
Ossicle at lambda	–	–	0 (0/13)	0 (0/13)
Bregmatic bone	–	–	0 (0/13)	0 (0/13)
Palatine torus	–	–	25.0 (2/8)	25.0 (2/8)
Metopism	–	–	19.0 (4/21)	19.0 (4/21)
Lambdoid ossicle	42.8 (3/7)	66.6 (4/6)	–	55.5 (5/9)
Coronal ossicle	0 (0/7)	0 (0/7)	–	0 (0/9)
Epipteric bone	0 (0/1) (left?)	–	–	0 (0/1)
Asterion ossicle	0 (0/2)	33.3 (1/3)	–	33.3 (1/3)
Parietal notch	0 (0/1) (left?)	–	–	0 (0/1)
Fronto-temporal articulation	0 (0/1) (left?)	–	–	0 (0/1)
Parietal foramina	54.5 (6/11)	45.4 (5/11)	–	64.2 (9/14)
Access infraorbital foramina	0 (0/2)	–	–	0 (0/2)
Multizygomatic foramina	46.6 (7/15)	38.4 (5/13)	–	47.0 (8/17)
Auditory torus	0 (0/22)	5.2 (1/19)	–	4.5 (1/22)
Mandibular torus	20.0 (4/20)	19.0 (4/21)	–	19.0 (4/21)
Maxillatry torus	33.3 (3/9)	33.3 (3/9)	–	33.3 (3/9)
Supraorbital foramen	41.6 (5/12)	21.4 (3/14)	–	40.0 (6/15)
Supraorbital notch	81.8 (9/11)	93.3 (14/15)	–	93.7 (15/16)
Mastoid foramen	38.4 (5/13)	40.0 (4/10)	–	53.8 (7/13)

Table 3.11   Frequency of post-cranial traits.

Trait	Side prevalence		Skeletal prevalence % (n/N)
	Left % (n/N)	Right % (n/N)	
Septal aperture	7.6 (1/13)	25.0 (4/16)	25.0 (4/16)
Supracondyloid process	0 (0/13)	0 (0/16)	0 (0/17)
Atlas double facet	55.5 (5/9)	66.6 (6/9)	66.6 (6/9)
Atlas lateral bridge	0 (0/7)	0 (0/7)	0 (0/9)
Atlas posterior bridge	12.5 (1/8)	14.2 (1/7)	12.5 (1/8)
Atlas bipartite foramen	0 (0/5)	0 (0/4)	0 (0/6)
Allen's fossa	0 (0/11)	0 (0/9)	0 (0/12)
Poirier's facet	10.0 (1/10)	14.2 (1/7)	18.1 (2/11)
Plaque	20.0 (2/10)	16.6 (1/6)	20.0 (2/10)
3rd trochanter	8.3 (2/24)	28.5 (6/21)	23.0 (6/26)
Hypotrochanteric fossa	31.0 (9/29)	31.8 (7/22)	33.3 (10/30)
Exostosis in intertrochanteric fossa	42.8 (6/14)	33.3 (3/9)	46.6 (7/15)
Vastus notch	20.0 (1/5)	33.3 (2/6)	28.5 (2/7)
Vastus fossa	0 (0/4)	0 (0/6)	0 (0/6)
Emarginate patella	0 (0/5)	0 (0/7)	0 (0/8)
Tibia lateral squatting facet	60.0 (3/5)	60.0 (3/5)	66.6 (4/6)
Tibia medial squatting facet	0 (0/5)	0 (0/4)	0 (0/5)

element that could not be associated with a specific skeleton at the time of recording; See Chapter 2) represented less than 25% of a complete skeleton. Most small finds comprised crania (8.3%; 35/419); mandibles (7.3%; 31/419); ribs (21.7%; 91/419); and major long limb bones (32.9%; 138/419). Hand and foot bones, sternums and vertebrae were infrequent (Table 3.13).

Most of the articulated skeletons were in a good or very good condition (Table 3.14). This means that bone surface erosion was minimal or slight and bones generally had a fresh appearance and clearly visible surface morphologies (McKinley 2004, 16). Fragmentation was considerable across all condition categories.

Nine skeletons (4.4%) were in an excellent condition and, of these, all but one (1518) were less than 25% complete. Interestingly, amongst these nine skeletons, were three subadults. The excellent preservation of subadult skeletons is unusual because their small,

Table 3.12 Completeness of the articulated skeletons within the mass grave.

Completeness	Number of skeletons	% of the assemblage (N = 201 skeletons)
>75%	17	8.4
75–50%	23	11.4
50–25%	29	14.4
<25%	132	65.6
Total	201	

Table 3.13 Composition of the skeletal small finds assemblage within the mass grave.

Element	Number (% of 419 elements)
Skull	11 (2.6)
Cranium	35 (8.3)
Mandible	31 (7.3)
Small finds that are only one loose tooth	8 (1.9)
Sternum	1 (0.2)
Vertebrae	10 (2.3)
Ribs	91 (21.7)
Scapula	18 (4.2)
Clavicles	21 (5.0)
Pelvis	11 (2.6)
Long bones (Humerus, Radius, Ulna, Femur, Tibia, Fibula)	138 (32.9)
Patella	19 (4.5)
Hand bones (carpals, metacarpals, phalanges)	11 (2.6)
Foot bones (carpals, metacarpals, phalanges)	14 (3.3)
Total	419

Table 3.14 Condition of the articulated skeletons within the mass grave.

Category	Number of skeletons	%
Excellent	9	4.4
Very good	72	35.8
Good	82	40.7
Fair	29	14.4
Poor	9	4.4
Destroyed	0	0
Total	201	

fragile bones do not usually survive as well as those of adult skeletons (Chamberlain 2000). The subadults from the mass grave may be an exception because the burial of many individuals together may have provided a more protected environment than a single grave. The overall better condition of the skeletons from the mass grave compared to the discrete skeletons, may also be explained by this.

Table 3.15 Condition of the skeletal small finds within the mass grave.

Category	Number of skeletons	%
Excellent	8	1.9
Very good	141	33.6
Good	148	35.3
Fair	94	22.4
Poor	26	6.2
Destroyed	2	0.4
Total	419	

The condition of the small finds and disarticulated elements (Tables 3.15 and 3.16) was similar to that of the articulated skeletons. Thus, regardless of location and human remains category (articulated skeleton, small find or disarticulated element), all bones in the mass grave were fairly homogenous in terms of their condition.

Taphonomy

There were no obvious cases where fragments of a single bone found in different locations within the pit conjoined. This may be because no formal conjoining exercises (see White 1992, 65–77) were undertaken and thus such information has been missed. Alternatively, this may indicate that fragments of the same bone were not dispersed within the pit, just bones from the same skeleton.

Attempts at matching met with limited success. During excavation, several records were made that suggested possible matches between elements, and these were confirmed during macroscopic examination and by application of *Crossbones*. In all of these cases, the matches occurred between elements that were in approximate anatomical alignment with one another. Thus, for example, Skeleton 1569, represented by a left leg was matched with the remains comprising Skeleton 1560, and the remains that comprised Skeleton 1521 were matched to the bones recorded as Skeleton 1591 and small find 390.

Based on the recommendations of Wright (2003), measurements of the humerus and femur were employed to match dispersed elements and bone units. However, the incompleteness of these elements meant that the full set of required measurements for

Table 3.16 Condition of the disarticulated elements within the mass grave.

Category	Number of Elements	%
Excellent	1	0.3
Very good	41	13.0
Good	85	27.1
Fair	151	48.2
Poor	33	10.5
Destroyed	2	0.6
Total	313	

each bone (seven for each) could not be taken in all but one case (a humerus from Skeleton 1668). Thus, the remains did not provide any metrical data that could be employed to match elements.

There was no evidence that any of the remains had been modified by scavengers, exposure in daylight or deliberate disarticulation with a blade or other sharp tool. This suggests that corpses had not skeletonised or partially decomposed prior to their deposition in the pit. This is supported by a preliminary analysis of the occurrence of articulating joints in the entire assemblage (based on sketches made of the bone in the field). This indicates that there were at least 35 articulated crania and mandibles, 27 right hips, 24 left hips, 16 right knees and 14 left knees. Shoulders, elbows, wrists and ankles scored between 12 and three occurrences.

Three dimensional analysis of the assemblage did not identify any matches between elements but provided information regarding the spatial relationship of elements. This primarily relates to two separate queries that were run using *Crossbones*. The first explored horizontal and/or vertical relationships between articulated skeletons with lower limb bones and articulated skeletons that lacked lower limb bones. The second explored horizontal and/or vertical associations between articulated skeletons with upper limb bones and articulated skeletons that were without upper limb bones. No obvious relationships were observed in the vertical plane for both analyses. Patterns were, however, observed in the horizontal plane for both analyses.

In general, this showed that upper limb bones were more dispersed than lower limb bones (Figs 3.2 and 3.3). The latter were concentrated in the western side of the pit in the same area as skeletons that lacked lower limbs. The former were located comparatively further from skeletons that lacked upper limb bones. Some skeletons without upper limbs were located in the middle of the pit, some distance from the western half where the majority of the small finds were located.

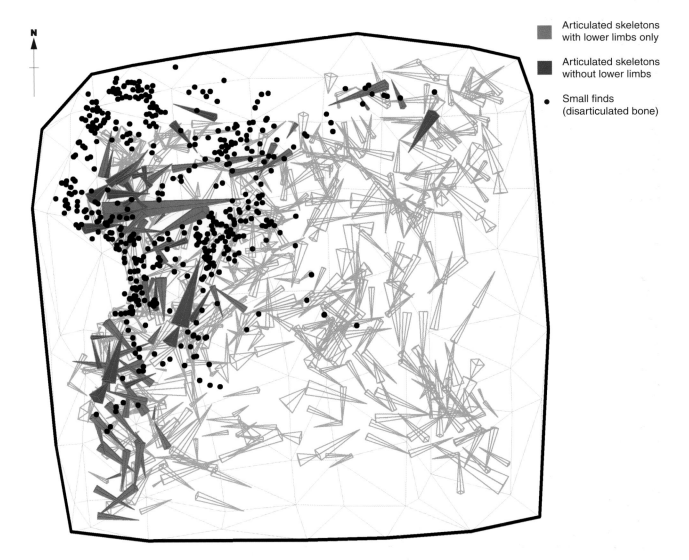

Articulated skeletons with lower limbs only

Articulated skeletons without lower limbs

Small finds (disarticulated bone)

Figure 3.2   Three dimensional analysis of articulated skeletons with and without lower limb bones in the mass grave.

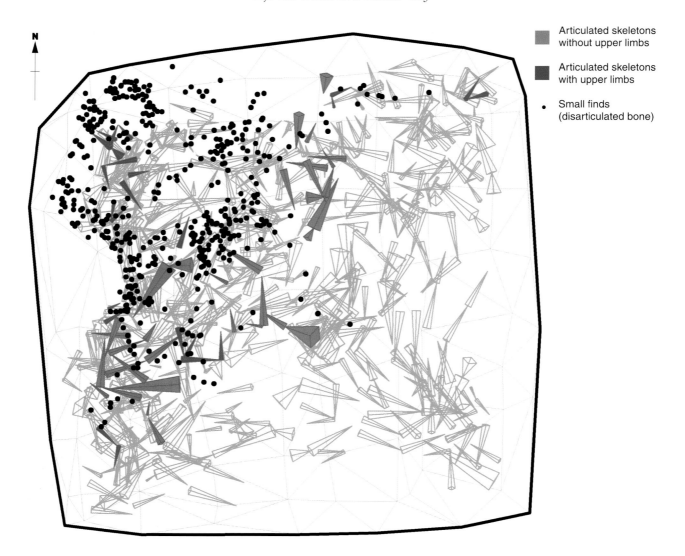

Figure 3.3 Three dimensional analysis of articulated skeletons with and without upper limb bones in the mass grave.

Despite the limited success at matching elements and skeletal units from the pit, this basic taphonomic analysis of the remains suggests that the individuals had been deposited in the pit as articulated fleshed, fresh, corpses. The disassociation of elements is, most likely, the result of post-depositional processes relating to body decomposition (Duday 2006). This is a plausible explanation for the concentration of partial skeletons and skeletal elements in the same area of the pit.

Minimum number of individuals

To avoid duplication, the minimum number of individuals (MNI) was calculated for the entire assemblage, including articulated skeletons, small finds and disarticulated bones. This was based on the number of repeated elements, whilst taking into account age, sex and bone morphology. Owing to the fragmented nature of the sample, it was important to ensure that a bone was not counted more than once. This analysis, therefore, has employed the calculation

of specific anatomical landmarks such as the glabella, the external occipital protuberance, the radial notch of the left ulna and the *fovea capitis* of the left femur.

The highest MNI achieved by the most frequent anatomical landmark or bone segment, the mid-shaft of the right femur, was 87 individuals (Table 3.17) and was based on femoral mid-shafts that were over 50% complete. Of these, 73 belonged to articulated skeletons, 13 were small finds and one was disarticulated. The mid-shaft of the femur, which comprises a thick cylinder of compact bone (White 2003), is the strongest bone in the skeleton. It is therefore not surprising that this element should yield the highest MNI count in the present sample. This MNI was followed by a lower count for the left femur (n=84) and the mental eminence of the mandible (n=78).

Based on the number of right femora (87) there was a minimum of 76 adults and seven subadults (four were of unknown age). The number of subadults was, however, higher than this, as indicated by repeated counts of the mental eminence. This suggests a minimum number of 10 subadults. Although other

Table 3.17   MNI calculation for the mass grave assemblage according to repeated anatomical landmarks in different bone elements.

Specific skeletal region	Number of repeated elements			MNI Total
	Subadult	Adult	Age unknown	
Right femur mid-shaft (>50% complete)	7	76	4	87
Left femur mid-shaft (>50% complete)	9	71	4	84
Mental eminence (mandible)	10	68	0	78
Right Mastoid process (temporal bone)	9	61	4	74
External protuberance (occipital bone)	8	64	0	72
Left mastoid process (temporal bone)	7	64	0	71
Glabella (frontal bone)	8	51	0	59
Left talus (>50% complete)	3	39	5	47
Right talus (>50% complete)	5	33	4	42
Radial notch (left ulna)	3	34	1	38
Radial notch (right ulna)	5	31	1	37
Fovea capitis (right femur)	5	31	1	37
Fovea capitis (left femur)	3	33	0	36
Nutrient foramen (left tibia)	1	30	2	33
Olecranon fossa (right humerus)	3	25	1	29
Radial tuberosity (right radius)	5	22	2	29
Nutrient foramen (right tibia)	2	21	2	25
Tibial tuberosity (left tibia)	0	23	2	25
Radial tuberosity (left radius)	3	18	0	21
Tibial tuberosity (right tibia)	1	18	2	21
Olecranon fossa (left humerus)	3	17	0	20

subadult bone fragments, such as those from the left temporal and left parietal, were repeated among 19 skeletons and 20 small finds numbers, these were less than 50% complete and are therefore unreliable for estimating the minimum number of subadults (Dobney and Reilly 1988).

The minimum number of subadults is increased further to 15 individuals based on age indicators rather than repeated bone elements. There were no perinatal or neonatal remains, but an MNI for all other subadult age groups could be established (Table 3.18). Estimations were based on dental development for one skeleton in the young child age category, three in the older child age category

Table 3.18   MNI calculation of the subadult sample from the mass grave.

Age category	MNI (based on most frequently repeated elements)	Elements employed in the MNI calculation
Infant	1	Not applicable
Young child	3	Repeated left femora
Older Child	4	Several repeated elements including the mandible, the atlas and axis vertebrae
Adolescent	7	Several repeated skull elements, the atlas and axis vertebrae
Total	15	

and six in the adolescent age group. The remainder were aged based on skeletal maturity and/or long bone lengths. Adding these 15 subadult individuals to the 76 adult individuals, as inferred from the right femur middle shaft, the total minimum number of individuals from the mass grave is 91.

Recovery rate

Based on an MNI of 91 individuals, the recovery rate of bones from the grave pit was calculated (Table 3.19) to explore whether partially complete skeletons or corpses had been deposited. This was undertaken by dividing the number of elements present by the total number that would be expected for 91 individuals. This calculation assumes that all individuals were complete when they were buried. Only the long bone segments that provided the highest count were included.

Recovery rates were highest for femora and skull bones. All other elements had a recovery rate of around 50%. This is with the exception of very small bones, such as foot phalanges, which had a low recovery rate. Some bias may have been introduced into these results because elements that were <50% complete were not counted. Further, bone fragments from some parts of the skeleton, for example, the skull, are more easily identified by the Osteologist than others such as hand and foot bones.

Despite these caveats, overall patterns of recovery would seem to be reflective of characteristic preservation patterns of the skeleton resulting from

Table 3.19 Skeletal representation and bone recovery rates for the mass grave assemblage.

Bone element/anatomical landmark	Number recovered/ number expected	%
Femora (middle shaft >50%)	171/182	93.9
mental eminence (mandible)	78/91	85.7
Temporal bone (mastoid process)	145/182	79.6
Occipital bone (Nuchal crest area)	72/91	79.1
Clavicles (shafts)	144/182	79.1
Humeri (distal shaft >50%)	128/182	70.3
Frontal bone (glabella)	59/91	64.8
Zygomatics	117/182	64.2
Patellae	109/182	59.8
Vertebrae	1274/2184	58.3
Ulnae (proximal shaft >50%)	104/182	57.1
Tibiae (middle shaft >50%)	101/182	55.4
Radii (middle shaft >50%)	99/182	54.3
Fibulae (middle shaft >50%)	98/182	53.8
Scapulae (glenoid fossa)	81/182	44.5
Metacarpals	371/910	40.7
Ribs	850/2184	38.9
Metatarsals	340/910	37.3
Tarsals	449/1274	35.2
Hand phalanges	680/2548	26.6
Pubis	49/182	26.9
Carpals	356/1456	24.4
Foot phalanges	184/2548	7.2
Nasal bones	10/182	5.4
Vomer	4/182	2.1
Palatines	4/182	2.1
Hyoid	2/91	2.1
Sternum	2/91	2.1
Lacrimal bones	0/182	0

Table 3.20 Age-at-death distribution in the mass grave sample.

Age category	Number of skeletons	% of individuals (N=91)
Foetus	0	
Perinate	0	
Neonate	0	
Infant	1	1.0
Young child	3	3.2
Older Child	4	4.3
Adolescent	7	7.6
Young Adult	36	39.5
Middle Adult	13	14.2
Mature Adult	7	7.6
Older Adult	5	5.4
Adult	15	16.4
Total	91	

All subadults were assigned to an age category as described above.

Almost 40% (N=36) of the skeletons were assigned to the young adult age category (Table 3.20 and Fig. 3.4). The number of skeletons assigned to the infant and younger child age categories was lower than expected (N=1) and only five skeletons were estimated to have been older adults when they died. Sex estimation was based on a combination of pelvic and skull indicators for the more complete skeletons, but relied on a limited number of skull indicators for the small finds and disarticulated elements (Table 3.21, Fig. 3.5). Most of the individuals were male, although 35.5% of the adult skeletons were of undetermined sex.

Deaths were highest for both males and females in the young adult age category. Out of a total of 14 females and 35 males, seven females (50%) and 19 males (54.2%) were assigned to this age category.

Metrical analysis

A limited number of measurements could be taken from skulls and long bones and have been recorded for the archive. No statures could be estimated. This is with the exception of skeleton 1668 which had a complete left humerus that provided a maximum length of 30.5 cm. The absence of a skull and pelvis meant that it was not possible to estimate the sex of this skeleton. Applying the humeral length to regression equations for both females and males suggests a female height of 160 cm (5' 2.4") and a male height of 164 cm (5' 3.8").

Non-metric traits

Limited data on non-metric traits could be obtained (Tables 3.22 and 3.23). The small size of the sample precluded analysis of the data by sex and age. Several traits including the coronal ossicle, epipteric bone, asterion ossicle, parietal notch and the

the inherent structural properties of bone (Bello and Andrews 2006, 10). Thus, large, dense bones, such as the femur and skull, have a higher survival rate than do less dense, smaller bones, such as those from the hands and feet (ibid.). These patterns are similar to recovery rates that are observed among discrete medieval skeletons that were interred as complete corpses and were not subsequently removed or deliberately disturbed until archaeological excavation (ibid., 9). These findings therefore suggest that corpses had probably not skeletonised before they were interred in the mass grave and that no selection of elements for burial had taken place.

Biological age and sex

The ages of adult skeletons were primarily estimated by employing the most frequently occurring skeletal indicator; wear patterns on the molar teeth combined with ante-mortem tooth loss. This is with the exception of 17 articulated skeletons for which ages could be estimated based on a combination of indicators including dentitions and pelves. Only dentitions that had the mental eminence present were counted for this analysis, so as to avoid any duplication.

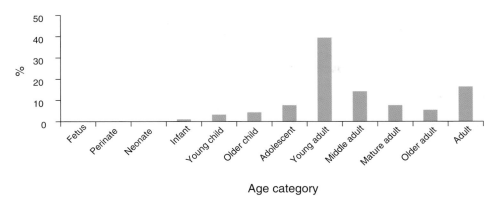

Figure 3.4 Mortality profile (mass grave).

fronto-temporal articulation could not be scored owing to the incompleteness of the remains.

The most frequently occurring cranial traits were the parietal foramina, multizygomatic foramina, access infraorbital foramina and the lambdoid ossicle. However, for the latter two, only one bone was available for each observation. The most frequently occurring post-cranial traits were the hypotrochanteric fossa, the tibial squatting facet and the vastus notch. Again, for the latter, observations were biased by the small number of skeletal elements that were available for examination.

Overall, the range and frequency of cranial and post-cranial non-metric traits is broadly similar to that which has been recorded for the discrete skeletons. This suggests that both populations were exposed to similar genetic and environmental influences.

Dental health status
by Nicholas Márquez-Grant

Introduction

Examination of conditions such as dental caries, *antemortem* tooth loss and dental calculus can provide information on the diet of the population as well as the levels of oral hygiene. Moreover, lesions called hypoplasias, which can be present on tooth enamel, may provide an insight into living conditions and levels of nutrition, infection and hygiene during the childhood years. In addition, data on oral pathology provide information on the social, cultural and economic context in which a population lived and may be a means of inferring cultural change (Emery 1963).

The examination of the dentitions that belonged to the discrete skeletons and the mass grave skeletons focused on enamel hypoplasia, dental caries, ante-

Table 3.21 Age distribution in the adult sample (N=76) according to biological sex.

Age category	Female	?Female	Unknown	?Male	Male	% Females (n)	% Males (n)
Young Adult	5	2	10	11	8	9.2 (7)	25.0 (19)
Middle Adult	3	1	2	4	3	5.2 (4)	9.2 (7)
Mature Adult	0	2	3	2	0	2.6 (2)	2.6 (2)
Older Adult	0	1	1	3	0	1.3 (1)	3.9 (3)
Adult	0	0	11	1	3	0 (0)	5.2 (4)
Total	8	6	27	21	14	18.4 (14)	46.0 (35)

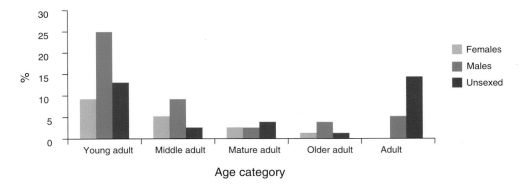

Figure 3.5 Sex distribution of the adult sample (mass grave).

Table 3.22 Cranial non-metric trait frequencies in the mass grave assemblage.

Trait	Side prevalence		Unilateral trait prevalence % (n/N)
	Left % (n/N)	Right % (n/N)	
Highest nuchal line			0 (0/2)
Ossicle at lambda			0 (0/1)
Bregmatic bone			0 (0/7)
Palatine torus			25.0 (1/4)
Metopism			9.3 (4/43)
Lambdoid ossicle	100 (1/1)	–	
Parietal foramina	80.0 (4/5)	100 (9/9)	
Access infraorbital foramina	100 (1/1)	–	
Multizygomatic foramina	68.0 (17/25)	72.7 (16/22)	
Auditory torus	0 (0/32)	0 (0/30)	
Mandibular torus	40.0 (2/5)	33.3 (1/3)	
Maxillary torus	–	–	60.0 (3/5)
Supraorbital foramen	53.8 (7/13)	46.6 (7/15)	
Supraorbital notch	69.5 (16/23)	75.0 (15/20)	
Mastoid foramen	0 (0/3)	50.0 (2/4)	

mortem tooth loss, dental calculus, periodontitis, periapical cavities, dental attrition and dental anomalies such as tooth agenesis or chipping. Data are presented separately for subadult and adult individuals, and for the discrete burial assemblage and the mass grave assemblage.

Materials

Subadult sample

Of the nine subadult skeletons in the discrete burial assemblage, only four (skeletons 1066, 1086, 1277,

Table 3.23 Post-cranial non-metric trait frequencies in the mass grave assemblage.

Trait	Side prevalence	
	Left % (n/N)	Right % (n/N)
Septal aperture	0 (0/10)	0 (0/18)
Supracondyloid process	6.2 (1/16)	5.2 (1/19)
Atlas double facet	18.7 (3/16)	21.4 (3/14)
Atlas lateral bridge	0 (0/14)	0 (0/11)
Atlas posterior bridge	0 (0/14)	0 (0/11)
Atlas bipartite foramen	0 (0/4)	0 (0/2)
Allen's fossa	14.2 (1/7)	11.1 (1/9)
Poirier's facet	0 (0/7)	0 (0/8)
Plaque	14.2 (1/7)	0 (0/9)
3rd trochanter	3.5 (1/28)	6.6 (2/30)
Hypotrochanteric fossa	20.4 (10/49)	24.0 (12/50)
Exostosis in intertrochanteric fossa	0 (0/3)	0 (0/3)
Vastus notch	18.1 (2/11)	23.0 (6/26)
Vastus fossa	0 (0/7)	0 (0/25)
Emarginate patella	0 (0/25)	0 (0/36)
Tibia lateral squatting facet	100 (1/1)	100 (2/2)
Tibia medial squatting facet	0 (0/1)	0 (0/1)

1317) provided dental information, since in the other skeletons the dentitions were not preserved. In the mass grave, dental information came from small finds 540, 564, 588 and 6873, and skeletons 1526, 1547, 1559, 1570, 1584, 1595, 1608, 1615, 1623, 1642, 1672 and 1685.

A total of 38 deciduous and 63 (21 unerupted) permanent teeth from the discrete burial assemblage were available for examination. The total sample examined for the subadult individuals from the mass grave consisted of 79 deciduous teeth and 197 (three unerupted) permanent teeth.

Adult sample

There were 51 adult individuals in the discrete burial assemblage and 76 adult individuals from the mass grave sample. Of these, 36 from discrete samples and an MNI of 68 from the mass grave provided information regarding dental health.

Table 3.24 provides a breakdown of the number of teeth present in these adult samples. The number of teeth expected in this table has been determined by counting the number of common teeth in a human being (32 permanent teeth) and multiplying this by the number of adult individuals in the sample.

In total, 557 and 1913 adult teeth were examined from the discrete burial and the mass grave assemblages respectively.

Methods

All observations were made macroscopically and employed standard published criteria (Brickley and McKinley 2004). For subadults, deciduous and permanent teeth were analysed separately. A full description of the methods employed is presented in Appendix 1.

Table 3.24 Number of teeth present, number lost ante-mortem, number lost post-mortem and number generally missing (no data).

	Discrete cemetery (51 adults) n (%)	Mass grave (76 adults) n (%)
Total teeth expected for 100% preservation and recovery (n = 32 teeth per adult dentition)	1632	2432
Teeth present	557 (34.1)	1913 (78.6)
Teeth lost *ante-mortem*	42 (2.5)	107 (4.3)
Teeth missing *post-mortem*	120 (7.3)	–*
Agenesis (congenitally absent/unerupted)	15 (0.9)	22 (0.9)
Tooth status unknown (missing data)	898 (55.0)	441 (18.1)**

*teeth missing *post-mortem* in the mass grave. Since they are commingled, the number of loose teeth is greater than the number of alveoli that were observed as having teeth lost *post-mortem* (108 alveoli, 4.4%). Since it cannot be determined whether the teeth that are missing were or were not among the loose teeth in the assemblage, this figure cannot be calculated. **This calculation has been obtained by totalling the number of teeth present with the number lost *ante-mortem* and the number of examples of agenesis and subtracting this from the total number of expected teeth. The number of teeth lost *post-mortem* was excluded from this calculation.

Results

All samples contained a cross-representation of adult ages and both sexes. Samples from the discrete burial assemblage and the mass grave are presented alongside each other to facilitate comparisons and discussions. Adult ages have been pooled as well as left and right teeth, and maxillary and mandibular teeth.

Data for the discrete burial assemblage are presented first, followed by those for the mass grave. These results are then compared. A discussion and interpretation of the results follows after.

The discrete burial assemblage

The adult sample

Enamel hypoplasia (EH)
Enamel hypoplasia is a dental enamel defect caused by generalised disruptions to the enamel matrix formation (Hillson 1996b). The prevalence of these lesions has been used to infer the level of physiological stress in a population (Skinner and Goodman 1992). Since these disruptions occur during tooth formation, these lesions provide an insight into health status during childhood.

There are several types of enamel defects, but pits and linear defects are those most common in archaeological populations. The aetiology of hypoplasias is multifactorial (Pindborg 1982). Amongst the factors contributing to the presence of these disruptions are malnutrition, infectious disease, genetic anomalies, diabetes, allergies, trauma, infections, neonatal disturbances, psychological stress and genetic background (Pindborg 1982; King *et al.* 2002). Generally speaking, the prevalence of these defects in a population is likely to result from a complex interaction of factors.

The sample examined for enamel hypoplasia was 279 teeth. This does not include teeth that were too poorly preserved, had surfaces that were obscured by calculus, or were too worn. The total prevalence rate was 35.1% (Table 3.25). In the majority of cases (>90%) the defects were linear, but the pitting form was also observed.

The total prevalence for London Road is higher than other Romano-British populations (Roberts and Cox 2003, 140), including the cemetery of Kingsholm, Gloucester where 10.4% of all teeth were affected (Roberts 1989).

Dental caries
Dental caries involves the destruction of the enamel surface, the dentine (internal part of the tooth) and the cement (outer layer of the roots). This is caused by the acid produced by bacteria present in dental plaque (Hillson 1996b, 269). Classified as an infectious disease, it usually progresses gradually.

The prevalence of dental caries is strongly influenced by diet and subsistence technology (Larsen 1997). In particular, the consumption of carbohydrates, especially sugar, is a well established cause of cavitations (Hillson 1996b; Moyniham 1998). Other factors, such as tooth crown shape, food texture, attrition, frequency of consumption of food and inheritance may also play a role in the manifestation of this condition (Powell 1985; Larsen *et al.* 1991).

Table 3.25 Prevalence of enamel hypoplasia in the discrete burial assemblage.

	Females % (n/N)	Males % (n/N)	Unsexed % (n/N)	Total % (n/N)
All anterior teeth	54.3 (25/46)	79.4 (31/39)	54.2 (13/24)	63.3 (69/109)
All posterior teeth	17.7 (14/79)	15.0 (9/60)	19.3 (6/31)	17.0 (29/170)
Total	31.2 (39/125)	40.4 (40/99)	34.5 (19/55)	35.1 (98/279)

Table 3.26 Dental caries prevalence in the discrete burial assemblage.

	Females % (n/N)	Males % (n/N)	Unsexed % (n/N)	Total % (n/N)
All anterior teeth	1.4 (1/70)	4.1 (4/96)	3.0 (1/33)	3.0 (6/199)
All posterior teeth	12.5 (17/135)	18.9 (30/158)	16.7 (9/54)	16.1 (56/347)
Total	8.8 (18/205)	13.4 (34/254)	11.5 (10/87)	11.4 (62/546)

(These are uncorrected rates which means that ante-mortem and post-mortem tooth loss have not been taken into account.)

The total prevalence for dental caries for the discrete skeletons was 11.3% (Table 3.26) which places London Road among the highest rates to have been recorded for Romano-British material (Roberts and Cox 2003, 131). Females had a lower frequency than males, although ten teeth with cavities belonged to individuals of undetermined sex. Most cavities were present on the coronal surfaces of teeth, or at the cemento-enamel junction (Table 3.27). 'Gross' refers to the involvement of the entire surface of the tooth.

Ante-mortem tooth loss
The loss of a tooth before death is the end result of several disease processes. Calculus deposits can irritate the soft tissue and the underlying bone, which may lead to the reduction of the bone (periodontal disease) and ante-mortem tooth loss (AMTL) (Roberts and Manchester 1995, 45). Teeth may also be lost as a result of peri-apical abscesses formed through the exposure of the pulp cavity, caused by caries or excessive attrition coupled with localised resorption of the alveolar margin. AMTL is regarded as a degenerative disease where the main contributory factors are old age and poor oral hygene.

AMTL was identified as partial or complete remodelling of the alveolar bone and tooth socket, which occurs after a tooth is lost (Costa 1980, 580). The calculation of AMTL prevalence rates usually involves observing the number of regenerated alveoli in the assemblage and dividing it by the number of alveoli present, the former indicating that the teeth were lost before death. However, in the present assemblage, the alveoli were extremely poor. Thus, there were discrete skeletons that did not have any alveoli preserved but had all of their teeth present. The calculation of AMTL was therefore determined by dividing the number of regenerated alveoli by the total number of teeth present, added to the total of number of teeth lost post-mortem and number of alveoli with AMTL in the sample.

A total of 42 alveoli showed complete regeneration or initial signs of regeneration (teeth lost in a relatively short time before death). The total prevalence was 5.8% (42/719). Females were less affected than males (Table 3.28).

Dental calculus
Dental calculus consists of mineralised plaque composed of micro-organisms that accumulate in the mouth and become imbedded in a matrix of protein and saliva. Sugar in the diet accelerates this process (Hillson 1996b, 254–55).

A total of 66.7% of the teeth from the discrete assemblage had deposits of calculus (Table 3.29). This frequency is among the highest to be reported for Romano-British material (see Roberts and Cox 2003, 132). This is particularly high when taking into account the fact that the prevalence of calculus in once living populations is underestimated in archaeological material because it is easily flaked off during excavation and post-excavation handling. Calculus was judged to have been considerable for 3.2% of all teeth. Rates were similar for both males and females.

Periodontal disease
The principal predisposing factor in periodontal disease is the accumulation of calculus in dental pockets. The disease begins as gingivitis (an inflammation of the soft tissues), which is transmitted to the jaw itself. Resorption of the bone commences, followed by tooth loss. There is a strong link between increase in age and the increase in the prevalence

Table 3.28 AMTL frequencies in the discrete burial population.

	Females % (n/N)	Males % (n/N)	Unsexed % (n/N)	Total % (n/N)
All teeth	2.4 (6/242)	8.6 (30/346)	4.6 6/131	5.8 (42/719)

Table 3.27 Distribution of pattern of carious lesions in the discrete burial assemblage.

Lesion distribution	Occlusal n/N (%)	Coronal n/N (%)	CEJ n/N (%)	Root n/N (%)	Gross n/N (%)
Anterior teeth (6 teeth; 6 lesions)	–	4/6 (66.6)	1/6 (16.6)	0/6 (0)	1/6 (16.6)
Posterior teeth (56 teeth; 59 lesions)	11/59 (18.6)	13/59 (22.0)	19/59 (32.2)	1/59 (1.6)	15/56 (26.7)

(Frequencies have been calculated by dividing the number of observed dental surfaces by the number of carious lesions present. Gross lesion frequencies were based on the number of teeth observed rather than the number of lesions observed since there was no indication as to the initiation site of the lesions.)

Table 3.29 Dental calculus frequencies in the discrete burial assemblage.

	Females % (n/N)	Males % (n/N)	Unsexed % (n/N)	Total % (n/N)
All teeth	68.8 (139/202)	73.0 (165/226)	45.3 (39/86)	66.7 (343/514)
Considerable cases (considerable/ teeth with calculus)	2.9 (6/202)	2.2 (5/226)	0 (0/39)	3.2 (11/343)

of periodontal disease in modern populations, and this is also the case with past populations. However, the aetiology is multifactorial with genetic predisposition, environment, diet and hygiene all being factors influencing the development of the disease.

Most jaws in the present sample were very fragmented and this meant that the number that could be examined for periodontal disease was limited. The total prevalence was high (Table 3.30), although advanced recession (considerable cases) was of relatively low prevalence. There was no marked difference between males and females.

Periapical cavities
Periapical cavities have often, in anthropology, been erroneously referred as abscess cavities, since it is unlikely that abscesses form these cavities in the majority of cases (Dias and Tayles 1997). They are identified as openings or holes in the periapical bone of the mandible or maxilla at the apex of the tooth root. They arise as a result of inflammation of the dental pulp that can occur as a result of trauma, caries or attrition. Depending on severity, these cavities may contain granulation tissue (a 'granuloma'), a fluid filled sac (a 'periapical cyst') or a pus filled sac (an 'abscess'). Granulomata and periapical cysts are usually asymptomatic. Abscesses may result in a persistent fever, a general feeling of being unwell and, when they burst and discharge their contents, halitosis. Acute abscesses may lead to osteomyelitis (bone infection) which can be fatal if, for example, it leads to septicaemia.

The fragmentation of maxillae and mandibles limited the number of observations. Only 0.7% of the alveoli observed had a periapical cavity (Table 3.31) and involved just three skeletons (1103, 1153 and 1328). This prevalence is the lowest of those presented for Romano-British populations by

Roberts and Cox (2003, 136). This is with the exception of Kingsholm, Gloucester which has a total prevalence of 0.6% (ibid.).

Dental anomalies
Dental anomalies may be inherited but can also be culturally induced. At least seven skeletons revealed agenesis (congenital absence) of the third molar. Due to fragmentation and poor preservation, it can only be stated that at least one tooth was unerupted in the adult dentitions of skeletons 1057 (male), 1131 (female), 1206 (female) and 1381 (not sexed). Determination of whether these teeth had not developed or had developed but were unerupted would require radiology. Three third molars were absent in skeleton 1165 (female) and the four molars were evidently absent in skeletons 1337 (female) and 1360 (not sexed). The total number of teeth, therefore, that had not erupted was 15. Agenesis of third molars may be inherited (eg Lasker 1951; Bermúdez de Castro 1989).

The subadult sample

Data are presented for dental caries and enamel hypoplasia only (Table 3.32). No carious cavities were identified among the deciduous teeth and only one example was observed among the permanent teeth. The very high prevalence of hypoplasia has been biased by the dentition belonging to skeleton 1277 which had severe EH involving all 13 (eight anterior and four posterior) un-erupted permanent teeth (Plate 3.1). The deciduous teeth from this individual also displayed EH (2/4 anterior dentition; 3/5 posterior dentition). Severe enamel hypoplastic defects may be observed among individuals with congenital syphilis (Hillson *et al.* 1998; Aufderheide and Rodríguez-Martín 1998), but the nature of the lesions, the incompleteness of other diagnostic

Table 3.30 Periodontal disease frequencies in the discrete burial assemblage.

	Females % (n/N)	Males % (n/N)	Unsexed % (n/N)	Total % (n/N)
All alveoli with teeth present post-mortem	56.2 (63/112)	55.8 (38/68)	13.2 (5/38)	48.6 (106/218)
Considerable cases (considerable/alveoli with periodontitis)	7.9 (5/63)	5.2 (2/38)	0 (0/5)	6.6 (7/106)

Table 3.31 Periapical cavity frequencies in the discrete burial assemblage.

	Females % (n/N)	Males % (n/N)	Unsexed % (n/N)	Total % (n/N)
All alveoli observed	0.5 (1/177)	1.4 (2/139)	0 (0/107)	0.7 (3/423)

Table 3.32 Dental health status in the subadult sample from the discrete burial assemblage.

Deciduous	Anterior dentition		Posterior dentition	
Age range	Dental caries % (n/N)	Enamel Hypoplasia % (n/N)	Dental caries % (n/N)	Hypoplasia % (n/N)
Young Child	0 (0/15)	13.3 (2/15)	0 (0/16)	23.0 (3/13)
Older Child	0 (0/4)	0 (0/4)	0 (0/3)	0 (0/3)
Total	0 (0/19)	10.5 (2/19)	0 (0/19)	18.7 (3/16)
Permanent	Dental caries	Enamel Hypoplasia	Dental caries	Hypoplasia
Young Child	–	91.6 (11/12)	–	66.6 (4/6)
Older Child	–	100 (1/1)	0 (0/5)	16.6 (1/6)
Adolescent	0 (0/10)	100 (10/10)	8.3 (1/12)	91.6 (11/12)
Total	0 (0/10)	95.6 (22/23)	5.8 (1/17)	66.6 (16/24)

features of the examined skeleton and the need for future work cannot, at present, pinpoint a specific cause for these defects. Skeleton 1277 was less than 25% complete and was represented by the skull, vertebrae, and a humerus and femur shaft. No pathological lesions were identified on these remains apart from cribra orbitalia.

The mass grave assemblage

Enamel hypoplasia
Discounting poorly preserved teeth and those that were too worn or had surfaces that were obscured by calculus, 1222 teeth could be examined for enamel hypoplasia. The total prevalence was 28.5% (Table 3.33). Like the discrete burials, this is high for a Romano-British population (Roberts and Cox

2003). The majority (>90%) of the cases were classified as linear enamel hypoplasias, the remaining being pit defects of the enamel. Females had higher frequencies than males. There were also 34 teeth belonging to skeletons of unknown age (ie adult or subadult). The frequency of hypoplasia for the anterior sample was 45.4% (5/11) and for posterior teeth 4.3% (1/23).

Dental caries
The total prevalence rate for dental caries was 7.9% (Table 3.34). This prevalence is higher than Kingsholm (5.3%), Cirencester north (4.8%), Cirencester south (5.1%), and is average for this period (Roberts and Cox 2003, 131). Teeth from skeletons of undetermined age (ie adult or subadult) had no (0/15) carious teeth in the anterior dentition and 7.4% (2/27) in the posterior teeth.

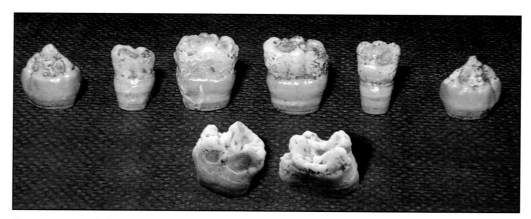

Plate 3.1 Permanent teeth from Skeleton 1277, a two to five year old displaying considerable enamel defects.

Table 3.33 Prevalence of enamel hypoplasia in the mass grave assemblage.

	Females % (n/N)	Males % (n/N)	Unsexed % (n/N)	Total % (n/N)
All anterior	50.5 (47/93)	42.6 (96/225)	33.7 (61/181)	40.8 (204/499)
All posterior	32.6 (51/156)	20.0 (67/334)	11.6 (27/233)	20.0 (145/723)
Total	39.4 (98/249)	29.2 (163/559)	21.3 (88/414)	28.5 (349/1,222)

Table 3.34   Dental caries prevalence in the mass grave assemblage.

	Females % (n/N)	Males % (n/N)	Unsexed % (n/N)	Total % (n/N)
All anterior	0 (0/137)	0.3 (1/331)	3.9 (10/225)	1.5 (11/693)
All posterior	7.7 (17/218)	11.7 (66/563)	14.7 (51/347)	11.8 (134/1128)
Total	4.8 (17/355)	0.8 (7/894)	10.7 (61/572)	7.9 (145/1821)

Carious lesions were most common at the cemento-enamel junction (CEJ) in the anterior teeth, whilst cavities on the coronal surfaces as well as gross lesions were more abundant in the posterior teeth (Table 3.35).

Ante-mortem tooth loss
AMTL was calculated in the same way as described for the discrete skeletons (Table 3.36). A total prevalence of 5.3% was observed which is low for a Romano-British population.

Dental calculus
Like the discrete skeletons, rates for calculus were high for this period with 59.4% of the teeth identified as having deposits (Table 3.37). Only 3.2% of the teeth in the assemblage had deposits that were recorded as considerable. Teeth that belonged to individuals of unknown age (ie they were adults or subadults) yielded a prevalence of 39.4% (15/38). Only one tooth had a considerable amount (6.6% of the teeth with calculus).

Periodontal disease
The prevalence of periodontal disease was relatively high (Table 3.38). Males had a higher prevalence than females. Five alveoli from the age unknown group had periodontitis. Since these are likely to belong to adult individuals, this was added to the unsexed group and the total count. There were no considerable cases.

Periapical cavities
In total 1.6% of the alveoli that could be observed had a periapical cavity (Table 3.39). This figure is similar to that in other Roman populations from Gloucestershire (Kingsholm and Cirencester south), but low compared to samples from the rest of

Table 3.35   Distribution of pattern of carious lesions in the mass grave assemblage.

Lesion distribution	Occlusal n/N (%)	Coronal n/N (%)	CEJ n/N (%)	Root n/N (%)	Gross n/N (%)
Anterior teeth (11 teeth, 12 lesions)	–	3/12 (25.0)	6/12 (50.0)	0/12 (0)	3/11 (27.2)
Posterior teeth (134 teeth, 156 lesions)	35/156 (22.4)	38/156 (24.3)	32/156 (20.5)	2/156 (1.2)	49/134 (36.5)

Table 3.36   AMTL frequencies in the mass grave assemblage.

	Females % (n/N)	Males % (n/N)	Unsexed % (n/N)	Total % (n/N)
All teeth	2.9 (11/372)	3.7 (37/994)	7.1 (44/618)	5.3 (107/1984)

Table 3.37   Dental calculus frequencies in the mass grave assemblage.

	Females % (n/N)	Males % (n/N)	Unsexed % (n/N)	Total % (n/N)
All teeth	66.5 (231/347)	53.4 (636/1191)	68.3 (372/545)	59.4 (1239/2083)
Considerable cases (considerable/ alveoli with calculus)	1.7 (4/231)	5.5 (35/636)	4.6 (17/372)	4.5 (56/1239)

Table 3.38   Periodontal disease frequencies in the mass grave assemblage.

	Females % (n/N)	Males % (n/N)	Unsexed % (n/N)	Total % (n/N)
All alveoli with teeth present post-mortem	19.1 (9/47)	78.3 (116/148)	70.4 (81/115)	66.4 (206/310)
Considerable cases (considerable/alveoli with periodontitis)	22.2 (2/9)	13.7 (16/116)	0 (0/81)	8.7 (18/206)

Table 3.39   Periapical cavity frequencies in the mass grave assemblage.

	Females % (n/N)	Males % (n/N)	Unsexed % (n/N)	Total % (n/N)
All alveoli observed	0 (0/134)	1.6 (5/300)	3.8 (4/104)	1.6 (9/538)

Roman Britain (Roberts and Cox 2003, 136). Amongst the alveoli from the unaged individuals, two out of three (66.6%) had periapical cavities.

Dental anomalies

Twenty-two teeth had not erupted and might have been congenitally absent. These are third molars from adult dentitions. The presence of abnormalities that involved the enamel surfaces of the anterior and posterior teeth belonging to skeleton 1672 (Plate 3.2) was an exceptional finding. The abnormalities were reminiscent of the notched incisors and mulberry molars that appear in congenital syphilis (Langsjoen 1998, 405–6, figs 14.10 and 14.11; Hillson *et al.* 1998). This skeleton, a 15–18 year old, was represented by its skull, vertebrae and a left tarsal, all of which displayed no pathological lesions. The individual

was buried in the north-west quadrant of the pit and in the lower layer. Histological analysis would be required to explore this diagnosis further.

Comparison with the discrete skeletons

Examination of the total sample frequencies calculated for adult dentitions from the discrete burial assemblage compared to the mass grave indicates that the discrete burials had higher prevalences for all conditions, except for periodontitis and periapical lesions (Table 3.40). The females from the mass grave had higher rates of enamel hypoplasia on their posterior teeth but less periodontitis than the females from the discrete assemblage (Table 3.41). With regard to males, poorer oral health was indicated

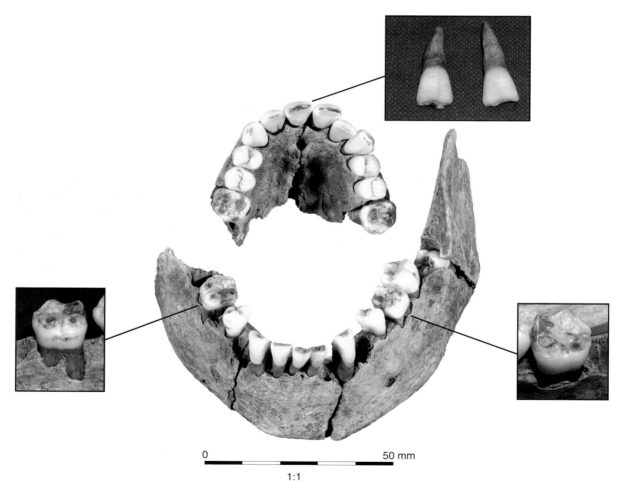

Plate 3.2   Dentition belonging to Skeleton 1672, a 15 to 18 year old with enamel defects. Of particular note are the molars and central incisors (detail).

Table 3.40   Comparison between the discrete burials and the mass grave adult dental assemblages.

Oral condition		Total adult sample	
		Discrete burials % (n/N)	Mass grave % (n/N)
Enamel hypoplasia	Anterior	63.3 (69/109)	40.8 (204/499)
	Posterior	17.0 (29/170)	20.0 (145/723)
Dental caries	Anterior	3.0 (6/199)	1.5 (11/693)
	Posterior	16.1 (56/347)	11.8 (134/1128)
Ante-mortem tooth loss		5.8 (42/719)	5.3 (107/1984)
Dental calculus		66.7 (343/514)	59.4 (1239/2083)
Periodontitis		48.6 (106/218)	66.4 (206/310)
Periapical cavities		0.7 (3/423)	1.6 (9/538)

Table 3.41   Comparison between the females and males from the discrete burial and the mass grave assemblage.

		Females		Males	
Oral condition		Discrete burials % (n/N)	Mass grave % (n/N)	Discrete burials % (n/N)	Mass grave % (n/N)
Enamel hypoplasia	Anterior	54.3 (25/46)	50.5 (47/93)	79.4 (31/39)	42.6 (96/225)
	Posterior	17.7 (14/79)	32.6 (51/156)	15.0 (9/60)	20.0 (67/334)
Dental caries	Anterior	1.4 (1/170)	0 (0/137)	4.1 (4/96)	0.3 (1/331)
	Posterior	12.5 (17/135)	7.7 (17/218)	18.9 (30/158)	11.7 (66/563)
Ante-mortem tooth loss		2.4 (6/242)	2.9 (11/372)	8.6 (30/346)	3.7 (37/994)
Dental calculus		68.8 (139/202)	66.5 (231/347)	73.0 (165/226)	33.4 (636/1191)
Periodontitis		56.2 (63/112)	19.1 (9/47)	55.8 (38/68)	78.3 (116/148)
Periapical cavities		0.5 (1/177)	0 (0/134)	1.4 (2/139)	1.6 (5/300)

among the discrete burials, with the exception of periodontitis (Table 3.41).

The subadult sample

In the mass grave assemblage caries affected two deciduous teeth (5.4%) and five permanent teeth (4.4%). The prevalence of caries affecting deciduous teeth was higher than that calculated for the discrete skeletons (Tables 3.42 and 3.43). Enamel hypoplasia was confined to permanent teeth only and was less prevalent than in the discrete assemblage.

Palaeopathology
by Louise Loe

Methods

All skeletons were examined for pathology or bony abnormality based on the recommendations of Roberts and Connell (2004). When present, lesions were described and diagnosed by employing standard definitions (eg Aufderheide and Rodríguez-Martín 1998; Ortner and Putschar 1985; Roberts and Connell 2004). Conditions were broadly classified thus: infection, metabolic disorders, trauma, congenital and

Table 3.42   Dental health status in the subadult sample from the mass grave.

Deciduous	Anterior dentition		Posterior dentition	
Age	Dental caries % (n/N)	Enamel Hypoplasia % (n/N)	Dental caries % (n/N)	Enamel Hypoplasia % (n/N)
Infant	0 (0/7)	–	–	–
Young Child	0 (0/15)	–	0 (0/13)	–
Older Child	0 (0/18)	–	8.3 (2/24)	0 (0/4)
Total	0 (0/40)	–	5.4 (2/37)	0 (0/4)
Permanent	Dental caries	Enamel Hypoplasia	Dental caries	Hypoplasia
Young Child	–	–	–	–
Older Child	0 (0/30)	22.2 (2/9)	0 (0/19)	0 (0/10)
Adolescent	0 (0/60)	–	5.8 (5/93)	–
Total	0 (0/90)	22.2 (2/9)	4.4 (5/112)	0 (0/10)

Table 3.43   Comparison between dental conditions observed among subadults from the discrete burial assemblage and the mass grave.

Oral condition		Deciduous teeth		Permanent teeth	
		Discrete burials % (n/N)	Mass grave % (n/N)	Discrete burials % (n/N)	Mass grave % (n/N)
Enamel hypoplasia	Anterior	10.5 (2/29)	–	95.6 (22/23)	22.2 (2/9)
	Posterior	18.7 (3/16)	0 (0/4)	66.6 (16/24)	0 (0/10)
Dental caries	Anterior	0 (0/19)	0 (0/40)	0 (0/10)	0 (0/90)
	Posterior	0 (0/19)	5.4 (2/37)	5.8 (1/17)	4.4 (5/112)

(While enamel hypoplasia and dental caries have been calculated based on the number of observed teeth. Calculus, periodontitis and periapical cavities have been calculated by counting the number of alveoli available for examination.)

developmental conditions, joint disease, circulatory disorders, neoplastic disease, miscellaneous conditions and unclassified pathological changes.

Results

Discrete inhumations

Infection

Infection manifests on bone in the form of inflammation and may involve the entire bone ('osteomyelitis'), the cortical bone ('osteitis') or the fibrous sheath that covers bone, the periosteum ('periostitis'). These changes may be observed as a result of tuberculosis, leprosy and syphilis (among others) or, where the pattern of change is non-diagnostic and the pathogen is unknown, non-specific infection. Infection may arise as a result of pathogens spreading from an adjacent lesion via the blood stream (for example, as seen in trauma, chronic skin ulceration, paranasal sinusitis, middle ear cavity infection, a dental abscess and visceral rib surface inflammation), or as a result of direct implantation into bone (for example, as seen in puncture and penetrating injuries). Periostitis is the most commonly observed lesion in archaeological populations. This surface inflammation may be identified on dry bone as fine pitting, longitudinal striations, swelling and/or plaque-like new bone formation on the original bone surface. Surface inflammation may also affect the cranium but, owing to a difference in anatomy, the term periostitis does not apply here. These changes may occur as the result of infection, or may accompany other conditions of a metabolic, neoplastic or traumatic nature (Resnick and Niwayama 1995). The level of non-specific infection in a population is generally regarded as an indicator of adaptation or

mal-adaptation to environmental conditions, or more specifically, malnutrition, poor sanitation and generalised health stress (Roberts and Manchester 1995).

Non-specific inflammation involving the skull: Three skeletons, one 18 to 25 year old male (Skeleton 1386), one adolescent (Skeleton 1317) of undetermined sex and one 25 to 35 year old female (Skeleton 1181), had inflammatory changes involving ectocranial and/or endocranial surfaces of the skull vault (Table 3.44). The female had spiculated and porous new bone on both the endocranial and the ectocranial surfaces of the pars basilaris and the ectocranial surface of the left pars lateralis of the occipital bone. The changes on the male and subadult involved the endocranial surfaces of their parietal bones and were in the form of capillary-like new bone. Inflammation involving the cranial vault may be the result of a number of different conditions including scurvy, chronic meningitis, trauma, anaemia, neoplasia, venous drainage disorders and tuberculosis (Lewis 2004; Ortner and Erikson 1997). There were no changes on other parts of these skeletons that suggest which of these diagnoses is more likely here.

Skeleton 1181 also had inflammation affecting the alveolar bone around the third mandibular molars. Both molars had been lost post-mortem and the empty sockets did not display any pathological changes. Inflammatory changes were also observed on the mandibles of Skeleton 1232, an 18–25 year old female, and Skeleton 1328, a 25–35 year old male. Skeleton 1232 had active and healed new bone on the internal and external surfaces of the right ascending ramus bone and the damaged socket of the right third molar. No dental conditions were observed in association with these lesions, but the bone was incomplete. On Skeleton 1328, active new bone was

Table 3.44   Non-specific inflammation involving the skull.

Element involved	Total	%	Unsexed adults		Male %		Female %		Subadults %	
Ectocranium	2/48	4.2	0/8		0/24		1/11 (9.1)		1/5	
Endocranium	1/48	2.1	0/8		0/24		1/11 (9.1)		0/5	
Mandible	5/77	6.5	R: 0/6	L: 0/8	R: 1/18 (5.6)	L: 1/17(5.9)	R: 2/9 (22.2)	L: 1/10 (10)	R: 0/4	L: 0/5

present on the alveolar bone (buccal aspect) below the sockets for the left first molar and the right first and second molars. There was a periapical cavity associated with the right first molar and all teeth were associated with carious cavities. An erupting tooth, dental disease and scurvy are among the conditions that may cause inflammatory changes involving the mandible.

Sinusitis: Skeleton 1181 also presented changes that were consistent with maxillary sinusitis. This is in addition to Skeleton 1381, a 25 to 35 year old of undetermined sex and Skeleton 1328, a 25 to 35 year old male. Maxillary sinusitis is diagnosed based on the presence of new bone in the nasal sinuses. Upper respiratory tract infections, poor living conditions, environmental pollution, congenital abnormalities, dental disease and specific infectious diseases such as tuberculosis and leprosy are among the aetiological factors associated with this condition (Lewis 2002, 21). In addition to new bone on a fragment of nasal sinus, the same changes were also present on a poorly preserved fragment of skull bone belonging to Skeleton 1328. The fragment could not be precisely identified. It was either an additional piece of sinus bone, or it may have been a piece of sphenoid bone.

Periostitis: Periostitis was observed on 28 out of 63 skeletons (44.4%), 25 adults (49%) and three subadults (33.3%). It was encountered on more females (seven out of eleven females, or 63.6%) than males (12 out of 23 males, or 50%), although six adults were of unknown sex. The most frequently involved elements were the lower long limb bones and the bones of the feet (Table 3.45).

The tibia was the most frequently affected element (TPR 28.9%). This finding is typical for most archaeological skeletal assemblages and is explained by the fact that the tibia is more easily affected by mild trauma compared to other bones in the skeleton (Roberts and Manchester 1995, 130). However, in the present sample, few tibiae were affected unilaterally. Further, the plotted distribution of element involvement indicates that at least 16 of the affected individuals had changes that involved more than one element (Table 3.46), this being a minimum number because the plot does not take into account

observations that could not be made owing to preservation. This therefore suggests that something other than just mild trauma was causing periosteal reactions in the present sample. Multiple element involvement is indicative of systemic disease, although the patterns of involvement in the present skeletons are not exclusive to any one particular disease process.

The affected innominate bones (Plate 3.3) were from one individual, Skeleton 1372, an adult male. This individual also had periosteal new bone deposits on all of his lower major limb bones and most of his metacarpals and metatarsals. On all bones the changes were typical of inflammation of the periosteum (ie striae, pitting and lamellar bone formation), with the exception of the innominate bones where the changes, in the region of the attachment site for the ischiofemoral ligament, included capillary-like new bone formation. Because of the location of these changes, it is just possible that they are the result of ligament trauma at this site. However, owing to the fact that the changes involved both sides, non-specific systemic disease is the preferred diagnosis.

Comparison with other Romano-British populations indicates that London Road has a high prevalence of periostitis for this period. For example, a prevalence of 24.2% (TPR) has been reported for tibiae and 17.2% (TPR) for fibulae from Kingsholm and 25% (TPR) has been reported for tibiae and 12.2% (TPR) for fibulae from Kempston (Roberts and Cox 2003). Wells (1982a, 182) reports that between 10 and 12 percent of all adult tibiae in the Cirencester south assemblage had periostitis and that there was little difference between males and females. These figures are compared to a TPR of 28.9% for tibiae and 16% for fibulae from the present site. The TPR for 124–130 London road was not available but a CPR of 7.1% has been reported (Clough 2003). Overall, out of 5,716 skeletons from 52 different Romano-British sites, 381 (CPR 6.7%) had non-specific infection (Roberts and Cox 2003, 124). These figures are far lower than the CPR of 44.4% for London Road.

Osteomyelitis: There were no definite examples of osteomyelitis (non-specific bone infection). However, it is possible that some of the more thorough-going

Table 3.45 Periostitis, absolute prevalence.

Element involved	Total	%	Unsexed adults		Males		Females		Subadults	
			Right	Left	Right %	Left %	Right %	Left %	Right	Left
Ribs	5/316	1.6	0/10	0/8	1/62 (1.6)	0/87	1/60 (1.7)	1/47 (2.1)	1/16	1/26
Innominate	2/61	3.3	0/4	0/4	1/13 (7.7)	1/15 (6.7)	0/9	0/9	0/4	0/3
Femur	9/86	10.5	1/9	1/9	1/17 (5.9)	1/18 (5.6)	1/10 (10)	1/11 (9.1)	2/6	1/6
Tibia	24/83	28.9	4/13	2/9	1/18 (33.3)	6/16 (37.5)	3/10 (30)	2/11 (18.2)	0/3	0/3
Fibula	12/75	16.0	3/11	1/7	4/17 (23.5)	4/14 (28.6)	0/10	0/10	0/3	0/3
Metacarpals	2/172	1.2	0/13	0/5	1/34 (2.9)	1/52 (1.9)	0/27	0/27	0/6	0/8
Metatarsals	8/162	4.9	0/22	1/15	3/45 (6.7)	4/39 (10.3)	0/16	0/25	0	0
Calcaneus	3/41	7.3	0/6	0/5	0/11	0/10	1/4 (25.0)	2/5 (40.0)	0	0

Table 3.46   Distribution of elements with non-specific inflammation by skeleton.

Age	Sex	Skeleton number	En-cranial	Ec-cranial	Mandible	R Orbit	L Orbit	Ribs	CV	TV	LV	R innom.	L innom.	R humerus	L humerus	R radius	L radius	R ulna	L ulna	R MCs	L MCs	Hand phals.	R femur	L femur	R tibia	L tibia	R fibula	L fibula	R MTs	L MTs	Foot phals.	Tarsals
5–12	u/k	1086						X																								
46+	M	1089																							X							
35–45	F	1103																					X									
25–35	M	1109																							X		X					
25–35	F	1131																					X	X								X
18–25	u/k	1138																					X									
18–25	F	1165																														X
25–35	F	1181	X	X	X			X																								
46+	M	1216						X																					X	X		
18–25	F	1232			X																											
25–35	M	1262																					X	X	X	X	X					
Adult	u/k	1279																													X	
111	M	1286																							X	X		X				
108	u/k	1317		X																			X	X								
25–35	M	1328			X																											
25–35	F	1337																					X	X								
Adult	M	1372										X	X										X	X	X	X						
25–35	F	1390																					X	X								
Adult	M	1393																					X	X								
12–18	u/k	1396																					X									
Adult	u/k	1401																					X	X	X	X	X	X				
Adult	u/k	1405																							X		X					
Adult	M	1453																								X		X		X		
46+	M	1459																					X									
25–35	M	1496																					X	X								
Adult	M	1499																											X			
Adult	u/k	1510																									X					
Adult	u/k	1709																					X	X								

examples of periostitis were caused by this. In particular, this concerns Skeleton 1286, a 25–35 year old male (Plate 3.4). This skeleton displayed considerable, long-standing, new bone formation, suggestive of marrow involvement. However, there was no evidence for a draining sinus (a cloaca), or sequestra (areas of dead bone) and there was no involucrum (proliferative new bone) around the affected bones. Radiography to demonstrate the extent of the changes would be required to explore this further.

Metabolic disorders

These are triggered by either an excess or a deficiency in the body's dietary requirements and hormones and result in specific changes to the skeleton, such as in the form of increased or decreased bone turn over. Included in this category are scurvy (vitamin C deficiency) and cribra orbitalia. No definite cases of scurvy were identified, but the lesions may be fairly subtle in archaeological bone and, therefore, difficult to detect (Roberts and Manchester 1995). There was no evidence for inflammation on those parts of the skeleton (for

example, the scapula and the sphenoid bone) that are affected in this disease (Ortner and Erikson 1997). However, the inflammatory changes that were identified on the skulls, as described above, are seen in this condition. On their own, these changes cannot be considered diagnostic of the disease.

Cribra orbitalia and porotic hyperostosis: Cribra orbitalia and porotic hyperostosis refer to small porosities or large interconnected trabeculae on the roof of the orbits (cribra orbitalia) and the frontal, parietal and occipital bones of the cranial vault (porotic hyperostosis) (Stuart-Macadam 1991). These changes are believed to represent the skeletal manifestation of iron deficiency anaemia which may arise as a result of dietary deficiency, malabsorption (due to gastro-intestinal infection or parasites), blood loss and chronic disease (Roberts and Cox, 2003, 234). Iron deficiency anaemia may also be inherited, but this form in rare in British material (Boylston *et al.* 1998). In the present sample, cribra orbitalia was idenfitied on one or both of the orbital bones of 11/51 adults (21.6%) and 2/9 subadults

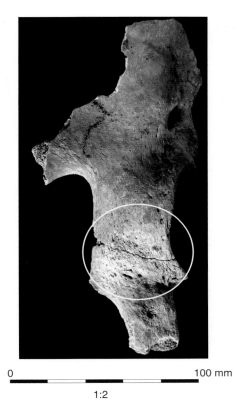

0   100 mm

1:2

Plate 3.3   Non-specific inflammation (highlighted) involving the right innominate bone of Skeleton 1372, an adult male.

(22.2%) (Table 3.47). There were no examples of porotic hyperostosis.

The youngest individual with cribra orbitalia was approximately two to five years old and the oldest, over 45 years old. The higher prevalence among subadults is to be expected because cribra orbitalia does not develop in adult bone (Stuart Macadam 1985). The changes, therefore, all represent a childhood condition.

In five cases both orbits were involved and in four cases only the right orbit was involved. There were no cases where only the left orbit was involved. However, two skeletons only had their right orbits available for examination and one only had its left orbit available. An additional skeleton only had one orbit present, but this was unsided.

The prevalence rates for cribra orbitalia were similar to those reported for Poundbury (Stuart-Macadam 1991) which were 24.4% (TPR) for males, 27.7% (TPR) for females and 36.4% (TPR) for subadults (ibid., 102). However, rates were higher than those reported for Kempston, Bedfordshire (Boylston and Roberts 1996) where the TPR for males was 18.3%, for females 10.5% and for subadults 26.7%. Males, females and subadults from Cirencester (Wells 1982a, 186) also had lower rates. The true prevalence rates observed among these groups were 19.9%, 13.3% and 35.1% respectively. Four out of 56 skeletons from 124–130 London Road

0   100 mm

1:2

Plate 3.4   Thorough-going periosteal reaction involving right and left tibiae of Skeleton 1286, a 25–35 year old male.

are reported to have had the condition (CPR 7.1%) (Clough 2003), which is drastically lower than the CPR for the present sample (20.6%). These differences may be explained by the fact that there were more older adults among the populations from Kempston and 124–130 London Road. Lesions heal with age and are thus less common among the older adult age categories.

Trauma

Trauma refers to any injury or wound to the body that may affect the bone and/or soft tissues (Roberts 1991, 226). Dislocations, ligament trauma in the form of new bone formation and fractures are some of the types of change in this category. The most common of these are fractures and these represent the main type of trauma identified in the present sample.

Table 3.47   Cribra orbitalia, absolute prevalence.

Orbit	Male	%	Female	%	Unsexed adult	%	Unsexed and unaged	%	Subadult	%
Right	3/9	33.3	4/8	50	3/3	100	0/1	0	1/2	50
Left	2/9	22.2	0/8	0	3/4	100	0/0	0	1/4	25
Total	5/18	27.8	4/16	25	6/7	100	0/1	0	3*/6	50

* includes one orbit that could not be sided.

A fracture is defined as a complete or partial break in the continuity of bone (ibid.). Fractures may result from underlying pathology, repeated stress or acute injury (Roberts and Manchester 1995). Fractures occurring around the time of death, when the organic matrix of the bone is still present, are termed peri-mortem, while those occurring after death, when the organic matrix has decomposed, are termed post-mortem. Ante-mortem fractures occur before death and may be identified based on evidence for healing. The identification of these different types of fracture in archaeological human bone provides enormous scope for furthering knowledge of the lives of past populations including, their social interactions, activities, socio-economic status and treatment of the dead. For example, certain types of ante- or peri-mortem fracture are indicative of inter-personal violence, while others could be from accidents (such as a fall from a height) (Crawford Adams 1983; Galloway 1999; Walker 1997). The alignment of an ante-mortem break and evidence for secondary pathology (among other changes) may indicate quality of diet and treatment (Grauer and Roberts 1996) while, in certain burial contexts (for example, a mass grave), some types of peri-mortem break may be associated with post-mortem dismemberment (Villa and Mahieu 1991; White 2003).

Ante-mortem fractures: Healed ante-mortem fractures were observed on the bones of nine skeletons (14.1% of all individuals); seven out of 24 males (29.2%) including three adults, one adolescent, one old adult and three middle adults. Two skeletons were unsexed individuals (both adults). Fractures were not identified on the skeletons of any females. This is despite the fact that the survival of the different female skeletal elements was proportional to that of male skeletal elements. Fractures were less frequent among adult females from Cirencester (south) (CPR 6.6%) than they were among adult males (CPR 26.7%) (Wells 1982a, 167). At 124–130 London Road 30% of all males had sustained a fracture compared to 14.3% of all females (Clough 2003).

A total of 14 elements displayed macroscopic evidence for a fracture, identified as a break in the continuity of the alignment of the bone. However, of these, five (see Table 3.48) require radiography to confirm their diagnosis. For the purposes of the present analysis, all of these elements have been counted as definite fractures.

All fractures were well healed and showed good alignment suggesting that they had been sustained a

Table 3.48   Summary of possible fractures.

Skeleton Number	Sex	Age	Element(s)
1118	Male	Adult	Third and fourth left metacarpals
1281	Unsexed	Adult	One unsided hand phalanx
1286	Male	25–35 years	Right tibia
1405	Unsexed	Adult	Right tibia

long time before death. There was also no evidence for associated thorough-going bone infection, although two tibiae (Skeletons 1286 and 1405) and two fibulae (Skeletons 1089 and 1453) had associated periostitis. Only one skeleton with a possible fractured hand phalanx (Skeleton 1281) had osteoarthritis in an associated joint. There were probably more cases like this, however, because associated joint surfaces were frequently missing. Fractures that become infected may result in septicaemia and ultimately in death. They may also disrupt the mechanics of a joint and result in arthritis, leading to deformity and debilitation. There is no evidence in the present sample that the secondary changes had a significant impact on the population.

The most frequently affected elements were the fibula (2.9%) followed by foot phalanges (2.6%) and the tibia (2.6%) (Table 3.49). The prevalence of upper limb bone (humerus, radius, ulna and clavicle) fractures was 0.4% (1/246), compared to 2.3% (5/220) for the lower limb bones (femur, tibia and fibula). Fibulae and tibiae were also the most frequently fractured elements among the skeletons from Cirencester south (Wells 1982a, 168). Here, 4.7% (13/274) of all fibulae and 2.4% (8/334) of all tibiae had sustained ante-mortem fractures. This trend is also seen among other Romano-British assemblages (Roberts and Cox 2003, 157).

Foot phalanges are susceptible to fracturing being '...ideally positioned to collide with a variety of objects' (Galloway 1999, 222). It is unlikely that the fractures involving feet would have greatly incapacitated the individuals that they involved (ibid.). Both of the tibia fractures (skeleton 1405 and skeleton 1286) require confirmation radiologically (see Plate 3.5). Both presented swelling that was located on the middle portion of the shafts. A subperiosteal haematoma or bone infection are

Table 3.49 Distribution of fractures, absolute prevalence.

Skeletal element	Total n/N	%	Males				Females				Unsexed adults			
			Right n/N	%	Left n/N	%	Right n/N	%	Left n/N	%	Right n/N	%	Left n/N	%
Clavicle	1/61	1.6	1/17	5.9	0/17		0/8		0/8		1/6	16.7	0/5	
Ribs	2/274	0.7	1/62	1.6	1/87	1.1	0/60		0/47		0/10		0/8	
Humerus	0/75		0/20		0/20		0/8		0/9		0/10		0/8	
Radius	0/56		0/14		0/18		0/8		0/9		0/4		0/3	
Ulna	0/54		0/13		0/18		0/8		0/7		0/3		0/5	
Mcs	4/158	2.5	0/34		2/52	3.8	0/27		0/27		0/13		2/5	40
Hand phalanges	1/254	0.4	0/113				0/79				1/62			1.6
Femur	0/74		0/17		0/18		0/10		0/11		0/9		0/9	
Tibia	2/77	2.6	1/18	5.6	0/16		0/10		0/11		1/13	7.7	0/9	
Fibula	2/69	2.9	0/17		1/14	7.1	0/10		0/10		0/11		1/7	14.3
MTs	0/162		0/45		0/39		0/16		0/25		0/22		0/15	
Foot phalanges	1/38	2.6	0/20				0/9				1/9			11.1

MCs = metacarpals; MTs metacarpals

other conditions that may result in bony swelling, but the preferred diagnosis is old trauma. The shaft is the most common part of the tibia to be fractured and the middle or distal portions are usually involved (ibid., 193).

Fractures that involve the fibula usually show little displacement and therefore the good alignment shown by the examples in the present sample is not surprising. Further, where the tibia was not involved, it is unlikely that the fibula fractures caused the individuals to experience significant mobility problems. This is because the un-fractured tibia would have acted as a natural splint, providing support and stability to the broken fibula. In modern clinical settings, fractures that involve the fibula often go undetected by the patient (Crawford Adams 1983). It is possible that this was also the case for individuals from London Road. Fibula fractures may result from direct force trauma such as a blow, if they occur without the involvement of other elements (ibid.). Rotation of the ankle round an axis provided by the stationary tibia is another mechanism, such as may occur accidentally whilst walking on rough ground, or in a modern setting, skiing (Boylston and Roberts 1996). For the present

0   100 mm

Plate 3.5   Possible old healed fracture involving the right tibia shaft belonging to Skeleton 1405, an adult of undetermined sex.

skeletons, it is impossible to say what may have caused them because lower limb bone elements are missing and thus the pattern of element involvement (for example, whether they were isolated fractures or whether other associated bones were also affected) is not known.

Rib fractures were generally infrequent and involved two individuals out of 63 skeletons (CPR 3.2%), or two ribs out of a total of 274 (TPR 0.7%). This is lower than the percentages calculated for skeletons from 124–130 London Road (CPR 7.1%) (Clough 2003); Kempston, Bedfordshire (TPR 10%) (Boylston and Roberts 1996); Kingsholm, Gloucester (CPR 12.5%); Cirencester (north) (CPR 4.4%) and Cirencester (south) (CPR 7.7%) (Roberts and Cox 2003). The rate was, however, higher than that reported for Poundbury (CPR 2.0%) (Farwell and Molleson 1993), Eastern Cemetery, London (CPR 1.3%) (Conheeney 2000), Cassington (CPR 1.4%) and Ancaster (CPR 2.1%) (Roberts and Cox 2003). The rib fractures in the present sample involved the lateral portion of the shaft of one unidentified right rib (Skeleton 1109) and the neck, or vertebral end, of one unidentified left rib (Skeleton 1089). Fractures that involve the shaft (rather than the neck) of the rib are likely to be the result of interpersonal violence (Wells 1982a).

The absence of radial and ulnar (forearm) fractures is unusual. Clough (2003) reports a CPR of 1.8% (1/56) for the assemblage from the 124–130 London Road cemetery. For Kempston, Bedfordshire, the TPR was 2.8% and 2.6% for radial and ulnar fractures respectively (Boylston 1996). Similarly, Wells (1982a) reports that 2.9% of all ulnae and 1.7% of all radii were fractured among the elements examined from Cirencester (south). The crude prevalence rate for ulnar and radial fractures observed in Romano-British populations is between approximately one and three percent (Roberts and Cox 2003, 154–55). Generally, forearm fractures were infrequent during the Romano-British period compared to other periods (Wells 1982a).

Defence injuries and accidental falls onto an out-stretched hand are the most common causes of forearm fractures (Crawford Adams 1983).

Two skeletons had more than one fractured element. Skeleton 1089, a male aged over 45 years, had sustained fractures to his left rib, left third metacarpal and right fibula shaft. Fractures involving the left third and fourth metacarpals were recorded for Skeleton 1118, an adult male. It is not possible to say whether these skeletons sustained these breaks at the same time, or whether they were the victims of more than one traumatic event.

Cranial trauma: One skeleton, Skeleton 1112, had a small elliptical depressed fracture that was superior to the nuchal line of the left occipital bone (Plate 3.6). The lesion was healed and was probably the result of an impact from a blunt object. The individual was an adolescent male. Very similar traumatic lesions were identified on four skulls from Cirencester (south) by Wells (1982a). These were attributed to '....an accidental blow on the head....or.....a fall against the corner of a table....[or]....a battle wound caused by an accurately directed slingshot' (ibid., 163–4).

Spondylolisis: Spondylolisis is a stress fracture in which the neural arch separates from the body of the fifth lumbar vertebra. It may be caused by an underlying congenital weakness in this part of the spine (Aufderheide and Rodríguez-Martín 1998). One skeleton, an adult male (Skeleton 1118), showed evidence for this condition which gives a crude

prevalence rate of 1.6% for the population overall. This is higher than the total overall CPR (0.9%) calculated for the Romano-British period by Roberts and Cox (2003).

Peri-mortem trauma: The *in situ* location of the skull belonging to Skeleton 1232, an 18–25 year old female, suggested that she may have been decapitated prior to her burial. However, there was no evidence on her skeletal remains that this had been the case. Decapitation may be identified on dry bone as cut or chop marks on the cervical vertebrae, clavicles, basioccipital of the skull and the mandible. The remains of Skeleton 1232 were in a fragmentary condition, although the cortical bone was well preserved and all of the aforementioned elements were available for examination. None of these displayed changes that were consistent with cut or chop marks.

Peri-mortem cut marks: Formal analysis of the London Road skeletons for peri-mortem modification was beyond the scope of the present report, but any observations relating to this were noted in passing. Of particular note were the remains of Skeleton 1496, a 25 to 35 year old male, that had numerous parallel and sub-parallel linear incisions that cut into the cortical surfaces of several bones. These striations were located perpendicular to the long axis of the right and left femora, right ilium and left ulna. Most were sharp, straight and had 'v' shaped profiles. Striations that have this appearance and occupy a perpendicular orientation are indicative of deliberate anthropogenic

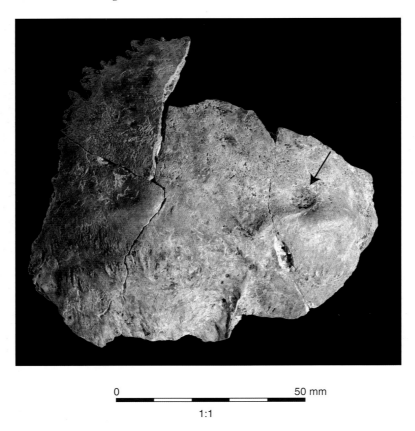

0   50 mm

1:1

Plate 3.6   Healed blunt trauma involving the occipital bone of the skull from Skeleton 1112, an adolescent male.

cut marks, such as may be observed as a result of dismemberment. However, in the present example, the striations tended to be located away from articulations, which is where the marks of dismemberment are usually observed. Further, some of the marks had distinctly eroded margins and were quite shallow. These factors would combine to suggest that they were the result of excavation damage rather than any deliberate modification that had occurred in antiquity. They have been classified as pseudo-cut marks (Plate 3.7).

<u>Congenital and developmental conditions</u>
This refers to abnormalities in growth or development. They may not become evident until the period of growth or young adulthood, or they may be present at the fetal stage or at birth. The most common abnormalities are relatively minor and involve the spinal column (Barnes 1994).

Spina bifida occulta and lumbarisation: Two skeletons exhibited bony changes that place them in this category. Spina bifida occulta, in the form of incomplete fusion of the posterior neural arches of the third, fourth and fifth sacral segments, was identified on Skeleton 1390, a female of between 25 and 35 years of age. Skeleton 1393, an adult male, showed evidence for shifting of the lumbosacral border in a caudal direction, a condition also known as lumbarisation. In this condition, the first sacral

0   50 mm

1:1

Plate 3.7 Pseudo-cut marks observed on the left femur from Skeleton 1496, a 25–35 year old male.

vertebra is separated from the rest of the sacrum and assumes the form of the last lumbar vertebra (Aufderheide and Rodríguez-Martín 1998). The assimilation may involve one side only or both sides, it may be complete or incomplete, unlateral or bilateral and symmetrical or asymmetrical. The condition would not have caused any symptoms and is more common among females (Aufderheide and Rodríguez-Martín 1998). Only the right side of the sacrum was present and, therefore, it was not possible to determine what the involvement was.

<u>Joint disease</u>
Osteoarthritis: Osteoarthritis (OA) is the most common pathological condition in both archaeological and modern populations (Rogers and Waldron 1995). It is therefore not surprising to find that it involved the most skeletons of all other disease categories described in this report. Seventeen skeletons (32.1% of all adults); 10 males (41.7%), four females (36.4%) and three of undetermined sex, presented changes that are diagnostic of this condition (Table 3.50). The changes included eburnation (polished bone) or a combination of pitting, bony contour change and/or osteophytosis (new bone growth around the margin of a joint or, less commonly, on a joint surface) (Rogers and Waldron 1995).

Two skeletons (1153 and 1206), who were young adults of between approximately 18 and 25 years of age, had OA affecting their costovertebral joints. OA is not usually observed among young adult skeletons because it is associated with old age. Thus, activity and trauma may have played a significant role in the manifestation of the disease in these individuals.

Compared to 124–130 London Road, rates for OA were higher. For 124–130 London Road the CPR was 17.4% for all adult males and no females (out of a sample of 21) were affected (Clough 2003). London Road rates were, however, similar to those calculated for the Cirencester population which had a CPR for males of 51.5% and for females, 32.9% (Wells 1982a). These comparisons should be viewed with caution because they may be biased by the different methods employed to diagnose OA between observers (Rogers and Waldron 1995).

The most frequently affected joints were the cervical spine (TPR 17.1%), followed by the hip (TPR 15%) (Table 3.51). It was not possible to identify the number of vertebrae involved for each spine owing to fragmentation. Skeleton 1281 had OA that involved the metacarpophalangeal joint (the knuckle) of the third finger. The proximal and middle phalanges belonging to this finger bone had ankylosed (fused). The changes may be secondary to trauma.

It is not unusual to find that the knee was rarely affected. This is typical of archaeological populations where both the hip and cervical spine are frequently involved (Rogers *et al.* 1981). Rates for the knee are, however, perhaps low for this period, whereas rates for the hip would seem to be high for this period. For example, Roberts (1989) reports a TPR of 4.2% for both the hip and the knee for skeletons from

Table 3.50   Age and sex distribution of skeletons with OA.

	Males	Females	Unsexed	Total
Adult (any adult age category)	3	1	2	6
Young adult	1	1		2
Middle adult	3	1		4
Mature adult		1		1
Old adult	3		1	4
Total	10/24 (41.7%)	4/11 (36.4%)	3/18 (16.7%)	17/53 (32.1%)

Kingsholm, and the calculated TPR for Poundbury is 1.1% for the hip and 3.1% for the knee (Farwell and Molleson 1993).

Three individuals (1089, 1216 and 1262) had generalised OA which means that the disease had affected multiple joints in their skeletons. Skeleton 1089, a male aged over 45 years, showed involvement of the right and left hips and the cervical vertebrae. The right and left hips were also involved on Skeleton 1216, a male aged over 45 years, who also had costovertebral involvement. Finally, skeleton 1262, a 25–35 year old male, showed involvement in the right and left hips, the right elbow, left knee and cervical and lumbar spines.

Great attention has been focused in the archaeological literature on the association between OA and activity and occupation (see Jurmain 1999). However, it is very unlikely that occupation and activity will have played a unique role in the manifestation of OA in this population (possibly with the exception of Skeletons 1153 and 1206 described above). Many factors, including age, sex, ancestry and genetic predisposition, as well as activity or occupation, play a part in the manifestation and course of the disease. Except in rare instances, when a pattern of OA occurs that is unique to an activity or occupation, it is usually impossible to determine which of these factors was

responsible for this disease (Waldron and Cox 1989). The distribution of the disease in the present sample would not seem to be directly associated with a specific activity or occupation.

Spondylosis deformans and Schmorl's nodes: Spondylosis deformans and Schmorl's nodes are two conditions that involve the spine and are extremely common in both modern and archaeological populations. Schmorl's nodes are caused by intervertebral disc herniation into the vertebral body. They appear on dry bone as depressions, either on the superior or inferior surface of the body. Although associated with degenerative disease, Schmorl's nodes have been linked to activity and trauma, especially in adolescence, or metabolic disorders (Jurmain 1999). Four skeletons, three males and one female, showed evidence for this condition. They ranged in age from 18–25 years (one male), to 25–35 years (one female and one male). One male could not be aged more specifically than adult. The changes involved the thoracic spine of three skeletons and the lumbar spine of one skeleton.

Spondylosis deformans is identified on dry bone as increased porosity on the surfaces of the vertebral bodies. The condition is mainly caused by degeneration of the intervertebral disc and is associated with increasing age. There were four skeletons with this condition, including one female adult, a 25–35 year

Table 3.51   Frequency of joints affected with OA.

Skeletal element	Total	%	Males				Females				Unsexed adults			
			Right	%	Left	%	Right	%	Left	%	Right	%	Left	%
Costovert.	11/274	4.0	3/62	4.8	3/87	3.4	2/60	3.3	2/47*	4.3	0/10		0/8	
Cervical spine	6/35	17.1	4/18			22.2	1/10			1.0	1/7			14.3
Thoracic spine	1/30	3.3	1/17			5.9	0/8				0/5			
Lumbar spine	1/28	3.6	1/16			6.3	0/9				0/3			
Shoulder	0/37		0/8		0/12		0/7		0/6		0/3		0/1	
Elbow	1/56	1.8	1/14	7.1	0/15		0/8		0/7		0/7		0/5	
Hand	1/61	1.6	0/15		0/17		0/9		0/9		1/6	16.7	0/5	
Hip	9/60	15.0	4/15	26.7	4/16	25.0	0/9		0/9		1/11**			9.1
Knee	1/58	1.5	1/16	6.25	0/15		0/9		0/10		0/4		0/4	

Key: costovert. = costovertebral joints

*excludes one unsided costovertebral joint (this has been included in the total); **hip bone is unsided; Hand = any carpal or metacarpal joints; or more joints; All spines = number of skeletons with one or more vertebrae present old individual of undetermined sex and two males of 18 to 25 years and over 45 years old. In all, the changes involved the cervical spine. Spondylosis is uncommon on young individuals and is probably the result of trauma.

Possible Legg-Calvé-Perthes disease: The osteoarthritis that was observed on the left hip bone (Plate 3.8) belonging to Skeleton 1286, a male aged between 25 and 35 years, may have been secondary to Legg-Calvé-Perthes disease (Perthes). Perthes affects children between three and 12 years of age, is more common among males and is associated with growth retardation. Repeated trauma, infection and endocrine disease have all been implicated in the aetiology of Perthes, but it is generally regarded as an idopathic condition (of unknown cause). It arises when impaired blood supply during growth of the femoral head causes necrosis and deformity leading to premature joint disease in this part of the hip. In the present example, the changes included a mushroom shaped, flattened femoral head and osteophytosis (new bone growth around the margin of the joint). However, not enough of the bone had survived to determine whether it displayed coxa vara (an abnormal femoral neck angle), or whether the femoral neck was shortened and widened, and there were no metaphyseal cysts. These are other changes that are seen in this condition. Right and left acetabulae were shallow but both were too incomplete to determine whether they were lengthened (also diagnostic of Perthes). The left femur was missing from the top of the diaphyseal shaft upwards. Differential diagnoses include bad osteoarthritis and hip dislocation.

Other joint disease: There were five skeletons that presented changes involving their joints that do not fit into the above categories. Two smooth-walled antemortem oval, lytic lesions were observed in the region of the fibula articular surface of the right talus bone of

Skeleton 1510, an unsexed adult (Plate 3.9). The lesions had penetrated the cortical bone and were large (approximately six millimetres by 13 millimetres). This skeleton was less than 25% complete and was represented by the right tibia and fibula and an incomplete set of foot bones. No changes were observed on the other bones that were present. In the absence of any inflammation, the changes are unlikely to be the result of infection involving this joint. Diagnosis is difficult in the absence of other hand and foot bones, but an erosive joint disease is a possibility. This includes gout, which commonly involves the feet and presents punched-out oval or round lesions.

Peri-articular scalloped erosions were present on the heads of the right and left first metatarsals belonging to Skeleton 1453, an adult male (Plate 3.10). The same changes also involved the phalanx of the left great toe. Periostitis was present on the shaft of the first left metatarsal, in addition to the left tibia and fibula (the latter may have been fractured). The skeleton was represented by lower limb bones and forearm bones and had incomplete sets of hand and

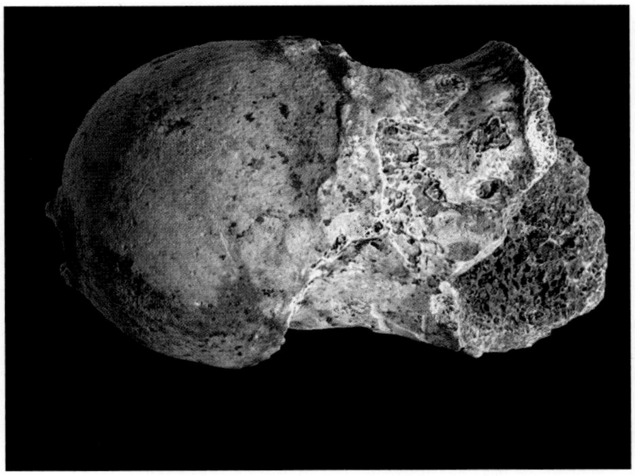

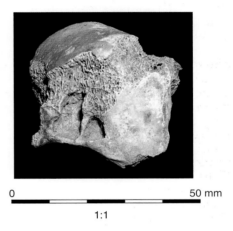

0   50 mm

1:1

Plate 3.9   Oval, lytic lesions involving the lateral side of the right talus bone of Skeleton 1510, an unsexed adult.

0   50 mm

1:1

Plate 3.10   Scalloped erosions involving the heads of the right and left great toes from Skeleton 1453, an adult male.

0   50 mm

1:1

Plate 3.8   Possible Legg-Calvé-Perthes disease involving the left femur belonging to Skeleton 1286, a 25–35 year old male.

foot bones. Erosive changes affecting foot bones may be caused by relatively minor conditions such as hallux valgus (bunions) or may be the result of something more systemic such as gout. In the present case, the erosions were not typical of those seen in gout (Rogers and Waldron 1995). However, bones of the feet are typically involved in this disease. Gout, therefore, cannot be ruled out.

A small circular ante-mortem lytic lesion was also observed on the joint surface of each of two left wrist bones (scaphoid and lunate) belonging to Skeleton 1328, a 25–35 year old male. There was no indication that these changes were present on other joints from this skeleton which was mostly complete but had a very limited number of hand and foot bones surviving. This was a relatively mild lesion that was probably the result of a benign cyst.

Left temporomandibular joint dysfunction of the jaw bone was identified on Skeleton 1112, an adolescent male (Plate 3.11). Here, extension of the joint surface area, a possible pseudo-joint, and a lytic defect may have been the result of temporomandibular joint dislocation with secondary cystic formation. Alternatively the lytic defect may have been caused by neoplastic disease.

Early ankylosis (fusion) involving the left hip and sacrum belonging to Skeleton 1367, a male adult, was indicated by the presence of a spur of new bone on the left iliac joint surface of the pelvis. This skeleton also had osteoarthritis of the left hip. Ankylosis involving the sacroiliac joint is observed in ankylosing spondylitis, a joint disease in which the spine fuses in a characteristic way so that is resembles bamboo. The disease begins in the sacroiliac joints and then progresses up the spine. It usually affects people between the ages of 15 and 35 years and involves more males than females (Rogers and Waldron 1995). Inheritance has a strong influence over the manifestation of this disease which is of unknown cause. It is impossible to say whether the changes that were observed in Skeleton 1367 were a result of this disease because the lower spine had not survived. The sacrum and innominate bones were also very incomplete. Other conditions that may cause ankylosis include diffuse idiopathic skeletal hyperostosis (DISH), another condition that involves fusion of the spine in a characteristic way, and trauma. DISH tends to affect males over the age of 45 years and is associated with obesity and diabetes.

Circulatory disorders

Reduction or loss of the blood supply to bone may result in necrosis (bone death) in the affected area and subsequent joint dysfunction. Examples of this in the London Road inhumations were present in the form of osteochondritis dissecans and possible Legg-Calvé-Perthes disease.

Osteochondritis dissecans: Osteochondritis dissecans involved 1.6 % (CPR) of the population and was observed on the right capitulum of the humerus (the elbow) of a possible female aged between 25 and 35 years (Skeleton 1337). In this condition, necrosis occurs in a small focal area on the convex surface of diarthrodial joints and results in partial or complete detachment of a segment of the subchondral bone and articular cartilage. The aetiology of this condition is not fully understood but it may be caused by low grade chronic trauma or micro-trauma. In the Roman period, this condition is seen in increasing frequency in the knee joint, possibly the result of occupational trauma (Roberts and Cox 2003, 151).

In modern populations, the elbow is the third most common site to be involved and the condition is more common among males and individuals aged between 10 and 25 years old. The predominant involvement of the right side is possibly as a result of right-sided dominance in strong activities involving the arms (Aufderheide and Rodriguez 1998). In the present example, the lesion would not have greatly impacted on the daily life of the individual, who may have experienced a clicking in the joint and some pain with movement. For the Romano-British period, the crude prevalence rate, based on seven populations, ranges from between 0.2% for the Eastern Cemetery, London and 5.2% for Baldock 2 (Roberts and Cox 2003, 152), with an overall prevalence of 0.4%. The prevalence for London Road, therefore, is among the highest.

Neoplastic disease

The only form of neoplastic disease that was identified in the sample were two ivory osteomas (or button osteomas), one on each of the cranial vaults of Skeleton 1114, a 25–35 year old of unknown sex, and Skeleton 1537, an adult female. Ivory osteomas are benign tumours and are common among archaeological and modern populations. They may be described as smooth dense expansions

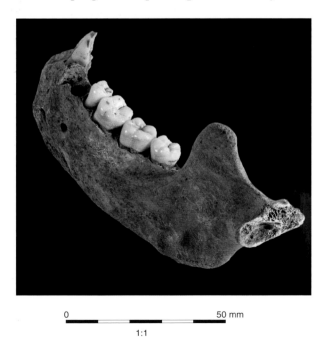

0   50 mm

1:1

Plate 3.11 Lytic lesion involving the head of the left mandibular condyle. Skeleton 1112, an adolescent male.

of cortical bone that are usually small and tend to occupy the outer table of the skull or the sinuses. Their cause is unknown but some have suggested that they are a response to trauma (Aufderheide and Rodríguez-Martín 1998).

Miscellaneous conditions
Hyperostosis frontalis interna: Hyperostosis frontalis interna (HFI) was present on the endocrania of four skeletons (TPR 8.3%, 4/48; CPR 6.3%, 4/63) including a young adult female, a middle adult female and a young adult and a mature adult of unknown sex. HFI is identified on dry bone as thickening and nodule formation on the endocranial surface of the frontal bone. This condition has associations with virilism and obesity and it is common among post-menopausal women. Its cause is unknown but it has been known to occur in pregnancy and accompany changes associated with acromegaly, thereby implicating some sort of pituitary gland disorder in its aetiology (Aufderheide and Rodríguez-Martín 1998).

Unclassified pathological changes
Changes that do not fit into any of the above categories in this section are discussed here. They concern skeletons that would require radiography to explore diagnoses. The cranial fragments belonging to Skeleton 1238, a male aged over 45 years, were very light and had a woolly appearance, both suggestive of poor bone turnover. One condition that results in poor bone turnover is Paget's disease, a disease that results in the progressive enlargement and thickening of bones as a result of disruption to cellular activity.

Skeleton 1337, a 25 to 35 year old female, had shallow, oval lytic lesions on the anterior surfaces of right and left femoral necks adjacent to the margin of the femoral heads (Plate 3.12). These lesions were very subtle, were not associated with any inflammation and had regular margins. Lytic lesions in the region of the femoral necks can occur in pathological conditions such as tuberculosis. However, the subtlety of the

present lesions, their relatively benign appearance and smooth margins, suggest that non-pathological skeletal variation is a more likely explanation.

The mass grave
This analysis includes a minimum number of 76 adults and 15 subadults. Sexed individuals include a minimum number of 15 females (including one adolescent) and 38 males (including three adolescents). Crude prevalence rates have been calculated based on the minimum number of individuals by employing the methods described above.

Infection
Non-specific inflammation involving the skull: This was observed on the outer surface of skull vaults only and affected two skeletons (CPR 2.2%; TPR 1.6%) including two males aged 35–45 years (Skeleton 1518) and 18–25 years (Skeleton 1541). On both, the changes included porous new bone formation that was located on the frontal and parietal bones. The changes involving Skeleton 15 were associated with trauma involving the frontal bone of the cranial vault.

Periostitis: At least 16 (CPR 17.6%) individuals had periostitis involving one or more elements. Periostitis was more frequent among males (18.4%) than it was among females (13.3%) and it involved few individuals who were below the age of 18 years (Table 3.52). The most frequently affected element was the tibia (TPR 11.3%), followed by the fibula (TPR 6.5%) (Table 3.53). In one case periostitis was associated with healed trauma involving the fifth metatarsal (1516).

Compared to the discrete skeletons, a similar range of skeletal elements were affected with periositis (Fig. 3.6). However, unlike the discrete skeletons, there was involvement of the forearms but not the innominate bones, the metacarpals, or the calcaneus—patterns that are probably not significant owing to the small numbers involved. Based on the crude prevalence, the rate for periostitis is high for a Romano-British population (Roberts and Cox

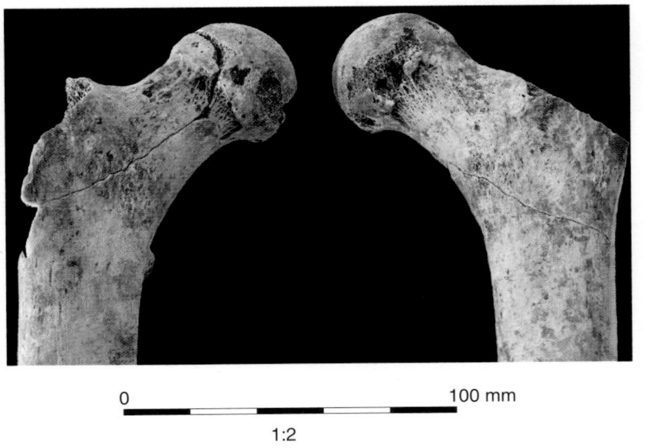

Plate 3.12 Oval lytic lesions involving the necks of right and left femora. Skeleton 1337 a 25–35 year old female.

Table 3.52 Age and sex distribution of skeletons with periostitis.

	Male (%)	Female (%)	Unsexed (%)	Total (%)
Infant	0/0	0/0	0/1	0/1
Young child	0/0	0/0	0/3	0/3
Older child	0/0	0/0	1/4	1/4
Adolescent	1/3	0/1	0/3	1/7
Young adult	1/19	0/7	1/10	2/36
Middle adult	3/7	1/4	0/2	4/13
Mature adult	1/2	1/2	0/3	2/7
Older adult	0/3	0/1	1/1	1/5
Adult	1/4	0/0	4/11	5/15
Total	7/38	2/15	7/38	16/91
	(18.4)	(13.3)	(18.4)	(17.6)

Table 3.53 Periostitis, absolute prevalence.

Element involved	Total (%)	Unsexed adult		Male		Female		Subadults	
		Right (%)	Left (%)	Right (%)	Left (%)	Right (%)	Left (%)	Right (%)	Left (%)
Ribs	1/793 (0.1)	0/77	1*/77 (0.6)	0/195	0/172	0/116	0/101	0/28	0/27
Ulna	1/123 (0.8)	0/20	0/18	1/25 (4.0)	0/29	0/10	0/12	0/5	0/4
Radius	1/111 (0.9)	0/18	0/14	1/24 (4.2)	0/27	0/9	0/11	0/4	0/4
Femur	3/199 (1.5)	1/30 (3.3)	0/40	1/38 (2.6)	0/34	0/22	0/21	0/7	1/7 (14.3)
Tibia	16/142 (11.3)	0/26	3/31 (9.7)	4/26 (15.4)	3/20 (15.0)	2/14 (14.3)	2/15 (13.3)	1/2 (50.0)	1/8 (12.5)
Fibula	8/124 (6.5)	1/18 (5.6)	4/28 (14.3)	1/21 (4.8)	0/20	1/12 (8.3)	1/16 (6.3)	0/4	0/5
Metatarsals	3/319 (0.9)	0/34	3/68 (4.4)	0/69	0/57	0/36	0/42	0/8	0/5

* rib fragment is unsided; APR calculated out of a total of 154

2003, 124). However, true prevalence rates for the tibia are lower than Kempston and Kingsholm but similar to Cirencester (see above).

It is impossible to explore evidence for multiple element involvement in this group owing to the fact that the sample comprises articulated and disarticulated elements. However, consideration of only the articulated skeletons with periostitis and/ or inflammation on the cranial vault (twelve in total), suggests that, like the cemetery population, multiple element involvement (and hence systemic disease) was also common to this group (but less frequent) (Table 3.54).

Other infection: There was a small fragment of innominate bone (possibly ilium) that displayed significant remodelled lamellar bone. Small proliferative erosions were also present. The fragment was so small that it was not possible to tell exactly what the full extent of the changes were (ie whether they involved a joint and/or were in an area of muscle attachment). The changes may have been associated with infection, or they may have been the result of trauma. There was no evidence for osteomyelitis.

Metabolic disorders
Cribra orbitalia: Cribra orbitalia affected a minimum number of six skeletons, four males (CPR 10.5%) and two females (CPR 13.3%). The females were aged between 18 and 25 years and 25 and 35 years and the males included one adult, one adolescent, one aged between 18 and 25 years and one aged between 25 and 35 years. No sub-adults were affected by the condition. The condition was also not observed on any older adults. The lack of sub-adult involvement is unusual given that cribra orbitalia develops in childhood and has usually healed by the time individuals reach adulthood.

More left orbits were involved than right orbits (Table 3.55). There was little difference between the number of affected male orbits (10.1%) compared to the number of affected female orbits (10.7%). True prevalence rates for males, females and subadults

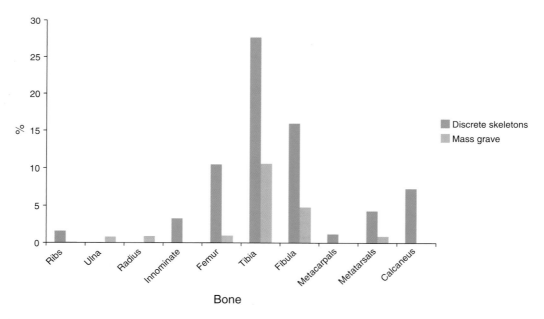

Figure 3.6 Periostitis distribution: discrete burials and mass grave (TPR).

Table 3.54   Distribution of elements with non-specific inflammation by skeleton (articulated skeletons only).

Age	Sex	Skeleton number	En.-cranial	Ec.-cranial	R Orbit	L Orbit	Ribs	CV	TV	LV	R ilium	L ilium	R humerus	L humerus	R radius	L radius	R ulna	L ulna	R MCs	L MCs	Hand phals.	R femur	L femur	R tibia	L tibia	R fibula	L fibula	R MTs	L MTs	Foot phals.	Tarsals
Adult	u/k	1516																											X		
Adult	u/k	1517																							X				X		
35–45	M	1518			X	X																	X									
25–35	F	1539																					X	X								
25–35	M	1540														X	X						X									
18–25	M	1541	X																				X	X								
Adult	u/k	1543																								X		X				
25–35	M	1544																					X		X							
46+	u/k	1546																				X										
12–18	M	1547																					X	X								
35–45	F	1552																					X	X	X	X						
25–35	M	1553																					X	X								
Adult	u/k	15162																									X					
18–25	u/k	15652																						X			X					
Adult	M	15762																				X										

Table 3.55   Cribra orbitalia, absolute prevalence.

Orbit	Male	%	Female	%	Unsexed adult	%	Sub-adult	%
Right	4/36	11.1	1/13	7.7	0/7	0	0/10	0
Left	3/33	9.1	2/15	13.3	0/8	0	0/7	0
Total	7/69	10.1	3/28	10.7	0/15	0	0/17	0

were low compared to Poundbury, Kempston and Cirencester (see above).

Porotic hyperostosis: Increased porosity was frequent on outer skull vaults throughout the assemblage, a change that may have been caused by porotic hyperostosis (this also applies to the discrete skeletons). However, none of these displayed the thinned outer tables and expanded diploic space that is consistent with the disease. This porosity was probably not of any great consequence to the overall health of the individuals and was probably related to conditions such as minor scalp infection.

Trauma

Ante-mortem fractures: Healed fractures were identified on at least seven skeletons (CPR 7.8%) including one 18 to 25 year old male (1524), two 25 to 35 year old males (1544 and 1648) and four unsexed adults (427, 609, 1516 and 1543). Thus, the CPR for males was 7.8% (3/38) which is far lower than rates observed at 124–130 London Road (CPR 30%) (Clough 2003) and Cirencester (south) (CPR (26.7%) (Wells 1982a, 167). There was no macroscopic evidence that any of the females had sustained fractures.

Fractures involved a total of nine elements (excludes sternal end of clavicle), three from the upper limbs, one from the torso and five from the lower limbs (Table 3.56). All fractures had probably been sustained a long time before death owing to the fact that they displayed long term bone turnover. All were well aligned except for the fractured humerus belonging to Skeleton 1524 which displayed marked angular deformity and shortening (Plate 3.13). This skeleton may also have had a dislocated right shoulder, but fragmentation has prevented a conclusive diagnosis. No fractured bones displayed evidence for OA in associated joints, although many joint surfaces were missing. Three fractured elements, a fifth metatarsal (Skeleton 1516) and a left tibia and left fibula (Skeleton 1543), were associated with periostitis.

The distribution of fractures was similar to that described for the cemetery population: no females were affected, rib fractures were infrequent, there were no radial or ulnar fractures and the overall fracture rate for upper limb bones was lower than that for lower limb bones (0.3% compared to 0.7%). With the exception of the clavicle, frequencies were consistently lower for all elements among the mass grave population compared to the cemetery population (Figure 3.7).

The most frequently fractured elements were the clavicle (TPR 1.8%) and the fibula (TPR 0.9%) followed by the tibia (TPR 0.8%) (Table 3.57). Compared to other populations, the crude prevalence rate for clavicle fractures is higher: 3.2% compared to 1.8% for Ancaster, 4.2% for Kingsholm (Roberts and Cox 2003), 0.8% for Cirencester (south) (Wells 1982a), and 2.3% for Poundbury (Farwell and Molleson 1993).

Generally speaking, clavicles may fracture in three places; at the sternal end of the shaft, along the mid

Table 3.56   Distribution of fractures, absolute prevalence.

Skeletal element	Total	%	Males				Females				Unsexed adults			
			Right	%	Left	%	Right	%	Left	%	Right	%	Left	%
Clavicle	2/109	1.8	1/24	4.2	1/27	3.7	0/10		0/12		0/19		0/17	
Ribs	1/738	0.1	0/195		0/172		0/116		0/101		1*/154			
Humerus	1/135	0.7	0/29		1/32	3.1	0/11		0/11		0/24		0/28	
Radius	0/103		0/24		0/27		0/9		0/11		0/18		0/14	
Ulna	0/114		0/25		0/29		0/10		0/12		0/20		0/18	
Hand phalanges	1/585		0/313				0/148				1/124			
Femur	2/185	1.1	0/38		2/34	5.9	0/22		0/21		0/30		0/40	
Tibia	1/132	0.8	0/26		0/20		0/14		0/15		0/26		1/31	3.2
Fibula	1/115	0.9	0/21		0/20		0/12		0/16		0/18		1/28	3.6
MTs	1/321	0.3	0/69		0/57		0/57		0/36		0/34		1/68	1.5
Talus	1/76	1.3	0/18		0/14		0/9		0/10		0/9		1/16	6.3

* rib is unsided. Prevalence calculated out of all ribs.

Plate 3.13   Fractured left humerus belonging to Skeleton 1524, an 18–25 year old male.

shaft, or at the acromial end of the shaft (the end nearest the scapula). Most common are those that involve the mid shaft and these are often associated with a blow as a result of a fall or being struck with an object (Galloway 1999, 115). In the present sample, one fracture involved the acromial end of the left clavicle that belonged to Skeleton 1544, a 25–35 year old male. The sternal end of the right clavicle may also have been fractured (and has been counted here), but requires radiological investigation. Fractures that involve the acromial end may result from being displaced following a considerable pull on associated muscles, most often as a result of a blow to the shoulder (Galloway 1999, 115). Fractures that involve the sternal end tend to arise as a result of direct violence (ibid.).

Cranial trauma: There was little evidence for cranial trauma. Skeleton 1518 had healed trauma on the superior aspect of the left orbital margin. The lesion, a remodelled linear defect, was consistent with sharp force trauma, such as that which might be delivered by someone yielding a blade. The skeleton was a 35–45 year old male. Healed sharp force trauma was also identified by the presence of a healed linear lesion on a parietal bone fragment of a small find (number 2032), and identified as a 25–35 year old male. Taken together, the lesions indicate an overall

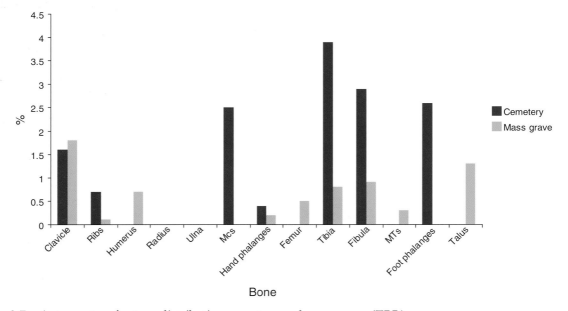

Figure 3.7   Ante-mortem fracture distribution: cemetery and mass grave (TPR).

Table 3.57   OA frequency of sites affected.

Skeletal element	Total	%	Males				Females				Unsexed adults			
			Right	%	Left	%	Right	%	Left	%	Right	%	Left	%
Costovert.	0/738		0/195		0/172		0/116		0/101		0/154			
Cervical spine	2/80	2.5	0/47				0/19				2/14			14.3
Thoracic spine	1/72	1.4	0/37				0/19				1/16			6.3
Lumbar spine	2/68	2.9	0/34				0/20				2/14			14.3
Shoulder	1/90	1.1	0/19		0/22		0/12		0/10		0/12		1/15	7.7
Elbow	0/99		0/24		0/26		0/9		0/10		0/13		0/17	
Hand	1/104	1.0	0/25		0/25		0/10		0/13		1/14	7.1	0/17	
Hip	0/158		0/37		0/35		0/26		0/24		0/15		0/21	
Knee	1/114	0.9	0/21		0/23		0/12		0/14		1/20		0/24	

crude prevalence rate of 2.2% (2/91) and an absolute prevalence rate of 1.6% (2/122).

Dislocations: A 25 to 35 year old male (1553) had a dislocated right finger that involved the joint between the first and second phalanges (metacarpal unidentified). The dislocation had resulted in abnormal articulation between these two bones and secondary changes included osteoarthritis and periostitis. One other skeleton (1554) had a possible dislocated right shoulder and has been mentioned above.

Peri-mortem fractures: No peri-mortem fractures were identified. Breakage patterns were not formally studied (this was beyond the scope of the present report) but in general, there were numerous transverse breaks among the long bones, a feature that is typical of post-mortem fracturing (Galloway 1999) and is usually the result of soil compaction (Trinkhaus 1985).

Congenital and developmental anomalies
Skeleton 1547, an adolescent male, had one bifid unidentified left rib.

Joint disease
Osteoarthritis: Owing to fragmentation, the prevalence for spinal OA was calculated based on the number of cervical, thoracic and lumbar spines that were available for analysis among the articulated skeletons that were excavated from the pit only. Only one small find had spinal OA (701). This was an adult male who had changes involving the cervical spine (this has not been included in Table 3.57). All other spinal OA was observed on skeletons that had been articulated (ie were not small finds). The prevalence for all extra-spinal OA has been calculated based on the total number of all joints that were present among the articulated skeletons and the small finds.

At least three individuals had OA involving one or more of their joints (articulated Skeletons 1516, 1546 and 1555). These were two adults and one old adult (<45 years), all of undetermined sex (three out of 76 adults, or 3.9%). The old adult had OA affecting multiple joints including the right hand, the left shoulder, the cervical spine and thoracic spine. This is perhaps not surprising given the age of the individual. The CPR (3.9%) is low compared to

other Romano-British populations. For example, Wells (1982a) calculated a CPR of 44.8% for adults from Cirencester (south), although inter-observer variability in diagnosing OA should be borne in mind here.

Unlike the skeletons from the cemetery, the skeletons from the mass grave displayed a different pattern of joint involvement (Table 3.57). The spine was the most frequently affected, but instead of the cervical spine, the lumbar spine showed the highest prevalence (2.9% compared to 2.5%). There was no evidence for hip OA and, unlike the cemetery population, there was evidence for shoulder OA.

Schmorl's nodes and degenerative disc disease: Five skeletons (CPR 5.5%) had changes in their spines that were consistent with Schmorl's nodes (Table 3.58). They involved one unsexed adult (Skeleton 1517), two adult males (Skeletons 1542 and 1551) and one male (Skeleton 1518) and one female (Skeleton 1552) who were both 35–45 years of age. Three skeletons 1517, 1518 and 1542) had thoracic and lumbar spine involvement and two (1551 and 1552) had thoracic spine involvement only. Spines were too incomplete to allow calculation of the number of affected vertebrae from each spine.

Degenerative disc disease affected just one skeleton (CPR 1.2%), an individual of over 45 years and of unknown sex. The changes involved the cervical spine (TPR 1.3%) and the thoracic spine (TPR 1.4%).

Circulatory disorders: The distal joint surface of the left tibia belonging to Skeleton 1540, a 25–35 year old adult, had a single delineated pit that resembled the

Table 3.58   frequency of spines affected with Schmorl's nodes.

	Total (%)	Males (%)	Females (%)	Unsexed (%)
Cervical spine	0/80	0/47	0/19	0/14
Thoracic spine	5/72 (6.9)	3/37 (8.1)	1/19 (5.3)	1/16 (6.3)
Lumbar spine	3/68 (4.4)	2/34 (5.9)	0/20	1/14 (7.1)

changes seen in osteochondritis dissecans. However, in this disease the changes affect the concave surface of diarthrodial joints, not the convex surface (Aufderheide and Rodríguez-Martín 1998). The talus bone belonging to this skeleton did not show any changes.

Neoplastic disease: One skeleton (1542) had an ivory osteoma on the cranial vault. This was an adult male. One upper thoracic vertebra belonging to this individual had destructive lesions that involved the superior surface of the body (the laminae were missing) (Plate 3.14). The height of the vertebral body was also uniformly reduced. There was no involvement of other vertebrae. Infection and neoplasms are among the diseases that may cause these changes. The latter is the favoured diagnosis here because of the solitary involvement of the vertebra and the absence of inflammatory changes.

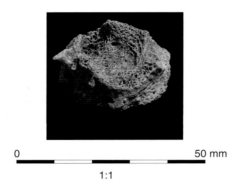

0   50 mm

1:1

Plate 3.14 Destructive lesions involving a thoracic vertebra from Skeleton 1542, an adult male.

A further adult mandible (small find 716) had a large lytic lesion that involved the alveolar bone of the left mandible (at the site of the second premolar and the left molars) and is consistent with an ameloblastoma (Plate 3.15) (Dias and Tayles 1997). Ameloblastomas are rare, benign neoplasms that are slow growing and cause severe abnormalities to the face and jaw. The mandible was incomplete and lacked the right mandibular ramus and both ascending rami. All the incisors, canines and left premolars had been lost post-mortem. The amenoblastoma was 28 mm in diameter. A periapical cyst (approximately 7.83 mm wide) was located on the site of the left canine and has been counted among the dental conditions recorded in the relevant section above.

The disarticulated material
by Nicholas Márquez-Grant

Disarticulated human remains (bones and teeth) were recovered from 45 contexts throughout the site (except for the mass grave) and are listed in Appendix 2. All contexts but four provided a minimum of one individual. Contexts (1182), (1454) and (1457) had a minimum of two individuals represented, while (1409) had a minimum of three adult individuals. Thus, adding all the MNI calculations for each context, the total MNI is 50. However, it is unlikely that these bones represent discrete skeletons that are additional to the number of skeletons from the cemetery overall. They probably belong to the discrete skeletons, or may form part of a skeleton that has remains in various contexts due to post-mortem disturbance.

All individuals were adult except in contexts (1285) and (1418) where they were subadult

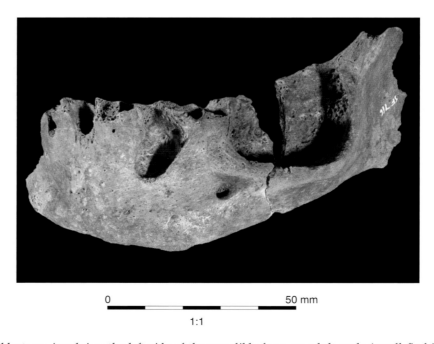

0   50 mm

1:1

Plate 3.15 Ameloblastoma involving the left side of the mandible from an adult male (small find 716).

(>18 years) individuals. A possible subadult was also represented by the remains in context (1182). The bones from five contexts (1247, 1341, 1361, 1387, 1397) did not provide any age estimates. In addition, bone recovered from contexts (1282) and (1365) provided a narrower adult age range, suggesting that the remains represent young adult individuals (18–25 years). Sex determination was possible for contexts 1333 (sf 154), 1182 and 1457 which suggest male, male and a possible female respectively.

The only pathological changes that were observed on these remains was periostitis. This involved the left tibia and left fibula bones that were recovered from the fill of grave 1402. The changes were considerable and are in the same league as those identified on the remains of Skeleton 1286 and illustrated in Plate 3.4 above. No changes were identified macroscopically that would confirm that the lesions had been caused by osteomyelitis, although this is likely.

Isotope analysis

A single molar tooth was taken from 21 skeletons, including 10 discrete inhumations and 11 mass grave skeletons, for analysis of oxygen and strontium isotopes at the NERC Isotope Geoscience Laboratory. A detailed report is provided in Appendix 3. The main findings are summarised here.

The analyses were undertaken to explore the geographic origin of the skeletons. In particular, they were undertaken to identify any 'non-local' individuals and, if present, establish their origin. Origin was explored in relation to cultural (for example, burial location and associated artefacts) and biological (for example, age and sex) variables.

The findings of the analyses indicated two distinct groups, as reflected by their combined strontium and oxygen values (see Figure A3.1, Appendix 3). The first group comprised eight discrete skeletons and six mass grave skeletons. Among these individuals $^{87}Sr/^{86}Sr$ values were wide ranging but most referred to geology that lies within a 20 km radius of Gloucester, in particular the Malvern Hills (Chenery, Appendix 3). Oxygen values related to drinking water zones throughout the UK, therefore suggesting wider geographic origin. Overall, the results would suggest that the individuals probably originated from the UK.

The second group comprised two discrete skeletons and three mass grave skeletons. Strontium values tended to cluster, suggesting a common geographic origin for these individuals that has a different geology to Gloucester. This is confirmed by Oxygen values which exceeded the expected range for the UK and were reflective of drinking water that might be found on the extreme western or southern coast of Europe, North Africa, or extremely arid locations. However, very few values have been published for these locations to say with confidence whether or not the London Road values relate to drinking water zones in these areas. Other areas that

have similar high values are Cornwall, Ireland and the east coast of Italy.

These analyses do not point with confidence to the geographic location of the individuals from either the cemetery or the mass grave. There is no pattern in the distribution of isotope values of different skeletons in terms of age, sex, burial type and associated artefacts. However, sample size was small.

Overall, the results would suggest that individuals from the mass grave and cemetery were of diverse origin and possibly include individuals from regions with climates that are warmer than the UK. The fact that values did not show any correlation with burial location would indicate that individuals from the mass grave and the cemetery were part of the same population. Thus, the selection of individuals for burial in the mass grave was random rather than one determined by geographic origin.

Discussion of the unburnt human remains
by Louise Loe, Nicholas Márquez-Grant and Jonny Geber

A summary of the main findings described in this report is presented in Table 3.59. Overall, the mass grave skeletons and the discrete inhumations did not differ significantly in terms of their physical attributes, demography and disease. They shared a similar range of non-metric traits, both groups comprised males and females, the young and the old, and, although frequencies differed, they shared the same range of pathological conditions. These osteological findings therefore suggest that there is no reason to believe that the discrete inhumations and mass grave skeletons were from different populations.

Some caveats

Of the discrete skeletons that could be assigned to an age category, few were assigned to the older adult age range. In addition, infants were under-represented. These findings were also observed among the mass grave assemblage. When interpreting these trends there are several caveats that should be considered. Perhaps the most important is the fact that estimating biological age is fraught with problems, not least because present standards have been derived using populations that are distanced in time and space from archaeological populations (Bocquet-Appel and Masset 1982). Studies using adult skeletons of documented age have demonstrated that present methods tend to over-age the young and under-age the old (Cox 2000), and this must also be borne in mind in relation to the present results.

In the present assemblage, most age estimations were based on observations relating to dental attrition. This method is widely recognised for its tendency to under-age skeletons (Cox 2000). More relevantly, it has been noted for its tendency to under-age Roman populations in particular (Boston

Table 3.59   Summary of the main osteological findings.

Criteria		Summary	
		Discrete inhumations	Mass grave
Minimum number of individuals		64 (63 analysed)	91 (422 small finds and 201 skeletons)
Preservation		Most very good or fair and almost half less than 25% complete	Most good or very good
Sex		11 females, 24 males	14 females, 35 males
Age		Deaths highest among young adults and middle adults. Few children below the age of five years. More older adult deaths than the mass grave. More females than males in all adult age categories, except older adults (more males). Many more un-aged male adults than female adults.	Deaths highest among young adults. Few deaths among children under five years and among older adults. Young adult and older adult age categories have more males than females. Middle and mature adult age categories have more females than males.
Stature		Average female height: 160 cm (5'3'') Average male height: 169 cm (5'5'')	One unsexed skeleton: 160 cm (5'2'') F or 164 cm (5'3'') M
Non-metric traits		Most frequent cranial traits: Parietal foramen and supraorbital notches. Most frequent post-cranial traits: tibial squatting facets.	Most frequent cranial traits: Lambdoid ossicles, parietal foramen and Access infraorbital foramen. Most frequent post-cranial traits: Hypotrochanteric fossa, tibial squatting facets and vastus notch.
Dental health and disease		More enamel hypoplasia among subadults than mass grave. More carious cavities, ante-mortem tooth loss, calculus and periodontitis among adults than mass grave.	More carious cavities among subadults than discrete inhumations. More periapical cavities among adults than discrete inhumations.
Pathology	Trauma	Ante mortem fractures: 14.1% of population (CPR) 29.2% of males (CPR) No female fractures Tibia most common (TPR 3.9%). More lower limb than upper limb.	Ante mortem fractures: 7.8% of population (CPR) 7.9 % of males (CPR) No female fractures Clavicle most common (TPR 1.8%). More lower limb than upper limb.
	Non- specific Infection	Periostitis: 44.4% of population (CPR) 63.6% females (CPR) 50% males (CPR) Tibia most frequently involved element (TPR 28.9%). Frequent multiple element involvement.	Periostitis: 17.6% of population (CPR) 13.3% females (CPR) 18.4% males (CPR) Tibia most frequently involved element (TPR 11.3%). Frequent multiple element involvement.
	Metabolic conditions	Cribra: 21.6% of all adults (CPR) 22.2% of all subadults (CPR) males 27.8% (TPR) females 25% (TPR) subadults 50% (TPR) No porotic hyperostosis	Cribra: 7.9% of all adults (CPR) No subadults affected males 10.5% (CPR) females 13.3% (CPR) No porotic hyperostosis
	Joint disease	OA: 32.1% of adults (CPR) 41.7% of males (CPR) 36.4% of females (CPR) CV most common (TPR 17.1%) followed by hip (TPR 15.0%)	OA: 3.9% of adults (CPR) All unsexed skeletons LV most common (TPR 2.9%) No hip OA Shoulder OA (TPR 1.1%)

pers com.). Furthermore, many skeletons, both discrete and commingled, were incomplete. This has meant that age had to be estimated by employing fewer indicators than the desired range. This is reflected in the large number of adult skeletons that could not be assigned to an age category. If it had been possible to estimate more precise ages for these skeletons, and employ more accurate methods, the mortality profiles for the discrete inhumations and the mass grave may appear quite different. The fact that some of the younger adults had pathological conditions (for example OA) that are more typical of older age groups, may suggest that the individuals from London Road were not dying at such young ages as the mortality profiles would perhaps otherwise suggest.

The under-representation of the youngest

The under-representation of the youngest individuals (from two years and below) is not unique to the London Road assemblage and has been observed among other Roman cemetery populations (Clough 2003; Mays 2000). Several factors may have caused this including excavation bias, cultural practices and preservation. For example, it was common practice to bury infants in settlements rather than afford them burial in a cemetery (Philpott 1991). It has been suggested that the practice of burying babies beneath doorsteps was adopted during the Roman period because of the belief that they would bring good luck to the inhabitants (Scott 1991; Scheuer and Black 2000, 15). Infanticide may have resulted in the disposal of infants in sewers and ditches, or their abandonment outside the settlement (Mays 1993; Smith and Kahila 1992; see Chapter 6). Driven by a belief in 'changelings' mothers may have also temporarily abandoned their infants and this would have resulted in deaths and, by proxy, infanticide (Mays 2000, 185). Philpott (1991) considers that, during the Roman period, infants below the age of about 18 months were given burials that were often casual and separate from cemeteries because they were not regarded as full members of society. There may perhaps have been separate child cemeteries, not yet discovered (Dennehy 2001; Pearce 2001).

The full extent of the London Road cemetery was not identified during excavation and it is therefore entirely possible that young infants were buried in areas that were not excavated. Further, infants may not have survived the burial environment because their small, fragile bones are more susceptible to disintegration in the ground (Chamberlain 2000). Although these factors have probably contributed to the rate of recovery, the fact that the small, fragile bones of older children were recovered suggests that these factors did not significantly affect this.

The mortality profiles

For un-biased, pre-industrial populations the mortality profile should approximate the U-shaped curve that is characteristic of undeveloped countries where the highest deaths occur in the youngest and oldest age categories (Waldron 1994). The mortality profile for the discrete burials is broadly compatible with this. As discussed above the youngest are under-represented for various reasons (in particular cultural), and adults are probably under-aged because of the methods that have been employed.

Obstetric casualties and in- and out-migration are factors that may explain the higher numbers of deaths among the 25–35 year olds and the 35–45 year olds (Grauer 1991; Chamberlain 2000). In- and out-migration are very plausible influences given the socio-economic and cultural activities taking place in Gloucester at this time.

The mortality profile for the mass grave does not conform to the usual curve for Roman populations, but reflects the profile of a living population. Unlike the mortality profile for the discrete burials the majority of individuals, both males and females, died before they had reached 35 years of age. The kolmogorov-Smirnov statistical test (at the significance level of $p < 0.05$ the maximum difference between the two samples (0.183) was less than $D_{m,n}$ (0.263)) indicated that there was no significant difference between the mortality profiles. However, this does not mean that the profiles are the same, rather there is insufficient evidence to suggest that they are different (Shennan 1997, 61).

A peak in deaths in young adulthood is compatible with the mortality profiles of other populations dying as a result of a catastrophic event (Margerison and Knüsel 2002). Catastrophic events that might cause sudden death in a population include war, massacre and plague. War may be identified in skeletal remains by a high mortality among young males, high frequencies of peri-mortem trauma, embedded weapons and partially articulated skeletons (Boylston *et al.* 2000; Hurlburt 2000; Ostendorf Smith 1997). These trends were reflected among skeletons from a mass grave in Towton, Yorkshire (Fiorato *et al.* 2000). Sharp, blunt and projectile traumas, largely involving the skull, were frequent among this group, who were victims of the Battle of Towton (1461). Similar patterns have been observed for a Napoleonic period mass grave in Lithuania (Signoli *et al.* 2004) and an early/middle Bronze Age multiple burial from Wassenaar, the Netherlands (Kooijmans 2005). No such patterns were observed among the remains from London Road.

Epidemics such as famine or plague result in acute death, thus pathological changes associated with these conditions do not show on skeletal remains. Famine tends to affect the most vulnerable members of a community, these being the oldest and the youngest (Margerison 1997). This is not reflected in the mortality profile of the London Road assemblage, although problems with age estimation and the under-representation of infants means that this suggestion cannot be fully explored with the present data. Nevertheless, the overall impression is of a mixed population that comprised both sexes spanning all ages. An epidemic, such as plague, that did not target either sex or any particular age group, therefore provides a more powerful explanation for the deaths among this random cross section of the population. A similar cross section of the East Smithfield population died as a result of the Black Death during the 14th century, and supports this interpretation (Kausmally 2007).

The date of the mass grave is contemporary with the Antonine Plague, which may have been an outbreak of measles or smallpox (see Chapter 6 for discussion). Measles causes no unique or recognisable changes in the skeleton, although smallpox may be identified skeletally. Changes include osteomyelitis and arthritis which tend to involve the limb bones, in particular those from the arm (Aufderheide and Rodríguez-Martín 1998). However, such lesions are not seen in adult skeletons and they tend to disappear up to a year following the virus (ibid.). Secondary changes include bone ankylosis (or fusion), degenerative joint disease and retarded growth. In the present sample, there was no confirmed evidence for osteomyelitis and changes that involved joints were not consistent with those described for smallpox (Resnick and Niwayama 1989). Evidence for secondary changes were present in the form of growth arrest (manifested as enamel hypoplasia), osteoarthritis and bony ankylosis. However, these changes may arise in association with many other conditions. Without any primary evidence, the presence of smallpox cannot be proved or disproved from osteological evidence alone.

Taphonomy

It was suggested during the excavation of the mass grave that some bodies were in the early stages of putrefaction prior to being buried. Basic analysis of the remains to explore whether they had been deposited as fleshed corpses or skeletonised remains was undertaken. In particular, the remains were analysed to explore why the disarticulation of skeletons had occurred. The results revealed that the condition of all bones was not markedly different between the different burial types (articulated skeletons, small finds and disarticulated bone) implying uniformity in their treatment. There was no evidence that human remains had been exposed to scavengers or sunlight and there was also a high recovery rate of elements. Environmental evidence indicated that the pit had contained a distinct lack of snails, insect remains, or other factors that would point to a mass of decomposing bodies. However, this does not necessarily mean that skeletons rather than corpses had been deposited in the pit, particularly if the pit was filled in quickly (Nicholson pers com.).

Overall, these observations suggest that fleshed corpses had been buried in the pit, probably around the same time, and that all were complete when deposited. Thus, the pit and remains therein probably represent a primary, rather than secondary, burial.

The results of the matching and conjoining exercises unfortunately do not lend support to this conclusion. These did not identify any matches between elements or fragments and this therefore may suggest that incomplete skeletons or corpses were buried in the pit. However, it is more likely that these results are a reflection of the preliminary nature of the present analysis. For example, match-ing exercises were limited to large bones only (for example, skulls and major limb bones), whereas Duday (2006, 52) considers that small bones, namely the patellae and those of the hands and feet, provide the most matches in assemblages of commingled remains. The fragmentary nature of the assemblage has also severely hindered element matching which would benefit from a dedicated programme of reconstruction. There was limited opportunity to fully integrate biological and archaeological data with the three-dimensional representation of the mass grave, *Crossbones*. Again, this more specialised analysis would, no doubt, yield positive results.

The high level of incompleteness observed among the mass grave skeletons is probably the result of a combination of *in situ* decomposition and recording. Post-excavation analysis has determined that, in many cases, different parts of the same skeletons were assigned a different skeleton number during excavation. This is a result of the sheer complexity of the deposit which could not be fully understood until it had been excavated and digitally analysed. This has therefore artificially increased the apparent high level of incompleteness.

In situ decomposition relates to environmental factors combined with the physical and chemical properties of the skeleton. The same skeleton may have had its elements displaced to different areas of the grave as a result of piled cadavers decomposing (Duday 2006, 50). Other factors that have probably resulted in the pattern of disarticulation of bones in the mass grave relate to variation in the resilience of ligaments between some articulations in the skeleton compared to others, the effects of gravity and the creation of empty spaces for bones to fall into as soft tissues decayed (Galloway 1999; Duday 2006). Rising and falling water tables and body fluids also probably contributed to the displacement of elements, particularly of lighter spongy bones and skulls which float more easily than other elements (Boaz and Behrensmeyer 1976; Duday 2006).

These conclusions are consistent with the fact that displaced elements, recorded as small finds, were found in the part of the pit where there would have been the highest water levels (the western side), being the deepest part. In addition, spatial analysis showed that upper limbs had been dispersed more than lower limbs which are denser and have more resilient connecting soft tissues. Skulls were also among the most frequent type of element amongst disassociated bones that comprised the small finds.

An interesting observation was the fact that many broken bones displayed fracture margins that were indicative of having been broken when there was still some organic matrix in them (ie they were 'dry' rather than 'green'). This implies that some of the breakage did not occur immediately around the time of death, but neither during recent times. These are most likely to be natural fractures resulting from environmental processes (for example, soil compaction) rather than the result of deliberate human activity. Galloway (1999, 16) points out that bone may not necessarily always completely dry out in its burial environment, if it is lying below the water table or is in a constantly wet environment. Further, in the context of a mass grave, body fluids and moisture can be trapped for many years and thereby reduce the degree to which bones dry out (Galloway 1999). Thus, in these cases, dry fracture properties of bone may be retained and may result in some of the changes described here.

Pathology and physical attributes among the discrete skeletons and the mass grave skeletons

Compared to the discrete inhumations, prevalence rates for pathological conditions among the skeletons from the mass grave were lower. However, a similar range of conditions was experienced by both groups. For example, periostitis was more common among the discrete skeletons than the mass grave skeletons, but several skeletons from both groups showed a pattern of skeletal involvement that implicated systemic disease, rather than mild trauma, in its aetiology. Thus, similar disease processes were being experienced by both groups. It is possible that the mass grave skeletons had fewer pathological lesions because they represented those individuals of the population who had weaker constitutions and were more susceptible to acute disease. Interestingly, enamel hypoplasia was more frequent among the discrete inhumations than the mass grave skeletons. Some have suggested that this evidence for growth arrest during childhood shows in the skeletons of individuals who had robust constitutions, or were 'survivors', not those who were more susceptible to ill health and acute death (Duray 1996; Lewis and Roberts 1997).

A low prevalence of pathology among the mass grave skeletons is not an uncommon finding for this type of burial. This has also been observed among other mass graves resulting from natural disasters such as an epidemic. For example, a low prevalence was also observed among the medieval skeletons from the East Smithfield Black Death cemetery (1348–50) (Kausmally 2007).

Compared to other Romano-British populations, the London Road population is notable for its high levels of non-specific infection, with a crude prevalence rate of 44.4% for the discrete skeletons and 17.6% for the mass grave skeletons. These rates are higher than that (CPR 6.7%) reported by Roberts and Cox (2003, 124) for 5,716 skeletons from 52 different Romano-British sites. Patterns of element involvement suggest that systemic disease, including infection, was prevalent. That few cases seem to have been associated with infection resulting from trauma supports this suggestion. High levels of infection are typical of close-contact societies whereby overcrowding and poor sanitation facilitate the transmission of disease (Larsen 1997). A review of the evidence by Roberts and Cox (2003) concludes that sanitation (for example, sewerage management) was inadequate in many urban Romano-British environments, despite the 'apparent 'superficial' sanitary organisation for this period' (2003, 125). The evidence from London Road is in keeping with this.

Two skeletons, one from a discrete burial (Skeleton 1277) and one from the mass grave (Skeleton 1672) had severe enamel defects which are possibly indicative of congenital syphilis. Syphilis is diagnosed on dry bones and teeth based on the presence of proliferative and destructive lesions. Involvement of the entire skeleton and 'caries sicca' (distinctive lesions on the outside surface of the skull) are common in the veneral form of the disease and dental defects ('mulberry molars' and 'Hutchinson's teeth'), perforations in the nasal area and palate, joint involvement and changes involving the tibia ('sabre shin') are common in the congenital form of the disease (Aufderheide and Rodríguez-Martín 1998). Apart from the enamel defects, there were no skeletal changes identified in the assemblage that match those observed in either congenital of venereal forms of the disease. If these cases are confirmed they will join an increasing number of important palaeopathological examples which, if the diagnoses are correct, suggest that congenital syphilis was present in the Old World before 1493 (see Erdal 2006, 30).

Overall, the prevalence of ante-mortem fractures among the male skeletons from the discrete burials (CPR 29.2%) was similar to other Romano-British assemblages including 124-130 London Road (30%) (Clough 2003) and Cirencester (26.7%) (Wells 1982a, 167). This was not reflected in the prevalence that was calculated for the mass grave skeletons (CPR 7.8%), although fragmentation has probably reduced the number of fractures that could be identified here.

Fracture patterns suggest limited interpersonal violence in the population (just three skull wounds) and involved only males. This may suggest that males engaged in particular activities that predisposed them to trauma, unlike the females. Patterns of trauma (in terms of elements involved) were similar to those reported by Wells (1982a;b) for Cirencester (south and north), namely the blunt force skull trauma, the under-representation of forearm fractures and the frequency of lower limb fractures. While the CPR for trauma was low among the individuals from the mass grave, fragmentation has probably reduced the number of fractures that could be identified here.

Evidence for nutritional status indicated a population that may have had high levels of iron deficiency anaemia compared to other Roman groups. The true prevalence for the cemetery population was 27.8% for males, 25% for females and 50% for subadults. These figures are higher than those reported for Kempston, Bedfordshire (18.3% for males, 10.5% for females and 26.7% for subadults) (Boylston and Roberts 1996) and Cirencester (19.9% for males, 13.3% for females and 35.1% for subadults) (Wells 1982a, 186); and similar to Poundbury (24.4% for males, 27.7% for females and 36.4% for subadults) (Stuart-Macadam 1991). However, rates for the mass grave are lower (10.1% for males, 10.7% for females and 0% for subadults).

Iron deficiency anaemia may be caused by a deficient diet. However, there was no convincing evidence in the assemblage for malnourishment. In fact, the evidence (as it stands) indicated that the population enjoyed an adequate diet. The high levels of iron deficiency anaemia may therefore be a result of increased pathogen loads. For example, there were no confirmed cases of scurvy or rickets, as has been observed among other Roman populations including, Kingsholm, Gloucester (Roberts and Cox 2003, 142–3) and Kempston, Bedfordshire (Boylston and Roberts 1996). Compared to other populations, there were high rates of caries and this may suggest that the London Road skeletons consumed higher levels of carbohydrates, or employed different dietary regimes and food preparation techniques compared to their contemporaries. Evidence for the quality and quantity of diet is also indicated, if the erosive joint changes that have been described turn out to have been caused by gout. Gout is a disease that is associated with excessive alcohol intake, obesity, high blood pressure and kidney problems (Roberts and Cox 2003, 137). Interestingly, gout is common in the Cotswolds (both today and in the past) and the oldest examples date from the Roman period (Roberts and Cox 2003, 137–8).

Fragmentation provided little opportunity to explore the physical attributes of the population. However, limited data for stature indicate that the population may not have experienced significant growth disruption during childhood because male and female statures tended to fall above the average that has been reported for males (1.69 m) and females (1.59 m) from this period (Roberts and Cox 2003). Growth disruption can be caused by prolonged periods of malnutrition, disease and/or heavy manual stress (Steckel 1995). The range of non-metric traits in the population suggest that perhaps inheritance was a more significant component in their manifestation in this population than mechanical stress.

Conclusions and future potential

The human skeletons from London Road represent a highly significant group that includes discrete articulated skeletons and commingled skeletons from a mass grave that are probably from the same population. This has afforded a unique opportunity to compare patterns of demography and disease between attritional and catastrophic groups from a single population. The mass grave comprises individuals who probably died over a relatively short period of time and therefore affords the opportunity to explore aspects of demography and disease among individuals who lived at the same time.

The assemblage has considerable potential for further research. A more dedicated programme of element matching and reconstruction to explore the burial taphonomy of the mass grave has already been discussed above. Several pathological conditions would benefit from radiography to explore differential diagnoses. In particular, this concerns joint disease and infection to explore the presence or absence of specific infections (for example syphilis and tuberculosis) and gout. The possible examples of congenital syphilis would benefit from histological analysis. The study of DNA from the mass grave has the potential to make a significant contribution to the question of why the individuals were afforded this type of burial, once problems such as contamination are resolved (Thomas *et al.* 2005; but see Drancourt *et al.* 2004). Palaeopathology is a rapidly expanding field in which knowledge of skeletal involvement in certain diseases is constantly being developed (for example Brickley *et al.* 2007). Those pathological skeletons in the present assemblage, in particular those which presently remain of uncertain diagnosis (for example, with endocranial lesions), will surely benefit from future advances in understanding.

THE BURNT HUMAN BONE
by Nicholas Márquez-Grant

Introduction

In accordance with recommended practice (McKinley and Roberts 1993), cinerary urns (1061 and 1251) were lifted largely intact and the contents of cremated bone were excavated under controlled laboratory conditions. These deposits were excavated in 20 mm spits, each of which was planned at a scale of 1:10 and a total soil sample taken. The samples were then wet sieved and sorted into >10 mm, >5 mm and >2 mm size categories. The sorted bone and the residues were then assessed.

The fragmentation and/or truncation of the other four cinerary urns (1068, 1223, 1200, 1191), meant that it was not possible to excavate and process the remains in the same way. In some cases, the deposits were excavated in spits. In others, the bone and surrounding soil was bulk sampled as a single unit. These samples were wet-sieved and residues sorted into bone and other material such as charcoal and artefacts. All bone was sorted into >10 mm, >5 mm and >2 mm size categories.

The colour of bone fragments, the weight of each deposit, fracture patterns, fragment sizes and the skeletal and dental elements present were recorded to explore the cremation process and pyre technology. Colour is a reflection of the temperatures achieved during cremation (see below). All deposits were examined to determine the MNI and estimate ages and sexes, where possible. Bones were also examined for any evidence of bony abnormality or pathological lesions.

Methods

Where possible, each fragment was identified and classified by anatomical region (eg neurocranium, splanchnocranium, upper limb and lower limb). The presence of any specific anatomical landmark (eg orbit, *linea aspera*) was noted. The representation of skeletal elements may indicate whether certain parts of the skeleton were favoured over others for burial (see below), although it must be taken into account that the prevalence of unidentifiable bone is largely dependent on the degree of fragmentation, whereby larger fragments are easier to identify than smaller ones. It must also be taken into consideration that some skeletal elements (for example cranial fragments) are more diagnostic and more easily identified than others and therefore more often recorded. This may create bias in calculations of the relative quantities of skeletal elements collected for burial.

Bone fragments were weighed to the nearest 0.5 g. Skeletal remains were classified as 'unidentified' if the specific element they represented was unclear. This largely relates to fragments of trabecular bone structure. The average thickness of the cranial vault bones was also measured using a sliding calliper to the nearest 0.01 mm. The presence of pyre goods, grave goods and faunal remains within the deposits was also noted.

Material smaller than 5 mm was not sorted. Analysis at this level focused on the general colour and bone elements only. A note was also made of any identifiable fragments, such as dental crowns, hand and foot bones and other fragments that may provide additional information regarding the MNI count and estimation of biological parameters. The methods described for the unburnt human remains also apply to the burnt remains in terms of estimating the MNI, biological parameters and diagnosing pathological conditions. One method, based on cranial vault thickness (Gejvall 1963), which is specifically aimed at cremated bone deposits, was not employed because the preservation of the remains was not sufficient.

Background: the cremation process

The information that may be derived from cremated bone is less extensive than that derived from unburnt bone. However, it is possible to make inferences about pyre technology and what happened to the bone during and after the cremation process. When a body is cremated, the skeleton is not destroyed but changes occur to the colour and composition of the bones. During the cremation, all the moisture evaporates out of the bone and the organic component (chiefly collagen) is combusted, leaving only the mineral portion. The bones also fragment and can become distorted in shape with some shrinkage occurring.

It is mostly the body fat that fuels the combustion. Observations in modern crematoria suggest that once the temperature has reached about 800°C the fat will ignite, and the fuel jets can actually be turned off (McKinley 2000a). When the body has been cremated, and the pyre has cooled down, the bone fragments are collected. These may be buried directly in the ground, in a small pit, but more usually they are collected together and placed inside an urn or an organic container (for example, a cloth bag or a wooden box). If they have been collected in an organic container, this will not survive the burial process, so it will appear that the cremated bone is 'loose' in the soil. Collection of the entire cremated skeletal remains for burial rarely occurs. This may have been because the relatives (or undertakers) were not very efficient at collecting all the cremated bone from the pyre (the pyre would comprise a heap of charcoal, partially burnt wood, and possibly stones or burnt clay from the lining of the fire pit). Alternatively it may have been unimportant to collect all of the burnt bone, only a token handful or two. Perhaps only certain body parts were deliberately selected for burial. Cremated human bone may be recovered from a number of different contexts and these are summarised in Table 3.60. It is not always possible to determine the type of deposit (particularly if it is not contained within an urn) during excavation. Only by considering, during analysis, factors such as the degree of fragmentation, the skeletal elements that are present, and the minimum number of individuals buried is it possible to establish the most likely type.

Results

There were six urned and three un-urned cremation burials (Table 3.61). A detailed record for each is provided in Appendix 4. In addition, contexts throughout the site included scatters of human cremated bone. These are discussed separately.

Condition and completeness

All but two (1266, 1767) burials were incomplete, having undergone considerable truncation. The ceramic containers in cremation burials 1766, 1196 and 1209 were fragmented *in situ*, and it is unclear whether the deposits had been dispersed. This means that it is impossible to distinguish between the effects of taphonomy and the weight of bone originally selected for burial. Overall, bone preservation was good, there was no marked weathering on the cortical surface of the bones and large quantities of trabecular bone were present in most deposits.

Weight and skeletal part representation

The deposits ranged in weight from 1.5 g to 1255.5 g (Table 3.62). The weight of bone of an adult cremation from a modern crematorium ranges from about 1000 to 3600 g (McKinley 2000b, 404). Therefore, only context 1767 can be considered to represent one complete cremated adult human skeleton.

The highest represented bone fragments were those from the upper and lower limb bones (919.5 g or 38.7% of the entire assemblage). The skull vault was represented mainly by the frontal, parietal and occipital bones (335 g or 14.1% of the entire assemblage). Temporal bones were rarely represented by the petrous pyramid (cremation burial 1766), which is usually a characteristic anatomical landmark that is

Table 3.60   Definitions of deposit types.

Deposit type	Definition
Bustum	Pyre site which also functioned as a grave. The pyre burnt down into the under-pyre pit and the human remains are buried *in situ*. Where no secondary manipulation has occurred, the cremated remains are expected to lie in the correct anatomical position on a bed of charcoal. The effect of the burning has been observed to penetrate the soil by 2–5 cm. The average weight of bone retrieved from cremated adult is between 1600–2000 g but may be as little as 1000 g.
Urned burial	Deposit of cremated bone within a container. May be surrounded by, on top of, or overlain by a deposit of redeposited pyre debris.
Unurned burial	Concentrated deposit of bone, which may have been in an organic container, which may also include a secondary deposit of pyre debris within the backfill.
Unurned burial or redeposited pyre debris	An apparently mixed deposit of cremated human bone and charcoal which may represent the remains of one or more cremated individuals.
Pyre site	Large quantity of charcoal with relatively small amount of burnt bone fragments situated on the ground surface or in under-pyre pits. The pits may also be T or L-shaped to aid draught and are shallow (0.10–0.20 m deep). The soil beneath the pyre should show evidence of burning that may penetrate the soil by 2–5 cm.
Redeposited pyre debris	A mixture of fuel ash, fragments of cremated bone and pyre goods, and possibly burnt flint, burnt stone, burnt clay, fuel, ash and slag depending on the local environment. May contain a relatively large quantity of bone since a small deposit of bone may have been collected for burial. The deposit may be present in the backfill of the burial, over the cremation burial, within pre-existing features, uncontained in spreads and in deliberately excavated features.
Redeposited cremated remains	Small amounts of cremated bone situated or recovered from features, such as pits and ditches, and in the backfill of intercutting cremation burials.
Cremation-related deposit	Unknown deposit type including cremated human bone.

Table 3.61   Summary of cremated human bone.

Cremation burial	Context(s)	Weight of human bone	MNI and identifiable fragments	Predominant colour/ Observations
1196 (late 1st-early 2nd AD)	1189 (fill of pot 1191), 1190 (backfill), 1193 and 1194 (residues of fill of pot)	269.5g	MNI = 1 Skull, vertebrae, ribs, pelvis, shoulder girdle, long bones	White; Fauna present (1g)
1209 (late 1st-early 2nd AD)	1197 (disturbed backfill), 1201 (fill of ancillary pot), 1202 (fill of pot sf 71)	281.5g	MNI = 1 Skull, vertebrae, ribs, pelvis, long bones	White; Fauna present (7.5g)
1227 (late 1st-early 2nd AD)	1225 (disturbed back fill)	1.5g	MNI = 1 Skull	White
1266 (late 1st-early 2nd AD)	1251 (fill of pot 1252), 1258 (backfill)	143g	MNI = 2 Skull, vertebrae, ribs, shoulder girdle, long bones	White
1766 (Pre-Flavian AD 49–68)	1049 (fill of pot 1068)	132.5g	MNI = 1 Skull, vertebrae, ribs, pelvis, shoulder girdle, long bones	White; Fauna present (78.5g)
1767 (Pre-Flavian AD 49–68)	1062 (fill of pot), 1377 (backfill)	1255.5g	MNI = 3 Skull, vertebrae, ribs, pelvis, shoulder girdle, long bones	White; Fauna present (11g)
1768	1095 Unurned cremation deposit	17.5g	MNI = 1 Skull, ribs, long bones	White; Fauna present (1g)
1769 (AD 60–220)	1187 Unurned cremation deposit	261g	MNI = 1 Skull, vertebrae, ribs, pelvis, long bones	White; Fauna present (130.5g)
1770 (50 BC–AD 70)	1324 Unurned cremation deposit	8.5g	MNI = 1 Skull, ribs, long bones	White

present in human cremated bone deposits. There were very few identifiable skeletal landmarks, condyles and some portions of orbit (cremation burial 1767) being amongst these. Some skull fragments that had the coronal and sagittal sutures were present. There was one occipital protuberance amongst the occipital fragments (cremation burial 1196) and fragile, facial bones, such as the sphenoid and maxilla

Table 3.62   Summary of weights (g) for each of the human cremated bone deposits.

Anatomical area	Burial number									
	1196	1209	1227	1266	1766	1767	1768	1769	1770	Total (g)
Cranium	42.5	51	0.5	32	18.5	156.5	6	27	1	335
Mandible	0.5	1	0	0.5	0.5	3.5	0	0	0	6
Teeth	0	1	0	3	2.5	5	0.5	7	0	19
Rib	4	6	0	8.5	5	55	0.5	3.5	0.5	83
Vertebra	2	1	0	1	2	23.5	0	1	0	30.5
Scapula/pelvis	4.5	2.5	0	0.5	6.5	60	0	0.5	0	74.5
Long bone	125.5	92.5	0	37	40	527	8.5	83	6	919.5
Patella	0	2	0	0	0	0	0	0	0	2
Hand/foot	0.5	6.5	0	1	0.5	23.5	0	2.5	0	34.5
Unidentified	90	118	1	59.5	57	401.5	2	136.5	1	866.5
Total (g)	269.5	281.5	1.5	143	132.5	1255.5	17.5	261	8.5	2370.5

(palate fragments in cremation burials 1766 and 1767), were rarely present or could not be identified. A right zygomatic (cremation burial 1766) was present.

Few mandibular fragments were identified (6 g or 0.2% of the total weight of the assemblage), mainly fragments of the body, the ascending ramus, gonion and the condyles (cremation burials 1766 and 1767). Some dental roots were recovered which provided information on biological age.

Vertebrae and ribs were very fragmented and not complete. Most remains belonged to spinous processes or pedicles, bodies of vertebrae and shafts of ribs. Two odontoid processes from two axis vertebrae were identified in cremation burial 2. Atlas fragments were also identified in cremation burials 5 and 7.

The shoulder and pelvic girdle accounted for 74.5 g or 3.1% of the total weight. Some body portions of the scapula and some clavicle shaft fragments represented the shoulder girdle. With regard to the pelvis, most fragments were from the body of the ilium and the acetabulum. There was no sciatic notch identified.

All the major long bones were present, although many of the epiphyses were missing post-mortem. There was a portion of the proximal epiphysis of the radius (cremation burials 1766 and 1767), and several specific landmarks in cremation burial 1767: a portion of the fovea capitis of a femur, distal radius, the radial tuberosity and nutrient foramen of the radius, olecranon of the ulna, proximal tibia, proximal and distal humerus, and distal femur. Humerus, radius, ulna, femur, tibia and fibula shaft fragments were clearly identified in most of the cremations. The skeletal catalogue in Appendix 4 states what bones were present for each cremation burial. So that, for example, in cremation burials 1768 and 1769 only upper limb bones could be identified. One portion of patella (2 g or 0.08% of the total assemblage weight) was identified in cremation burial 1209.

Hand metacarpals and phalanges were present in cremation burials 1209 and 1767. Hand phalanges

were also found in cremation burial 1266. Amongst the foot bones, metatarsals, tarsals (talus, calcaneous) and phalanges were present in cremation burial 1209. Metatarsals, metacarpals and phalanges were also identified in cremation burials 1266, 1767 and 1769.

Many fragments (36.5%) could not be identified. These came largely from the unsorted 4–2 mm sieve size bulk, which were mostly long bone fragments. Other common unidentified fragments were portions of trabecular bone.

Minimum number of individuals, sex and age determination

The material represented a minimum of 12 individuals (Table 3.63). Only two deposits contained material that indicated the presence of more than one individual. These were contexts 1266 and 1767 and they contained a minimum of two and three individuals respectively.

The assemblage comprised nine adults, two subadults and one individual of unknown age. The adults were assumed to be over the age of approximately 15 years because of the dimensions of the long bones and dental formation. Unfortunately, no epiphyses were preserved to assess their degree of fusion to the metaphyses or shafts of the long bones, and also no third molars were present to confirm the adult age of the individuals. The subadult age was established from dental formation. Tentatively, the presence of first and second molars in cremation burial 1769, the lack of exposed dentine in a portion of a molar, the non-edentulous state of the mandible and the non-obliteration of the cranial sutures, suggest a young adult individual (18–25 years). Considerable tooth loss may be regarded as an indicator of old age (over 45 years). Despite several factors, for example cultural practices, which may influence tooth loss in younger adults, mandibles or maxillae with over 50% of teeth lost ante-mortem have been assigned by some to the older age categories (Miles 2001; Mays 2002; also see Wols and Baker 2004). If considerable ante-mortem tooth

Table 3.63   Summary of cremated human bone assemblage.

Cremation burial	MNI	Age	Sex	Observations (ageing criteria)
1196	1	?Adult	?	Bone dimensions
1209	1	?Adult	?male	>12 (dental formation)
1227	1	?	?	–
1266	2	2–6 years and >6–12 years	?	Dental formation
1766	1	?Adult	?	>15 years (dental formation)
1767	3	?Adult	2 x ?male; 1 x ?	>12 (dental formation)
1768	1	?Adult	?	>12 (dental formation)
1769	1	?Adult	?	>15 (dental formation)
1770	1	?Adult	?	Bone dimensions

loss can be considered to be an indicator of old age (<45 years), the skeleton from this latter cremation burial did not show any signs (regeneration) of a considerable (<50%) number of teeth having been lost during life. This is based on three tooth sockets (alveoli) observed for the anterior dentition and 29 dental fragments, which probably correspond to a minimum of nine teeth. Hence, this adult may not be regarded as an old adult.

The sex of the adults could not be determined with any certainty owing to the absence of diagnostic bones. Based on robusticity and the dimensions of long bones and mandible fragments, it is tentatively suggested that the remains from context 1767 represent the remains of male individuals. In addition, certain cranial features (for example, the supraorbital margin, the posterior zygomatic arch and the nuchal crest) that were identified in context 1209 suggested a possible male, although all of these reflected a degree of ambiguity.

Non-metric traits

Only one non-metric trait, the multi-foramina in the zygomatic, could be scored for presence or absence. The right zygomatic found in cremation burial 1766 presented multi-foramina. No ossicles were found in any of the portions of cranial sutures that were observed.

Fragmentation

Fragments between 10 and 5 mm were the most frequent, with the exception of cremation burials 1767 and 1770 which were mainly represented by fragments larger than 10 mm (Table 3.64). The

longest shaft fragment measured 59 mm and was from a tibia from burial 1209. This was followed by fragments from burial 1767 which included a fibula fragment measuring 58 mm and others from the femur and the tibia which were 55 mm in length.

Colour

Most of the cremated bone was white or predominantly white with hues of blue/grey (93.2% of all classified fragments) (Table 3.65). Fragments that were a darker colour, ranging from deep blue through to grey, brown and black, accounted for 6.7% of all classified fragments (143 g/2109 g). Thus for most of the assemblage complete or intense combustion of all the organic component of the bone had taken place. This generally occurs at temperatures above 700°C (Holden *et al.* 1995).

Palaeopathology

Most of the recovered fragments could be observed for pathological changes. Conditions that were present include periostitis and joint disease.

Periostitis

Periostitis was observed on the bones from three deposits (context numbers 1767, 1769 and 1770). Their distribution is summarised in Table 3.66. In addition to the usual periosteal changes, some bone fragments, in particular one metatarsal from burial 1769, showed a 'coral reef' appearance. This is reminiscent of pulmonary osteoarthropathy. However, this diagnosis, which relies on being able to establish the pattern of skeletal involvement, cannot be

Table 3.64   Percentage (in brackets) of bone fragments larger than 10 mm, between 10–4 mm and smaller than 4 mm.

	Context number								
	1196 (%)	1209 (%)	1227 (%)	1266 (%)	1766 (%)	1767 (%)	1768 (%)	1769 (%)	1770 (%)
>10 mm	98g (36.3)	103g (36.5)	0g (0)	24g (16.7)	36g (27.1)	730.5 (58.1)	8g (45.7)	74g (28.3)	5g (58.8)
10–4 mm	153.5g (56.9)	145.5g (51.6)	1.5g (100)	86g (60.1)	87.5g (66.0)	468 (37.2)	9g (51.4)	145g (55.5)	3g (35.2)
<4 mm	18g (6.6)	33g (11.7)	0g (0)	33g (23.0)	9g (6.7)	57 (4.5)	0.5g (2.8)	42g (16.0)	0.5g (5.8)
Total (g)	269.5	281.5	1.5	143	132.5	1255.5	17.5	261	8.5

Chapter Three

Table 3.65 Percentage of fragments according to weight that presented a particular colour.

| | \multicolumn{9}{c}{Context number} | | | | | | | | |
	1196	1209	1227	1266	1766	1767	1768	1769	1770
Black	0g	0.5g	0g	0g	0g	0g	0g	0g	0g
Blue	10g	0g	0g	10g*	7g	42g	0g	6g	0.5g*
Brown	0g	1g	0g	0g	0g	18g	0g	1g	0g
Grey	1g	18.5g	0g	0g	1g	22g	0g	15g	0g
White	177g	94g	1.5g	86.5g	111.5g	251g	17.5g	22g	8g
White + blue/grey	76g	91g	0g	36g	12g	830g	0g	152g	0g

*Dark blue with shades of light grey

Table 3.66 Periostitis distribution in the human cremated bone assemblage.

Context	Bones affected	weight	% of weights in each deposit (long bones)
1767	Tibia Fibula	2.75g	0.5%
1769	Long bones	16g	19.2% (of long bones)
	Hand and foot bones	1.5g	60% (of hand/foot bones)
1770	Long bone (humerus?)	5g	8.5g

confirmed with the present remains. The periosteal reactions that were identified for burials 1767 and 1770 were typical of this condition.

Joint disease

Joint disease, in the form of osteoarthritis (OA), was observed on the bones from context 1767. The changes, osteophytosis and an altered bony contour, involved the first metatarsophalangeal joint (the joint at the base of the great toe). No other joints from this deposit 1767 had OA. This includes two vertebral facets, two rib facets and a left mandibular fossa of the temporo-mandibular joint.

Dental conditions

Dental elements were obtained from six cremation burials (1196, 1209, 1266, 1766, 1767 and 1769) and these are included in the skeletal catalogue in Appendix 4. No pathological conditions were obvious on the dental fragments. No *ante-mortem* tooth loss was observed in 15 sockets from adult individuals corresponding to six mandibular (contexts 1196 and 1209) and nine maxillary alveoli (contexts 1766, 1767 and 1769). Periapical cavities could not be scored because of the incompleteness of the remains.

Further observations

Increased porosity was present in the ectocranial surface of several fragments of skull from cremation burial 1769. This was present on three fragments (2 g) from the skull, including one occipital bone

fragment. In cremation burial 1196 there was one parietal fragment (2 g) with ectocranial pitting. These examples of ectocranial pitting were probably not caused by porotic hyperostosis because they did not display all of the features that are characteristic of this condition.

Discussion of the cremation burials

A minimum of nine adult individuals, two subadults and one of unknown age composed the human cremated bone assemblage.

Skeletal biology and palaeopathology

As previously stated, amongst the 12 individuals identified from the nine cremated human bone deposits, two were subadults younger than 15 years of age, the age of one skeleton was unknown and the remainder were likely to be adults based on bone dimensions and dental formation. Three adults were possible males while the remainder were of unknown sex. Thus the assemblage includes the remains of individuals of different ages, subadult and adult, and at least of male individuals.

Health indicators were present in the form of periostitis and OA. In terms of periostitis, the involvement of the tibia may suggest that relatively inconsequential factors, such as mild trauma, were causing this bony reaction. However, multiple element involvement and the suggestion of more thorough-going periosteal reactions (in the form of 'coral reef' bone), indicates that systemic, chronic disease was experienced by some of these individuals. This finding is in keeping with that observed for the unburnt human remains from London Road.

Gross dental caries has a key role in the development of ante-mortem tooth loss. Thus, although no complete teeth survive it is possible to say that none (0/15 sockets) had been lost during life as a result of dental caries or abscesses. Caries and abscesses are heavily influenced by a diet high in carbohydrate and poor oral hygiene. In the absence of information pertaining to more precise age estimates and without the complete dental crowns and the sockets for posterior rather than anterior teeth, more detailed information on diet cannot be obtained. None of the

77

seven alveoli from the adult individuals presented any regeneration indicative of ante-mortem tooth loss.

Overall, the limited pathological conditions reported to be present may be reflective of living conditions perhaps associated with inadequate nutrition and an environment which would have facilitated the spread of infection. However, a larger sample size would be required to confirm this statement together with a further exploration of the living conditions at the time as inferred by other sources such as material culture and environmental data for the period (see Chapter 5).

Efficiency of cremation and the funerary rite

Overall, there was no apparent pattern with regard to the presence or absence of skeletal elements. The relatively high proportion of cranial fragments is most probably a result of the relative ease with which they are identified compared to other bones, and the small quantity of fragments from the axial skeleton is probably the result of preservation and identification rather than deliberate exclusion. Collection of the bones seems to have been undertaken with care because there has clearly been an attempt to select as many bones as possible, including small fragments such as dental crowns and roots.

Cremated bone may range in colour from brownish-black (slightly charred), through hues of blue and grey, to white, or fully calcined bone (McKinley 2000b, 405). Colour may indicate the temperature at which the body was burnt, although this also depends on how much soft tissue is around the bone. On human

cremated bone, different temperatures are correlated with different colours. These range from orange (200°C), through to black (300°C), grey (600°C) and finally white at a temperature usually between 700°C and 800°C (Shipman *et al.* 1984; Holden *et al.* 1995). In modern crematoria where temperature, fuel availability and air circulation are optimised, full cremation of an adult corpse generally takes between 1 and 1.5 hours to complete when the temperature within the cremator is maintained between 700–1000° C (McKinley 2000b, 404). The colour of the bone in the London Road assemblage was predominantly white reflecting successful cremation at a temperature over 600–700°C. Limited incomplete burning was indicated by the presence of some brown/black/blue fragments. This would suggest that although the mourners and/or funerary attendants took considerable pains to ensure thorough burning of the corpse, some body parts escaped complete cremation, probably depending on the depth of overlying soft tissue and/or their position on the pyre. Other factors that may influence colour variation are the temperature of the firing, oxygen supply, the size of the pyre, the duration of exposure and proximity of the body to the flames, the amount of soft tissue, position of the corpse, and movements of body parts during the cremation (McKinley 2000a and 2000b).

Fracture patterns and surface texture may indicate whether a body was burnt with its flesh or whether only the dry skeleton was selected for the pyre after decomposition or defleshing of the soft tissue. As opposed to dry bones, burning a skeleton covered with flesh produces curved transverse fracture lines, irregular longitudinal splitting, twisting and marked

Table 3.67 Human bone from non-cremation burial contexts.

Context	Sample/ SF	Sieve size (mm)	Bone	Weight (g)	Colour	Observations
1063	3	10–4, 4–2	1 rib shaft 14 unidentified fragments	1	White + grey	Dimensions = >10 years
1106	–	>10, 10–4	2 upper limb, 1 long bone. 4 unidentified fragments	4.5	White	Adult dimensions. Longest fragment = 38 mm
1132	11	10–4	1 ?radius shaft	0.5	White	Adult dimensions
1166	28	>10, 10–4	3 skull vault fragments	1.5	White	Dimensions = >10 years
1166	29	>10, 10–4	1 skull vault, 1 rib shaft, 5 unidentified fragments	2	White + hues of blue	–
1166	30	10–4, 4–2	3 skull vault fragments, 1 unidentified	1	White	–
1201	53	>10 mm	1 long bone shaft, 1 vertebral body, 2 unidentified fragments	3	White-light grey	Spit 2
1212	112	10–4	1 ulna or fibula shaft fragment	<0.5	White	–
1246	95	10–4	1 rib shaft, 2 unidentified	0.5	Light grey	–
1333	145	10–4	2 long bone shaft fragments	<0.5	White	–
1515	242	10–4	2 unidentified and 2 long bone fragments	0.5	Light brown, grey	–
1707	–	>10, 10–4	1 ulna, 1 tibia, 1 long bone, 1 metatarsal? shaft fragments	4	White, white + grey, hues of blue (MT shaft)	Adult dimensions. Longest fragment = 28 mm. 2 fauna fragments (5 g)

warping (Ubelaker 1989; Buikstra and Ubelaker 1994). This latter was the case at London Road.

Investigations in modern crematoria have found that the average bone weight of a cremated adult female individual weighs on average 1615.7 g and a male body an average of 2283.5 g (McKinley 1993). Predictably, individuals of smaller and more gracile build, such as children, or those older individuals with osteoporosis will have a lower bone weight and possibly poorer bone survival (McKinley 2000b, 404). Overall, bone weights were low in the London Road, Gloucester, assemblage with the exception of one undisturbed, urned adult cremation burial (burial 1767, context 1062), which weighed approximately 1255.5 g. This may suggest that, at least for those undisturbed burials, collection and deposition of the entire cremated remains of these individuals was not deemed important, and that only 'token' deposits had been buried.

Fragment size represents the measurements taken by the human osteologist during analysis. Factors that affect fragmentation include the cremation process, collection and burial of the human remains, deliberate fragmentation by the mourners or grave diggers, taphonomic factors (for example, soil characteristics and ploughing), and the much later process of archaeological excavation and post-excavation processing (McKinley 1994). It is possible that cremated bone was fragmented deliberately in order to fit it into the urn but there is no evidence to suggest this was the case. In fact, while most fragments were larger (>10 mm) than would perhaps be expected if they had been deliberately treated in this manner, the size of the aperture of most vessels was around *c*100 mm and the size argument here may be irrelevant (Booth, pers. comm.). In addition, McKinley (1997, 251) points out that fragment sizes recorded during post-excavation analysis will unlikely represent the size of the fragments during the time of deposition due to a number of factors including site disturbances and the excavation process.

Cremated human bone from non-cremation burial contexts

A number of non-cremation burial related deposits with human cremated bone were present and are merely listed here (Table 3.67). The estimated biological ages are based on bone dimensions only. In no case was sex determined and no further information could be obtained other than that included in Table 3.67.

In addition, three bags were analysed containing human cremated bone from the mass grave fill (1545). From this context, sample 244 contained one trabecular bone fragment (10–4 mm, >0.5 g). The remaining fragments from the other two bags included apparently adult bones. These comprised long bones smaller than 10 mm and two unidentified fragments, in total weighing 6 g. The colour varied according to the fragment from black to light blue, grey and white. There is also 5 g of skull vault (two fragments possibly of frontal bone) which are white in colour with hues of blue and grey. Due to the contextual information and the small quantity of these remains it is likely that the inclusions in the mass grave are accidental rather than deliberate.

Chapter 4   The Grave Catalogue

INTRODUCTION

Each grave is referred to in the catalogue by its grave group number, the number used throughout the text. Each entry gives details of the grave, comprising orientation; shape and dimensions; the nature of the fill; stratigraphic relationships with other features; evidence for grave furniture; a description of any grave goods, pyre goods and other finds recovered from the grave; date where this could be established from artefactual evidence or radiocarbon dating. The location of each grave is indicated on Figure 4.1 and plans (Figs 4.2–8) are only provided for those graves containing grave goods.

The following information is given for each skeleton, when applicable: a description of the posture of the body, including the position of the arms and legs; sex; age; an indication of the completeness of the skeleton as recovered; an assessment of the condition of the bone; and details of any pathological abnormalities. The completeness of discrete skeletons was categorised as >75%, 75–50%, 50–25% or <25%. Bone condition was assessed according to criteria proposed by McKinley (2004).

For cremations the following information is given: the weight of the calcined fragments; maximum dimension of the largest fragment; a brief note of identifiable fragments; colour of the bone; the minimum number of individuals (MNI) represented by the remains; the age and sex of the individual(s).

Age at death and biological sex were estimated as described in Chapter 3.

Every object is described in detail with the exception of material derived from the backfill of the grave. The bracketed numbers following each entry are the context number and small find number ascribed to the object (the latter prefixed by sf), and a reference to any illustration of the item located within the relevant specialist report.

CATALOGUE OF GRAVES

Inhumation grave 1143

Grave cut 1111

Orientation: NE-SW
Shape: Rectangular. Straight vertical sides, flat base
Dimensions: 1.97 x 0.69 m, 0.25 m deep
Fill: Greyish-brown silty clay back-fill (1113)
Relationships: Cuts grave 1759, cut by grave 1144. Relationship with grave 1167 uncertain

Skeleton 1112

Posture: Prone, extended. Legs extended and parallel, truncated at mid-tibia
Arm position: Hands and forearms absent but the angle of the upper arms suggests that they were behind the back

Sex: Male
Age: 13–17 years
Completeness: 50–75%
Condition: Good
Pathological conditions: healed blunt cranial trauma, temporo-mandibular joint anomaly, enamel hypoplasia

Finds: Five sherds of 1st–early 2nd century pottery were recovered from the back-fill.

Inhumation grave 1144

Grave cut 1122

Orientation: SSW-NNE
Fill: Greyish-brown silty clay back-fill (1123=1269)
Relationships: Cuts grave 1143

Skeleton 1114=1270

Posture: Supine, legs extended and parallel
Arm position: Left arm extended beside body, right arm absent
Age: 26–35 years
Completeness: 25%–50%
Condition: Very good
Pathological conditions: cribra orbitalia, neoplastic disease (button osteoma), enamel hypoplasia, dental caries, dental calculus, periodontitis
Musculo-skeletal markers: enthesophytes on calcanei

Charnel 1115

Shafts of left and right tibia, which had been placed directly on the skull of skeleton 1114=1270

Finds: An assemblage of 11 hobnails and a fragment of colourless glass that may be a modern intrusion were recovered from the back-fill.
Date: 2nd century AD or later
Comments: The middle part of the grave was truncated by a modern feature, leaving only the head and left upper arm and the lower parts of the legs.

Inhumation grave 1145 (Fig. 4.2)

Grave cut 1126

Orientation: SW-NE
Shape: Sub-rectangular. Vertical sides, flat base
Dimensions: 1.52 x 0.54 m, 0.12 m deep
Fill: Orange-brown silty clay back-fill (1129)

Skeleton 1127

Posture: Prone, extended. Lower parts of legs removed by later truncation
Arm position: Left arm extended beside body, right flexed beneath torso with hand lying beneath left shoulder.
Sex: ?Male
Age: 18–25 years
Completeness: 25–50%
Condition: Fair
Pathological conditions: dental calculus
Musculo-skeletal markers: enthesophytes on ulnae and femora

Grave goods: Part of a ring-necked flagon in oxidised TF 11A (1128, Fig. 5.2, no. 10) lay on its side against the side of the skull. The rim has an old chip out of the circumference.

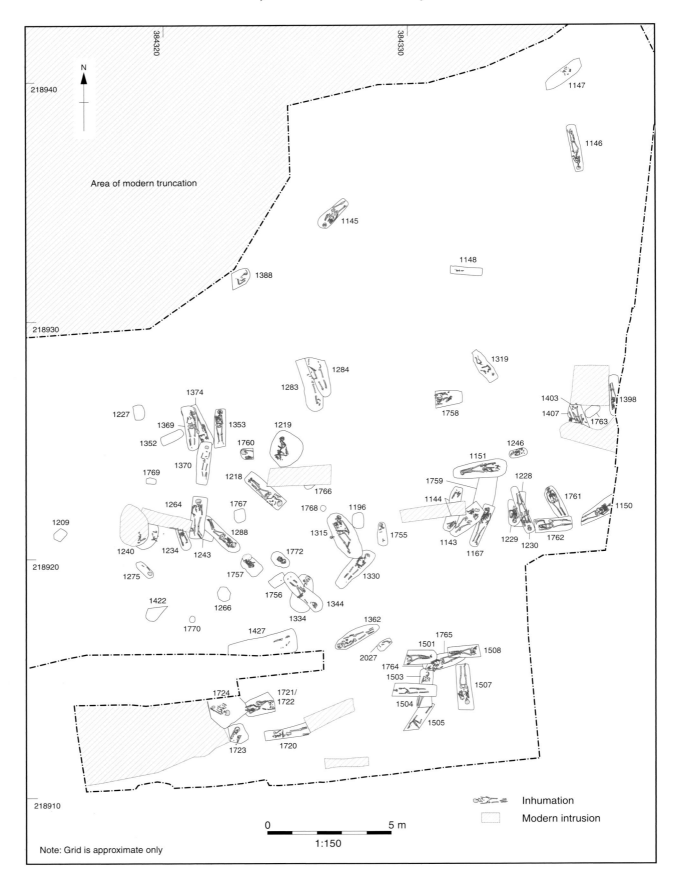

Figure 4.1   Plan of all burials.

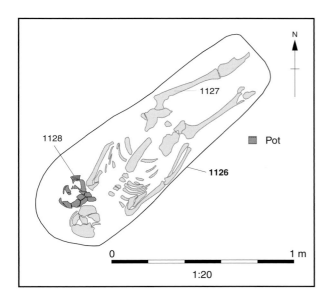

Figure 4.2   Plan of inhumation burial 1145.

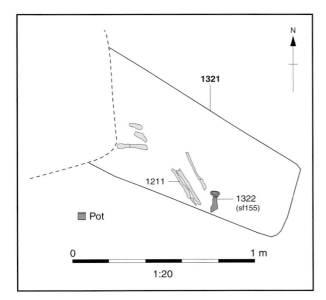

Figure 4.3   Plan of inhumation burial 1243.

Other finds: A single iron nail (sf 24) was recovered from the backfill.
Date: 1st–early 2nd century

Inhumation grave 1146

Grave cut 1130

Orientation: N-S
Shape: Sub-rectangular, concave base
Dimensions: 1.90 x 0.40 m, 0.18 m deep
Fill: Greyish-brown clay back-fill (1132)

Skeleton 1131

Posture: Supine, legs extended with feet together
Arm position: Left arm extended beside body, right arm absent
Sex: Female

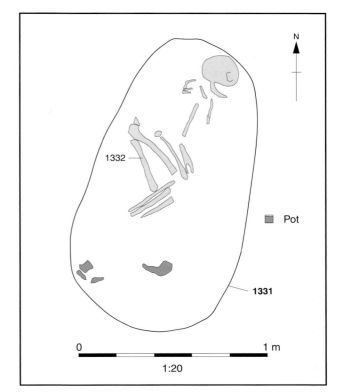

Figure 4.4   Plan of inhumation burial 1334.

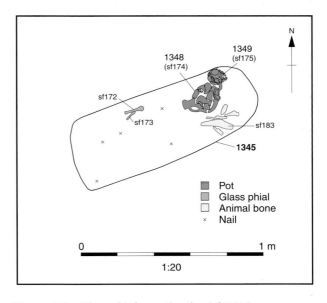

Figure 4.5   Plan of inhumation burial 1352.

Age: 26–35 years
Completeness: <25%
Condition: Fair
Pathological conditions: active periostitis on left femur and left calcaneous, healed periostitis on right femur, dental calculus.

Finds: Three sherds of 1st century pottery were recovered from the back-fill, as well as eight hobnails and a single structural nail (sf 23).
Comments: This individual has been buried in a very narrow grave. The legs and feet are very close together, suggesting that they may have been bound within a shroud.

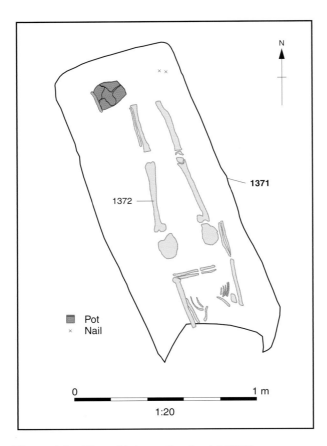

Figure 4.6 Plan of inhumation burial 1374.

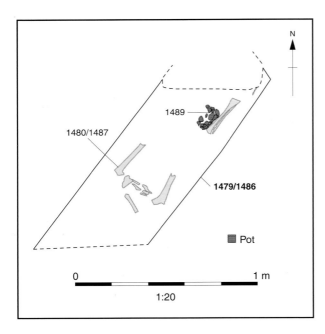

Figure 4.7 Plan of inhumation burial 1505.

Inhumation grave 1147

Grave cut 1134

Orientation: NE-SW
Shape: Sub-rectangular

Dimensions: 1.80 x 0.50 m, 0.10 m deep
Fill: Orange-brown clay back-fill (1136)

Skeleton 1135

Posture: Supine
Age: Adult (>18 years)
Completeness: <25%
Condition: Good
Pathological conditions: enamel hypoplasia, dental calculus, periodontitis

Finds: One sherd of 1st century pottery and two structural nails (sfs 25, 26) were recovered from the back-fill.

Inhumation grave 1148

Grave cut 1137

Orientation: E-W
Shape: Indeterminate due to severe truncation
Dimensions: Indeterminate due to severe truncation
Fill: Orange-brown silty clay back-fill (1139)

Skeleton 1138

Posture: Supine, extended
Arm position: Left arm extended beside body, right side of body absent
Age: 18–25 years
Completeness: <25%
Condition: Good
Pathological conditions: healed periostitis on tibiae, enamel hypoplasia, dental caries, dental calculus

Finds: A single nail was recovered from the back-fill.
Comments: Grave severely truncated by modern disturbance, only the left side of the body surviving.

Inhumation grave 1150

Grave cut 1104

Orientation: NE-SW
Shape: Rectangular. Vertical sides, flat base
Dimensions: >1.5 x 0.6 m, 0.1 m deep
Fill: Orange-brown silty clay back-fill (1102)

Skeleton 1103

Posture: Prone, legs extended and parallel
Arm position: Left arm extended beside body, right arm slightly flexed with hand beneath pelvis
Sex: Female
Age: 36–45 years
Completeness: 50–75%
Condition: Very good
Pathological conditions: osteoarthritis on ribs and vertebrae, osteophytosis on ribs, vertebrae and long bones, active and healed periostitis on right tibia, enamel hypoplasia, dental caries, dental calculus, periodontitis, periapical cavity

Finds: A single sherd of 1st–2nd century pottery was recovered from the back-fill.
Comments: The north-eastern end of the grave was truncated by the foundation of a modern wall and the south-western end by machining, the latter having removed the feet.

Inhumation grave 1151

Grave cut 1108

Orientation: E-W
Shape: Sub-rectangular. Steep sides, flat base
Dimensions: 2.16 x 0.76 m, 0.21 m deep
Fill: Yellowish brown silty clay back-fill (1110)
Relationships: Cuts grave 1759

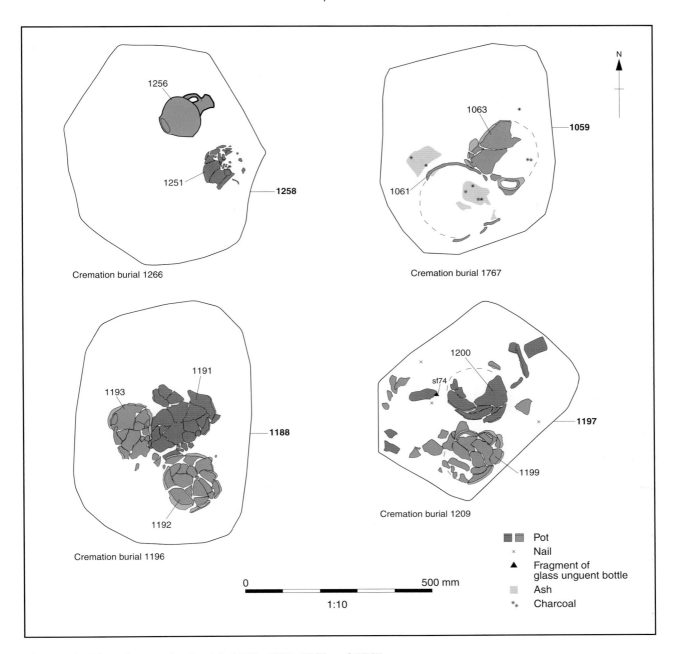

1256

1251

1258

Cremation burial 1266

1063

1059

1061

Cremation burial 1767

1191

1193

1188

1192

Cremation burial 1196

1200

sf74

1197

1199

Cremation burial 1209

■■ ▫▫ Pot
×   Nail
▲   Fragment of
         glass unguent bottle
▨   Ash
*⁎⁎   Charcoal

0   500 mm

1:10

Figure 4.8   Plan of cremation burials 1196, 1209, 1266 and 1767.

Skeleton 1109

Posture: Supine, legs extended with feet together
Arm position: Arms slightly flexed, hands crossed over pelvis
Sex: ?Male
Age: 26–35 years
Completeness: >75%
Condition: Very good
Pathological conditions: healed trauma on right rib, healed periostitis on tibiae and fibulae, dental caries, dental calculus
Musculo-skeletal markers: enthesophytes on tibiae and left patella

Grave furniture: The remains of a coffin were represented by four iron nails (sfs 16–19) located *in situ* around the left side and foot of the burial. sf 19 was located above the skeleton, indicating that this was a coffin rather than a bier.
Other finds: A damaged and incomplete copper alloy mount (sf 20) was recovered from the back-fill.

Comments: A small patch of green staining indicating the former location of a degraded copper alloy object was observed in the chest region. Skull absent due to truncation.

Inhumation grave 1167

Grave cut 1164

Orientation: NNE-SSW
Shape: Sub-rectangular. Vertical sides, flat base
Dimensions: 1.76 x 0.42 m, 0.22 m deep
Fill: Orange-brown clay back-fill (1166)
Relationships: Relationships with graves 1143 and 1759 are uncertain

Skeleton 1165

Posture: Supine, legs extended and parallel
Arm position: Arms flexed with hands crossed over pelvis

Sex: ?Female
Age: 18–25 years
Completeness: >75%
Condition: Poor
Pathological conditions: healed periostitis on left calcaneous, enamel hypoplasia, dental calculus

Grave furniture: The remains of a coffin were represented by five iron nails (sfs 35–39) lying *in situ* around the lower part of the skeleton.
Grave goods: A total of 20 hobnails were recovered. A group of 17 hobnails (sf 34) were located at the foot of the grave and may represent an item or items of footwear placed as grave good(s). The location of the remaining three hobnails (sf 28) was not recorded.
Other finds: A rim sherd of 1st century Dorset black burnished ware was recovered from the back-fill, which joined with a sherd recovered from grave 1230.

Inhumation grave 1218

Grave cut 1215

Orientation: SE-NW
Shape: Rectangular. Vertical sides, flat base
Dimensions: 1.93 x 0.55 m, 0.28 m deep
Fill: Orange-brown silty clay back-fill (1217)

Skeleton 1216

Posture: Supine, legs extended with feet together
Arm position: Left arm flexed with hand near right shoulder, right arm extended beside body with hand beneath pelvis
Sex: Male
Age: 45+ years
Completeness: >75%
Condition: Fair
Pathological conditions: cortical defect on left clavicle, osteoarthritis on ribs, vertebrae and hip joints (femora and os coxa affected), healed periostitis on ribs and metatarsals, cribra orbitalia, enamel hypoplasia, dental caries, dental calculus, periodontitis
Musculo-skeletal markers: enthesophytes on patellae

Grave furniture: Three iron nails (sfs 78–80) were recovered from the back-fill.
Other finds: Four sherds of 1st–2nd century pottery were recovered from the back-fill.

Inhumation grave 1219

Grave cut 1208

Shape: Sub-circular
Dimensions: 1.40 x 1.22 m, 0.15 m deep
Fill: Reddish-brown silty clay back-fill (1207)

Skeleton 1206

Posture: Crouched. Lying on right side with head to NE and legs flexed
Arm position: Left arm flexed, right arm extended
Sex: ?Female
Age: 18–25 years
Completeness: 50–75%
Condition: Fair
Pathological conditions: rib osteoarthritis, possible healed trauma on right humerus, possible abnormal healed inflammation on sphenoid, cribra orbitalia, enamel hypoplasia, dental caries, dental calculus, periodontitis

Finds: A single unclassified nail was recovered from the back-fill.

Inhumation grave 1228

Grave cut 1183

Orientation: S-N
Shape: Rectangular. Vertical sides, flat base

Dimensions: 1.47 x 0.4 m, 0.18 m deep
Fill: Orange-brown clay gravel back-fill (1185)
Relationships: Cut by graves 1229 and 1230

Skeleton 1184

Posture: Supine, legs extended
Completeness: <25%
Condition: Poor

Date: AD 70–240 (NZA 27006) (radiocarbon assay)
Comments: The middle and south-western parts of this grave were removed by the digging of subsequent graves 1230 and 1229 respectively.

Inhumation grave 1229

Grave cut 1154

Orientation: S-N
Shape: Sub-rectangular
Dimensions: 1.18 x 0.58 m, 0.07 m deep
Fill: Orange-brown clay back-fill (1155)
Relationships: Cuts grave 1228, cut by grave 1230

Skeleton 1153

Posture: Supine. Lower part of body absent from mid-pelvis
Arm position: Left arm flexed across pelvis, right arm absent
Sex: ?Male
Age: 18–25 years
Completeness: <25%
Condition: Very good
Pathological conditions: rib osteoarthritis, Schmorl's nodes, enamel hypoplasia, dental caries, dental calculus, periodontitis, periapical cavity

Grave furniture: The remains of a coffin were represented by five nails (sfs 29–33) located *in situ* around the edge of the grave.
Other finds: A single small sherd of 1st century pottery and two nails were recovered from the back-fill.
Comments: The northern and eastern parts of the grave have been truncated by the digging of subsequent grave 1230, removing the right side and lower part of the body.

Inhumation grave 1230

Grave cut 1180

Orientation: SSW-NNE
Shape: Sub-rectangular. Vertical sides, concave base
Dimensions: 2.06 x 0.41 m
Fill: Brownish-orange clay gravel back-fill (1182)
Relationships: Cuts grave 1229

Skeleton 1181

Posture: Prone, legs extended with feet together
Arm position: Left arm extended beside body, right arm flexed with hand beneath pelvis
Sex: Female
Age: 26–35 years
Height: 1.62 m
Completeness: >75%
Condition: Very good
Pathological conditions: healed rib periostitis, periostitis on occipital bone, vertebral osteophytosis, healed maxillary sinusitis, enamel hypoplasia, dental caries, dental calculus, periodontitis
Musculo-skeletal markers: enthesophytes on left femur

Finds: An iron ring (sf 141), a coin dated *c* AD 270–295, four fragments of tile, an iron nail, a hobnail head and seven sherds of 2nd century pottery were recovered from the back-fill, the latter including a rim sherd from a Dorset black burnished ware vessel that joined with a sherd from the back-fill of grave 1167.
Date: Late 3rd–4th century

Inhumation grave 1234

Grave cut 1231

Orientation: NNW-SSE
Shape: Rectangular. Vertical sides, flat base
Dimensions: >0.92 x 0.38 m, 0.12 m deep
Fill: Orange-brown silty clay back-fill (1233)

Skeleton 1232

Posture: Prone, legs extended and parallel. Severely truncated, only the legs surviving. Skull placed on backs of knees
Sex: ?Female
Age: 18–25 years
Completeness: 25–50%
Condition: Good
Pathological conditions: possible active periostitis on mandible, cribra orbitalia, hyperostosis frontalis interna, enamel hypoplasia, dental caries, dental calculus

Grave goods: Two groups of hobnails were found, representing items of footwear worn at the time of burial—a group of 32 (sf 87) associated with the right foot and a group of 37 (sf 91) associated with the left foot.
Other finds: A total of 27 sherds of 1st century pottery and three iron nails were recovered from the back-fill.
Comments: The northern half of this grave has been truncated by a modern pit, leaving only the southern end.

Inhumation grave 1240

Grave cut 1237

Shape: Sub-circular. Steep sides, flat base
Dimensions: 0.90 m diameter, 0.22m deep.
Fill: Brownish-yellow sandy clay back-fill (1239)
Relationships: Overlain by Roman soil layer 1106

Skeleton 1238

Posture: Crouched, lying on left side with the head to the east
Sex: ?Male
Age: 45+ years
Completeness: <25%
Condition: Fair
Pathological conditions: cortical defects on left femur, possible Paget's disease, enamel hypoplasia, dental caries, dental calculus

Finds: Three sherds of 1st century pottery were recovered from the back-fill.
Comments: Truncated by a modern pit.

Inhumation grave 1243 (Fig. 4.3)

Grave cut 1321

Orientation: WNW-ESE
Shape: Sub-rectangular
Dimensions: 2.0 x 0.60 m, 0.30 m deep
Fill: Orange sandy clay back-fill (1322)
Relationships: Cut by grave 1264

Skeleton 1211

Posture: Supine, legs extended
Arm position: Right arm extended beside body. Left arm absent
Age: Adult (>18 years)
Completeness: <25%
Condition: Poor

Grave goods: The upper part of a ring-necked flagon in oxidised fabric TF 11A (sf 155, Fig. 5.2, no. 11) lay on the right foot.
Other finds: Two sherds of 1st century pottery were recovered from the back-fill.

Date: AD 1–130 (NZA 27005) (radiocarbon assay)
Comments: The western half of grave was truncated by a modern pit, which had removed the upper part of body with the exception of the right forearm and hand.

Inhumation grave 1246

Grave cut 1245

Orientation: E-W
Fill: Greenish-orange clay (1246)

Skeleton 1235

Posture: Crouched, lying on left side with head to east
Arm position: Tightly flexed in front of torso
Age: 5–12 years
Completeness: <25%
Condition: Good

Finds: An iron finger ring (sf 88), lacking its intaglio, was recovered from the grave and is likely to have been placed as a grave good.
Comments: Southern side of grave truncated by modern concrete pad, removing legs.

Inhumation grave 1264

Grave cut 1261

Orientation: N-S
Shape: Rectangular. Vertical sides, flat base
Dimensions: 1.82 x 0.50 m, 0.22 m deep
Fill: Orange-brown silty clay back-fill (1263)
Relationships: Cuts graves 1243 and 1288

Skeleton 1262

Posture: Supine, legs extended and parallel
Arm position: Left arm extended beside body, right arm flexed with hand over pelvis
Sex: ?Male
Age: 26–35 years
Completeness: <25%
Condition: Fair
Pathological conditions: osteoarthritis (including both eburnation and osteophytosis) on vertebrae, left os coxa, right humerus, right radius and right femur, healed trauma on right clavicle, active and healed periostitis on right tibia and fibula, healed periostitis on right metatarsal, enamel hypoplasia, dental caries, dental calculus, periodontitis
Musculo-skeletal markers: enthesophytes on femora and patellae

Grave furniture: The possible remains of a coffin were represented by four nails (sfs 106, 110, 111, 116) located around the foot of the grave and a fifth (sf 112) at the head.
Other finds: A single small sherd of 1st century pottery was recovered from the back-fill.
Date: Assigned a 3rd–4th century date on the basis of its apparent spatial association with grave 1370.

Inhumation grave 1275

Grave cut 1276

Orientation: SE-NW
Shape: Sub-rectangular. Steep sides, flat base
Dimensions: 0.95 x 0.36 m, 0.17 m deep
Fill: Yellow clay back-fill (1278)

Skeleton 1277

Posture: Supine. Left leg absent, right leg extended
Arm position: Left arm absent, right arm extended beside body
Age: 2–5 years

Completeness: <25%
Condition: Fair
Pathological conditions: cribra orbitalia, enamel hypoplasia

Date: AD 50–220 (NZA 29423) (Radiocarbon assay)

Inhumation grave 1283

Grave cut 1210

Orientation: N-S
Shape: Sub-rectangular. Steep sides, flat base
Dimensions: 1.70 x 0.73 m, 0.16 m deep
Fill: Brownish-grey silty clay back-fill 1212
Relationships: Cut by grave 1284

Skeleton 1279

Posture: Supine, extended
Arm position: Right arm extended beside body, left arm absent
Age: Adult (>18 years)
Completeness: <25%
Condition: Fair
Pathological conditions: healed periostitis on left metatarsal

Grave goods: An assemblage of 44 hobnails was recovered from a soil sample taken from around the feet.
Other finds: Four nails and ten sherds of 1st century pottery including a single fragment from an amphora were recovered from the back-fill.
Comments: The northern end of the grave is truncated by a modern feature and the eastern side by grave 1284, leaving only the feet, right leg and right arm.

Inhumation grave 1284

Grave cut 1280

Orientation: N-S
Shape: Sub-rectangular. Steep sides, flat base
Dimensions: 1.80 x 0.75 m, 0.44 m deep
Fill: Brownish grey silty clay back-fill (1282)
Relationships: Cuts grave 1283

Skeleton 1281

Posture: Supine, legs extended and parallel
Arm position: Left arm extended beside body, right arm slightly flexed with hand over pelvis
Age: Adult (>18 years)
Completeness: <25%
Condition: Fair
Pathological conditions: osteoarthritis on metacarpal and hand phalanx, osteophytosis on matacarpals, phalanges, right femora and left os coxa, possible trauma (followed by anky-losis) on hand phalanges
Musculo-skeletal markers: enthesophytes on left ulna and femora

Grave goods: Three hobnails were recovered from the area of the feet (sf 130, 133).
Other finds: Eleven sherds of 1st century pottery and three frag-mentary iron nails (sfs 94, 113 and 127) were recovered from the back-fill.
Comments: The northern end of the grave is truncated by a modern feature.

Inhumation grave 1288

Grave cut 1287

Orientation: SE-NW
Shape: Sub-rectangular. Near vertical sides, flat base
Dimensions: 2.00 x 0.60 m, 0.29 m deep
Fill: Brown clay back-fill (1285)
Relationships: Cut by grave 1264

Skeleton 1286

Posture: Extended on left side but slumped slightly onto front. Legs slightly flexed, feet together
Arm position: Left arm beneath torso, right arm extended beside body
Sex: ?Male
Age: 26–35 years
Completeness: 50–75%
Condition: Good
Pathological conditions: rib osteoarthritis, osteophytosis on vertebrae and femora, trauma, periostitis on right tibia, osteo-myelitis on left tibia and fibula, cribra orbitalia, enamel hypoplasia, dental calculus, periodontitis, circulatory disease (possible Perthes' disease).
Musculo-skeletal markers: enthesophytes on femora.

Grave furniture: The remains of a coffin were represented by an assemblage of 15 coffin nails (sfs 119–125, 128, 129, 131, 132, 136–8, 140) located *in situ* around the edges of the grave.
Grave goods: The partial remains of a domestic fowl were placed behind legs.
Other finds: Ten sherds of 1st century pottery were recovered from the back-fill.
Date: AD 60–240 (NZA 27007) (radiocarbon assay)

Inhumation grave 1315

Grave cut 1314

Orientation: NW-SE
Shape: Sub-rectangular. Steep sides, flat base
Dimensions: 2.10 x 0.50 m, 0.37 m deep
Fill: Greyish yellow clay back-fill (1312)
Relationships: Cuts grave 1330

Skeleton 1313

Posture: Supine, right leg extended, left leg flexed with foot beneath right ankle
Arm position: Left arm extended at slight angle to body, right arm flexed with forearm across pelvis
Sex: Male
Age: 18–25 years
Completeness: 50–75%
Condition: Good
Pathological conditions: vertebral osteophytosis, degenerative disc disease, enamel hypoplasia, dental caries, dental calculus, periodontitis
Musculo-skeletal markers: enthesophytes on ulnae and femora

Grave goods: An assemblage of 37 hobnails was recovered from a soil sample taken from around the feet.
Other finds: Two iron nails (sfs 139 and 143) were recovered from the back-fill.
Comments: The irregular posture may result from the body shift-ing inside a coffin, although only two possible coffin nails were recovered.

Inhumation grave 1319

Grave cut 1316

Orientation: SE-NW
Shape: Sub-rectangular. Steep sides, flat base
Dimensions: 1.48 x 0.52 m, 0.14 m deep
Fill: Orange-brown gritty clay back-fill (1318)

Skeleton 1317

Posture: Supine, legs extended and truncated at approximately the knees
Arm position: Left arm flexed at an angle to body, right arm flexed across stomach
Age: 13–17 years
Completeness: 25–50%
Condition: Good

Pathological conditions: healed periostitis in femora, endocranial lesions, enamel hypoplasia, dental caries, dental calculus

Grave furniture: The remains of a coffin were represented by eight nails located around the edges of the south-eastern half of the grave (sfs 141, 144–150).

Other finds: A single sherd of 1st century pottery was recovered from the back-fill.

Comments: The NW end of the grave has been truncated by a modern feature, removing the lower parts of the legs.

Inhumation grave 1330

Grave cut 1329

Orientation: NE-SW
Shape: Sub-rectangular. Steep sides, flat base
Dimensions: 2.00 x 0.65 m, 0.18 m deep
Fill: Greenish yellow clay back-fill (1327)
Relationships: Cut by grave 1315

Skeleton 1328

Posture: Supine, legs extended and parallel
Arm position: Both arms flexed, crossing over pelvis
Sex: Male
Age: 26–35 years
Completeness: 50–75%
Condition: Fair
Pathological conditions: osteoarthritis in vertebrae, benign cysts in carpal bones, healed infection in frontal sinus, cribra orbitalia, dental caries, dental calculus, periodontitis, periapical cavity

Grave goods: Two groups of hobnails were found, representing footwear worn at the time of burial—a group of 22 (sf 156) associated with the right foot and a group of 13 (sf 157) associated with the left foot.

Other finds: Three iron nails (sfs 158–160) were recovered from the back-fill.

Inhumation grave 1334 (Fig. 4.4)

Grave cut 1331

Orientation: NNE-SSW
Shape: Oval
Dimensions: 1.52 x 0.83 m, depth not recorded
Fill: Reddish-brown gravelly clay back-fill (1333)
Relationships: Cut by grave 1344

Skeleton 1332

Posture: Crouched, lying on left side with legs flexed
Arm position: Left arm absent, right arm flexed
Age: Adult (>18 years)
Completeness: <25%
Condition: Poor
Musculo-skeletal markers: enthesophytes on femora

Grave goods: The base of a well-fragmented grey ware jar with a triangular-shaped rim in fabric TF11A was positioned at the base of the grave near the feet.

Other finds: A single sherd of 1st century pottery was recovered from the back-fill.

Date: 1st–early 2nd century AD (Radiocarbon date AD 50–230 (NZA 27004))

Inhumation grave 1344

Grave cut 1339

Orientation: SE-NW
Shape: Sub-rectangular. Steep sides, flat base
Dimensions: 1.96 x 0.38 m, 0.23 m deep
Fill: Greyish-yellow clay gravel back-fill (1341)
Relationships: Cuts grave 1334 and probably grave 1756

Skeleton 1340

Posture: Supine, legs extended and parallel
Arm position: Arms extended beside body
Age: 36–45 years
Completeness: <25%
Condition: Poor
Pathological conditions: cribra orbitalia, hyperostosis frontalis interna, neoplastic disease (button osteomata)
Musculo-skeletal markers: enthesophytes on femur

Grave furniture: The remains of a coffin were represented by five iron nails (sfs 163, 168–71, 182, 203) located around the edges of the north-western end of the grave.

Grave goods: An assemblage of 178 hobnails (sf 170) was recovered from the area of the feet.

Other finds: Two sherds of 1st century pottery were recovered from the back-fill.

Inhumation grave 1352 (Fig. 4.5)

Grave cut 1345

Orientation: NE-SW
Shape: Sub-rectangular. Steep sides, flat base
Dimensions: 1.10 x 0.60 m, 0.18 m deep
Fill: Yellowish-brown gravely clay back-fill (13470)

Skeleton: No skeletal material was present

Grave furniture: The remains of a box or coffin were represented by an assemblage of seven nails (sfs 176–81, 247) located around the edges of the grave.

Grave goods:

1. Ring-necked flagon in oxidised TF 11A, represented by the upper part only (1348, sf 174, Fig. 5.1, no. 8)
2. Upper portion of a flagon in oxidised TF 11A (1349, sf 175, Fig. 5.2, no. 9)
3. Tubular unguent bottle in blue/green glass. sf 173
4. Tall conical unguent bottle in blue/green glass. sf 172
5. Some mammal bone (sf 183) that was lost prior to identification

Other finds: Three sherds of 1st century pottery were recovered from the back-fill.

Date: 1st–early 2nd century AD

Inhumation grave 1353

Grave cut 1336

Orientation: S-N
Shape: Rectangular. Near vertical sides, flat base
Dimensions: 1.76 x 0.44 m, 0.10 m deep
Fill: Orange-brown gravelly clay back-fill (1338)
Relationships: Relationship with grave 1374 could not be established

Skeleton 1337

Posture: Supine, legs extended and parallel
Arm position: Left hand extended with hand on pelvis, right arm flexed across pelvis
Sex: ?Female
Age: 26–35 years
Completeness: >75%
Condition: Very good
Pathological conditions: Schmorl's nodes, osteochondritis dissecans, active periostitis in tibiae, erosive lesions in femoral neck, cribra orbitalia, hyperostosis frontalis interna, enamel hypoplasia, dental caries, dental calculus, periodontitis

Grave furniture: The remains of a coffin were represented by seven iron nails (sfs 206–12) located around the western side and ends of the grave.

Grave goods: A group of 17 hobnails (sf 204) was found associated with the right foot and a further two (sf 205) associated with the left foot, as well as 19 recovered from a soil sample.

Other finds: Four sherds of 1st century pottery were recovered from the back-fill.

Inhumation grave 1362

Grave cut 1359

Orientation: SW-NE
Shape: Sub-rectangular. Moderate-steep sides, concave base
Dimensions: 2.08 x 0.83 m, 0.20 m deep
Fill: Brownish-grey silty clay back-fill (1361)

Skeleton 1360

Posture: Supine, legs extended and parallel, left tibia displaced toward right leg
Arm position: Left arm extended beside body, right arm slightly flexed across pelvis
Age: 18–25 years
Completeness: 25–50%
Condition: Poor
Pathological conditions: cribra orbitalia, hyperostosis frontalis interna, dental caries, dental calculus.

Grave furniture: The remains of a coffin were represented by six iron nails (sfs 213–5, 217, 218 and 241) located *in situ* around the edges of the grave.
Grave goods:

1. A copper alloy bracelet (sf 216) worn on the left arm
2. A copper alloy finger ring (?) sf 219

Other finds: Eleven sherds of 1st–2nd century pottery were recovered from the back-fill.
Date: 3rd–4th century AD

Inhumation grave 1369

Grave cut 1366

Orientation: N-S
Shape: Sub-rectangular. Steep sides, flat base
Dimensions: 1.92 x 0.48 m, 0.21 m deep
Fill: Reddish-brown gritty clay back-fill (1368)
Relationships: Cuts grave 1374

Skeleton 1367

Posture: Supine, legs extended and parallel
Arm position: Left arm extended beside body, right arm flexed behind back
Sex: Male
Age: Adult (>18 years)
Completeness: >75%
Condition: Very good
Pathological conditions: osteoarthritis on acetabula, cortial defects on right humerus, dental caries, periodontitis
Musculo-skeletal marker: enthesophytes on femora

Grave furniture: The remains of a coffin were represented by 14 iron nails (sfs 184, 227–37, 242, 243) located *in situ* around the edges of the grave and two nails recovered from environmental samples.
Grave goods: An assemblage of 104 hobnails was found in the area of the feet.
Date: 3rd–4th century AD

Inhumation grave 1370

Grave cut 1363

Orientation: N-S
Shape: Rectangular. Near vertical sides, flat base
Dimensions: 1.82 x 0.54 m, 0.35 m deep
Fill: Orange-brown gravely clay back-fill (1365)
Relationships: Cuts grave 1374

Skeleton 1364

Posture: Supine, legs extended
Arm position: Both arms flexed at right angles across stomach
Sex: ?Female
Age: 18–25 years
Completeness: 50–75%
Condition: Very good
Pathological conditions: dental caries, dental calculus

Grave furniture: The remains of a coffin were represented by nine iron nails (sfs 220–6, 245, 246) located around the edges and northern end of the grave.
Other finds: Three sherds of 1st century pottery were recovered from the back-fill.
Comments: It is difficult to establish the original position of the legs as the tibia and fibula of both legs have become displaced after deposition.

Inhumation grave 1374 (Fig. 4.6)

Grave cut 1371

Orientation: SSE-NNW
Shape: Rectangular. Vertical sides, flat base
Dimensions: 1.72 x 0.77 m, 0.37 m deep
Fill: Brownish-yellow gravelly clay back-fill (1373)
Relationships: Cut by graves 1369 and 1370

Skeleton 1372

Posture: Supine, legs extended and parallel
Arm position: Left arm flexed at a right angle across the stomach, right arm extended beside body
Sex: Male
Age: Adult (>18 years)
Completeness: 50–75%
Condition: Good
Pathological conditions: possible ligament trauma on os coxae, healed periostitis on metacarpals, femora, tibiae and metatarsals

Grave furniture: The remains of a coffin were represented by nine iron nails (sfs 289–97) located around the east side and foot of the grave.
Grave goods: The substantial part of a flared rim jar in micaceous greyware fabric TF 5 (1375, sf 239, Fig. 5.2, no. 12) was placed beside the feet, possibly within the coffin.
Other finds: Four iron nails were recovered from environmental samples.
Date: 3rd–4th century AD

Inhumation grave 1388

Grave cut 1385

Orientation: NE-SW
Shape: Sub-rectangular with a rounded end
Dimensions: 0.8 x 0.63 m, 0.27 m deep
Fill: Yellowish brown gravely clay back-fill (1387)

Skeleton 1386

Posture: Supine
Arm position: Left arm flexed at a right angle across the stomach, right arm absent
Sex: Male
Age: 18–25 years
Completeness: <25%
Condition: Poor
Pathological conditions: endocranial lesions, enamel hypoplasia

Other finds: Two small sherds of 2nd century pottery were recovered from the back-fill.
Date: 2nd century AD or later.
Comments: A modern foundation trench had removed the right side and lower part of the body.

Inhumation grave 1398

Grave cut 1395

Orientation: S-N
Shape: Sub-rectangular
Dimensions: 1.70 x 0.10 m, 0.10 m deep
Fill: Brownish-orange silty clay back-fill (1397)
Relationships: Cut by pit 1408

Skeleton 1396

Posture: Supine, legs extended and parallel
Arm position: Arms slightly flexed, hands crossing over pelvis
Age: 13–17 years
Completeness: 25–50%
Condition: Poor
Pathological conditions: possible active periostitis on femora

Grave furniture: The possible remains of a coffin were represented by four iron nails (sfs 302–5) located in situ around the western edge of the grave.
Comments: The grave was truncated by the foundation of a modern wall defining the eastern boundary of the site, which has removed the head and the upper right part of the chest.

Inhumation grave 1403

Grave cut 1400

Orientation: NW-SE
Shape: Sub-rectangular
Dimensions: 1.30 x 0.45 m, 0.33 m deep
Fill: Brownish-orange clay back-fill (1402)
Relationships: Cut by pit 1408. Cuts grave 1407

Skeleton 1401

Posture: Supine, legs parallel
Age: Adult (>18 years)
Completeness: <25%
Condition: Good
Pathological conditions: active periostitis on right femur, healed periostitis on tibiae and fibulae
Musculo-skeletal marker: enthesophytes on femora, tibia and left patella

Finds: Two sherds of 2nd century pottery and an intrusive medieval sherd were recovered from the back-fill.
Date: 2nd century AD or later.

Inhumation grave 1407

Grave cut 1404

Orientation: N-S
Shape: Grave cut not seen, but inferred from the presence of skeleton 1405
Dimensions: Grave cut not seen, but inferred from the presence of skeleton 1405
Fill: Brownish-orange clay back-fill (1406)
Relationships: Cut by grave 1403

Skeleton 1405

Posture: Supine, the left foot crossed over the right
Age: Adult (>18 years)
Completeness: <25%
Condition: Fair
Pathological conditions: healed periostitis on right tibia and fibula, possible healed trama/haematoma on right tibia
Musculo-skeletal markers: enthesophytes on left calcaneous

Finds: A single small sherd of 1st–2nd century pottery was recovered from the back-fill.

Comments: Severely truncated grave, only the feet and the lower part of the right leg surviving.

Inhumation grave 1422

Grave cut 1419

Orientation: SW-NE
Shape: Sub-rectangular. Vertical sides, flat base
Dimensions: 0.70 x 0.60 m, 0.07 m deep
Fill: Orange-brown silty clay back-fill (1421)
Relationships: Cuts gully 1358

Skeleton 1420

Posture: Supine
Arm position: Left arm flexed across stomach. Right arm extended beside body
Completeness: <25%
Condition: Poor

Grave furniture: The possible remains of a coffin were represented by five iron nails (sfs 310–3, 319) located *in situ* at the south-western end of the grave and a further three recovered from environmental samples.

Inhumation grave 1427

Grave cut 1424

Orientation: E-W
Shape: Sub-rectangular, tapering to west. Vertical sides, flat base
Dimensions: 2.63 x 0.92 m, 0.19 m deep
Fill: Orange-brown silty clay back-fill (1426)
Relationships: Relationship with pit 1301 uncertain

Skeleton 1425

Posture: Supine
Completeness: <25%
Condition: Fair
Musculo-skeletal markers: enthesophytes on left femur

Comments: Preservation was very poor and only the legs survive.

Inhumation grave 1501

Grave cut 1452

Orientation: W-E
Shape: Cut not seen, inferred from the presence of skeleton 1453
Fill: Brown silty clay back-fill (1454)
Relationships: Cuts grave 1764. Cut by ditch 1055

Skeleton 1453

Posture: Supine, legs extended with feet together
Arm position: Arms extended beside body
Sex: Male
Age: Adult (>18 years)
Completeness: 25–50%
Condition: Good
Pathological conditions: osteoarthritis on left os coxa, osteophytosis on os coxa, erosive lesions on left and right metatarsals and phalanges, possible trauma on left foot phalanx, healed periostitis on left tibia and left metatarsal, active and healed periostitis on left fibula
Musculo-skeletal markers: enthesophytes on femora, tibiae and patellae

Finds: A total of 43 sherds of 3rd–4th century pottery and a single iron nail were recovered from the back-fill.
Date: 3rd–4th century AD
Comments: The western half of the grave was truncated by ditch 1055, removing the upper part of the body.

Inhumation grave 1503

Grave cut 1458

Orientation: N-S
Shape: Sub-rectangular. Steep sides, flat base
Dimensions: 1.59 x 0.50 m, 0.10 m deep
Fill: Brown silty clay back-fill (1460)
Relationships: Cuts graves 1505 and 1764. Cut by grave 1504

Skeleton 1459

Posture: Supine, legs extended with feet together
Sex: Male
Age: 45+ years
Completeness: <25%
Condition: Good
Pathological conditions: osteoarthritis on vertebra, osteophytosis on vertebrae, healed periostitis on right tibia, enamel hypoplasia, dental caries, dental calculus
Musculo-skeletal markers: enthesophytes on patellae

Finds: Three sherds of 1st century pottery and three sherds of 3rd–4th century pottery were recovered from the back-fill.
Date: 3rd–4th century AD
Comments: The central part of this grave has been truncated by the digging of grave 1504.

Inhumation grave 1504

Grave cut 1466

Orientation: W-E
Shape: Rectangular. Flat base
Dimensions: >1.60 x 0.60 m, 0.10 m deep
Fill: Brown silty clay back-fill (1468)
Relationships: Cuts grave 1503

Skeleton 1467

Posture: Supine, legs extended and parallel
Arm position: Arms flexed with hands crossed over pelvis
Age: 45+ years
Completeness: <25%
Condition: Fair
Pathological conditions: osteoarthritis on vertebra, vertebral osteophytosis, enamel hypoplasia, dental caries, dental calculus

Grave furniture: The possible remains of a coffin were represented by seven iron nails (sfs 312–8) located along both sides of the skeleton.
Other finds: Nine sherds of pottery dating from the 2nd century or later, two iron nails and a single hobnail were recovered from the back-fill.
Date: 3rd–4th century AD
Comments: Ditch 1055 truncates the western end of the grave, removing the top of the skull of skeleton 1467.

Inhumation grave 1505 (Fig. 4.7)

Grave cut 1479=1486

Orientation: SW-NE
Shape: Sub-rectangular. Near vertical sides, flat base
Dimensions: 1.70 m x 0.50 m. 0.12 m deep
Fill: Brown sandy clay back-fill (1481=1488)
Relationships: Cuts mass grave pit 1483. Cut by grave 1503

Skeleton 1480=1487

Posture: Supine
Arm position: Left arm flexed with forearm over left side of pelvis, right arm flexed at a right angle across stomach and the hand resting on the left forearm. Left hand displaced, located beneath the right side of the pelvis

Age: Adult (>18 years)
Completeness: 25–50%
Condition: Fair
Pathological conditions: osteoarthritis on unsided os coxa and femur, osteophytosis on unsided os coxa and femur
Musculo-skeletal markers: enthesophytes on left ulna
Grave goods:

1. 1489 (sf 323). Several sherds from a DOR BB1 jar decorated with an oblique burnished line lattice. Most of the rim is missing. Placed between the legs. The vessel contained a partial domestic fowl skeleton (28 fragments including foot phalanges, a carpal a tarsometatarsus and indeterminate fragment)
2. A copper alloy finger ring (sf 319) worn on the third or fourth finger of the left hand

Other finds: Eight sherds of pottery dating from the 2nd century or later and three iron nails (sf 321–3) and a hobnail recovered from the back-fill.
Date: 3rd–4th century AD
Comments: The north end of the grave had been truncated by graves 1503 and 1504 and the south end by ditch 1729, removing the head and most of the torso and the left leg.

Inhumation grave 1507

Grave cut 1495

Orientation: S-N
Shape: Rectangular. Flat base
Dimensions: 1.96 x 0.56 m, 0.12 m deep
Fill: Orange-brown silty clay back-fill (1497)
Relationships: Cuts mass grave pit 1483

Skeleton 1496

Posture: Supine, legs extended and parallel
Arm position: Left arm flexed with hand over sternum, right arm extended beside body
Sex: ?Male
Age: 26–35 years
Completeness: 50–75%
Condition: Very good
Pathological conditions: Schmorl's nodes, osteophytosis on right femur, healed periostitis on tibiae, enamel hypoplasia, dental caries, dental calculus
Musculo-skeletal markers: enthesophytes on right femur

Grave furniture: The remains of a coffin were represented by five iron nails (sfs 327, 329–31 and 335) located in a halo around the north end of the grave and a single nail (sf 328) at the south end.
Other finds: A single iron nail was recovered from an environmental sample.
Date: 3rd–4th century AD

Inhumation grave 1508

Grave cut 1498

Orientation: E-W
Shape: Grave cut not seen, but inferred from the presence of skeleton 1499
Fill: Orange-brown silty clay back-fill (1500)
Relationships: Cuts mass grave pit 1483

Skeleton 1499

Posture: Supine, legs extended with feet together
Arm position: Left arm flexed with hand across pelvis, right arm tightly flexed with forearm over chest
Sex: Male
Age: Adult (>18 years)
Completeness: 50–75%
Condition: Fair
Pathological conditions: active periostitis on left metatarsal
Musculo-skeletal markers: enthesophytes on right ulna, right patella and tibiae

Grave goods: An assemblage of 15 hobnails (sf 332, 333), was recovered but their location within the grave were not recorded.
Other finds: A single sherd of Dorset black burnished ware was recovered from the back-fill.
Date: 3rd–4th century AD
Comments: The upper part of the skeleton has been removed by truncation.

Inhumation grave 1720

Grave cut 1705

Orientation: W-E
Shape: Sub-rectangular. Steep sides, flat base
Dimensions: >1.76 x 0.50 m. Depth not recorded
Fill: Brownish-yellow sandy clay back-fill (1707)
Relationships: Cut by ditch 1729

Skeleton 1706

Posture: Supine, legs extended and parallel
Arm position: Left arm flexed at a right angle across the stomach. Right arm absent
Sex: ?Male
Age: 18–25 years
Completeness: 50–75%
Condition: Poor
Pathological conditions: enamel hypoplasia, dental calculus

Grave furniture: The remains of a coffin were represented by an assemblage of 18 iron nails (sfs 1000–17) located along the north side and both ends of the grave.
Other finds: A total of 26 sherds of pottery were recovered from the back-fill, including a fragment from an amphora of 2nd century date.
Date: 2nd century AD or later.
Comments: The south side of the grave has been truncated by ditch 1729 and the east end by a modern feature, removing much of the right side of the skeleton, the feet and the ends of the legs.

Inhumation grave 1721

Grave cut 1708

Orientation: E-W
Shape: Rectangular. Near vertical sides, flat base
Dimensions: > 1.77 x 0.62 m, 0.14 m deep
Fill: Orange-brown sandy clay back-fill (1710)
Relationships: Cut by grave 1722

Skeleton 1709

Posture: Supine, legs extended and parallel
Arm position: Arms extended beside body
Age: Adult (>18 years)
Completeness: <25%
Condition: Good
Pathological conditions: active periostitis on tibiae

Other finds: Three iron nails (sfs 1026, 1027, 1030) were recovered from this grave.
Comments: The grave has been severely affected by truncation. The feet have been removed by grave 1724, the central part of the body from the knees to the abdomen by grave 1722 and the head during machine stripping of the site.

Inhumation grave 1722

Grave cut 1711

Orientation: W-E
Shape: Rectangular. Near vertical sides, flat base
Dimensions: >1.41 x 0.60 m, 0.08 m deep
Fill: Orange-brown sandy clay back-fill (1713)
Relationships: Cut by grave 1724. Cuts grave 1721

Skeleton 1712

Posture: Supine
Arm position: Left arm flexed with hand resting on pelvis, right arm extended beside body with the forearm displaced somewhat
Age: Adult (>18 years)
Completeness: <25%
Condition: Poor

Grave furniture: The remains of a coffin were represented by ten iron nails (sfs 1018–25, 1028, 1029) located *in situ* along the sides of the grave.
Comments: The west end of the grave has been truncated by the digging of grave 1724, removing the head of the skeleton.

Inhumation grave 1723

Grave cut 1714

Orientation: NNE-SSW
Shape: Sub-rectangular
Dimensions: >0.75 x 0.60 m, 0.10 m deep
Fill: brownish-orange silty clay back-fill (1716)
Relationships: Cut by ditch 1729. Relationship with grave 1724 not established

Skeleton 1715

Posture: Supine
Arm position: Arms beside body, truncated at elbows
Sex: ?Male
Age: 18–25 years
Completeness: 25–50%
Condition: Fair
Pathological conditions: enamel hypoplasia, dental calculus

Finds: Two sherds of pottery and three iron nails were recovered from the back-fill.
Comments: The grave is truncated by ditch 1729 to the south and modern disturbance 1700 to the west, leaving only the upper part of the body.

Inhumation grave 1724

Grave cut 1717

Orientation: SE-NW
Shape: Sub-rectangular. Steep sides, flat base
Dimensions: > 1.40 x 1.38 m
Fill: back-fill (1719)
Relationships: Cuts grave 1722, relationship with grave 1723 not established

Skeleton 1718

Posture: Supine
Arm position: Left arm extended beside body, right arm extended beyond the edge of the trench at mid-humerus
Sex: Male
Age: 45+ years
Completeness: <25%
Condition: Poor
Pathological conditions: enamel hypoplasia, dental caries, dental calculus

Grave furniture: The remains of a coffin were represented by 10 iron nails (sfs 1035–44) located in a halo around the surviving south east end of the grave.
Other finds: Two iron nails and a single hobnail were recovered from the back-fill.
Comments: The north-west part of the grave, containing the lower part of the body, lay beyond the edge of the trench and so this part of the skeleton was not recovered. The end of the left arm had been removed by modern truncation 1700.

Inhumation grave 1755

Grave cut 1065

Orientation: N-S
Shape: Oval. Steep sides, flat base
Dimensions: 0.90 x 0.32 m, 0.23 m deep
Fill: Orange-brown silty clay back-fill (1067)
Relationships: Cuts soil layer 1020=1106. Cut by pit 1003

Skeleton 1066

Posture: Crouched, lying on left side
Arm position: Both arms flexed in front of face
Age: 2–5 years
Completeness: 25–50%
Condition: Very good
Pathological conditions: enamel hypoplasia

Comments: The grave had been truncated by pit 1003, causing some damage to the skull.

Inhumation grave 1756

Grave cut 1071

Orientation: NE-SW
Shape: Rectangular, tapering from NE to SW. Vertical sides, flat base
Dimensions: 0.65 x 0.40 m, 0.25 m deep
Fill: Yellowish-brown sandy silt back-fill (1078)
Relationships: Cut soil layer 1020=1106. ?Cut by grave 1344

Skeleton 1073

Posture: Insufficient remains were present to determine the posture
Age: 0 years (perinate)
Completeness: <25%
Condition: Poor

Grave furniture: Cist formed from five pieces of limestone measuring between 0.25 x 0.17 x 0.05 m and 0.42 x 0.21 x 0.05 m. Five of these stones were set on edge to form a trapezoidal cist measuring *c* 0.5 x 0.3 m and 0.2 m high, and the sixth placed flat to form a base for the south-west end of the grave.
Other finds: sf 12 (Iron object) recovered from the back-fill between the cist and the grave cut (1080).

Inhumation grave 1757

Grave cut 1088

Orientation: NW-SE
Shape: Sub-rectangular. Sloping ides, concave base
Dimensions: 0.87 x 0.53 m, 0.13 m deep
Fill: Orange-brown silty clay back-fill (1090)

Skeleton 1089

Posture: Skeleton 1089 was a tightly packed cluster of disarticulated bones
Sex: Male
Age: 45+ years
Completeness: 50–75%
Condition: Good
Pathological conditions: osteoarthritis on vertebrae and on os coxae, osteophytosis on left femur, right humerus and left auricular surface, degenerative disc disease, healed trauma on left rib, on right fibula and on left metacarpal, healed periostitis on right fibula
Musculo-skeletal markers: enthesophytes on right ulna, femora and tibiae

Other finds: Animal bone (sf 14) recovered from the back-fill.

Inhumation grave 1758

Grave cut 1117

Orientation: E-W
Shape: Sub-rectangular
Dimensions: >1.10 x 0.73 m. Depth not recorded
Fill: Reddish-brown silty clay back-fill (1119)
Relationships: Cut by ditch 1055

Skeleton 1118

Posture: Supine
Arm position: Left arm absent, right arm extended beside body
Sex: Male
Age: Adult (>18 years)
Completeness: <25%
Condition: Very good
Pathological conditions: spondylolysis, possible healed trauma on left metacarpals
Musculo-skeletal markers: enthesophytes on right ulna

Finds: Two iron nails (sfs 21 and 22) were recovered from the back-fill.
Comments: The western half of the grave had been truncated by ditch 1055, removing the lower part of the body, and the left arm and head had been removed by truncation.

Inhumation grave 1759

Grave cut 1170

Orientation: N-S
Shape: Sub-rectangular. Near vertical sides, flat base
Dimensions: 1.89 x 0.84 m, 0.27 m deep
Fill: Brownish-grey silty clay back-fill (1171)
Relationships: Cut by graves 1143 and 1151. Relationship with grave 1167 not established

Grave goods: A partial domestic fowl skeleton was recovered.
Other finds: A single small sherd of 1st century pottery was recovered from the back-fill.
Comments: No skeletal remains were recovered from this grave.

Inhumation grave 1760

Grave cut 1382

Orientation: W-E
Shape: Sub-rectangular
Dimensions: >0.60 x 0.45 m, 0.15 m deep
Fill: Yellowish-brown sandy clay back-fill (1380)

Skeleton 1381

Posture: Supine
Age: 26–35 years
Completeness: <25%
Condition: Very good
Pathological conditions: degenerative disc disease, remodelled new bone on zygomatic bones, cribra orbitalia, enamel hypoplasia, dental caries, dental calculus

Comments: The eastern part of the grave was truncated by a modern foundation, leaving only the upper part of the body.

Inhumation grave 1761

Grave cut 1391

Orientation: NW-SE
Shape: Sub-rectangular with rounded ends
Dimensions: 1.80 x 0.60 m, 0.15 m deep
Fill: Yellowish-brown silty clay back-fill (1389)
Relationships: Cut by grave 1762

Skeleton 1390

Posture: Supine, legs extended and parallel
Arm position: Both arms extended beside body
Sex: ?Female
Age: 26–35 years
Completeness: >75%
Condition: Very good
Pathological conditions: rib osteoarthritis, rib osteophytosis, pseudo-joint surface on left os coxa, healed periostitis on tibiae, spina bifida occulta on sacrum, enamel hypoplasia, dental caries, dental calculus, periodontitis

Comments: The south-west corner of the grave was truncated by grave 1762, removing the right foot.

Inhumation grave 1762

Grave cut 1394

Orientation: W-E
Shape: Sub-rectangular
Dimensions: >1.30 x 0.60 m, 0.12 m deep
Fill: Yellowish-brown silty clay back-fill (1392)
Relationships: Cuts grave 1761

Skeleton 1393

Posture: Supine, legs extended and parallel
Arm position: Left arm flexed across stomach, right arm extended beside body
Sex: ?Male
Age: Adult (>18 years)
Completeness: 50–75%
Condition: Very good
Pathological conditions: rib osteoarthritis, vertebral osteophytosis, Schmorl's nodes, possible haematoma on left femur, healed periostitis on tibiae, congenital conditions (lumbarisation).
Musculo-skeletal markers: enthesophytes on tibiae and left femur

Comments: The west end of the grave had been truncated by a modern feature, removing the head.

Inhumation grave 1763

Grave cut 1410

Orientation: NE-SW
Shape: Sub-rectangular with rounded ends.
Dimensions: 0.65 x 0.35 m. Depth not recorded.
Fill: Brownish orange clay back-fill (1411).

Skeleton: No skeletal material was present.
Finds: Fourteen sherds of 1st century pottery were recovered from the back-fill.

Inhumation grave 1764

Grave cut 1509

Orientation: SSW-NNE
Shape: Grave cut not seen, but inferred from the presence of skeleton
Fill: Orange-brown silty clay back-fill (1511)
Relationships: Cuts grave 1765. Cut by graves 1501, 1503 and 1508

Skeleton 1510

Posture: Posture not established as only the lower part of the right leg survived
Age: Adult (>18 years)
Completeness: <25%

Condition: Fair
Pathological conditions: healed lytic lesions on right talus, possible osteochondritis dissecans on foot phalanges, healed periostitis on right fibula

Grave goods: A hobnail shoe comprising 42 nails (sf 334) was worn on the surviving foot.
Date: 3rd–4th century AD
Comments: The grave has been severely truncated by subsequent burials, leaving only the lower part of the right leg.

Inhumation grave 1765

Grave cut 1535

Orientation: E-W
Shape: Oval. Vertical sides, flat base
Dimensions: 1.88 x 0.60 m, 0.30 m deep
Fill: Mottled brown and orange silty sand back-fill (1536)
Relationships: Cut by grave 1764

Skeleton 1537

Posture: Prone, legs parallel
Arm position: Left arm extended beside body, right arm flexed behind back with the hand resting on the back of the pelvis
Sex: Female
Age: Adult (>18 years)
Completeness: >75%
Condition: Good
Pathological conditions: osteoarthritis on vertebrae, vertebral osteophytosis, degenerative disc disease, cribra orbitalia, neoplastic disease (button osteoma), enamel hypoplasia, dental calculus, periodontitis
Musculo-skeletal markers: enthesophytes on left patella

Grave furniture: The probable remains of a coffin were represented by 12 iron nails (sfs 354–63, 368 and 369).
Grave goods: A group of 42 hobnails (sf 367) was located in the area of the left foot.
Date: 3rd–4th century AD

Inhumation grave 1772

Grave cut 1077

Orientation: SE-NW
Shape: Oval
Dimensions: 0.83 x 0.56 m, 0.23 m deep
Fill: Orange-brown silty clay back-fill (1087)
Relationships: Cuts soil layer 1020=1106

Skeleton 1086

Posture: Crouched, lying on left side with legs drawn up tight to the chest
Arm position: Arms wrapped around legs
Age: 5–12 years
Completeness: 50–75%
Condition: Very good
Pathological conditions: active rib periostitis, cribra orbitalia, enamel hypoplasia.

Comments: The upper part of the grave was filled by a deposit of limestone rubble that was visible in the surface of soil layer 1020=1106 and may have acted as a grave marker.

Inhumation grave 2027

Grave cut 2000

Orientation: SW-NE
Shape: Grave cut not seen, but inferred from the presence of skeleton 2001

Fill: Yellowish-brown silty clay back-fill (2002)
Relationships: Cut by ditch 1725

Skeleton 2001

Posture: Supine
Age: Subadult (<18 years)
Completeness: <25%
Condition: Fair

Comments: The grave has been severely truncated by modern disturbance, which has left only the right femur, right side of the pelvis and part of the left femur.

In addition to the skeletal remains recovered from graves, three partial skeletons were recorded which had been disturbed and for which no grave could be identified. These are listed below.

Skeleton 1057

Sex: ?Male
Age: 36–45 years
Completeness: <25%
Condition: Fair
Pathological conditions: enamel hypoplasia, dental caries, dental calculus, periodontitis

Skeleton 1116

Sex: ?Female
Age: 45+ years
Completeness: <25%
Condition: Very good
Pathological conditions: None

Skeleton 1294

Completeness: <25%
Condition: Fair

CATALOGUE OF CREMATIONS

Cremation burial 1196 (Fig. 4.8)

Grave cut (1188)

Shape: Sub-rectangular, oriented N-S
Dimensions: 0.70 x 0.50 m, 0.08 m deep
Fill: Light yellowish-red silty clay back-fill (1190)

Cinerary urn (1191, sf 61): A grey, necked jar in the local Gloucester kiln ware TF 11A. The vessel is fragmented and most of the rim is missing. Fig. 5.1, no. 5.
Cremation deposit (1189)
Weight: 269.5 g
Largest fragment: 43 mm
Identified bones and teeth: Skull, vertebrae, ribs, pelvis, shoulder girdle, long bones
Colour: White
MNI: 1
Age: Adult (>18 years)
Pyre goods: Five fragments of calcined probable pig bone including cranial and long bone fragments were recovered from the cremation deposit.
Grave goods:

1. An oxidised flagon in fabric TF 11A (1192, sf 62), well fragmented and missing the rim
2. An oxidised flagon in fabric TF 11A (1193, sf 63), well fragmented and missing the rim

Other finds: The cremation backfill contained 24 sherds of 1st century pottery, one small intrusive sherd of medieval date and a single iron nail, as well as eleven fragments of burnt medium and large mammal long bone and 14 fragments of unburnt large mammal long bone.
Date: 1st–early 2nd century AD

Cremation burial 1209 (Fig. 4.8)

Grave cut (1197)

Shape: Sub-rectangular, oriented NE-SW
Dimensions: 0.55 x 0.40 m, 0.17 m deep
Fill: Orange-brown clay back-fill (1198)

Cinerary urn (1200, sf 71): The lower part only of a greyware jar in fabric TF 25. The cremation urn also contained one small sherd of grey sandy ware (TF 39).
Cremation deposit (1202)
Weight: 281.5 g
Largest fragment: 59 mm
Identified bones and teeth: Skull, vertebrae, ribs, pelvis, long bones
Colour: White
MNI: 1
Age: Adult (> 18 years)
Sex: Male?
Pyre goods:

1. The lower neck and reservoir of a tubular unguent bottle in blue/green glass, melted and collapsed
2. A melted drop of blue/green glass
3. A base fragment from a tubular unguent bottle in blue/green glass (sf 74)
4. Two fragments of blue/green glass
5. Two fragments from a large mammal skull fragment (possibly human) and a pig phalanx from a juvenile animal were recovered from the cremation deposit, which may represent the remains of pyre goods

Grave goods:

1. An oxidised flagon in fabric TF 11A with no surviving rim (1199, sf 70). An indeterminate medium mammal sized fragment, a single hobnail and a fragment of nail shank were inside the vessel
2. Body fragments of glass unguent bottle

Other finds: The backfill produced 27 sherds of 1st century pottery including a handle from an oxidised flagon and two rim sherds from a Severn Valley ware lid, six iron nails, four hobnails and some burnt animal bone fragments.
Date: 1st–early 2nd century AD

Cremation burial 1227

Grave cut (1222)

Shape: Sub-rectangular, oriented N-S
Dimensions: 0.65 x 0.44 m, 0.05 m deep
Fill: Mid yellowish-brown silty clay back-fill (1225)

Cinerary urn (1223, sf 79): The lower part of an oxidised flagon in the local Gloucester kiln ware TF 11A.
Cremation deposit (1224)
Weight: 1.5 g
Largest fragment: <10 mm
Identified bones and teeth: Skull
Colour: White
MNI: 1

Finds: The cremation urn fill produced four sherds of TF 11A with a further small sherd from the cremation backfill.
Date: 1st–early 2nd century AD

Cremation burial 1266 (Fig. 4.8)

Grave cut (1253)

Shape: Sub-circular
Dimensions: 0.60 in diameter, 0.08 m deep
Fill: Brownish-orange silty clay back-fill (1258)

Cinerary urn (1251, sf 97): A reduced everted rim jar in fabric TF 11A (Fig. 5.1, no. 6) with a squared rim.. Most of vessel is present including the entire rim, but broken. Two small nails were inside the vessel.

Cremation deposit (1252)
 Weight: 143 g
 Largest fragment: 38 mm
 Identified bones and teeth: Skull, part of the mandible, vertebrae, ribs, shoulder girdle, long bones
 Colour: White
 MNI: 2
 Age: 5–10 years and 10–15 years
Grave goods:

1. A complete ring-necked flagon in oxidised TF 11A (1256, sf96). The rim circumference is complete apart from an old nick in one part. Fig. 5.1, no. 7
2. A gaming set comprising 43 bone and glass counters and two dice together with a frit melon bead were found in the cremation urn

Other finds: A medium mammal long bone fragment, one medium mammal or bird long bone fragment and five indeterminate fragments were recovered from the backfill.
Date: 1st–early 2nd century AD

Cremation burial 1766 (Plate 2.6)

Grave cut (1048)

 Shape: Circular
 Dimensions: At least 0.44 m in diameter, 0.13 m deep
 Fill: Orange-brown sandy clay back-fill (1072)
 Relationships: Cuts pit 1074

Cinerary urn (1068): Grey ware jar in fabric TF 25, a substantial part of which survives, with an everted thickened rim. Fig. 5.1, no. 1.
Cremation deposit (1049)
 Weight: 132.5 g
 Largest fragment: 47 mm
 Identified bones and teeth: Skull, vertebrae, ribs, pelvis, shoulder girdle, long bones
 Colour: White
 MNI: 1
 Age: Adult (>18 years)
 Non-metric traits: The only trait available for observation was the multi-foramina in the zygomatic which was present.
Pyre goods:

1. Melted and vesicular fragment of blue/green glass, possibly the collapsed reservoir of a tubular unguent bottle
2. A burnt sherd of everted rim jar in oxidised TF 11A was recovered from the fill of the cinerary urn
3. Animal bone was recovered from the cremation deposit representing at least two pigs. The pigs were represented by cranial and tooth fragments, a left tibia, a left astragalus, a calcaneum, a left humerus, and two left ulnae. Further medium or large mammal sized scapula, long bone, tooth and indeterminate fragments may also be pig.

Other finds: The fill of the cinerary urn contained four sherds of 1st century pottery, two very small fragments of fired clay and four iron nails.
Date: Pre-Flavian
Comments: The northern half of the feature was truncated by a modern pit.

Cremation burial 1767 (Fig. 4.8)

Grave cut (1059)

 Shape: Square
 Dimensions: 0.48 x 0.45 m, 0.15 m deep
 Fill: Back-fill (1377)

Cinerary urn (1061): Necked jar with a thickened rim in grey sandy ware TF 25. Most of the vessel is present. Traces of a thin white calcareous deposit are visible on the interior of the basesherds. Fig. 5.1, no. 2.

Cremation deposit (1062)
 Weight: 1255.5
 Largest fragment: 58 mm
 Identified bones and teeth: Skull, vertebrae, ribs, pelvis, shoulder girdle, long bones
 Colour: White
 MNI: 3
 Age: Adult (>18 years)
 Sex: Mandibular fragments from two individuals had male traits

Pyre goods: A total of ten fragments (48.6 g) of cremated animal bone were recovered from the cremation deposit, comprising the remains of a possible cattle rib and medium mammal-sized long bones and cranial fragments, as well as an unburnt fish rib/process and an unburnt indeterminate fragment.
Grave goods: Collared rim (Hofheim) flagon in oxidised sandy ware TF 25, almost complete although part of the base is missing (1063, Fig. 5.1, no. 3). The fill of the vessel contained a medium mammal long bone fragment and three indeterminate bone fragments weighing a total of 8 g.
Date: Pre-Flavian

Cremation burial 1768

Grave cut (1094)

 Shape: Circular
 Dimensions: 0.25 m in diameter, 0.03 m deep
 Fill: Cremation deposit 1095, a yellowish-brown silty clay with pieces of calcined bone
Cinerary urn: Un-urned
Cremation deposit (1095)
 Weight: 17.5 g
 Largest fragment: 28 mm
 Identified bones and teeth: Skull, ribs, long bones
 Colour: White
 MNI: 1
 Age: Adult (>18 years)

Pyre goods: A total of five fragments (1.8 g) of burnt medium mammal sized long bone and indeterminate bone fragments were recovered from the cremation deposit.

Cremation burial 1769

Grave cut (1186)

 Shape: Rectangular, oriented E-W
 Dimensions: 0.43 x 0.28 m, 0.05 m deep
 Fill: Cremation deposit 1187, a loose black charcoal-rich clay with calcined bone
Cinerary urn: Un-urned
Cremation deposit (1187)
 Weight: 261 g
 Largest fragment: 44 mm
 Identified bones and teeth: Skull, vertebrae, ribs, pelvis, long bones
 Colour: White
 MNI: 1
 Age: Adult (>18 years)

Pyre goods: The cremation deposit contained 325 fragments (119 g) of animal bone comprising pig skull, right radius and left tibia fragments, and further medium mammal-sized cranial, vertebral, rib, long bone and indeterminate fragments which may also be pig. A burnt possible bird long bone fragment was also recovered.
Grave goods: An assemblage of 27 hobnails was scattered throughout the cremation deposit.
Other finds: Eight iron nails were recovered.
Date: AD 60–220 (OxA-16811) (radiocarbon assay)

Cremation burial 1770

Grave cut (1323)

 Shape: Sub-circular
 Dimensions: 0.22 m in diameter, 0.07 m deep

Fill: Loose yellowish-brown silt clay with some charcoal and calcined bone (1324)
Cinerary urn: Un-urned
Cremation deposit (1324)
    Weight: 8.5 g
    Largest fragment: 39 mm

Identified bones and teeth: Skull, ribs, long bones
Colour: White
MNI: 1
Age: Adult (>18 years)

Date: 50 BC – AD 70 (OxA-16792) (radiocarbon assay)

Chapter 5   The Finds and Environmental Evidence

THE POTTERY
by Jane Timby

Introduction

The excavation resulted in the recovery of 2156 sherds of pottery weighing 18.1 kg. Most of the pottery dates to the Roman period but also present are 61 sherds of medieval and 80 sherds of post-medieval date. The post-Roman material is not considered in detail other than where it has provided dating evidence.

The Roman pottery ranged in date from the Claudio-Neronian period through to the late 3rd–4th century. Approximately 77% of the assemblage by sherd count came from burial contexts, the remainder deriving from pits and post-Roman features. The condition of the material is thus quite variable. Nearly all the vessels deliberately deposited as grave goods or as containers for the cremated remains were in semi-complete state and only one vessel, a small flagon (1256, sf 96, Fig. 5.1, no. 7), had survived intact.

Fabrics and forms

The pottery assemblage as a whole is fairly typical for Gloucester for the periods covered in terms of the fabrics and forms present, although slightly atypical in the balance of wares present. Locally made Gloucester kiln wares, notably TF 11A, a fine textured ware made in both oxidised and reduced versions (Timby 1991), dominate the early Roman assemblage (Table 5.1). With the sandier counterpart TF 25, the local Gloucester kiln wares account for 55.4% by count of the total recovered assemblage, with 52.9% being the finer TF 11 variant. This is slightly unusual away from the kiln sites and demonstrates the preference shown for these vessels as burial urns and accessory vessels. Also local in source and potentially slightly earlier are fabrics 24, 36, 39 and 213 which are all associated with the legionary fortress at Kingsholm and are military wares, again produced locally in the Neronian period (Hurst 1985; Timby 1999). Other contemporary wares include very small quantities of imported fineware (South Gaulish samian and Lyons ware) and a small amount of amphora. A fine white ware flask from the fill of gully 1358 could also possibly be an import. Four sherds of grog-tempered handmade native ware (TF 2A) are also typical for 1st century Gloucester, and it is possible that the nearby river crossing was the site of a native settlement prior to the establishment of the Kingsholm fortress (cf Timby 1990).

Other local wares at this time include a black sandy burnished ware (TF 201) which tends to appear from the Neronian period through to the early 2nd century. Small amounts of Dorset black burnished ware (DOR BB1) were reaching Kingholm in the 1st century but the bulk of such material coming to Gloucester dates from the Hadrianic period through to the late Roman period. This together with the south-west variant (SOW BB1) account for 21.6% of the London Road assemblage and largely comes from the later Roman features. Severn Valley ware is quite poorly represented at 6.2%. This is surprising as once the Gloucester kilns had ceased production Severn Valley wares tended to flood the market, but can probably be explained by the chronology of the site and a general absence of mid-later 2nd and 3rd century wares. All other wares are present in very small amounts. The only other fabric, occurring as a complete (broken) vessel in a flared rim jar in TF 5, is a micaceous grey ware, which may come from south Gloucestershire.

Pottery from burials

Pottery vessels were recovered from six cremation burials (1196, 1209, 1227, 1266, 1766, 1767). None of the vessels survived intact and in many cases only a few sherds were present so it was unclear whether these represented fragmented and dispersed burial urns or accessory vessels, were deliberately deposited isolated sherds connected with the burial ritual, or were simply stray finds. At least six inhumation graves may have also had deliberately deposited vessels (grave groups 1145, 1243, 1334, 1352, 1374 and 1505), while an inverted pot was placed in a possible 'memorial' pit (1149; see Chapter 6). In addition, potsherds were recovered from the fills of 31 inhumation burials.

Pottery from cremation burials

Group 1196. Cremation urn: grey, necked jar in the local Gloucester kiln ware TF 11A (1191, sf 61, Fig. 5.1, no. 5). The vessel is fragmented and most of the rim is missing. Accompanying the urn were two oxidised flagons in fabric TF 11A (1192, sf 62 and 1193 sf 63), both well fragmented and missing the rims. The fill of the cinerary urn also produced four sherds of oxidised TF 11A. The cremation backfill produced one small sherd of early Seven Valley ware, 24 very fragmented sherds of oxidised TF 11A and one small intrusive sherd of medieval date. Date: Flavian-Trajanic.

Group 1209. Cremation urn: The lower part only of a greyware jar TF 25 (1200, sf 71). The urn was accompanied by an oxidised flagon, TF 11A with no

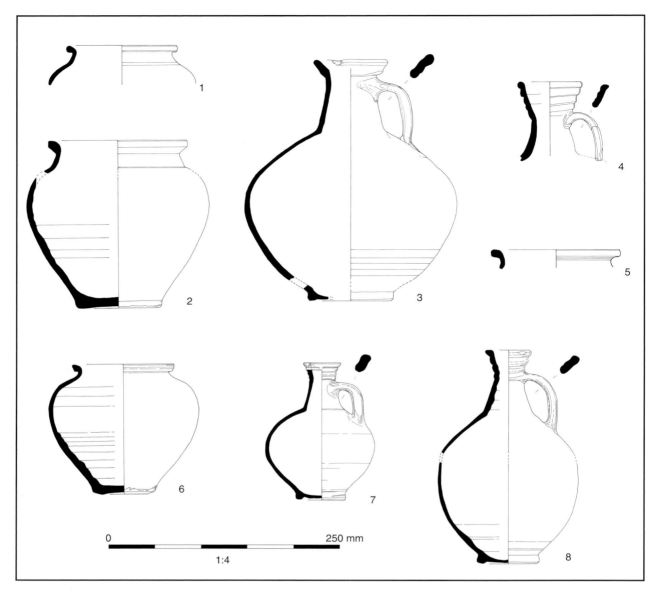

Figure 5.1   Roman pottery (1–8).

surviving rim (1199, sf 70). The cremation urn backfill produced one small sherd of grey sandy ware TF 39. The cremation backfill produced further sherds of oxidised flagon, including a handle in TF 11A, one sherd of grey TF 11A, five sherds of TF 39, one of TF 25 and six sherds from an early Severn Valley ware jar as well as two rimsherds from a Severn Valley ware lid. Date: Flavian-Trajanic.

Group 1227. Cremation urn: the lower part of an oxidised flagon in the local Gloucester kiln ware TF 11A (1223, sf 79). The cremation urn fill produced four further sherds of TF 11A with a further small sherd from the cremation backfill. Date: Flavian-Trajanic.

Group 1266. Cremation urn: everted rim jar with a squared rim in reduced fabric TF 11A (1251, sf 97, Fig. 5.1, no. 6). Most of vessel is present including the entire rim, but broken. Accompanying the urn is a

complete ring-necked flagon in oxidised TF 11A, (1256, sf 96, Fig. 5.1, no. 7). The rim circumference is complete apart from an old nick in one part. Date: Flavian-Trajanic.

Group 1766. Cremation urn: Substantial part of a grey ware jar with an everted thickened rim, TF 25 (1068, Fig. 5.1, no. 1). A sherd of everted rim jar in oxidised TF 11A was mixed in with these sherds. The cremation backfill produced four oxidised sandy sherds TF 25. Date: Neronian.

Group 1767. Cremation urn: Necked jar with a thickened rim in grey sandy ware, TF 25 (1061, Fig. 5.1, no. 2). Most of the vessel is present. Traces of a thin white calcareous deposit are visible on the interior of the base sherds. The ancillary vessel is a collared rim (Hofheim) flagon in oxidised sandy ware TF 25, almost complete although part of the base is missing (1063, Fig. 5.1, no. 3). Date: Neronian.

Table 5.1   Quantification of the pottery assemblage by fabric.

Roman	Fabric	Description	No	%	Wt (g)	%	Eve	%
Imports	SGSAM	South Gaulish samian	4	0.2	10	0.1	3	0.2
	CGSAM	Central Gauilsh samian	4	0.2	18	0.1	0	0.0
	LYO CC	Lyons ware	1	0.0	9	0.1	0	0.0
	GAL AM	Gallic amphora	1	0.0	68	0.4	0	0.0
	10	miscellaneous amphorae	5	0.2	263	1.6	0	0.0
Regional	DOR BB1	Dorset black burnished ware	257	12.8	1592	9.6	148	8.9
	SOW BB1	South-west black burnished ware	178	8.8	1333	8.0	101	6.1
	OXF RS	Oxon red slipped ware	9	0.4	43	0.3	0	0.0
	5	grey micaceous ware	43	2.1	654	3.9	90	5.4
	19	wheelmade Malvernian ware	2	0.1	30	0.2	0	0.0
Native ware	2A	hm grog-tempered ware	4	0.2	36	0.2	13	0.8
Glos kilns	7	white slipped oxidised ware	2	0.1	10	0.1	0	0.0
	11A (ox)	fine oxidised ware	897	44.5	5835	35.2	576	34.8
	11A (gy)	fine grey ware	170	8.4	1126	6.8	190	11.5
	25 (ox)	sandy oxidised ware	42	2.1	884	5.3	213	12.9
	25 (gy)	sandy grey ware	79	3.9	1528	9.2	133	8.0
	24	Kingsholm flagon fabric	53	2.6	340	2.1	0	0.0
	36	Kingholm oxidised ware	4	0.2	15	0.1	0	0.0
	39	Kingsholm grey sandy	80	4.0	1118	6.7	29	1.8
	213	Kingsholm grey ware	3	0.1	14	0.1	0	0.0
Local	SVW OX	Severn Valley ware	114	5.7	1305	7.9	63	3.8
	11D	early Severn Valley ware	13	0.6	153	0.9	11	0.7
	11E	limestone-tempered SVW	1	0.0	2	0.0	0	0.0
	23	hm Severn Valley ware	1	0.0	27	0.2	0	0.0
	201	wm black burnished sandy	29	1.4	70	0.4	3	0.2
	12R	local colour-coated ware	3	0.1	9	0.1	12	0.7
Unknown	WW	miscellaneous whiteware	9	0.4	27	0.2	50	3.0
	WWF	fine whiteware	1	0.0	10	0.1	0	0.0
	GREY	unattributed grey sandy wares	6	0.3	54	0.3	19	1.1
Roman total			2015	100.0	16583	100.0	1654	100.0
Med			61	0.0	793	0.0	0	0.0
Pmed			80	0.0	710	0.0	0	0.0
Total			2156	0.0	18086	0.0	1654	0.0

Pottery from inhumations and 'memorial'

Grave group 1145. The prone inhumation burial was accompanied by several sherds from a ring-necked flagon in oxidised TF 11A (1128, Fig. 5.2, no. 10). The rim has an old chip out of the circumference. Date: Flavian-Trajanic.

'Memorial' 1149. Ring-necked flagon represented by the upper part of the vessel in oxidised TF 11A (1141, sf 80, Fig. 5.1, no. 4). Date: Neronian-early Flavian.

Grave group 1243. The upper part of a ring-necked flagon in oxidised TF 25 (1322, sf 155, Fig. 5.2, no. 11). Date: Flavian-Trajanic.

Grave group 1334. A well-fragmented grey ware jar in fabric TF11A with a triangular-shaped rim. Only the base survived *in situ*, positioned at the base of the grave near the feet. Date: Flavian-Trajanic.

Grave group 1352. Ring-necked flagon in oxidised TF 11A (1348, sf 174, Fig. 5.1, no. 8). Accompanying the flagon is the upper portion of a second flagon in the same fabric (1351, sf 175, Fig. 5.2, no. 9). The backfill produced three sherds in the same fabric probably from the same vessels. Date: Flavian-Trajanic.

Grave group 1374. The substantial part of a flared rim jar (1375) in micaceous greyware TF 5 came from this burial. (1375, sf 239, Fig. 5.2, no. 12). Date: 3rd or 4th century.

Grave group 1505. Several sherds from a DOR BB1 jar (1489, sf 323). Most of the rim is missing. Decorated with an oblique burnished line lattice. Date: 3rd or 4th century.

Pottery from grave backfills

Pottery was recovered from the backfills of 31 of the inhumation graves. In most cases this appears to be isolated sherds rather than deliberate grave goods. The quantity ranged from single sherds to a maximum of 31 in grave 1501. A sherd join was observed between grave groups 1167 and 1230, which lie adjacent to one another but do not intercut.

Pottery from the mass grave

The mass grave produced a large assemblage of pottery amounting to some 267 sherds amongst

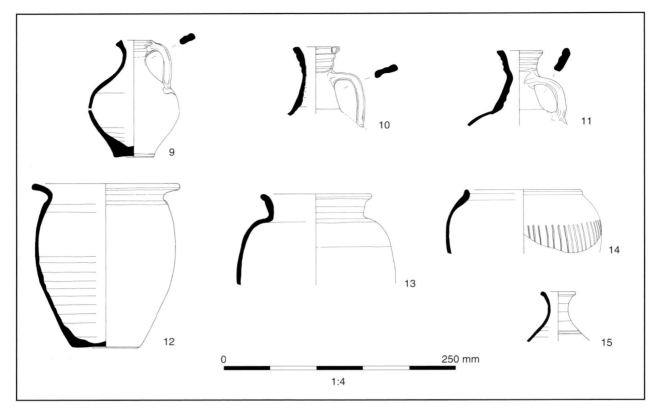

Figure 5.2   Roman pottery (9–15).

which were the substantial parts of at least six vessels (sf 64, sf 531–2, sf 619–20), all South-West black burnished ware jars (SOW BB1) (Fig. 5.2, no.13). Some of SOW BB1 jar sherds have right-angled to slightly oblique burnished lattice. Many sherds are heavily sooted and most of the rims are missing. The latticing would suggest a later 2nd–3rd century date. Other material from this deposit was confined to sherds of TF 11A and a DOR BB1 plain-rimmed dish. Pottery from the upper part of the backfill comprised a mixture of earlier and later Roman pottery, in particular TF 11A, SVW OX, DOR BB1 including a flanged conical bowl, SOW BB1, OXF RS, the latter mainly from a flask, and single sherds of samian and grey ware. The *terminus post quem* for this assemblage lies in the later 3rd–4th century, but its mixed nature suggests that it has been subject to some degree of contamination, probably associated with the later burials cut into the backfill.

Pottery from buried soils

Substantial amounts of Roman pottery were recovered from the various buried soils defined on the site. The soil layer associated with the use of the cemetery (1106/1020/1440) produced some 180 sherds (1310 g) of 1st–2nd century pottery including a significant number of DOR BB1 sherds. The fragmentation rate is quite high with an overall average sherd weight of 7 g suggesting well-disturbed material.

Medieval soil layer 1025/1105 produced 99 sherds (1131 g) including Malvernian ware cooking pot (Glos TF 40), Gloucester limestone-tempered ware (TF 41b) and Minety ware (TF 44), collectively suggesting a date in the 13th century. Residual Roman material from this layer spans the 1st to 4th centuries.

Discussion

Chronologically the assemblage falls into two main periods, the 1st–early 2nd century and the 3rd–4th century, with something of a hiatus from around the end of the Trajanic period through to the 3rd century. The earliest burials are dated to the pre-Flavian period on the basis of the fabrics present and the typology of the vessels. These include cremation groups 1766 and 1767, 'memorial' 1149 and pit 1306. Fabrics TF 24, 36, 213 and 39, represented in these features, all have direct links with the early military occupation at the Kingsholm fortress, occupied from *c* AD 49 through to AD 66/7 (Hurst 1985, 122; see Chapter 1), and are likely to have been produced by the army, probably locally. The products of these military kilns include flagons, jars, bowls, platters, mortaria and open lamps (ibid., 78 ff) but the examples found at 120–122 London Road are restricted to flagons, jars and one beaker.

Pottery recovered from the cremation burials entirely comprised products from local kilns, with the fine oxidised and reduced grey ware fabric TF

11A and its sandier counterpart TF 25 most prevalent. These wares have been identified from at least two kiln sites in Gloucester: the College of Art site (Rawes 1972) and Berkeley Street (Timby 1991). Both these sites were producing wares from the Flavian-Trajanic periods but an earlier phase of kilns at Berkeley Street would suggest a potentially earlier phase of production (ibid.). A third unpublished kiln from the Kingsholm rugby ground was also producing fine grey wares identical to TF 11A in the Flavian-Trajanic period.

There appears to be a pattern of using grey ware jars as cremation urns, accompanied by one vessel, or in the case of burial 1196 two vessels, of a contrasting colour, possibly hinting at some form of symbolism represented in the choice of form and colour. This pattern was also found in six of the 17 cremation burials excavated at 124–130 London Road, but the rest of the burials at that site displayed a greater variety of vessels, including at least four burials with Dorset black burnished ware jars, and one with two South Gaulish samian dishes. The number of vessels per grave also varied, ranging from one to a maximum of four, the latter including a flagon, jar, bowl and lamp (Timby forthcoming). There is some evidence that the use of no more than one or two vessels was fairly standard at this time: at the King Harry Lane cemetery at Verulamium, one of the largest late Iron Age-early Roman cremation cemeteries to be published, some 66% of the 455 cremation burials were urned and 64% of these comprised a single vessel, with a further 21% containing two vessels (Stead and Rigby 1989, table 3). A broadly contemporary cremation cemetery excavated at Caerleon contained 121 cremation burials dating to the later 1st–2nd century AD, of which over 75% of the urned cremation burials comprised a single vessel (Evans and Maynard 1997).

None of the vessels found with the burials can be considered exclusively made for the purpose of burial as they are moderately common forms and all occur in other 'domestic' contexts across Gloucester. It has been suggested that poorer quality vessels were often used for burial (Philpott 1991, 36) but none of the pots used at the London Road site appear to have been wasters or seconds, although their fragmented state may be masking slight deformities. The use of jars with relatively wide mouths for containing the cremated remains makes practical sense. The flagons accompanying them probably contained liquid, whether wine for the deceased or some other form of libation. Due to the poor preservation of most of the vessels it is impossible to determine whether they were deposited intact or whether the vessels were deliberately broken as part of the burial rites.

The limited range of vessels used in the sample excavated would strongly indicate a prescribed range of pots available for the burials and that these may have been specifically made available as a package on demand, perhaps with a pottery workshop having a contract with the overseers of the cemetery and of the burial procedures. It is possible that vessel colour had some relevance. Biddulph (2005, 37) has considered the possibility of vessels being provided through burial societies through which the costs and equipment of burial would be provided on a member's death, assuming regular payment of dues.

Catalogue of illustrated sherds (Figs 5.1 and 5.2)

1. Cremation urn 1068: jar with an everted thickened rim in grey ware TF 39. Cremation burial 1766.
2. Cremation urn 1061: necked jar with a thickened rim in grey sandy ware TF 25. Traces of a thin white calcareous deposit are visible on the interior of the base sherds. Cremation burial 1767.
3. Ancillary vessel 1063: collared rim (Hofheim) flagon in oxidised sandy ware TF 25. Cremation burial 1767.
4. Ancillary vessel 1141, sf 80: ring-necked flagon in oxidised TF 11A. 'Memorial' pit 1149.
5. Cremation urn 1191, sf 61: everted rim jar with a squared rim in grey ware TF 11A. Cremation burial 1196.
6. Cremation urn 1251, sf 97: jar in grey ware TF 11A. Cremation burial 1266.
7. Ancillary vessel 1256, sf 96: ring-necked flagon in oxidised TF 11A. Cremation burial 1266.
8. Grave good 1348, sf 174: ring-necked flagon in oxidised TF 11A. Grave group 1352.
9. Grave good 1351, sf 175: flagon in oxidised TF 11A. Grave group 1352.
10. Grave good 1128. upper part of a ring-necked flagon in oxidised TF 11A. Grave group 1145.
11. Grave good 1322: upper part of ring-necked flagon in oxidised TF 25. Grave group 1243.
12. Grave good 1375, sf 239: flared rim jar in micaceous greyware TF 5. Grave group 1374.
13. South-West black burnished ware jar (SOW BB1), sf 323. Context 1489, mass grave deposit, pit 1483.
14. Dorset black burnished ware beaded rim jar decorated with diagonal burnished lines. Joining sherds from contexts 1182 (grave group 1230) and 1166 (grave group 1167).
15. Whiteware flask of unknown provenance in a hard, fine white ware with a slightly sandy texture. Context 1265, curving gully 1358.

THE COINS
by Paul Booth

Four Roman coins were recovered during the excavation, all of late 3rd–4th century date. All were in poor condition and required cleaning and stabilisation before identification was possible. The coins are listed in approximate chronological order:

1. Irregular radiate, 13–16 mm. Obv: DIVO CLAUDIO, legend mostly off the flan. Rev: CONSECRATIO, altar 1b. *c* AD 270–295. Context 1182, grave 1230, sf 28.
2. Antoninianus, 22–25 mm. Obv: IMP CARAUSIUS PF AUG. Rev: PAX AUG, Pax standing l holding olive branch and vertical sceptre. Mint mark lost, but no letters in field. AD 286–293. Context 1254, pit 1255, sf 95.
3. AE2, 20 mm. Obv: ?]CONSTANTINUS[, head l. Rev: BEATA TR[ANQUILLITAS, altar. Mint mark lost. AD 321–324. Context 1300, pit 1301, sf 152.
4. Minim, 5 mm. No details visible. ?*c* 350–364. Context 1300, pit 1301, sf 134.

None of the coins is intrinsically remarkable, and the only item recovered from a burial feature was the irregular radiate from context 1182, the back-fill of inhumation grave 1230. For the type and date of the Consecratio issues of Claudius II see Bland and Burnett (1988, 144).

THE SMALL FINDS
by Hilary Cool

Introduction

Finds other than pottery, hobnails and coffin fittings were recovered from seven inhumation graves, three cremation burials and from the mass grave. It was only amongst the glass vessels that the same type was found with more than one burial. These can be more usefully considered as a whole. The other items are considered according to the burial they were found in.

The glass vessels

The most commonly occurring vessel type was the tubular unguent bottle (Price and Cottam 1998, 169–71). This is an extremely common form in the mid 1st century, going out of use during the 80s. They occurred as pyre goods in cremation burials 1209 and 1766, as a complete unburnt vessel in the somewhat enigmatic feature 1352 (sf 173; see Chapters 2 and 6), and as small unburnt fragments in cremation burial 1209 (sf 74). This type has been found at Kingsholm, where at least eighteen examples were recovered (Price and Cool 1985, 44) and at 124–130 London Road (Foundations Archaeology 2003) where examples were found in three of the burials. The examples found at 120–122 London Road were made in blue/green glass which is in contrast to those found during the earlier excavations, where one of the cremation burials had examples in light green, light yellow/green, and blue as well as blue/green. The other two burials only had blue/green examples as here.

Another type of unguent bottle also came from feature 1352 (sf 172). This had a tall conical reservoir but like the tubular form had a sheared rim. Conical unguent bottles were contemporary with the tubular form (Price and Cottam 1998, 172–4) with some examples continuing to be found into the 2nd century. The later examples tend to have rolled rims, and the sheared rim of this example would suggest that it is a 1st century AD example. The combination of the two in the grave-like feature would suggest that it dates before *c* AD 90.

These sorts of unguent bottles were used for holding oil for bathing prior to the development of the two-handled bath flask (Price and Cottam 1998, 188), and presumably the contents of those found on the pyres had been used to cleanse the body before burning. A total of 28 cremation burials have come from the excavations at 120–122 and 124–130 London Road, of which five definitely had tubular unguent bottles as pyre goods, another had an unguent bottle of uncertain type, and two others had glass vessels which were so completely melted that identification was impossible, but which are likely to have been unguent bottles given the pattern amongst the glass that has been identified. It would appear that the inclusion of unguent bottles as pyre goods was not universal, but does seem to have been a common part of the funeral rite in over a quarter of the cremation burials excavated. Given how common these little bottles must have been in the cemetery, the presence of a small unburnt fragment in cremation burial 1209 may be fortuitous rather than indicating the use of the contents both before and after burning.

The only other fragment of a glass vessel was found in the fill of inhumation grave 1144. If it is Roman, and the possibility of it being a modern intrusion can not entirely be ruled out, it would be most likely to be of 2nd or 3rd century date given that it is made of colourless glass.

Small finds from cremation burials

Cremation burial 1209

For discussion see the section on the vessel glass.

1. Tubular unguent bottle; lower neck and reservoir. Blue/green melted and collapsed. Length 39 mm, weight 5 g. 1198 Sample 68 spit 1. (Plate 5.1)
2. Melted drop of blue/green glass. Strain-cracked. Weight 1 g. 1202 sample 67.
3. Tubular unguent bottle (?); base fragment. Blue/green. Convex-curved thick fragment. Dimensions 10 x 7 mm, thickness 3 mm. 1198 sf 74.
4. Body fragments (2); blue/green. Convex-curved. Dimensions 15 x 4.5, 11 x 5.5 mm, wall thickness 2 mm. 1198 Sample 70 spit 2.

Plate 5.1 Melted unguent bottle from cremation burial 1209.

Cremation burial 1266

A gaming set comprising 43 bone and glass counters and two dice was found in the cremation urn of this grave together with a frit melon bead and a small scrap of unidentified iron (Plate 5.2). Neither the gaming set or the melon bead showed any signs of burning and so they can be regarded as grave rather than pyre goods.

All of the glass counters (nos. 12–43) have the typical plano-convex form with the exception of no. 42 which is a flat oval. In total there are 19 white counters, 11 of very dark glass which appears black, two of a mid blue shade appearing opaque, and one which is a very pale opaque blue/green (Plate 5.3;

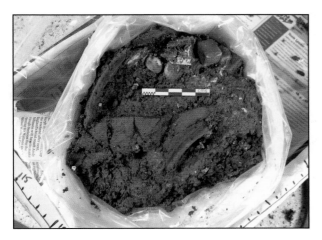

Plate 5.2 Cinerary urn 1252, burial 1266, before excavation of the contents in the laboratory.

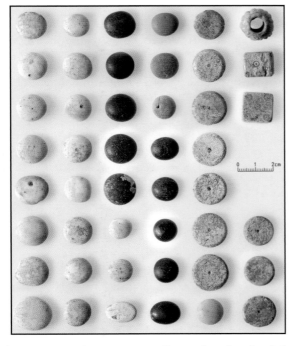

Plate 5.3 Gaming counters, dice and melon bead from cremation burial 1266.

Fig. 5.3). With the exception of nos. 15 and 16 which are oval, all the plano-convex counters are approximately circular in outline. There are also ten flat bone counters with a central dot on one face (nos 1–10). One of these (no.3) possibly has a graffito in the form of a single groove. The bone counters belong to Greep's Type 1 which he has identified as the early form in use during the 1st and 2nd centuries, being supplanted by his type 2 in the 2nd century (Greep 1998, 272). The number of glass counters would agree with a date in the 1st or earlier 2nd century for this set, as it can be shown that their use had declined markedly by the later 2nd century (Cool *et al.* 1995, table 125). It is likely that the set had been used for some time prior to deposition as one of the black counters (no. 11) showed a distinct area of wear on one edge, and some of the other counters also showed dulling or wear on their bases.

Both of the dice belong to the common form where the markings add up to seven on opposite faces. This type is not closely dateable. They are not a pair as no. 44 is cubic with the markings indicated by a double ring and dot, whilst no. 45 is more rectangular with single ring and dot markings. A small flake of no. 45 has become detached which enables it to be seen that it is made of ivory. It is unclear whether no. 44 was made of bone or ivory. The melon bead no. 46 is contemporary with the counters as such beads were in use during the mid 1st to mid 2nd centuries AD.

The range of sizes of the circular counters (ie excluding nos. 15, 16 and 42) is shown in Table 5.2. As can be seen the bone counters are, on the whole, larger than the glass ones. Though the black counters tend to be slightly smaller than the white ones there is no major difference in size between the different colours of glass used. In the gaming set found laid out on a board in the doctor's grave at Stanway one of the players had a special piece that was clearly much smaller than the rest of the counters (Crummy *et al.* 2007, 217), but in this set there is no obvious candidate for such a piece unless the flat oval counter no. 42 functioned in such a way.

A small number of the counters were recovered on site as some of the fill had spilled in antiquity. The rest were recovered during the excavation of the urn in the laboratory and so their position can be plotted (see Table 5.3). As can be seen the different types of counters were found at all depths of the urn. If the various spits are amalgamated into upper and lower fills, with those found on site considered as coming from the upper fill, it is possible to test formally whether there is any association between the type of counter and its position in the urn. Such tests show there is no association and so it is reasonable to assume they were added randomly as the calcined bones were poured into the urn. Both of the dice were added when the urn was almost full as was the melon bead no. 46.

The set shows some unusual features given the number of counters that are present. This can best be appreciated from Table 5.4 which summarises the gaming sets from burials of the 1st to early 3rd

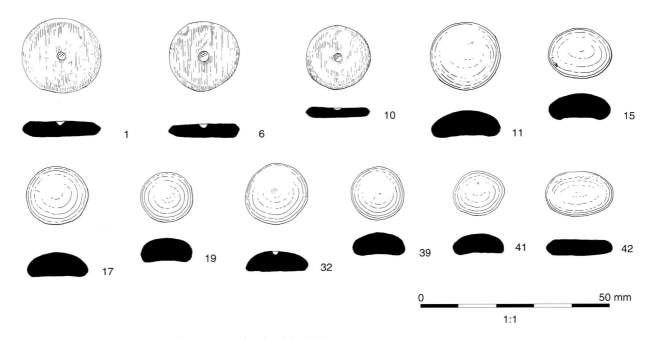

Figure 5.3   Gaming counters from cremation burial 1266.

century where we can be reasonably sure that everything deposited in the grave was recovered. It thus excludes the set discovered by metal detectorists as part of what appears to have been a rich later 2nd century grave at Elsenham, Essex (Hayes 1991; Frere 1992, 289) and that from Grave 66 at the St Pancras cemetery in Chichester as the grave was described as disturbed (Down and Rule 1971, 97). It also excludes a set from a Claudio-Neronian grave at Alton which was recovered from part of the deposit excavated in 1860 (Millett 1986, 51–8). No record of the find was made at the time. An early museum register records 19 counters and an unspecified number of dice (*ibid* 43) though only nine counters were catalogued when the cemetery was published in 1986. The set from Grange Road, Winchester has been included though it should be noted that the bag that contained the counters was found close to the point where the grave was cut by a pipe-trench, and so it is possible that other elements of the set could have been lost.

As can be seen from this table, where the set was designed for a game of chance using dice as here, the normal number of counters was 24. Three of the four dice graves in Table 5.4 have that number, and given that the bone counters in the grave at Chichester were described as very friable so that 'the exact number could not be determined', there must be the possibility that this grave too could have had 24

Table 5.2   The size of the counters in the gaming set within burial 1266.

Type	Number	Mean (mm)	Median (mm)	Range (mm)
Bone	10	18.8	19.0	21–17
White glass	18	16.5	16.5	19–14
'Black' glass	9	15.8	15.5	18–13
Blue glass	2	15.8	–	15.5–16
Pale glass	1	15.0	–	

Table 5.3   Distribution of the material in the urn (burial 1266). 'Site' refers to those recovered on site.

Location	White counter	Black counter	Blue counter	Pale green counter	Bone counter	Die	Melon bead	Total
Site	1	4	–	–	4	–	–	9
Spit 1	–	–	–	–	1	–	1	2
Spit 2	3	–	–	–	–	1	–	4
Spit 3	–	1	1	–	–	1	–	3
Spit 4	2	2	1	–	2	–	–	7
Spit 5	4	1	–	–	–	–	–	5
Spit 6	6	–	–	1	–	–	–	7
Spit 7	1	1	–	–	2	–	–	4
Spit 8	2	2	–	–	1	–	–	5
Total	19	11	2	1	10	2	1	46

Table 5.4 Gaming sets from selection of 1st to 3rd century burials.

Place	Date	Counter numbers	Dice numbers	Reference
Stanway	Claudian	26	None	Crummy *et al.* 2007, 217–20
London	40–80	24	4	Barber and Bowsher 2000, B435
Verulamium	80–90	22	None	Frere 1991b, 259 Anon 1990, 120
Winchester	85–95	18	None	Biddle 1967, 230–45
Colchester	Mid or late 1st century	24	4	May 1930, 275
Pins Knoll	Late 1st century?	20	None	Bailey 1967, 157–8
Chichester	Antonine	25 or 26	2	Down and Rule 1971, 117 no. 250
Ospringe	Later 2nd or earlier 3rd century	24	2	Whiting 1925, 39 Group XXXVIII

counters. Greep (1998, 272) has noted that despite the literary references to games played with dice such as *xii scripta* needing 15 pieces, the evidence of the sets themselves shows that they often consisted of multiples of six with 18 and 24 being the commonest. The set from this grave does not consist of a multiple of six, but it may be noted that it would do if only the 'normal' plano-convex glass counter and bone counters were considered, and the very unusual flat oval piece no. 42 was ignored. That no. 42 should be regarded as part of the set, however, is suggested by its position within the urn. It came from spit 5 and so was not added at a late stage as the dice and melon bead were.

The number of counters from this burial is exceptional and within Britain is only exceeded by the 46 bone counters found amongst the pyre debris in a late 2nd century cremation burial at Trentholme Drive York (Wenham 1968, 32 no. 41, 97 no. 46). The excavator suggested that these had been pyre goods, though the description of them makes no mention of whether they were burnt or not. If he was correct, the number in the set could have been much larger, given that not all of the pyre debris is likely to have been collected. This brings to mind the 126 counters that had been stored in a bag in a barrack block in the fort at Ravenglass when it burnt down in a fire during the late 2nd or early 3rd century (Potter 1979, 75–6). Based on the types present, it was suggested that the Ravenglass group included one set of 42 pieces and a second more miscellaneous group. Equally though the numbers recovered could have been the equivalent of three sets of 42. The figure is interesting in the light of the observation that this set consists of 42 standard counters and one unusual piece.

It is always possible that the large number of counters from this burial relates to the fact that it was the grave of two individuals although, given that all gaming sets assume that at least two people will be using them, the increased number of counters would not necessarily be required because of that. As Table 5.4 shows, two dice appear to have been regarded as the minimum needed for a set, so it seems unlikely that we are looking at two sets for the same type of game. A case could be advanced for the counters representing two different games, one needing dice and one which did not. Forty-two counters could represent one set of 18 and one set of 24 which, as Greep pointed out (see above), are the commonest

units found. That the different types found do not neatly divide into multiples of six would not necessarily have mattered as whilst some sets seem to divide neatly into two different sorts, others do not. Of the sets with dice in Table 5.4, only those from London and Ospringe are published in sufficient detail for the types to be divided. The London burial has 11 white and 13 black counters whilst that from Ospringe had four each in yellow and black glass, one each in blue and green glass, two bone counters with the rest being of white glass.

Table 5.4 suggests that a game requiring dice needed 24 counters. The set at Winchester did not have dice and consisted of 18 counters. A set found in a building occupied in the second quarter of the 2nd century at Castleford also consisted of 18 counters and lacked dice (Cool and Philo 1998, 362). The Winchester and Castleford sets do not divide neatly into two sets of nine counters. In the case of the Winchester counters (all of glass), there were twelve white, four black and two blue counters. The Castleford set consisted of seven bone counters decorated by a central dot (Greep type 1), nine bone counters with faces decorated by concentric rings (Greep Type 3) and two opaque white glass counters. Both of these sets thus divide into three recognisable groups but the numbers in each group are different.

If we assume the game needing dice took the London figures it would be easy to suggest that the Gloucester group had one set consisting of 13 white and 11 black, which would leave the second set consisting of eight glass counters (five white, one very pale blue/green, two blue) and ten bone ones. Given the very pale blue/green counter could easily pass as a white counter, the postulated second set would have three groups of clearly different counters just like the two groups from Winchester and Castleford described above. This is of course speculation which is not susceptible to proof, but given the fact that it is the burial of two individuals, it is a possibility. The age ranges given to the remains means that we could be dealing with two children in the age range of nine to eleven. Equally though there could have been a difference of almost ten years between them, and the board games a five or six year old plays tends to be more restricted than those available to a fourteen or fifteen year old. Two different sets might have been thought appropriate.

An interesting question is why these individuals were thought to be in need of one or two gaming sets. In general, though counters are a very common site find, they are rare in burials. Philpott's review of grave furnishings noted ten sets accompanying cremation burials and three accompanying inhumations (Philpott 1991, 185, 279). Since then a few others have been found including the ones from the London East Cemetery and Stanway (see Table 5.4). (See Crummy *et al.* 2007, table 5.5, which appeared whilst this was in press. Full consideration of the discussion has not been possible.) Recent excavations by Oxford Archaeology on the A2 near Springhead in Kent revealed another set (with 23 glass counters and two dice) from a rich early Roman cremation grave (Allen, pers com.). Despite these additional sets, this Gloucester find still only brings the total known from Britain to 26, so clearly they continue to be rare as a burial find. In cremation burials they occur primarily as grave goods rather than pyre goods, as is the case here. In the 1st century two different patterns of deposition can be identified. In the case of the Stanway, Alton, Verulamium, Springhead and Winchester graves they are occurring as part of the burial furnishings of elite members of native society. I have argued elsewhere (Cool 2006, 193) that these types of graves can be interpreted in terms of the native aristocracy in southern England exploring the parameters of what it meant to be 'Roman' and what was necessary for the good life. The Elsenham and Chichester finds continue this pattern into the Antonine period. The young man of between 15 and 17 years buried at Pins Knoll, Dorset may be exhibiting the same tendency in a different cultural milieu. He was buried in the Durotrigian tradition as a crouched inhumation burial, possibly in the second half of the 1st century. In the crook of his left arm there were 20 counters that had been in a bag, and an iron stylus and two studs. The counters were made of stone apart from two fashioned from potsherds and one from an oyster shell. The counters were thus not of the typical 'Roman' types but the inclusion of a stylus is paralleled in several of the contemporary elite graves further to the east where the inclusion of writing equipment seems to be another facet of what it was to be 'Roman'.

The other tradition of depositing gaming sets is seen at Colchester (Crummy *et al.* 1993, table 8.2), at London and here at Gloucester. This is where they form virtually the only offering. At Colchester the set had been on the pyre. At London the grave was suggested to be an inhumation but it was disturbed and no human bone was recovered. The only other find was a pottery vessel. The Colchester burial is not closely dated but the inclusion of burnt fragments of glass unguent bottles would strongly suggest it was of mid 1st century date or possibly a little later in the century. It will thus have been the burial of a colonist at the time when most of the inhabitants of Colchester can be assumed to be non-native. A similar origin might be proposed for the London individual, and the date proposed for this grave at Gloucester would suggest that they were either the children of someone attached to the legion or part of a family of an early colonist.

The difference in the deposition patterns between the native elite and the incomers suggests that the sets were perceived differently in the two communities. For native elite they could be viewed as being part of the 'Roman' cultural package alongside the writing equipment, items associated with visiting the baths, items for making sacrifice and tablewares for polite dining that are variously seen in these graves. For the incomers there was no need to flaunt symbols of *Romanitas* as they, self-evidently, were 'Roman'.

In the Gloucester burial the gaming set(s) are not indicating that the deceased were part of an elite family, but perhaps that these individuals were seen as in need of special care in their burial rite. It is noticeable that young people are often singled out for special treatment (see for example Martin-Kilcher 2000; Gowland 2001; Cool forthcoming), and this may be the reason for the deposition here. The melon bead also included might be a further indication of this. Melon beads occur in large quantities on domestic sites, occasionally in circumstances that suggest they may have been regarded as talismans. At both Scole and Colchester for example they have been found deposited with a bell in a manner that suggests they may have formed part of a foundation deposit (Seeley 1995; Crummy 1992, 187 no. 1663). They are also sometimes found singly or as parts of small assemblages of amulets in graves (Philpott 1991, 130). It is noteworthy that the individual buried at Grange Road, Winchester also had eight melon beads. These had been placed in a bag with the counters as well as various other trinkets including a finger ring, a seal box lid decorated with an animal, a bell and a banded flint. This group of material is very reminiscent of the *crepundia* that Martin-Kilcher (2000) has identified as being a feature of the burials of girls and young women in the Roman world who died before marriage. The inclusion of a bell in the group is also significant as when bells occur in graves they tend to be in those of children and an amuletic significance can be assumed (Cool 2004, 401).

There tends to be an assumption that gaming sets were appropriate for males. The (male) authors of the reports on both the Winchester and the Alton set make this explicit assumption (Biddle 1967, 248; Millett 1986, 51), though in the case of the Alton burial the bone specialist could only identify the remains as adult (unsexed) (Green in Millett 1986, 77 and table 4) and at Winchester the expert view was that the remains suggested 'immaturity (perhaps a teenager) or a fairly slender female' (Brothwell in Biddle 1967, 231). As already discussed the bag of trinkets which included the counters in the Winchester grave suggests the deceased may well have been an adolescent female. Of the graves with gaming sets where the sex of the deceased is known, few can be shown to be undoubtedly that of a male. At present the admittedly sparse evidence suggests that gaming sets were not seen as a gender specific type

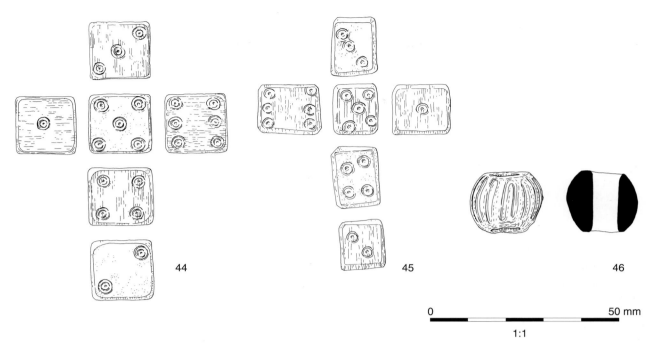

Figure 5.4   Other objects from cremation burial 1266.

of grave good but that they were seen as more appropriate for young people (here, Winchester, Pins' Knoll) than for adults (Alton).

Catalogue of small finds from grave 1266 (Figs 5.3–4)

1. Counter; worked bone. Circular with flat face and bevelled edges and central dot on one face. Diameter 21 mm, thickness 4 mm. sf 258. Level 4.
2. Counter; worked bone. Circular with flat face and bevelled edges and central dot on one face. Diameter 20 mm, thickness 3.5 mm. sf 280. Level 7. (not illustrated)
3. Counter; worked bone. Circular with flat face and bevelled edges and central dot on one face. Possible a deliberate groove on other face. Diameter 20 mm, thickness 4 mm. sf 281 Level 7. (not illustrated)
4. Counter; worked bone. Circular with flat face and bevelled edges and central dot on one face. Diameter 20 mm, thickness 4 mm. sf 103. Site find. (not illustrated)
5. Counter; worked bone. Circular with flat face and bevelled edges and central dot on one face. Diameter 19 mm, thickness 3 mm. sf 102. Site find. (not illustrated)
6. Counter; worked bone. Circular with flat face and bevelled edges and central dot on one face. Diameter 19 mm, thickness 4 mm. sf 279. Level 7.
7. Counter; worked bone. Circular with flat face and bevelled edges and central dot on one face. Diameter 18 mm, thickness 6 mm. sf 259. Level 4. (not illustrated)
8. Counter; worked bone. Circular with flat face and bevelled edges and central dot on one face. Diameter 17 mm, thickness 3.5 mm. sf 98. Site find. (not illustrated)
9. Counter; worked bone. Circular with flat face and bevelled edges and central dot on one face. Diameter 17 mm, thickness 4 mm. sf 100. Site find. (not illustrated)
10. Counter; worked bone. Circular with flat face and bevelled edges and central dot on one face. Diameter 17 mm, thickness 3 mm. sf 249. Level 1.
11. Counter, plano-convex. Very dark glass appearing black; base pitted, one edge worn smooth. Diameter 18 mm, thickness 7 mm. sf 256. Level 3.
12. Counter, plano-convex. Very dark glass appearing black; base pitted, some wear. Diameter 18 mm, thickness 7 mm. sf 264. Level 4. (not illustrated)

13. Counter, plano-convex. Very dark glass appearing black; base pitted. Diameter 17.5 mm, thickness 7 mm. sf 269. Level 5. (not illustrated)
14. Counter, plano-convex. Very dark glass appearing black; base pitted and dulled. Diameter 17.5 x 16.5 mm, thickness 7 mm. sf 101. Site find. (not illustrated)
15. Counter, oval plano-convex. Very dark glass appearing black; base pitted. Diameter 17 x 13 mm, thickness 6.5 mm. sf 286. Level 8.
16. Counter, oval plano-convex. Very dark glass appearing black; base smoothed. Diameter 16 x 13 mm, thickness 6.5 mm. sf 288. Site find. (not illustrated)
17. Counter, plano-convex. Very dark glass appearing black; base pitted. Diameter 15.5 mm, thickness 7 mm. sf 105. Site find.
18. Counter, plano-convex. Very dark glass appearing black; base pitted and dulled. Diameter 15 x 14 mm, thickness 7 mm. sf 104. Site find. (not illustrated)
19. Counter, plano-convex. Very dark glass appearing black; base pitted. Diameter 14 mm, thickness 6 mm. Sample 203. Spit 8.
20. Counter, plano-convex. Very dark glass appearing black; base pitted. Diameter 13.5 mm, thickness 6 mm. sf 262. Level 4. (not illustrated)
21. Counter, plano-convex; Very dark glass appearing black; base pitted. Half extant. Diameter 13 mm, thickness 5.5 mm. sf 282. Level 7. (not illustrated)
22. Counter, plano-convex. Cloudy mid blue appearing opaque, bubble voids on surfaces; base smooth. Diameter 16 x 15 mm, thickness 7 mm. sf 257. Level 3. (not illustrated)
23. Counter, plano-convex oval. Opaque mid blue, base pitted. Diameter 15.5 mm, thickness 13.5 mm. sf 260. Level 4. (not illustrated)
24. Counter, plano-convex. Opaque white glass; base pitted. Diameter 22 x 20 mm, thickness 7 mm. sf 284. Level 8. (not illustrated)
25. Counter, plano-convex. Opaque white glass; base smooth. Diameter 19 x 17 mm, thickness 7 mm. sf 271. Level 6. (not illustrated)
26. Counter, oval plano-convex. Opaque white glass; base pitted. One edge chipped. Diameter 19 x 16 mm, thickness 6.5 mm. sf 283. Level 7. (not illustrated)
27. Counter, plano-convex. Opaque white glass; base smooth; bubble voids on surface. Diameter 18.5 x 16.5 mm, thickness 7.5 mm. sf 276. Level 6. (not illustrated)

28. Counter, plano-convex. Opaque white; base smooth. Diameter 18 mm, thickness 6 mm. sf 267. Level 5. (not illustrated)
29. Counter, plano-convex. Opaque white glass; base pitted. Diameter 17 mm, thickness 6 mm. sf 275. Level 6. (not illustrated)
30. Counter, plano convex. Opaque white glass; slightly pitted base. Diameter 17 x 15 mm, wall thickness 6 mm. sf 99. Site find. (not illustrated)
31. Counter, plano-convex. Opaque white glass; base pitted. Diameter 17 x 15 mm, wall thickness 6.5 mm. sf 274. Level 6. (not illustrated)
32. Counter, plano-convex. Opaque white, bubble void on surface; base smooth. Diameter 16.5 mm, thickness 6 mm. sf 252. Level 2.
33. Counter, plano-convex. Opaque white glass appearing black; base pitted. Diameter 16.5 mm, thickness 6 mm. sf 268. Level 5. (not illustrated)
34. Counter, plano-convex. Opaque white glass; base smooth. Diameter 16 mm, thickness 7 mm. sf 272. Level 6. (not illustrated)
35. Counter, plano-convex. Opaque white glass; base smooth. Diameter 16 mm, thickness 6 mm. sf 261. Level 4. (not illustrated)
36. Counter, plano-convex. Opaque white; base smooth. Diameter 15.5 x 15 mm, thickness 6 mm. sf 285. Level 8. (not illustrated)
37. Counter, plano-convex. Opaque white glass; bubble void on surface; base smooth. Diameter 15.5 mm, thickness 6.5 mm. sf 251. Level 2. (not illustrated)
38. Counter, plano-convex. Opaque white glass; base smooth. In two joining pieces. Diameter 15 mm, thickness 7 mm. sf 263. Level 4. (not illustrated)
39. Counter, plano-convex. Opaque white glass, bubble void on surface; base smooth. Diameter 14.5 x 13.5 mm, thickness 6 mm. sf 250. Level 2.
40. Counter, plano-convex. Opaque white; nase smooth. Diameter 14 x 13 mm, thickness 6 mm. sf 266. Level 5. (not illustrated)
41. Counter, plano-convex. Opaque white glass; base pitted. Diameter 14 x 12 mm, thickness 6 mm. sf 273. Level 6.
42. Counter; opaque white glass. Oval flat. Dimensions 17 x 12 mm, thickness 4 mm. sf 265. Level 5.
43. Counter, plano-convex. Opaque glass appearing very pale blue/green; base smooth. Diameter 15 mm, thickness 6 mm. sf 277. Level 6. (not illustrated)
44. Die, worked bone or ivory. Cube with markings formed by double ring and dot; opposite faces adding to seven. Dimensions 16 x 16 x 16.5 mm. sf 253. Level 2.
45. Die, ivory. Rectangular-sided cube marked with ring and dot. Opposite faces add to seven. Dimensions 16.5 x 13 x 12 mm. sf 254. Level 3.
46. Melon bead, turquoise frit with glaze surviving. Complete. Diameter 18 mm, length 14 mm, perforation diameter 8 mm. sf 248. Level 1.
47. Unidentified. Iron strip (2 fragments) retaining fragment of copper alloy sheet. Lengths 17 and 14 mm, width 2 mm. sf 255. Level 3. (not illustrated)

Cremation burial 1766

For discussion see the section on the vessel glass.

1. Melted and vesicular fragment of blue/green glass. Possibly the collapsed reservoir of a tubular unguent bottle. Present length 37 mm, weight 2 g. 1049. (Plate 5.4)

Small finds from inhumation burials

Inhumation grave 1144

For discussion see the section on the vessel glass.

1. Body fragment; colourless body; strain-cracked. Possibly modern. Dimensions 21.5 x 17 mm, wall thickness 3 mm.

Plate 5.4   Melted unguent bottle from cremation burial 1766.

Inhumation grave 1151

The only item in this grave was a damaged and incomplete mount, fastened to whatever it decorated by a split pin. The configuration suggests it could have acted as some form of hinge. Whilst the depth of the split pin suggests it would have been fastened to something substantial such as a wooden board, it seems unlikely that this is a box mount as sheet mountings on those are normally fastened by studs (see for example Crummy 1983, 85–9). This item was recovered from the back-fill, and given its damaged and incomplete state, it seems most likely to have been a chance inclusion, rather than a deliberate grave good.

1. Mount. Copper alloy. Rectangular sheet with one short end broken; centrally perforated at other short end which is concave; perforation retains split pin through perforation; one leg of pin bent back for *c* 6 mm. Sheet has central vertical rib possibly formed from having been bent. Sheet: dimensions 43 x 23 mm. Split pin: length 27 mm, width 4 mm. 1110 sf 20.

Inhumation Grave 1230

The fragment from an iron ring was found in the abdomen area of the skeleton in the grave. Had it been a grave good more could have been expected to survive as it retains a solid metal core. Given the range of items found in the fill, it seems best to regard this item as an accidental inclusion rather than a deliberately placed grave good.

1. Ring; approximately one-third extant. Iron. Square-sectioned. Diameter *c* 25 mm. 1181 sf 141.

Inhumation grave 1246 (Fig. 5.5)

The type of finger ring found in this grave (sf 88) was in use primarily during the 1st and 2nd centuries AD (Henig 1974, 46 types II and III). It is currently incomplete, lacking a small part of the hoop but the part that is missing is where the hoop would have been narrowest and it may have disappeared through corrosion. The intaglio it would have held is also missing. It does not appear to be directly associated with the skeleton, but there are some grounds for thinking it was deliberately placed in the grave. Iron rings such as this were a mark of rank, as iron rings were appropriate for the ordinary citizen whereas gold ones were technically reserved for the senatorial and equestrian classes (Pliny *Natural History* 33.iv–viii). In a community such as the fortress and *colonia* at Gloucester it might be expected that status indicators such as the correct metal for a finger ring might be respected. There is also some evidence that iron may have been perceived as particularly appropriate for placing with the dead. A preliminary survey comparing the materials used for personal ornaments in domestic and in funerary contexts at Baldock shows that iron items are much more likely to be present in graves than would be expected in the domestic assemblages (Rosten 2007, 117–9).

The absence of an intaglio is also significant. As already noted, the incomplete state of the ring may have come about through corrosion. Normally complete rings such as this can be expected to retain their intaglios when found. This can be demonstrated in Table 5.5. This is derived from a survey of metal personal ornaments across southern Britain. As can be seen it is unusual for rings such as these to

Table 5.5   The occurrence of intaglios in complete and incomplete simple expanded finger rings (Source of data: Cool 1983, Finger ring group IVA excluding those with enamelled bezels).

State	Intaglio Present	Intaglio missing	Total
Complete	54	8	62
Incomplete	32	21	53
Total	86	29	115

be found with empty bezels when complete. As Henig has frequently observed, it is exceptional for intaglios to be found in Romano-British burials probably because they needed to be handed on to the heirs (eg Henig in Millett 1986, 57). The deliberate removal of the intaglio from this ring would fit this pattern and would explain why it is so much at variance with the pattern seen in Table 5.5. These factors, and the likely importance of it being made of iron, all argue for the ring having been deliberately included in the grave, rather than just being a chance inclusion.

It is not uncommon for children to be singled out for special treatment in their burial rite, and it is possibly the age of the deceased in this grave (5–12 years) that triggered the deposition of this ring. It might be thought that the child was too young to be in a position to have heirs to whom the intaglio passed, but there is epigraphic evidence in Britain for children as young as 13 having formal heirs (Collingwood and Wright 1965, no. 696).

1. Finger ring. Iron. Slender hoop expanding mainly at oval bezel, empty setting now infilled with corrosion products. In two fragments with part of back of hoop missing. Diameter *c* 27 mm, bezel dimensions 14 x 10 mm. 1244. sf 88.

Inhumation grave 1352 (Fig. 5.6)

For discussion see the section on the vessel glass.

1. Tubular unguent bottle; blue/green. Outbent rim, edge sheared; cylindrical neck; tubular body with slight flattening at base. Complete apart from a small fragment missing in the rim. Neck/body junction tooled. Rim diameter 15 x 14 mm, maximum body diameter 14 mm, height 74 mm. 1347. sf 173.
2. Tall conical unguent bottle; complete. Blue/green. Outbent rim, edge sheared; cylindrical neck; conical body with flattened base. Rim diameter 23 x 22 mm, maximum body diameter 29 mm, height 102 mm. 1347. sf 172.

Inhumation grave 1362 (Fig. 5.7)

Bracelet sf 216 belongs to the family of late 3rd and 4th century bracelets decorated with multiple units. These appear to be an insular fashion. The normal pattern is for there to be a zone of identical decoration behind each terminal, and for the central third of the circumference either to be decorated with a number of different motifs symmetrically arranged around the centre point or for it to be

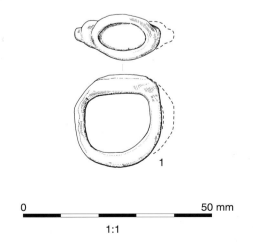

0   50 mm

1:1

Figure 5.5   Iron ring from inhumation burial 1246.

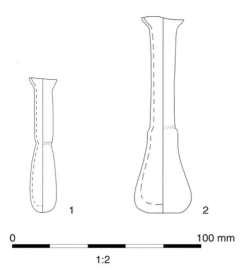

Figure 5.6 Unguent bottles from inhumation grave 1352.

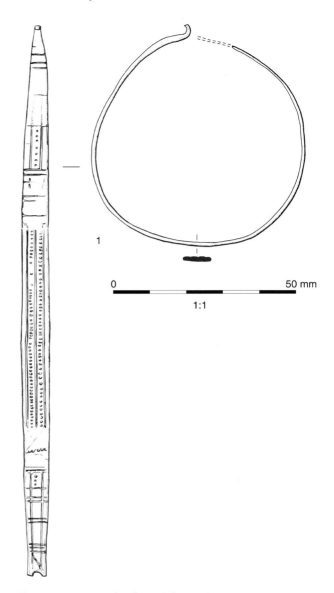

Figure 5.7 Bracelet from inhumation grave 1362.

occupied by just a single motif (Cool 1983, Bracelet Groups XXXI and XXXII; see also Swift 2000, 145). This example belongs to the latter group. The decoration is very faint but, insofar as can be judged, is unparalleled. Neither of the motifs occurred in the *c* 190 examples catalogued as part of my survey. The bracelet was worn on the left arm of an adult of 18–25 years. It was not possible to sex the individual from osteological data but elsewhere where the skeleton can be sexed, the association is normally with a female. This was certainly the pattern in the three graves with bracelets from the earlier excavations in this cemetery where two of the skeletons could be sexed as female. One was of the same age as the individual in 1362 (20–25 years) and the other a woman of *c* 50 years. The third individual was described as a mature adult and appears to have worn at least one of her bracelets, also on the left arm. The presence of a bracelet with an adult woman in this grave continues the trend seen in the earlier excavations that suggests that amongst this community bracelets were seen as appropriate for adults. At some sites such as Lankhills in Winchester bracelet wearing seems particularly associated with younger girls (Gowland 2001, 162), but this does not appear to be the case at Gloucester.

The function of ring sf 219 cannot be ascertained with certainty. The piece is broken across the area where the bezel would have been if it were a finger ring, but it is possible that these breaks represent damaged terminals of a penannular ring. If that is correct, then it could well have been an earring (Allason-Jones 1989a, Type 2b). Equally, however, it might have been an example of the light trinket rings popular in the 3rd and 4th centuries.

1. Bracelet (4 fragments). Copper alloy. Rectangular-sectioned, widest to wrist; hook and eye terminal, eye broken. Grooved and punched decoration in three zones, now very faint with unit of vertical grooves between them and behind terminals; central unit of three horizontal grooves with punching on two zones between them producing a milled appearance; zones between central unit and terminals probably consist of grooves parallel to each edge with a line of punched dots between; Diameter *c* 55 mm, section 7 x 1.5 mm. 1361. sf 216.

2. Finger ring (?), copper alloy. Rectangular-sectioned with rounded edges, vertical grooves across broken bezel. Central part of bezel missing. Diameter 18 mm, section 2.5 x 2 mm. 1361. sf 219. (not illustrated)

Inhumation grave 1505 (Fig. 5.8)

The ring found on the third or fourth finger of the left hand of the skeleton belongs to a group of trinket finger rings decorated with patterns similar to those on the light bangles in use during the later 3rd and 4th centuries (Cool 1983, Finger ring Group XX) and

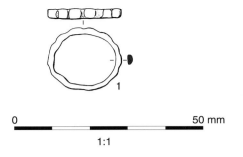

Figure 5.8   Finger ring from inhumation grave 1505.

is probably contemporary with them. A pair of rings decorated with vertical grooves were found apparently worn on the fingers of the left hand of an individual of about 20 to 25 years buried in the third quarter of the 4th century at Lankhills (Clarke 1979, 68 grave 326, fig. 87 nos. 401–2), and a similar ring from the Fordington cemetery at Dorchester is preserved still *in situ* around a finger bone (Cool 1983, 1108 no. 2). Unlike the intaglio rings such as sf 88 in grave 1246, whose function was to hold the

intaglio which was the seal of its owner, these trinket rings were purely decorative.

1. Finger ring. Copper alloy. D-sectioned band; oval outline. Wide vertical grooves forming a beaded outer face. Diameter 19 x 16 mm, section 2.5 x 1.5 mm. 1480. sf 319.

Small finds from the mass grave (Fig. 5.9)

The brooches from this feature suggest that burial took place in the later 2nd century. Wroxeter brooches such as Figure 5.9 no. 1 are 2nd century in date. The examples from dated contexts that Mackreth cites belong to the middle part of the century (Mackreth 1995, 963 no. 27) but they seem to have continued in use until at least the end of the century. An example came from a hoard of items dated to AD 200 at Chepstow (Bayley and Butcher 2004, 169) and another came from a ditch fill at Somerford Keynes with mid to late 2nd century pottery (Miles *et al.* 2007, 251 table 9.6 see also digital section 5.3). The knee brooch (Fig. 5.9, no. 2) belongs to the variety that appears to be a British development of the form (Hull form 171) though the bow is more angular than normal. A date in the later

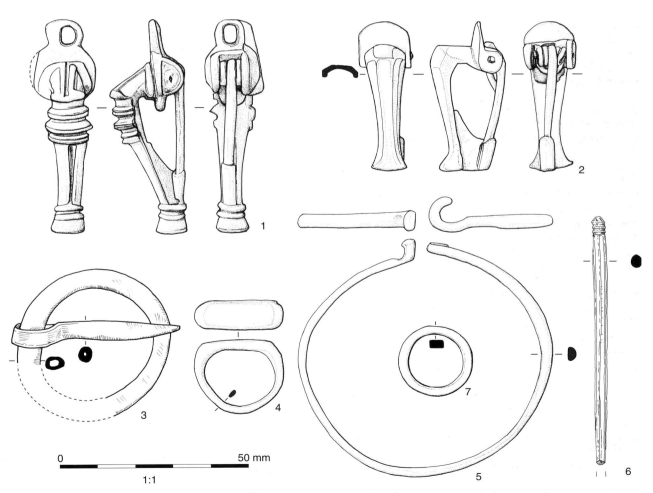

Figure 5.9   Small finds from mass grave 1483.

113

2nd to early 3rd century is appropriate (Bayley and Butcher 2004, 179–80). The third brooch is an iron penannular brooch which is not closely dateable (Fig. 5.9, no. 3). The proposed date would be in agreement with the hairpin found in the upper fill (Fig. 5.9, no. 6) as this is an example of a Crummy Type 2 (Crummy 1983, 21) which is the commonest 2nd century form.

None of the brooches was directly associated with any of the skeletons in the grave but all had their pins in the position that would be expected if they had been fastening items of dress. It seems likely that they entered the deposit as part of worn items of clothing.

An adult female aged 26–35 (1596) wore the bracelet (Fig. 5.9, no. 5) on her right forearm (Plate 5.5). It is a very simple form with hooked terminals. Most similar bracelets have been recovered from 4th century contexts (Cool 1983, 195 Bracelet Group XXXIII), but a complete example was recovered from an occupation level at Fishbourne dated to the early 2nd to later 3rd centuries (Cunliffe 1971, 107 no. 47, fig. 41). Figure 5.9, no. 5 provides very welcome evidence that the form was being worn in the later 2nd century. In general bracelet wearing was not fashionable for the majority of women before the end of the 3rd century but there is a growing body of evidence that in the Gloucestershire area it was a fashion that developed in the 2nd century (Cool in Miles *et al.* 2007, 346).

An adult male (skeleton 1542) had several items associated with him including the copper alloy ring (Fig. 5.9, no. 7) and two fragments of iron bar (nos. 8–9). Unfortunately quite what the iron fragments were part of cannot be identified, but as one of them was over the left hip, it might perhaps be suggested they were part of some form of belt or purse fitting.

The finger-ring (Fig. 5.9, no. 4) was not associated with any particular skeleton so it is not known whether it was worn at the time of deposition. It belongs to the same family of simple expanded rings

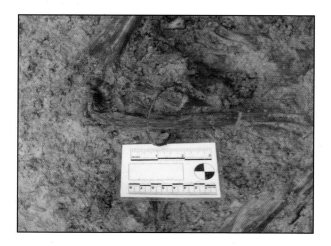

Plate 5.5 Copper alloy bracelet (sf 464) worn on the right forearm of skeleton 1596.

as that in grave 1246, so a 1st to early 3rd century date is appropriate.

The presence of three brooches in this deposit stresses how unusual it is. Despite brooch wearing being very common in the 1st to mid 2nd century judged by site finds, brooches seem almost to be actively shunned as grave or pyre goods at that time. 2nd or 3rd century cemeteries with brooch graves are not common as can be seen from Philpott's distribution maps (Philpott 1991, figs. 9 and 26). Though these were based on research carried out in the late 1980s, discoveries since then have not materially changed the picture. The habit of including brooches was commonest in the 1st century and in the 4th. To find three brooches in this burial pit would strongly suggest that the dead were not being prepared for burial in the normal way and there was a pressing need to dispose of them, perhaps in the garments they were wearing when they died. The dates of the brooches would suggest that if these unfortunate people were victims of a historically attested plague, then it is the Antonine one that is most likely (see discussion in Chapter 6). The later one in the mid 3rd century would be too late for these styles of brooches as by that time one would be expecting those people who chose to wear brooches to be favouring P-shaped brooches and light cross-bows.

1. Wroxeter brooch. Copper alloy. Cast headloop with flat D-shaped head plate. Two perforated lugs behind head plate holding spring of two turns, chord forms loop below spring; pin complete and fastened inside triangular catch plate. D-sectioned upper bow with three vertical grooves joins headplate with lentoid moulding on either side; junction of upper and lower bow marked by three transverse horizontally ribbed mouldings; Lower bow has one vertical groove. Cylindrical footknob with two mouldings at top. Length 55 mm, head width 15 mm. 1545. sf 406.

2. Knee brooch. Copper alloy. D-shaped headplate with two perforated lugs behind holding spring of four turns, cord forming a loop below spring; pin complete and fastened in trapezoidal catch plate. Slightly faceted, sharply angular bow expanding out to flat foot plate. Length 41 mm, head width 13 mm. 1483. sf 437.

3. Penannular or annular brooch, two joining fragments; iron. Square sectioned hoop with broken ends. Pin wrapped around hoop and tapering to point resting on hoop on opposite side. Diameter *c* 40 mm, hoop section 5 mm. 1485. sf 345.

4. Finger ring in four joining fragments. Copper alloy. Circular-sectioned hoop expanding to flattened rectangular bezel. Diameter 24 x 20 mm, bezel section 5.5 x 2 mm, hoop section 2 mm. 1526 sf 383.

5. Bracelet, copper alloy. D-sectioned hoop, double hook terminal, part of one hook broken. Diameter 66 x 64 mm, section 3.5 x 2 mm. 1596. sf 464.

6. Hair pin, worked bone (three joining fragments). Circular-sectioned shank; conical head with three grooves; broken tip. Present length 68 mm, shank section 3 mm. 1485. sf 341.

7. Ring, copper alloy. Rectangular-sectioned hoop. Diameter 19 mm, section 3.5 x 2.5 mm. 1545 sf 378

8. Bar. Iron. Rectangular-sectioned; three fragments, one curved. Largest fragment 21 mm, section 8 x 4.5 mm. 1545. sf 399. (not illustrated)

9. Bar. Iron. Rectangular sectioned, tapering to point Length 46 mm, section 8 x 4 mm. 1545. sf 408. (not illustrated)

10. Angle bracket? Iron. Length *c* 55 mm. 1544. sf 386. (not illustrated)

Small finds from other contexts

The only item from the non-funerary contexts that warrants discussion is the fragment which appears to be from a small barrel padlock from the cemetery soil. If this identification is correct, then it was lost or discarded when it was locked.

> Barrel padlock. Iron. Part of case with curved top and squared base retaining part of the haft, stop ridge and central internal rod. Present length 46 mm, casing 23 x 20 mm. 1440. (not illustrated)

THE NAILS
by Kelly Powell

Introduction

An assemblage of 1440 nails, including hobnails, was recovered from the excavation, of which 999 came from burial features. The condition of the nails was generally poor, the majority being heavily corroded and fragmentary. However, the lengths of most of the structural nails fell within the range 50–80 mm, typical of many Roman nail assemblages. A total of 145 were classified as Manning type 1 structural nails (47 of which were type 1b), with an additional five being tentatively identified as type 1 (Manning 1985). A total of 1146 nails could be positively identified as hobnails (Manning type 10) with five additional tentative identifications. The assemblage contained some complete hobnails, generally up to 18 mm long with head diameters of 9–10 mm. The remainder of the nails were unclassifiable due to their fragmentary nature and none of the less common nail types were positively identified within the assemblage.

Nails from cremation burials

An assemblage of 13 structural nails and 32 hobnails were recovered from five cremation burials. The largest group came from cremation burial 1769 and comprised 24 definite and three probable hobnails, and eight structural nails. Four structural nails were recovered from the cinerary urn in grave 1766 and two from the urn in grave 1766, and a single possibly complete hobnail and a fragment of nail shank were found within accessory vessel 1199 in burial 1209. The remainder of the assemblage came from grave backfills.

The majority were relatively small compared to those from inhumation graves, measuring less than 37 mm long, and could originate from a number of funerary fittings such as biers and boxes, as found at other Romano-British cemeteries such as the M6 Toll (Powell forthcoming), Pepper Hill, Kent (Biddulph 2006) and Brougham, Cumbria (Cool 2004). No clear examples of the use of boxes or caskets as containers for cremated bone or pyre goods were identified, and it is likely that the nails recovered from cremation burials were the remains of items included on the pyre.

Nails from inhumation burials

Structural nails

The majority of structural nails came from inhumation burials, a minimum of 224 definite and six possible nails being recovered from 40 graves. The size of groups from individual graves varied from one nail to 18. The nails in 19 graves were interpreted on the basis of their locations within the grave as being *in situ*, representing the remains of coffins. Mineralised wood was identified adhering to nails in seven of these graves (1330, 1353, 1369, 1374, 1422, 1505, 1507). The lengths of complete or near complete nails generally fell within the range of 50–80 mm, and indicated a high level of consistency in the construction of coffins. The overall lack of smaller nails suggests smaller wooden grave goods were unlikely to be have been interred with the burials.

Hobnails

A minimum number of 730 hobnails were recovered from a total of 20 inhumation graves. The groups of hobnails from six graves were recorded as representing items of footwear that were worn at the time of burial (see *Footware* in Chapter 2). The footwear worn by burial 1232 in grave 1234 were represented by groups of 32 hobnails associated with the left foot and 37 associated with the right foot, while 13 hobnails were associated with the left foot of burial 1328 in grave 1330 and 22 with the right foot, as well as a further 28 hobnails recovered from a soil sample. The only surviving foot of burial 1537 in grave 1765 was shod in an item of footwear comprising 42 hobnails. The burials in graves 1344, 1353 and 1369 wore footwear comprising 178, 38 and 104 hobnails respectively, and an unidentified iron object from grave 1353 may have been further corroded hobnails. Seventeen of the 20 hobnails recovered from grave 1167 were located beyond the feet and may come from an item of footwear placed at the foot of the grave rather than worn. Graves 1283, 1315 and 1765 produced assemblages of 44, 37 and 42 hobnails respectively that are also likely to represent footwear, whether worn or placed as grave goods. The hobnails from grave 1315 were mostly corroded together, some with possible mineralised organic material holding them in their original formation, but it is unclear whether this item of footwear was worn or simply placed with the burial. The remaining groups were smaller in number, and four graves contained only single hobnails, which are likely to be chance inclusions.

Nails from the mass grave

Five skeletons in the mass grave appear to have been shod at the time of burial. A group of 69 hobnails (sf 2004) associated with skeleton 2005 was found in its original formation, held together by corrosion and missing only the toe end. Hobnails were observed around the edge of the sole with three longitudinal rows at the toe end and a figure of eight at the heel. The patterning of hobnails on the soles of shoes has been discussed by van Driel Murray (1999), who argues that they were not merely fashionable decoration, but carried a variety of symbolic meaning, possibly associated with protection.

Skeleton 1666 was also shod, with two groups (sf 677, 676) of a minimum of 80 and 79 hobnails found associated with the left and right foot respectively. In addition to this 15 hobnails were recorded as being found in association with skeleton 1638, eight with skeleton 1552 and five with skeleton 2009. A further two groups of 41 hobnails (sf 2018) and 21 hobnails (sf 517) are likely to represent items of footwear that had become separated from their original wearers during or after burial, and a total of 59 stray hobnails (sf 249, 516, 517) were also found. The mass grave contained no obviously structural nails.

Discussion

Groups of *in situ* structural nails indicated that at least 19 burials were buried in coffins. Smaller numbers of nails recovered from a further 21 graves may be evidence for further coffined burials, the small size of these groups being the result of truncation or differential preservation, although it is also possible that some may represent residual material.

Hobnails indicate that shoes appear commonly as grave goods in the Roman period, though the relatively small numbers involved in many cases are unlikely to constitute whole pairs of shoes. In the case of cremation burials differential collection of material from the pyre for burial may result in the under-representation of hobnails, and deliberate selection may also play a part in the formation of the buried assemblage (McKinley 2000c, 41; Cool 2004, 391). In inhumation burials the presence or absence of hobnails may result from differing burial traditions related to the inclusion of grave goods. A number of the burials from London Road are entirely devoid of hobnails, suggesting that the individuals were not interred with shoes, or were buried with footwear whose construction did not involve the use of hobnails. The small numbers of hobnails in several graves may be the result of differential preservation, as also appears to have affected some of the skeletal material. In contrast some of the burials appear to have enough hobnails for more than one pair of shoes, a circumstance that has previously been noted in Romano-British cemeteries (Philpott 1991, 168).

THE SCULPTURAL STONE
by Martin Henig and Roger Tomlin

The two tombstones recovered during the course of the excavation have previously been published in the journal *Britannia*, largely from the standpoint of their inscriptions though incorporating a few comments on context and iconography (Tomlin and Hassall

2005). Photomicrographs of the tombstone geology can be found in Appendix 5.

Tombstone 1 (Plate 5.6)

Tombstone 1 was recovered from pit 1003, which was cut into the soil layer associated with the use of the cemetery (see Fig. 2.2 above). It is carved from a block of local oolitic limestone (from Painswick Hill, Glos, see Appendix 5), broken but mostly surviving in three main joining pieces with a number of smaller fragments. It measures 0.59 m in breadth, and the surviving height is 1.03 m though with a possibly gabled top and a base it may have reached some 1.30 m. The stele is 0.14 m thick.

The upper part of the stele displays within a niche, perhaps originally pedimented, a man reclining on a couch to the right and facing front. He wears a toga, pulled up to cover the back of his head, and holds the scroll containing his will in his left hand and a cup with fluted sides in his right hand. He is clean-shaven and his coiffure is characteristic of the Claudio-Neronian period though it should be noted that the banquet tombstones from Germany discussed below whose male subjects are shown with similar coiffure and physiognomy are all assigned Flavian or even Trajanic dates. The couch has a raised back with curved sides but the foot on the left of the stone is obscured by the figure of a slave-boy,

Plate 5.6   Tombstone 1 after cleaning and conservation.

while that on the right was on a missing portion of the stone. The head of the slave-boy is preserved, as is his left foot but the front of his body, which seems to have been wrapped in a cloak, has sheered off. In front of the man is a tripod table with curving widely-splayed legs, only two of which are shown, the position of the middle one being taken by a jug which stands on the ground line. The circular top of the table is depicted in flattened bird's eye view with two vessels, another cup, of scyphos form, and a bowl.

The stone was probably originally painted and there seems to be a reddish wash on the background to the head, though any other trace of colour appears to have been lost.
The inscription reads:

M[.]RTIALIS
C .[.]LONI Δ SERV[.]
[...]O Δ XIIII
[...] E
M[a]rtialis | G(ai) [Ci]loni serv[i] | [ann]o(rum) XIIII | [h(ic)] s(itus)] e(st)

'(To the shades of the dead and) of Martialis, the slave of Gaius Cilonius, aged 14. He lies here.'

The reading is fully discussed in Roman Inscriptions of Britain, III (forthcoming), but it may be noted that the absence of an introductory 'Dis Manibus', the genitive case of the name of the deceased, and Gaius Cilonius' lack of cognomen all point to a Claudio-Neronian date. His Italian nomen is uncommon, but probably cognate with the more common cognomen Cilo.

Discussion

The fact that the main figure is depicted wearing a toga and with his will suggests the tombstone was intended for a Roman citizen, though in the event it was used for a 14-year old slave. The carving must therefore have been executed prior to the inscription being added, and the tombstone was presumably bought 'off the peg'.

The character of the carving is of considerable interest. It is crisply cut, as is especially apparent in the folds of the toga, though the execution of the figure is much more schematised than, for example, the near-contemporary Legio XX tombstone of M.Favonius Facilis from Colchester (Huskinson 1994, 23). 1st century military grave stele from Germany include banquet scenes that are iconographically similar to the Gloucester stone, with a reclining clean-shaven man facing the spectator and a slave standing near the foot of the couch (Bauchhenss 1988, 43–9; Boppert 1992, 157–163), although stylistic contrasts between these thoroughly 'Roman' productions and what was produced at the same period in Gloucester are striking. It must be concluded that the latter workshop was a 'local' one with links to the army or indeed staffed by soldiers whose task was to produce tombstones, and perhaps also religious and commemorative monuments, for

the military community when required. It is surely significant that the closest parallels in terms of the shortened figure, the form of the table and the table top seen in bird's eye view are from Chester, although these do not date before the later 2nd century or even the 3rd century, and differ in points of detail, such as the position of the servant who is often behind the couch, or in front and not at the foot (Henig 2004, 14–16).

It is reasonable to see such stylistic links as there are between tombstones which are carved in different materials (those from Cheshire being of sandstone not limestone) as well as belonging to different periods as being due to a continuing tradition in Legio XX's lapidary workshop. The legion was stationed at Gloucester during the mid-1st century, but it should be noted that connections continued with legionaries retiring to the *colonia* as exemplified by a tombstone of a veteran, L. Valerius Aurelius found at Kingsholm some years ago.

Tombstone 2 (Plate 5.7)

Tombstone 2 is likewise carved from local oolitic limestone, and is broken into a number of pieces. It measures 0.51 m in width by at least 1.00 m in height and is some 0.11 m thick. The recessed panel on the front face of the stele is divided into two

Plate 5.7 Tombstone 2 after cleaning and conservation.

unequal parts. The upper edge of the top part is arched and displays a facing bust. Despite the brushed-forward Julio-Claudian hair, the style of presentation is native, as exemplified by the subject's jug-ears, ovoid eyes, small wide-open mouth and wedge-shaped nose. Immediately below the head he sports a large circular amulet. On the left edge a lobate leaf is inscribed.

The inscription reads:

L Δ OCTAVI
L Δ POL
MARTIALIS
EPOREDIA
M Δ LEG XX

L(uci) Octavi | L(uci fili) Pol(lia tribu) | Martialis | Eporedia | m(ilitis) leg(ionis) XX

'(To the shades of the dead and) of Lucius Octavius Martialis, son of Lucius, of the Pollian voting-tribe, from Eporedia, soldier of the Twentieth Legion.'

This reading again is fully discussed in Roman Inscriptions of Britain, III (forthcoming), and the absence of the introductory 'Dis Manibus', and the genitive case of the name of the deceased indicate a Claudio-Neronian date. The lack of the legion's cognomina V(aleria) V(ictrix) also suggests an early date, but the omission of the age of the deceased and his years of service, and perhaps of a concluding formula like h(ic) s(itus) e(st), is unusual rather than significant of date. Martialis' home town, Eporedia in Italia Transpadana, modern Ivrea north of Turin, is already known to have contributed soldiers to four other legions.

Discussion

The inscription shows that this was the tombstone of a soldier of the XXth legion, but it is far inferior in style to the other Gloucester tombstone, and perhaps the work of an amateur or novice mason. For the purpose of commemorating the dead, the portrait of the deceased was important, either as a free-standing bust or a relief, but accurate delineation of physiognomy was clearly not important as the subject of the 'portrait' would have been identified by the inscription which would be read out by those who came to pay their respects or by the traveller passing the grave. The bearded head of Q. Cornelius, probably also of Legio XX, from 3rd-century Chester provides a parallel of sorts (Henig 2004, 17).

The leaf like form is reminiscent of the decoration of an early Legio II tombstone from Alchester, Oxfordshire, ornamented with triangular motifs in the spandrels which look like carrot amphorae but are probably leaves (Sauer 2005, 103 and fig. 1). The contrast between the low level of artistic competence here and the relatively high level of the epigraphy is intriguing. While in the case of Tombstone 1 surely two men, a sculptor and a lapidarius were involved, it is possible that in the case of Tombstone 2 either there was a competent lapidarius and an amateur

sculptor, or else the lapidarius himself had a shot at carving the bust. Maybe something similar happened in the case at Alchester where a crescent moon was inscribed remarkably like a letter 'C'.

OTHER WORKED OR UTILISED STONE
by Ruth Shaffrey

The only item of worked stone apart from the tombstones was a fragment of roof tile recovered from back-fill of a cremation burial of 1st–early 2nd century date (1227). The tile was composed of Oolitic limestone weighing 401 g and had two surviving edges indicating a diamond shape.

Among the unworked stone recorded were three fragments of micaceous lower Old Red Sandstone, a stone known to have been used locally as roofing material, recovered from medieval and post-medieval contexts. They are all small fragments without clear evidence of working, although shallow grooves on one side of a thickish piece from the medieval soil layer (1025) indicate that it had been used as a whetstone.

THE CERAMIC BUILDING MATERIAL
by Cynthia Poole

A total of 154 fragments (7418 g) of ceramic building material of Roman to modern date was recovered from the excavation, as well as two fragments of fired clay (4 g). Roman material accounted for nearly half the assemblage by weight (3348 g), but only 38% of the Roman material occurred in Roman contexts, the remainder coming from features of later date.

No complete tiles were recovered, the assemblage comprising fragmentary and heavily abraded material, some pieces with score marks that may have derived from ploughing. Over half the material identified as Roman could not be positively identified to form, and could only be described as flat tile, brick or unidentified (Table 5.6). The remainder of the assemblage comprised pieces of tegula and inbrex, with a single ceramic tessera. No markings (signatures, stamps, tally marks, combing, imprints) were noted on any pieces.

No evidence was found for the use of tiles as grave covers or markers, which has been attested at Roman

Table 5.6 Quantification of Roman ceramic building material by form.

Form	Nos.	% Nos	Wt (g)	% Wt
Tegula	7	8.75	775	23.15
Imbrex	13	16.25	703	21.00
Flat / brick	32	40	1418	42.35
Brick	5	6.25	223	6.66
Tessera	1	1.25	14	0.42
Unid	22	27.5	215	6.42
Total	80	100	3348	100

cemeteries elsewhere (Philpott 1991, 10–11 and 66–7). If any had been employed in such a manner here more complete examples would be expected, whereas the pieces that were found in grave or cremation fills were small and already heavily abraded when deposited. The character of both the Roman and later material is more typical of a rural context subject to agriculture, with nearly two-thirds of the assemblage being moderately to heavily abraded, probably as the result of cultivation. This suggests that much of the material may have arrived through manuring or dumping of refuse from the town.

THE ANIMAL BONE
by Fay Worley

Introduction

The assemblage comprised 1464 fragments of unburnt animal bone, and a further 540 fragments (2.7 kg) of cremated animal bone were recovered from cremation burial deposits. The animal bone was identified as precisely as possible to taxon and element using faunal reference material and identification manuals (Cohen and Serjeantson 1996; Hillson 1996a; Schmid 1972). A full methodology for analysis can be found in the site archive.

Results

The assemblage comprised 883 hand collected bone fragments, dated from the Roman to the modern periods (Table 5.7), plus 581 fragments recovered from sieved residues (Table 5.8). In addition to these, 540 fragments (2.7 kg) of cremated bone were recovered from cremation burial deposits (Table

*Table 5.8 The animal bone assemblage from sieved residues quantified by NISP. * denotes that NISP count includes at least one partial skeleton. This table includes some burnt bones.*

Species	Roman	Post-medieval	Total
Cattle		3	3
Pig?	1		1
Mouse		1	1
Domestic fowl	90*		64
Bird	11	6	18
Megafauna	1		1
Large mammal	24	8	32
Medium mammal	1		1
Small mammal		1	1
Micro mammal		1	1
Unidentified	290	114	458
Total	418	134	581

5.9). The modest size of the post-Roman assemblages limits their potential for interpretation beyond presence or absence of taxa. The majority of data related to the Roman cemetery, although much of this material derived from grave backfills and may be accidental inclusions.

The condition of the assemblage was variable, ranging from very good to poor. The identified faunal assemblage was dominated by domestic mammals including cattle, sheep, sheep/goat and pig. No bones were identified as goat. Equid (probably horse) was also identified in the Roman and post-medieval assemblages, and dog in the Roman and medieval assemblages. Domestic fowl was prevalent in the Roman assemblage, but also

*Table 5.7 The hand collected animal bone assemblage. * denotes that NISP count includes at least one partial skeleton. This table includes some burnt bones.*

Species	Roman	Medieval	Post-medieval	Modern	Total
Cattle	28	11	13	5	57
Horse	20		5		25
Dog	1	1	2	41*	45
Sheep	1			1	2
Sheep/goat	8	13	10	7	38
Pig	6*	5	7	5	23
Hare				1	1
Rabbit			2		2
Hedgehog			1		1
Rat	1				1
Vole			1		1
Domestic fowl	29	1		1	31
Goose		1			1
Pigeon			1		1
Bird	15		1		16
Bird?			1		1
Large mammal	78	30	61	17	186
Medium mammal	40	25	30	32	127
Unknown	261	11	49	3	324
Total	488	98	183	114	883

Life and Death in a Roman City

Table 5.9 The cremated animal bone assemblage quantified by NISP, MNI, MNT and weight.

Data		Cremation burials						Inhumation	Total
Burial		1196	1209	1766	1767	1768	1769	1720	
Total number of fragments (NISP)		16	16	166	10	5	325	2	540
Total weight (g)		20.8	11.9	86.8	48.6	1.8	118.7	5.8	274.7
Taxa present	Pig			✓			✓		-
	?pig	✓		✓			✓		-
	?cattle				✓				-
	Medium mammal	✓	✓	✓	✓	✓	✓	✓	-
	?medium mammal			✓					-
	Medium/large mammal			✓	✓			✓	-
	?large mammal	✓		✓					-
	?bird						✓		-
	Indeterminate						✓		-
Minimum Number of Taxa (MNT)		1	1	2	2	1	2	1	-
Minimum Number of Individuals (MNI)		1	1	3	2	1	2	1	-

present in the medieval and modern assemblages. One goose bone was present in the medieval assemblage and one pigeon bone in the post-medieval assemblage. Other wild taxa identified include rabbit, rat, mouse and vole in Roman deposits.

Animal bone from cremation burials

Cremated animal bone was recovered from four of the five urned cremation burials and two unurned cremation burials (Table 5.9). Full details of these assemblages can be found within the cremation records in Appendix 4.

Animal bone from inhumation burials

Faunal remains, all comprising domestic fowl skeletons, were deposited as grave goods with three burials (Table 5.7). In burial 1505 the domestic fowl skeleton was recovered from within a vessel in the grave. The fowl in 1288 exhibited a small cut mark on its humerus. The third domestic fowl skeleton was recovered from the backfill of inhumation 1759, which may have been a cenotaph rather than a normal burial. Perhaps unsurprisingly with such a small dataset, there is no association of the fowl grave goods with a particular demographic profile.

Possible inhumation burial or 'memorial' 1149

It is uncertain whether this feature was a grave or some other form of deliberate 'memorial' deposit

(see Chapter 6), as no human bone was recovered. The feature contained a flagon and eight unburnt animal bones including a right forelimb pork joint (humerus, radius and ulna) from a pig aged between 12 and 42 months old at death. The context also included a cattle calcanuem and three medium mammal sized bone fragments.

Material from grave back-fills

Animal bone was recovered from the back-fills of 21 graves. The majority of this assemblage is unlikely to comprise grave goods but rather residual material incorporated into grave back-fills accidentally. This material is not considered further here. No burnt bones were recovered and only one bone exhibited butchery marks (see inhumation 1288 above).

Animal bone from the mass grave

The mass grave contained two groups of small-found animal bone. Small-find sf 340 comprised a fragmented sheep/goat left femur and tibia, a cattle carpal and some indeterminate bone fragments. The sheep or goat bones may have been deposited while articulated and may represent a meat joint or butchery/food debris. The bones were in fair to very poor condition and no butchery marks were observed. Small-find sf 405 comprised 24 domestic fowl bones from an adult cock skeleton. The identified skeletal elements comprised pelves, femora, tibiotarsi and tarsometatarsi (with spurs), a

120

right humerus and radius, a left carpometacarpus, the sternum and synsacrum and several vertebrae and foot phalanges. Soil samples from this deposit contained additional bird bones which may have originated from this skeleton. The burial pit also contained a dog-gnawed medium mammal long bone and three indeterminate bone fragments and two cattle carpals, a large mammal patella and eighteen further domestic fowl bones. Several large mammal, medium mammal and indeterminate bone fragments were recovered from sieved soil samples.

Animal bone from other features

An assemblage of 132 fragments of animal bone was collected from the soil layer associated with the use of the cemetery (1020/1106/1440) including cattle, sheep/goat, horse and dog. This group included an articulating horse right radius and ulna, left and right femora, a right humerus, left and right innominates, skull fragment and seven maxillary teeth. While epiphyseal fusion data could indicate that the long bones originate from a single animal aged approximately 36–42 months old at death, tooth attrition data suggests the presence of a considerably older horse's skull. The small size of this assemblage together with its provenance negates further interpretation of animal husbandry at Gloucester.

Discussion

Burnt animal bone was recovered from seven of the nine cremation burials. The amount of burnt animal bone in each burial varied from 1.8 g (5 fragments) to 118.7 g (325 fragments). The majority of the animal bone fragments were off-white in colour indicating complete calcination. A few fragments were less well burnt but this may be of no significance as variation in pyrolysis between fragments need not indicate that they originate from different pyre goods or different stages in the cremation process (Worley forthcoming a). The animal remains were all highly fragmented and exhibited fine fracture lines and fissures characteristic of burnt bone. No concentric fractures were identified and no conclusions can be drawn as to the fleshing levels of the pyre goods when cremated.

The vast majority of burnt bone fragments were unidentifiable but some fragments could be identi-

fied as pig, possible pig, possible cattle and possible bird. Further fragments were recorded as medium, medium/large or possible large mammal sized. The burnt bone grave assemblages each contain the remains of one or two taxa. Most contain a minimum of one individual of each taxon with the exception of 1766 which contains the remains of at least two pigs. No butchery marks or pathological lesions were noted in the burnt bone assemblages. Given the taphonomic pathways of cremation burials and problems of identification of the highly distorted and fragmented burnt bones, the pyre goods can be interpreted as complete pig carcasses in burials 1209, 1766 (together with remains of a second pig) and 1769, a minimum of a pig skull and limb in burial 1196, a minimum of a medium mammal skull and limb, with a large mammal rib in 1767 and a medium mammal limb in 1768. As no other medium mammals were specifically identified in the assemblage, the medium mammal pyre goods may also be pig.

Animal pyre goods have been recovered from Roman cremation burials elsewhere in Britain, the largest assemblage being that from the Eastern Cemetery of Roman London (Barber and Bowsher 2000). The frequency of cremation burials containing recognised faunal pyre goods at Roman cemeteries tends to be lower than that observed at London Road (typically 5–47% of burials in cemeteries where seven or more burials were analysed for faunal pyre goods: Worley forthcoming a), although 80% of urned burials at Ryknield Street, Wall, Staffordshire, contained faunal pyre goods (McKinley forthcoming). Many other sites include pig pyre goods, although they are generally less common than domestic fowl pyre goods in Roman Britain (Worley forthcoming a). The Severn region includes published Roman faunal pyre good assemblages from Cowbridge (Parkhouse and Evans 1996) and Lodge Hill Cemetery, Caerleon (Evans and Maynard 1997) in south Wales, the Bathgate (McWhirr *et al.* 1982) and Oakley Cottage (Reece 1962) cemeteries in Cirencester, and Abonae (Bennett 1985) in Bristol. None of these Severn region cemeteries exhibits a dominance of pig pyre goods as recorded for the London Road, Gloucester burials. However, pigs were the most common mammalian pyre goods at Roman cemeteries in Eastern London (Barber and Bowsher 2000), Derby Racecourse

Table 5.10 Fish bones recovered from soil samples taken from burials.

Burial	Context	Sample/spit	Context type	Quantity	Taxon	Element
1767	1062	<213>spit 5	Cremation deposit	1	pike	vertebra
1767	1062	<212>spit 4	Cremation deposit	1	?clupeid	vertebra
1196	1190	<59>	Cremation backfill	2	clupeid	vertebra
1209	1198	<68>	Cremation backfill	2	clupeid	vertebra
1114	1123	<22>	Inhumation: chest area	1	Eel	vertebra
1131	1132	<12>	Inhumation: abdomen	1	clupeid	vertebra
1360	1361	<172>	Inhumation: abdomen	1	clupeid	vertebra

(Wheeler 1985), St Stephens in Hertfordshire (author's observation) and Ryknield Street, Wall (Worley forthcoming b).

Animal grave goods are also often recovered from inhumations in Roman Britain. Birds, particularly domestic fowl, are often identified (Lauwerier 1993; Philpot 1991). Both domestic fowl and pigs provided a source of food in Roman Britain, consumption of pork and chicken may even have been relatively high status and an expression of Romanised identity. However, both species were also associated with deities and funerary sacrifice in Roman literature (although the literary sources refer to practice in Rome rather than Britain). Male domestic fowl were associated with chthonic deities and are often illustrated on tombstones (for example at Abonae; Bennett 1985, 62). While the pig and fowl pyre and grave goods at London Road may represent food offerings, their potential symbolic significance should not be forgotten. We cannot determine the intention of those arranging the funerals regarding the animal remains but the growing body of evidence suggests that the use of pig pyre goods and domestic fowl grave goods in Roman burials in Britain may have conformed to broad traditions.

THE FISH BONE
by Rebecca Nicholson

A small number of fish bones were recovered from several soil residues after processing soil samples from the cremations and inhumations (Table 5.10). In all cases the bones were unburnt. The bones from cremation burial 1767 were recovered from soil samples taken from the contents of the cinerary urn and may have been placed deliberately, but the material from cremation burials 1196 and 1209 comes from the back-fill and may be accidental inclusions. The bones from inhumation burials were recovered from samples taken from the chest and abdomen areas of the skeletons, but whether they were associated directly with the body or are accidental inclusions is uncertain. Species represented included small clupeids (herring *Clupea harengus* or sprat *Sprattus sprattus*), eel (*Anguilla anguilla*) and juvenile pike (*Esox lucius*). While pike and eel are both found in rivers and ponds and could have been fished locally, the clupeids were most likely to have been salted or pickled fish. Small oily fish such as clupeids were a common ingredient in *garum*, a fermented fish sauce much favoured by the Romans.

Chapter 6   Discussion of the Roman Cemetery

INTRODUCTION

The site at 120–122 London Road is the first substantial area of the Wotton cemetery to be excavated and published to modern standards. The excavation comprised an area of 0.1 hectares and resulted in the recovery of the remains of at least 165 individuals from graves, cremation burials and the mass grave. Although the existence of the cemetery has been known since the 19th century, discoveries have mainly been piecemeal, information deriving from observations made during the 19th century development of the area and from more modern records during small-scale ground disturbances. This has resulted in a rather unsatisfactory and disjointed hotchpotch of observations, with no overall coherence. The only previous excavation of a substantial area of the cemetery was carried out at the adjacent property, 124–130 London Road, but the results of this investigation have not yet been published (Foundations Archaeology 2003).

As one of only three *coloniae* established during the early part of the Roman period in Britain, Roman Gloucester had an unusual status and history, being a community of Roman citizens established *de novo* in a recently conquered territory. The excavation of part of one of its main burial grounds affords an opportunity to study the effects of the imposition of this alien community, and the resultant meeting of native and immigrant cultures as expressed through their funerary practices. The early date for the first burials, contemporary with the legionary fortress at nearby Kingsholm that preceded the establishment of the *colonia*, has provided a rare opportunity to examine the burial practices of the military community and the changes following the transition to civilian occupation. Furthermore, the discovery of a rare mass grave, possibly representing the victims of an epidemic, has afforded an opportunity to examine a cross-section of the population selected in all likelihood by chance rather than by rules governing access to the cemetery (See Chapter 3 and discussion below).

Certain caveats must be borne in mind when examining the evidence from the cemetery. Obviously, the area investigated by the excavation is only a small sample of a large cemetery, and conclusions based on the analysis of this sample may not hold true for the cemetery as a whole. In particular, it is considered likely that this area of the cemetery was used by a relatively low status section of the population (see below). Even within the area excavated, survival of graves may be only partial: the northern and western ends of the site have been truncated in modern times resulting in the loss of any burials in these areas. Some degree of horizontal truncation may have occurred across the remainder of the site due to later cultivation, and may have resulted in the loss of an unknown number of shallower burials, with the result that the burials excavated may be the survivors of an originally much greater concentration. Such destruction by later development is a feature of the Wotton cemetery, and indeed of Roman urban cemeteries in general. The customary siting of Roman cemeteries around the periphery of the urban area has made them particularly vulnerable to depredation from the effects of the expansion of the towns over the past two centuries. The development of 19th century suburbs may have exposed the existence and scale of these cemeteries, but it also inflicted permanent and widespread damage on many of them.

THE DEVELOPMENT OF THE WOTTON CEMETERY

The siting of the cemetery

The location of the cemetery at the junction of the main approach roads leading to both the fortress and the river crossing is unlikely to be accidental. Roman law dictated that cemeteries should be placed outside the city limits, and it was customary to locate them alongside the main roads approaching the settlement. Funerals in the Roman world were very public affairs, intended as a display of the social status of the deceased and his or her heirs, and it was also considered important for the well-being of the spirit of the deceased that the grave should be located where it would be visible to the most passers-by, who could then pay their respects while passing. The establishment of a burial ground at a very visible location in the landscape, on the crest of a hillock in the otherwise flat base of the Severn Valley, may also have been intended as a physical expression of the permanence of the Roman presence and their dominance of the surrounding landscape and its native population. Over the following three centuries the cemetery developed into a necropolis extending for more than 500 m along the road to the *colonia* and would have formed a dramatic sight for visitors approaching the city.

The growth of the cemetery

The cemetery appears to have been established on land previously used for farming, as indicated by the ploughmarks recorded in the north-eastern part of the site. The earliest burials recorded during the excavation are two cremation burials containing pottery datable on stylistic grounds to the pre-Flavian period

(AD 49–69) and a third that yielded a radiocarbon determination of 50 BC–AD 70 (OxA-16792 cal 2 sigma). These earliest burials, and six cremation burials of similar date recorded on the adjacent plot at 124–130 London Road (Foundations Archaeology 2003) are contemporary with the use of the fortress at Kingsholm, which is believed to have been occupied from AD 49 until the mid 60s. Their presence here suggests that the Wotton cemetery was one of the main burial grounds associated with the fortress, along with the eastern part of the cemetery which later occupied the Kingsholm area, where a small number of similarly early burials have been found (Rawes 1991, 231). A lone inhumation burial from 124–130 London Road was attributed to this period by the excavator on the basis of a stratigraphic relationship that indicated that it was earlier than a late 1st–early 2nd century cremation (Foundations Archaeology 2003), but its 1st century date is not certain, particularly as it contained sherds of 2nd century pottery. No other burials of this early date have been reported

from within the Wotton cemetery and it is possible that at this stage the cemetery was limited to a handful of burials in a small area to the south of the junction of Ermin Street with the road linking it to the site of a presumed crossing of the River Severn near the modern city centre (Fig. 6.1; and see Chapter 1, Fig. 1.3).

There appears to have been a substantial increase in both the number and the area of burials during the late 1st to early 2nd century AD. This expansion is broadly contemporary with the occupation of the legionary fortress at the city centre and the establishment of the *colonia*, and it is tempting to attribute it to a deliberate act of policy, extending the burial ground of the former fortress to serve the needs of the new settlement. However, the dating evidence for both the expansion of burials and the founding of the settlement is not sufficiently clear-cut to demonstrate this beyond doubt. Burials of this date have been found over an area measuring *c* 375 m in length, extending from 83–89 London Road to

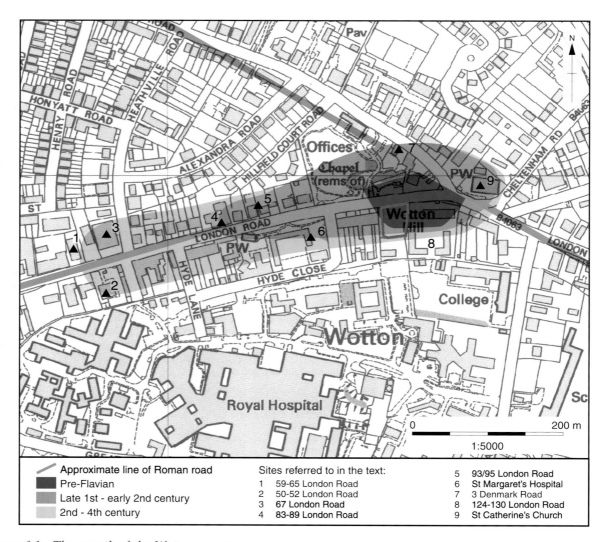

Figure 6.1 The growth of the Wotton cemetery.

St Catherine's Church at the junction with Ermin Street (Fig. 6.1). At 124–130 London Road the late 1st to early 2nd century burials extended further south, suggesting that the cemetery may also have expanded further back from the road at this time. It is also from this period that the earliest evidence has been found for burials located to the east of Ermin Street, at St Catherine's Church (Wills 2000, 226) and 3 Denmark Road (Atkins and Garrod 1988, 216; Rawes 1992, 221), and on the north side of the road linking the *colonia* to Ermin Street, at 93 London Road (Heighway 1980, 63). At St Margaret's Hospital, a group of five cremation burials of this date was arranged around the edge of an area of metalling, and this may be evidence that the formal layout of the cemetery was established at this time. The four crouched burials from the present site were also interred during this time and are likely to be the remains of members of the native population who had settled at the *colonia* or who had been integrated in some way into its population but continued to practice their traditional burial customs.

During the 2nd century cremation was gradually superseded by inhumation as the main funerary rite throughout the Roman empire (Jones 1987, 816), and the majority of the otherwise undated graves are likely to belong broadly within the 2nd–4th centuries AD. The area used for burial appears to have expanded again during this period, with inhumation graves having been recorded further along London Road toward the *colonia*, at 50–52 London Road and 67 London Road, as well as being found throughout the area already in use (Fig. 3.1). It is unclear whether the growth of the area used for burial represents expansion into an area that had been reserved for burials but had hitherto been unused, or the extension of the cemetery into an area formerly given over to some other use. Hurst (1999b, 121) has suggested that an area of open ground existed as a buffer between the *colonia*'s north-western suburb and the cemetery, but the discovery of the beam slots of a building during an evaluation at 59–65 London Road (Atkins and Garrod 1987, 233) may indicate that the suburb extended further than he allowed, and that the expansion of the cemetery in its final phase brought it almost into contact with the extra-mural settlement.

It is not possible to establish an accurate date for the end of the cemetery, although there is evidence that it continued in use well into the 4th century. This much is clear from the two sequences of graves in the south-eastern and western parts of the excavation, both of which started with burials accompanied by vessels dating from the 3rd to 4th century. In addition to this, the ring and bracelet worn by the individual buried in grave 1362 are of 4th century date. Three graves at 124–130 London Road contained 4th century coins, with two of these dating to no earlier than AD 348, indicating that burial continued until at least the middle of the century. Due to the small number of datable burials it is not possible to assess whether the use of the

cemetery petered out gradually or came to an abrupt halt, but the evidence indicates that it persisted until at least the mid-300s, and in all probability continued until organised urban life within the *colonia* had largely ceased around the end of the 4th century or early 5th century AD.

The layout and organisation of the cemetery

Little evidence survives to indicate how the cemeteries of Roman Britain were managed, but clearly a major urban cemetery such as that at Wotton, serving the population of the *colonia* and possibly of the surrounding *territorium*, would require some degree of centralised administration. Such management would be necessary to ensure that a sufficient area was available for burials, maintain its upkeep, administer the allocation of individual plots, possibly to provide for the proper carrying out of burial rites, and perhaps to ensure that only burials of eligible individuals were allowed within the prescribed area. A professional class of individuals entrusted with the task of burial is known to have existed in Rome (Bodel 2000, 135–44) but it is not known whether similar individuals existed in Britain.

The clearest surviving evidence for the management of the cemetery lies in its spatial organisation. The boundaries of the cemetery were not located within the excavation, and indeed no boundary features have been identified in other investigations within the Wotton cemetery. The provision of clearly defined physical boundaries to enclose the area given over to burial and separate it from land occupied by the living was an important consideration in the Roman world as contact with the dead was considered to be ritually polluting (Toynbee 1971, 50–1). Urban cemeteries elsewhere in Britain have been found to lie within boundaries defined by ditches, presumably accompanied by banks (eg Poundbury, Farwell and Molleson 1993, fig. 33; Butt Road, Colchester, Crummy *et al.* 1993, 13). At Winchester the boundaries of the cemetery at Lank-hills School were defined by both a ditch and a hedgeline (Clarke 1979, 109–10). It is likely that similar boundaries existed at Wotton and either await discovery or have been destroyed by the more recent development of the area. The excavation at 124–130 London Road demonstrated that burials did not extend much further south than the southern edge of the current site (Foundations Archaeology 2003) and it is likely that the southern boundary of the cemetery lies only a short distance away.

No evidence was found for the sub-division of the part of the cemetery within the area of the excavation, but urban cemeteries elsewhere have been found to be sub-divided internally by boundary ditches to form discrete plots or enclosures (eg Barber and Bowsher 2000; Farwell and Molleson 1993). However, three sides of a rectilinear ditched enclosure recorded at 124–130 London Road may be evidence for such enclosures at Wotton. The enclosure appears to have originated during the 2nd century as a single boundary ditch, oriented NNW-SSE at right angles to the line of Ermine Street. This was subsequently superseded by the north-western side of the enclosure, the ditch of which silted up during the 3rd century. The enclosure did not mark the edge of the cemetery, as further graves were identified beyond it to the east, but it appears to have been kept clear of graves, as the only burials identified within it were a pre-existing cremation burial, a 3rd or 4th century grave that may post-date the use of the enclosure, and a single undated inhumation. The function of this apparently empty enclosure within the cemetery is uncertain, although the identification of gravel surfaces elsewhere within the cemetery suggests that open areas were not uncommon. The excavators suggested that the enclosure may have been a private burial plot containing a high status burial, although no evidence of such a burial survived to support this interpretation (Foundations Archaeology 2003). Although it would have been a significant feature of this part of the cemetery, the enclosure does not seem to have had any influence on the orientation of nearby graves.

The distribution of burials is ostensibly hapha-zard, although some evidence for more deliberate organisation is apparent when examined in more detail. The earliest burials are too sparsely scattered to enable any coherent pattern to be identified, and a similar circumstance was recorded at 124–130 London Road, where the pre-Flavian cremations were quite dispersed, although they were generally located in the northern part of the excavation, nearest to the road linking Ermine Street with the site of the second fortress and *colonia*. Burials at this time appear to have been dotted around the area of the cemetery in a relatively dispersed distribution.

The layout of the cemetery from the 2nd century onward is more easily understood, due to the greater number of burials and the replacement of cremation by inhumation as the dominant rite. Graves lie on a variety of orientations, but two main trends can be identified (see also discussion on grave orientation below). The first of these is a number of graves oriented NE-SW or NW-SE, parallel and at right angles respectively to the line of the road linking the *colonia* to Ermine Street. The aligning of graves according to pre-existing boundaries is a common occurrence in Romano-British cemeteries, and this road would clearly have been a dominant feature in the layout of the cemetery, forming the route along which funeral processions would have proceeded from the *colonia* to the burial site. The eight inhuma-tion burials excavated at 3, Denmark Street were similarly aligned parallel and at right angles to the line of the adjacent part of Ermin Street.

A further group of graves was oriented N-S or E-W. These included the group of 3rd–4th century burials toward the western edge of the distribution of burials (1264, 1353, 1369, 1370) and most of the similarly dated graves in the south-eastern part of the excavation, as well as a number of graves at 124–130 London Road that may be an extension of the latter

group (Foundations Archaeology 2003). The apparent preference for cardinal orientations displayed by most of the graves to which a 3rd–4th century date could be assigned may suggest an increase in the level of organisation of the layout of the cemetery at this time, although the apparent clustering of the graves dated to this period in two distinct areas suggests that this still comprised discrete clusters of burials distributed sporadically across the cemetery, perhaps in individual plots, with unused areas or areas of older graves in between. A similar shift from scattered, haphazard burials to regular rows of east-west oriented graves also occurred at around this time at the cemetery at Kingsholm (Atkins 1987).

The burials were not distributed evenly across the area but were located in clusters of varying size and density, separated by 'blank' areas. While the effects of later truncation may have played some part in creating this pattern, it is likely that this is a true reflection of the layout of the cemetery as similar variations in the density of burials have been observed in cemeteries elsewhere in Roman Britain (eg Barber and Bowsher 2000, 300–1). This clustering may derive from the desire of members of family or other groups to bury their dead in close proximity, and may represent discrete plots within the cemetery that were maintained over a long period of time. The group of 3rd–4th century burials in the south-east part of the excavation has the appearance of being buried in such a plot, and the clusters of burials formed by graves 1143, 1144, 1151, 1167 and 1759, and graves 1228, 1229, 1230, 1761 and 1762 may be similar groups. In the latter group, dating evidence from 1st to 4th century suggests that these plots may have persisted over a considerable period of time.

The areas between graves may have been occupied by surface features that did not survive to be recorded during the excavation, such as trees or hedges, or may have resulted from the need to maintain open spaces in which to conduct funerary rites, to provide access to graves and to separate burial plots belonging to different groups. There is evidence from a number of locations within the Wotton cemetery for gravel surfaces, whether these were paths or more substan-tial open areas. A watching brief undertaken during the digging of service trenches at St Margaret's Hospital in 1976, for example, recorded an extensive metalled surface with cremations arranged around its fringes (Heighway 1980, 64) and parts of gravel surfaces associated with the cemetery have also been recorded at 50–52 London Road (Rawes 1983, 192) and St Catherine's Church (Wills 2000, 226). The largest open area thus far identified is the enclosure at 124–130 London Road, although no evidence was recovered to indicate that this area was metalled.

The overall pattern of burials at 120–122 London Road then is of a discontinuous and irregular distribution of burials, with little evidence for any attempt to impose a controlled layout. This con-trasts with the evidence from some urban ceme-teries, such as Lankhills School, Winchester (Clarke 1979, fig. 105) and Poundbury, Dorset (Farwell and

Molleson 1993, fig. 10), where the graves were placed in neatly regimented rows. Although some low level of organisation can be demonstrated at London Road, in the form of small groups of graves with common orientations, this seems more likely to result from the decisions or preferences of the groups conducting individual funerals than from any form of central control. This pattern may have arisen from sporadic use of this part of the cemetery over an extended period of time, although it is also possible that the site lay in a peripheral area of the cemetery where control was more lax.

The area examined is set back somewhat from the frontage of the road, particularly since the Roman road was located to the north of the line of the present London Road (Fig. 6.1, Spry 1971, 4). Burial plots on the road frontage are likely to have been the most prestigious, due to their greater visibility and the consequently increased opportunity for display that they afforded, and it is possible that the area investigated, being more marginal, was of lower status. This would explain the apparently rather modest treatment of the dead, with few grave goods and little in the way of exotic material, and in particular the absence of practices associated with higher status burials elsewhere during the late Roman period, such as lead or stone coffins, mausolea or plaster burials. Although the presence of tombstones to mark at least two graves hints at more provision for these burials, these date from the military phase and may not be relevant to the status of this part of the cemetery subsequently. The low status attached to this area may also explain why the mass grave was dug here.

Mausolea have been identified within the Wotton cemetery at 50–52 London Road (Rawes 1983), St. Margaret's Hospital (Heighway 1980, 63–4; Rawes 1993, 224) and 3 Denmark Road (Rawes 1992, 221) and may represent burials of a more high status part of the population. In addition to this, burials have also been discovered accompanied by multiple ancillary vessels at 3 Denmark Road (ibid., 221) and St Catherine's Church (Wills 2000, 226), and accompanied by ceramic lamps at St Margaret's Hospital (Rawes 1993, 224) suggesting that a wider range of funerary rites was practised by the population of the *colonia* than was evident within the area excavated. The burials in this area may therefore not be characteristic of the whole of the population of the *colonia*, or representative of the entire range of funerary customs practised within the cemetery, but perhaps represent the burials of only a lower stratum of society.

FUNERARY RITES

The funerary process

Roman traditions regarding the treatment and disposal of the dead are preserved in numerous written, epigraphic and iconographic sources, most of which refer to the practices of the upper echelons of society and are geographically biased toward the core provinces of Italy and the Mediterranean. Nevertheless they provide an indication of the sort of funerary ritual and practices that we might expect to encounter at an urban cemetery such as that at Wotton. Obviously this is not intended to suggest that all the individuals buried within the cemetery necessarily shared the same beliefs or were buried according to precisely the same rites, as it is clear from the physical evidence that a range of different customs was current within the cemetery. As a fortress, *colonia* and port Gloucester is likely to have had a diverse population with a corresponding variety of funerary and burial practices, but at its heart it was a community of individuals who are likely to have aspired to the values and customs of the classical world.

The funeral process began when the deceased breathed his or her last breath, and could last for a number of days until the remains were ultimately interred. During this period, the body was prepared and dressed in clothes appropriate to the status of the individual and was laid out in his or her house for mourners to pay their respects. On the day of the funeral the corpse was carried in a procession to the cemetery, where valedictory speeches may have been addressed to it before the final disposal, although it is uncertain how common the latter practice was outside aristocratic circles. During the early Roman period the body would then be cremated and the cremated bone buried, sometimes in a ceramic or glass vessel, but during the 2nd century cremation declined in popularity throughout the Roman world and was superseded by inhumation as the main burial rite (Jones 1987, 816).

Much of the funerary process will have left no archaeologically identifiable evidence. Clearly the lying-in-state and the funeral procession took place away from the place of burial, and even if artefacts buried with the body or otherwise deposited at the site of the grave had been used during these parts of the funerary process it would not be possible to establish this. This is particularly unfortunate as these may have been the most important parts of the funeral, with the act of burial itself being a relatively minor element. Certainly the lying-in-state and procession would have provided an opportunity for displays of grief and demonstrations of the wealth and status of the deceased to a far larger audience than could be accommodated at the graveside. It is important therefore to bear in mind that the evidence recovered from the excavation of the grave is likely to relate only to the final act of the funerary process, and to avoid assumptions that this was the focal part of the funeral.

Cremation burials

The pyre

Cremation burials during the Roman period took one of two forms: *in situ* cremation, in which the body was burnt at the place of burial with a pit dug beneath the pyre to receive the remains (a *bustum* burial), or cremation at a location reserved for this activity (an *ustrinum*), with the ashes subsequently buried elsewhere. All eight cremation burials discovered were of the latter type, representing burials of burnt remains collected from a pyre. No physical evidence for *ustrina* or dumps of pyre debris were excavated, and none has been identified elsewhere within the Wotton cemetery, although clearly such installations can be assumed to have existed somewhere in the vicinity. Possible evidence for the use of such sites was recovered from cremation burial 1767. The deposit of cremated bone in this grave contained three mandibular condyles from the right side of the mandible (see Chapter 3), and although this may represent the deliberate inclusion of three individuals in a single burial, it is equally possible that it results from the accidental incorporation of remains from individuals cremated previously on the same *ustrinum*. The absence of direct evidence for pyre sites is particularly unfortunate as items used in rituals conducted at the pyre may have been left on the pyre site itself (Polfer 2000). However, evidence for funerary rites conducted at the pyre can be extracted from material from the pyre incorporated, whether deliberately or accidentally, into the subsequent burial deposit (Pearce 1998).

The quantity of fuel required to cremate a human body represented a significant investment of resources, and the burning of the corpse would have provided a considerable spectacle within an important and dramatic part of the funeral. The colour of the bone recovered from the cremation burials was predominantly white, reflecting successful cremation at a temperature over 600–700°C, although limited incomplete burning was indicated by the presence of some brown/black/blue fragments (See Chapter 3 for discussion on efficiency of cremation). This would suggest that although some considerable pains were taken to ensure thorough burning of the corpse, some body parts escaped complete cremation, probably depending on the depth of overlying soft tissue and/or their position on the pyre.

Evidence for pyre goods incorporated into cremation burials is generally more common than the occurrence of grave goods in inhumations. This reflects the central role that the pyre played in cremation rites, as the main focus for the dedication and destruction of objects (Barber and Bowsher 2000, 308). The most common pyre goods recorded at 120–122 London Road were animal remains, which were recovered from six of the nine cremation burials. The quantity of the animal remains placed on the pyre is difficult to establish due to the partial nature of the collection of debris from the pyre for burial, but it is likely that these remains represent complete pig carcasses in three burials and at least part of a pig carcass in burial 1196. The evidence demonstrates a clear preference for pig as a pyre offering, particularly as the bones from medium sized mammals recovered from two further burials

are probably also the remains of pigs (See Worley, Chapter 5). The significance of these offerings is difficult to ascertain. In particular it is uncertain whether they were intended as food offerings for the deceased, or as offerings to the chthonic deities intended to ease the individual's passage into the underworld. In either case, the selection of a species whose consumption may have been associated with high status would have been appropriate. The possible presence of the entire carcass clearly indicates that the offerings were not limited to joints of meat, and may represent the remains of animals sacrificed as part of the funerary ritual.

Apart from the animal remains very few pyre goods were identified from the cremation burials, although this may partly be an accident of the process of collecting cremation remains for burial as there is no reason to believe that the inclusion of such items in the burial deposit was done intentionally. The remains of glass unguent bottles were found in three cremations, and there were two such vessels in feature 1352 which dated from the late 1st–early 2nd century and would have been contemporary with the use of cremation in the cemetery (See Cool, Chapter 5). Similar vessels have been recorded elsewhere within the Wotton cemetery at 124–130 London Road (Foundations Archaeology 2003) and 3 Denmark Road (Rawes 1992, 221). These sorts of bottles were commonly used for holding oil for bathing, and presumably those found with these cremation burials had been used to cleanse the body before cremation. It is possible that the deposition of these, and other items, involved deliberately throwing them onto the pyre in order to smash them, whether to symbolically kill them and thus transform them into the same state as the deceased, or to commit them to the deceased by placing them beyond the use of the living. In relation to this it is interesting to note that Wigg (1993) has suggested that material used in funerary feasts was deliberately destroyed, and has identified a number of deposits at cemeteries in Britain and elsewhere in the northern provinces as resulting from this practice. The only evidence for ceramic offerings at the pyre that was preserved in the buried remains was a single burnt rimsherd from a locally made jar recovered from cremation burial 1766. Although so workaday a vessel may appear out of place in the context of funerary ritual, it is likely to be the contents rather than the container that were of significance.

The pyre would have had to be left for some time to cool before the cremated bones could be collected for burial—perhaps it was left overnight and the funeral party, or some part of it, returned the following day for the final act of the funeral.

The grave

The weights of the deposits of cremated bone recovered from the cremation burials were consistently less than the average weight of *c* 1000–3600 g that would be expected from the cremation of a complete human body (see Chapter 3 for details). This may partly be explained by the truncation which had clearly affected most of the features, removing the upper parts of the cinerary urns in burials 1196, 1209 and 1227 and reducing the three unurned cremation burials to depths of no more than 70 mm. However, the two deposits of cremated bone that had not been truncated were similarly underweight. Deposit 1062 was more substantial but it may represent the combined remains of three adults (see above). The low weights for these untruncated bone deposits suggest that the apparent underrepresentation of bone in all nine cremation burials may be a product of funerary practice rather than of taphonomy. McKinley (1993b, 41–3) has suggested that all cremation deposits are essentially token, and the contemporary sources indicate that the burial of only a portion of the corpse was a requirement of cremation ritual (Toynbee 1971, 49). There is, then, evidence that the deposits of cremated bone buried at 120–122 London Road result from the collection from the pyre of only a portion of the cremated bone as a token to symbolically represent the entire individual. Evidence has been recorded at other sites for the disposal of the remainder of the debris from the pyre in a variety of locations including grave back-fills, pre-existing features, deliberately excavated features and as surface spreads (McKinley 2000a, 41–2), but no such remains were identified here.

Six of the nine cremation burials recorded in the course of the excavation were buried in ceramic containers (1196, 1209, 1227, 1266, 1766, 1767). This appears to have been the standard form of cremation burial at Wotton, although cremation burials in glass vessels have been recorded at St. Margaret's Hospital. At both this site and at St. Catherine's Church, cremation burials placed within urns were further contained inside stone cists (Heighway 1980, 63–4). Apart from the three examples excavated here, only two examples of cremation deposits without containers have been recorded within the Wotton cemetery, at 124–130 London Road (Foundations Archaeology 2003) and St. Margaret's Hospital (Heighway 1980, 64). However, it is possible that similar features have simply not been noticed elsewhere due to the nature of the investigations.

Five of the six cinerary urns at 120–122 London Road are locally made jars in a grey fabric, and there is some doubt as to whether the only exception, burial 1227, is in fact a grave (see below). It is possible that this consistency in the type of vessel used represents a deliberate choice. Similar vessels were used for cremation burials at 124–130 London Road (Timby forthcoming), and although urns from a greater range of sources have been recorded elsewhere within the Wotton cemetery, the preference for vessels in reduced fabrics is still common, with Black Burnished ware used at 124–130 London Road (ibid.), 83–89 London Road (Sermon 2003, 55) and 93–95 London Road (Heighway 1980, 63).

Ancillary vessels were placed with four of the six urned cremation burials (1196, 1209, 1266, 1767), and exclusively comprised flagons in oxidised fabrics. Three of these burials contained a single ancillary vessel and one (1196) was buried with two such vessels. Both cinerary urns and ancillary vessels were sourced locally, and there is some evidence that they may have been re-used rather than made specifically for deposition with burials. All are forms that are common in domestic assemblages in Gloucester, and cinerary urn 1061, in burial 1767, had traces of a thin white calcareous deposit on the interior of the base sherds that may be the result of prior use. These vessels were clearly not selected for deposition with burials due to any intrinsic value, and were presumably viewed as being as utilitarian in this context as in more domestic circumstances, serving simply as containers for offerings to accompany the dead. The preference for flagons suggests that these offerings were most commonly liquid, whether intended as a drink or libation. Strangely, the cinerary urns and ancillary vessels in burials 1266 and 1767 lay on their sides, having presumably been knocked over during the funeral or the backfilling of the grave pit and suggesting that little care was taken to avoid or correct such accidents.

The practice of using greyware jars as cinerary urns, accompanied by one, or in one case two vessels in a contrasting colour was also found in six of the 17 cremation burials excavated at 124–130 London Road (Timby forthcoming). The colours of these vessels may to some extent reflect the general trend in Roman Britain for using dark fabrics for cooking vessels, suitable for containing cremated remains, and oxidised fabrics for vessels used in serving and consumption, such as the flagons selected here to accompany the burials. However, the consistency of the pattern at Wotton raises the possibility that a standardised package of vessels was being used for deposition in burials, perhaps resulting from the employment of professional undertakers or representing a standard burial rite provided by a burial club (Biddulph 2005, 37). Membership of such a club was a means by which an individual could guarantee an appropriate funeral, in return for the payment of a regular subscription during life. Cremation burials elsewhere within the Wotton cemetery display greater numbers and types of vessels, an exceptional example including a burial at St. Catherine's Church that had been buried in a large pear-shaped storage vessel accompanied by three pear-shapes jars and two fine ware cups, as well as a samian dish placed within the urn (Wills 2000, 226) A burial at 3 Denmark Road in a large double-handled wine flagon was surrounded by an assemblage of ten samian vessels including two small and two large form 27 cups, three small form 35 dishes, and two large and one small form 18/31 bowls, with an additional form 27 cup inside the urn (Rawes 1992, 221).

The only non-ceramic grave goods recovered from cremation burials were an assemblage of 27 hobnails scattered throughout burial 1769 and four hobnails from burial 1209, including one that was inside the cinerary urn. Due to the corroded condition of the hobnails it is not possible to determine whether they are burnt, and so it is uncertain whether they accompanied the body on the pyre, perhaps worn, or were deliberately added to the deposit of burnt bone prior to burial. In either case, the symbolism of the provision of footwear is presumably associated with the belief that the deceased required footwear in order to undertake a journey to the afterlife (Philpott 1991, 173). The possibility that organic materials were placed in the grave which have not survived is raised by the positions of the cinerary urn and ancillary vessel in burial 1266, which were placed to one side of the grave pit, leaving a large space in the south-western half where such items could have been placed. Other grave goods recorded from cremation burials within the Wotton cemetery include ceramic lamps at 124–130 London Road (Foundations Archaeology 2003) and St. Margaret's Hospital (Heighway 1980, 64), coins at St. Margaret's Hospital (Heighway 1980, 64), 3 Denmark Road (Rawes 1992, 221) and St. Catherine's Church (Wills 2000, 226), and a metal pin and part of a copper spoon at 124–130 London Road (Foundations Archaeology 2003).

Additional sherds of pottery were recovered from the back-fills of four cremation burials (1196, 1209, 1227, 1766). These assemblages were more varied than the pottery placed in the burials, including products of the Severn Valley industry in addition to the more local wares. The inclusion of such sherds within cremation burials has also been noted at several sites within the Wotton cemetery (eg Sermon 2003, 55) and the likelihood is that at least some of this material was incorporated into the graves accidentally during back-filling. However, the presence of the smashed remains of two whole flagons in a burial at 3 Denmark Road (Rawes 1992, 221) suggests that some element of deliberate deposition may also be involved. This may be part of some ritual associated with the closing of the grave, possibly representing a separate form of offering from those accompanying the burial, or involving the deliberate destruction of vessels rendered 'unclean' by their use in the funeral rites.

Inhumation burials

Inhumation replaced cremation as the principal means of disposing of the dead throughout the Roman Empire between the late 2nd century and the late 3rd century (Jones 1987, 816), but there is some evidence that inhumation was practised at London Road at an earlier date. Five inhumations were attributed to the late 1st–early 2nd century, including a prone burial and four crouched burials. In addition, three extended inhumation burials produced radiocarbon determinations centred on the 2nd century, although the date ranges for the latter are admittedly rather large and do not discount

burial during the late 1st century or early 3rd century (see Chapter 2 for radiocarbon dates). The crouched burials are best seen as members of the native community, whose poorly understood funerary traditions seem to have comprised mainly excarnation, along with some evidence for crouched burial (Moore 2006, 111). Two examples of this practice are known elsewhere in the Wotton cemetery, from 124–130 London Road (Foundations Archaeology 2003, table 2), and St. Margaret's Hospital (Heighway 1980, 64). Slightly further afield seven crouched burials were found amongst an assemblage of 125 burials at Kingsholm (Garrod and Heighway 1984, 68). A similar 'native' interpretation might also be possible for the other early burials, as extended inhumations have been found in a 2nd century rural cemetery associated with a small native farmstead at Hucclecote, 5 km east of the *colonia*, where they surely represent members of the local population (Thomas *et al.* 2003, 65). These apparently early extended burials may be part of a local or regional native trend for such a burial rite pre-dating the widespread adoption of inhumation, although if so this tradition was clearly very circumscribed, as Booth's (2001) survey of the Oxfordshire Roman cemetery evidence identified no inhumations dated to before the 4th century.

The precise date of the widespread adoption of inhumation at London Road is uncertain due to the small number of burials accompanied by datable grave goods. No grave goods were found dating from the 2nd century, either at 120–122 London Road or in previous excavations within the cemetery, but it is unclear whether this is because few burials were made during this period or if the practice of depositing such items was not in vogue at this time. Inhumation was certainly the only burial practice identified during the 3rd and 4th centuries, when a number of burials were accompanied by grave goods.

Placing the body

The inhumations were placed in grave pits that were generally rectangular or sub-rectangular in plan and of a size to accommodate the body of the deceased. The choice of orientation for burial provides an opportunity for the expression of cosmological beliefs, as is found in the more recent Christian tradition of orienting burials west-east. Unlike some urban cemeteries from the Roman period (eg Clarke 1979; Farwell and Molleson 1993) the burials recorded during the excavation did not conform to a single consistent orientation, although this may partly be due to the graves representing a palimpsest of burials made over a considerable length of time. Nevertheless some patterns may be detectable.

Just over half the burials (50.8%) lay on cardinal orientations, divided almost equally between north-south and east-west. However there was little discernible patterning in the orientation of the bodies themselves in these groups, with at least five

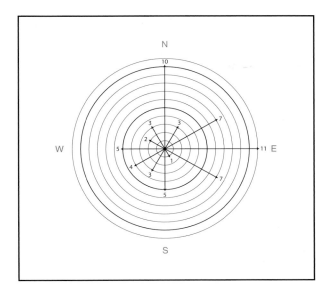

Figure 6.2 Orientation of inhumation burials, according to the position of the head (each segment represents an individual inhumation burial).

examples recorded of each of the four possible variations, although the placing of the head at the east and north ends of the graves was the most common with 11 and 10 examples respectively (Fig. 6.2). The current evidence is insufficient to establish whether these alignments contained some form of symbolism or simply resulted from an attempt to impose regularity to the arrangement of the cemetery through consistency of orientation. Of the remaining graves, 21 (34.4%) were oriented NW-SE or NE-SW, that is parallel or at a right angle to the line of the adjacent road, and it is likely that the alignments of these burials were influenced primarily by the physical boundaries of the cemetery and had no symbolic significance. As the majority of graves could not be assigned an accurate date it was not possible to analyse changes in orientation over time.

Beyond the selection of the location and orientation of the grave there is no evidence that the pit required further preparation before receiving the burial. Nevertheless, elsewhere within the Wotton cemetery a thin deposit of carbonised wood and fire-reddened soil on the base of the grave of a child aged *c* 6 years, associated with sherds of a Black Burnished ware jar, has been interpreted as the residue of a ritual preceding the placing of the body (Wills 2000, 226).

There is evidence that in some cases graves may have been deliberately re-opened for the insertion of new burials, perhaps due to a familial or other relationship between the individuals concerned (see discussion on grave markers below). A single example of the deliberate insertion of a later burial into an existing grave was noted at 124–130 London Road (Foundations Archaeology 2003).

The majority of the burials were placed in a supine posture, possibly due to a requirement for the body to be facing the mourners for the speeches which mourners addressed to the corpse (Barber and Bowsher 2000, 306).

Within the broadly uniform adoption of this posture, the position of the arms was somewhat more variable. The arrangement of the arms of those individuals that were sufficiently well preserved for this information to be established did not appear to be random, but conformed to a restricted range of positions (see Chapter 2 for details). These arrangements were presumably deliberately selected when the corpse was prepared for burial, but there appeared to be little consistency. Of the 20 adult burials in which both arms were preserved eight of the 16 possible combinations of arm positions were recorded, the most frequently encountered being with both hands resting on the pelvis (five instances), both beside the body (four instances) and with the left arm beside the body and the right flexed with the hand lying on the pelvis (four instances). No other combination was represented by more than two examples, and asymmetrical arrangements were slightly more common than symmetrical ones. There was no apparent correlation between arm position and other aspects of the burial. The three most frequent combinations of arm position are each divided equally between the sexes, excluding unsexed individuals, and do not correlate with specific age groups. Unfortunately too few graves could be dated sufficiently closely to establish whether there was any chronological patterning. The posture in which the body was placed in the grave was a matter of deliberate choice on the part of those conducting the burial (at least for non-shrouded bodies), and afforded an opportunity for subtle display of the status and identity of the individual, and the positions of the arms may have played a role in this. Unfortunately the apparent lack of coherent patterns in the arrangements recorded indicates that if this were so it is a code we are unable to read, although Barber and Bowsher (2000, 87) have pointed out that the asymmetric arm positions may mimic the 'toga position' of many Roman statues, with one arm folded across the waist and the other free, and it may be that the position of the arms is a consequence of the choice of clothing for the corpse. It may be relevant to note that the classical sources specifically state that a Roman citizen would be buried wearing a toga (Toynbee 1971, 44).

Discrepant burial rites: prone and decapitated burials

The burial of six individuals face down in a prone position represents a practice that was carried out on a minority of burials at many cemeteries of the Roman period (Philpott 1991, 71–6). The dates of these six burials span the period of use of the cemetery, ranging from the late 1st–early 2nd century, when burial 1145 was buried accompanied by a ring-necked flagon, until the 3rd–4th century, when a coin dated to AD 270–95 was incorporated into the back-fill of prone burial 1230 and burial 1537 was interred in grave 1765 in the group of late burials in the south-eastern part of the excavation. The remaining three examples (1143, 1150, 1234) were undated and consequently it is not possible to demonstrate whether the practice became more popular here during the later part of the Roman period, as has been found elsewhere (ibid., 78–9). Although the rite appears to have been more common on rural sites, some indication of the proportion of burials in urban cemeteries positioned in this way can be gathered from the 3.3% of the burials from the eastern cemetery of Roman London (Barber and Bowsher 2000, 87). In addition, 3.9% of the 308 burials at Lankhills School, Winchester for which a posture could be confidently established were prone (Clarke 1979, table 10), and a single example was excavated at Poundbury, Dorchester (Farwell and Molleson 1993, 65). A further six prone burials were found during the excavation at 124–130 London Road, including two from the preceding evaluation phase (Foundations Archaeology 2003), giving a combined figure of 12 prone burials for the two areas. This is a rather high figure, representing 11.2% of the 107 burials for which a posture could be established, although 8.8% of the burials excavated at the Bath Gate cemetery, Cirencester, were prone, and it is possible that the practice was more common in this region than elsewhere. Alternatively, the high proportion of prone burials recorded in the two excavations on London Road could be a function of the locations of the two excavated areas toward the southern margin of the cemetery, as it has been suggested that discrepant burials are often distributed toward the edges of the area of burial (Philpott 1991, 73). Although just over half the inhumation burials lay on cardinal orientations none of the prone burials was on these alignments, but it remains uncertain as to whether this is significant.

The remains of the individuals buried in this posture provide little evidence to explain why they were selected for this treatment. They range in age from an adolescent male (1112, grave 1143) to a mature female (1103, grave 1150), and although females outnumber males by four to two, a bias also seen at the eastern cemetery of London (Barber and Bowsher 2000, 87), the numbers of prone burials from both sites are not large enough to be considered statistically significant. At 124–130 London Road the sexes were represented equally and the age range was even greater, the assemblage comprising two juveniles and four adults aged 40 or over (Foundations Archaeology 2003).

The individuals buried prone in burials 1143 and 1765 were both interred with their hands behind their backs, and it is possible that they may have been bound, indicating some element of coercion, whether associated with sacrifice or judicial execution. (Philpott 1991, 72). Unfortunately the forearms of the individual in grave 1143 were truncated just

above the elbows during machining and consequently it is not possible to be certain whether they were tied together at the time of burial, while the evidence from burial 1765 is inconclusive as the arms of the individual are not sufficiently close together to demonstrate whether they were bound.

A number of possible explanations have been advanced for the practice of prone burial, including the possibility that they are accidental, resulting from undertaker error when dealing with sealed coffins or shrouded bodies or a simple lack of care on the part of those conducting the burial (McWhirr *et al.* 1982, 78–81; Philpott 1991, 72). Alternatively, the rite may have been intended as an act of disrespect toward the deceased. A lack of care could explain the slightly twisted posture of skeleton 1127 in burial 1145, and it is possible that the burial in grave 1230 was shrouded, but generally the prone burials appear to have been placed carefully, lying in fully extended postures in graves no different to those dug for supine burials. The positions of the arms are varied, but no more so than those of the supine burials, and there are no examples with the haphazard, sprawled postures to be expected from bodies carelessly thrown into the grave, and demonstrated on this site by the bodies in the mass grave. The apparently deliberate placing of the body, and the provision of a coffin in grave 1765 and pottery grave goods for this and burial 1145, suggest that the majority of the prone burials were interred with some degree of care, and that they represent a deliberate burial rite used for selected individuals.

A fear of the potentially malign influence that the dead could have on the world of the living was a concern that shaped many aspects of funerary practice in the Roman world (Toynbee 1971, 33–9). Esmonde Cleary (2000, 137–8) has suggested that the practice of enclosing cemeteries within physical boundaries was intended to prevent the dead from wandering. Prone burial may have been one measure taken to prevent this in the case of particular individuals, intended to prevent the deceased from escaping from the grave, whether bodily or in spirit form. The minority of the buried population who were selected for prone burial may thus be the remains of individuals for whom this was thought to be a particular concern, perhaps due either to the circumstances, timing or nature of the particular individual's death or to their being outcasts or in some way marginalised by society during life. Perhaps they were individuals who, though their appearance or behaviour, were feared or viewed as aberrant or unusual, but not so far beyond the pale as to be denied a place in the community's burial ground. If this is correct, then the marginal status of these individuals in life may be mirrored by their burial in a marginal part of the cemetery away from the more prestigious area on the road frontage.

The individual in grave 1234 had been decapitated in addition to being buried face down. Due to the loss of the upper part of the body there was no evidence from this grave to indicate the means by which the head was removed, but evidence from other Romano-British cemeteries indicates that decapitation usually took place after death: the removal appears most often to have been performed from the front, and was accomplished with a level of precision that would not be possible with a subject whose blood was still flowing (Harman *et al.* 1981, 166; Philpott 1991, 78). The reasons for decapitating the corpse are uncertain, although the occurrence of both rites in the same individual suggests that their purposes could overlap. Like prone burial, it may have been intended to prevent the dead from walking, but it is equally possible that the rite was believed to be beneficial to the deceased, perhaps intended to release the soul and enable it to pass on to the afterlife.

It is impossible to be sure whether those individuals who were buried prone or decapitated were afforded the funerary rites that other individuals were entitled to, but these unusual practices would have had certain implications for some aspects of the funerary process. At the very least, placing the body in the grave face down or with the head removed would appear to be inconsistent with addressing valedictory speeches to it, and the opportunity for display of the corpse at the grave would clearly have been diminished. It is also unknown at what stage in the funerary process of decapitated burials the head was removed. It could have been done at the death bed immediately after death, at the graveside, or even after the body was placed in the grave, and would have introduced an additional element to the process of burial, possibly one that formed the central act.

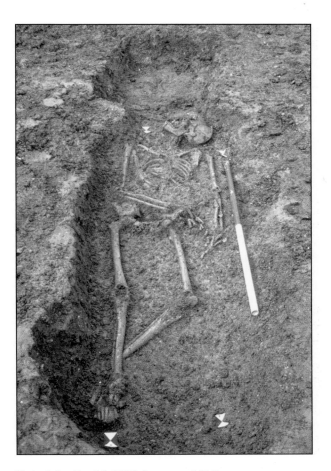

Plate 6.1   Burial 1313 in grave 1315.

Containing the body: coffins, cists and shrouds

Groups of nails indicative of the presence of coffins were recorded *in situ* in a total of 19 graves and smaller numbers of nails that may also indicate the former presence of coffins were recovered from a further 21 burials. Some of these assemblages may comprise material incorporated into the back-fills of graves accidentally and it is thus not possible to establish the exact number of graves that contained coffins. However, the presence of nails in 40 of the 66 inhumation graves within the area of the excavation indicates that a substantial proportion of the graves contained burials in coffins secured by nails, and is consistent with the results of the excavation at 124–130 London Road, where only five of the 37 graves failed to produce nails (Foundations Archaeology 2003). It is also possible that graves without nails may have contained coffins whose construction did not require nails, perhaps being secured by jointing or wooden pegs. The use of such techniques in the construction of coffins has been demonstrated elsewhere by the identification of graves containing coffin stains without nails (Farwell and Molleson 1993, 44–5). No coffin stains were identified at London Road, and in this case nothing would survive to indicate the presence of the coffin.

That some burials were made without the use of a coffin is demonstrated by bodies lying in positions that preclude the presence of a container, such as burial 1313 in grave 1315 which lies in a somewhat 'sprawled' posture and appears to have been deposited rather casually (Plate 6.1). Due to the uncertainty as to whether some of the smaller nail assemblages represent coffins it is not possible to establish the number of burials placed in nailed coffins and so comparison with other sites would be unproductive. This uncertainty and the large number of undated graves also hamper any attempt to assess changes in the prevalence of coffined burials over time.

The groups of nails from most of the graves were small, and none contained definite evidence for an upper layer used to secure the lid, raising the possibility that some burials were interred on biers or with open coffins, although coffins could have been covered with un-nailed boards once the appropriate rituals were complete. The only coffined burials with grave goods were burial 1374, which was accompanied by a pottery vessel, and burial 1360 in grave 1362, which was wearing a bracelet and ring. If the vessels were placed during the funeral, or were at least intended to be displayed during it, the coffins must have been open for at least part of the ritual; perhaps they were open when lowered into the grave, and the lid only secured once the coffin was in place, prior to back-filling. Barber and Bowsher (2000, 310) have suggested that coffins may not have been closed until the last possible moment in order to keep the dead person's face visible to the mourners while they recited the valedictory speeches.

A single burial (1756) was provided with a stone cist formed from five slabs of limestone set on edge to form a trapezoidal box, a practice not previously observed for inhumation burials within the Wotton cemetery. No capstones were found, but these may have been removed by subsequent truncation or deliberate robbing. Although examples of cist burial are known in the Gloucestershire area from the Iron Age the majority of datable instances recorded from Roman contexts belong to the 4th century (Philpott 1991, 61–2), and are thus too far separated in time from the pre-Roman examples to argue convincingly for continuity. The placing of an inhumation within a stone cist may have its origins in use of similar cists to contain cremation burials, examples of which have been recorded within the Wotton cemetery at St Margaret's Hospital (Heighway 1980, 63) and St Catherine's church (Heighway 1980, 64). Burial within a stone cist may have been regarded as equivalent to the provision of a coffin, albeit in a more robust material, but why this form of burial was chosen for a specific individual is uncertain. It is possible that the cist was intended to provide a chamber for the spirit of the deceased to inhabit, as it was popularly believed that the spirit remained at the place of burial (Toynbee 1971, 37–8). Alternatively the intention may have been to protect the body, as the late date of most burials of this sort would be contemporary with the increasing influence of Christianity and its doctrine of bodily resurrection, perhaps leading to a greater concern with ensuring the physical preservation of the body.

Evidence for the use of shrouds or winding-sheets is unlikely to survive in most circumstances due to the decomposition of the materials used. Some evidence has been preserved in the form of textile impressions in gypsum burials at York and Dorchester (Crowfoot 1981), but it uncertain how common the practice was. If the selection of clothes in which the deceased was dressed for burial was an expression of his or her status within society a shroud would clearly not be desirable, although such indications of status may not have been universal. No material evidence for the use of shrouds was found in the excavation, but it is possible that the posture of burials in which the arms are tight to the body and the legs close together indicates that they were wrapped in such a way. Seven such burials were identified (1146, 1151, 1218, 1230, 1501, 1503, 1508), including prone burial 1230. It is possible that these examples of discrepant postures result from undertaker errors caused by the shrouded bodies. All four potentially shrouded burials for which a date could be established were of 3rd–4th century

date, perhaps indicating that the use of shrouds at Wotton was a phenomenon of the later part of the Roman period, although the suggestion that any of these bodies were wrapped in shrouds is admittedly somewhat speculative. Burial 1151 was interred in a coffin, but as the gypsum burials demonstrate, the use of a shroud could be complementary to the provision of a coffin rather than the two representing alternative modes of burial.

Adorning the body

Three corpses were buried wearing or accompanied by items of jewellery. It is of course impossible to know whether these items were placed on the body specifically for burial or whether they were habitually worn during life, and perhaps at the time of death. The individual in burial 1362 wearing a copper alloy bracelet (sf 216) on the left arm could not be assigned a biological sex from osteological evidence, but the wearing of bracelets is normally associated with female burials. At Lankhills School, Winchester, the wearing of bracelets appeared to be particularly associated with younger girls (Gowland 2001, 162), but the individual at London Road was aged 18–25 years and may be part of a local tradition of adult women wearing such items, as the three individuals discovered previously at Wotton associated with bracelets were all adults (see Cool, Chapter 5). This burial also contained a ring or earring (sf 219), although it is uncertain from the excavation records whether this item was worn at the time of burial or simply placed with the corpse. In addition to this burial, an adult of indeterminate sex buried in grave 1505 was buried wearing a copper alloy ring on the third or fourth finger of the left hand and a child aged 5–12 years buried in grave 1246 was accompanied by an iron finger ring, minus its intaglio. The latter item was not worn at the time of burial but may have been deliberately placed as a grave good, as iron rings were worn as a sign that the wearer was a Roman citizen (see Cool Chapter 5). In burial contexts they are commonly lacking the intaglio as this was removed and handed on to the individual's heir.

Accompanying the body: food and drink

Six burials were provided with ceramic vessels, which presumably contained items of food or drink. This total includes burial 1352 which contained no human remains and may have been a cenotaph or memorial rather than a grave, and which is considered in more detail below. None of the burials contained more than one vessel, and the vessels themselves clearly played no part in displaying the wealth or status of the dead person as they appear to have been standard domestic types (see Timby, Chapter 5), and a chip missing from the rim of the flagon in burial 1145 suggests that they may not have been new when deposited. It is probable that the vessels were purely utilitarian in their role in the funerary rites, and that it was their contents that were significant. The Black Burnished ware jar placed in grave 1505 contained the partial skeleton of a domestic fowl, and parts of similar birds had been placed in burials 1374 and 1759. This would have been a particularly appropriate offering to accompany the dead due to its association with Mercury, who was believed to lead the souls of the dead to the underworld (Philpott 1991, 206). No evidence survived for the contents of the vessels in the other burials. The flagons in burials 1145 and 1243 would have been most appropriate to holding liquid, perhaps to quench the thirst during the journey to the underworld, although if drinking vessels were provided to decant the contents into, then they must have been of organic material as no evidence for them has survived.

The range of vessel types placed in the graves is limited to locally made flagons, which only appear to have been deposited with the earlier burials (1145, 1243), and jars. A jar produced at the Gloucester kilns was placed with crouched burial 1334 during the 1st–early 2nd century and jars from regional sources were used during the 3rd–4th centuries to accompany burials 1374 and 1505, reflecting the wider range of sources of pottery available during the later period.

Vessels were normally placed near the feet, the only exception being prone burial 1145, where the flagon lay beside the head, the inversion of the vessel's normal position perhaps mirroring the inversion of the body.

Accompanying the body: footwear

Items of footwear with hobnailed soles were provided in at least 12 graves, and in six of these the individual was demonstrably wearing the shoes/sandals at time of burial. The numbers of nails from individual graves varied, presumably representing different types of footwear (see Powell, Chapter 5). The largest assemblages, comprising 178 hobnails from grave 1344 and 104 from grave 1369, may represent heavily shod boots, but could alternatively be more than one pair of footwear. The groups of hobnails associated with the right (37) and left (32) foot of the burial in grave 1234 and the hobnails associated with the right (22) and left (13) foot of the burial in grave 1330 (the latter with a further 28 hobnails unlocated), are consistent with Mills' (1993, 99) observation that the number of nails per shoe/boot in graves at Poundbury indicated the presence of styles of footwear with approximately 10, 35 and 50 hobnails. The smallest group that is accepted as representing footwear placed in the grave is the 18 hobnails from grave 1508, which would be consistent with Mills' most lightly shod category, possibly a light sandal. Those burials lacking hobnails cannot be assumed to have been without footwear, as shoes constructed without hobnails are likely to have been common, and formed almost half of a sample of about 147 shoes from Billingsgate, London (Rhodes

1980, 103). Hobnailed footwear is recorded more commonly on rural sites than in urban cemeteries, albeit with some exceptions (Philpott 1991, 167), possibly because the more rigorous lifestyle of the agricultural population required more robust footwear. The presence or absence of hobnails in any individual grave may therefore be an indication not of the provision or lack of footwear but an indication of the type of footwear worn by the individual buried therein, and be dependent on his or her occupation or lifestyle rather than on liturgical requirements. This suggestion would be consistent with the age range of the individuals provided with hobnailed footwear, who are all adults. All six individuals that could be assigned a more accurate age were aged between 18 and 45 years, with only one aged over 35 years, and so would have been in the prime of their working lives. The biological sex of seven individuals could be established, of whom four were female and three male, but at 124–130 London Road males buried with hobnails outnumbered females by 4 to 2, giving a small overall majority of males for the combined burial group.

The practice of placing items of footwear in graves away from the feet and thus clearly not worn at the time of burial, as in burial 1167, indicates that they were of more than purely mundane significance in a funerary context. Presumably the deceased was expected to wear these items in the afterlife, or was required to undertake a journey to reach the afterlife. Either of these interpretations would imply that the afterlife was envisaged as a very physical reality in which the dead existed in some corporeal form.

Commemorating the dead

The dead were not forgotten once buried, but were commemorated both by the erection of physical memorials and by a number of festivals and feasts that were features of the Roman calendar. The most elaborate form of memorial was the construction of a mausoleum to house the grave. No evidence for such structures was found at 120–122 London Road, although parts of possible examples have been recorded elsewhere within the Wotton cemetery (eg Heighway 1980, 63–4). It is possible that gully 1358 formed the eastern side of a feature enclosing a grave or group of graves to the west (see Chapter 2 and below), as similarly shallow gullies of rectilinear plan surrounded burials at Lankhills School, Winchester and have been interpreted as bedding trenches for hedgelines (Clarke 1979, 109). Unfortunately this is not capable of proof as this part of the site had been subject to truncation associated with an adjacent track, and no features survive that could be confidently associated with the gully.

Grave markers

The two sculpted tombstones discovered during the course of the excavation (see Henig and Tomlin, Chapter 5) bring the total now known from the

Wotton cemetery to five. Sadly none of these can be associated with a specific grave. It is uncertain how common the use of stone grave markers was in the cemetery, as many more may have been removed and broken up during subsequent periods for use as building stone, such as the example incorporated into the chapel of the hospital of St Mary Magdalen (Sermon 1995). It may also be significant that three of the five known tombstones are dedicated to soldiers and one of the stones found at 120–122 London Road, although dedicated to a slave, has been dated on stylistic and epigraphic grounds to the Claudio-Neronian period, contemporary with the occupation of the Kingsholm fortress. This admittedly small sample may indicate that stone memorials were a phenomenon of the military phase of the cemetery that did not catch on with the civilian population of the *colonia*, a pattern that Mattingly has observed throughout Britain more generally (Mattingly 2006, 202).

Presumably markers in less durable materials were more common, and have now perished. The absence of direct evidence for markers in materials other than stone may simply mean that they did not penetrate deeply into the ground and that any evidence for their existence has been removed by subsequent truncation, although postholes found in proximity to two cremations at 124–130 London Road may have held wooden grave markers. That graves were marked by some means may be inferred from the deliberate locating of graves in relation to previous burials. Graves 1218, 1288 and 1344 share a common orientation and graves 1264, 1370 and 1353 may also have been deliberately placed in an approximate line, both of which would require the locations of the earlier graves in these groups to have been marked in some way.

It is also possible that some instances of intercutting graves may represent the deliberate re-opening of the earlier grave, again requiring a marker to indicate its location. Grave 1722 was dug directly into the back-fill of grave 1721 and may represent the deliberate opening of the earlier grave to receive a subsequent burial, perhaps suggesting a familial or other relationship between the two individuals. A similar situation may be represented by graves 1283 and 1284, while the digging of graves 1228, 1229 and 1230 in approximately the same location, albeit on slightly varying orientations, could also represent deliberate re-use of a single burial plot. In the latter group, the burial in the earliest grave (1228) produced a radiocarbon determination of AD 70–240 (NZA 27006 cal 2 sigma) and the latest grave (1230) was dated to no earlier than AD 270 by a coin in the back-fill, suggesting that the graves were dug over some considerable length of time, and that in order for graves to be deliberately placed at the locations of existing burials the earlier graves must have been marked.

The majority of occurrences of graves intercutting with earlier burials however appear to be accidental, as one would expect in view of the customary Roman prohibition on disturbing burials. It is likely that either the earlier graves in such instances were not marked, or the marker had decayed by the time the later grave was dug. The case of three intercutting burials toward the western edge of the distribution of graves demonstrates that the digging of graves in such sequences could be separated by a considerable period of time. The earliest grave in this group, grave 1243, contained a burial accompanied by a pot of Flavian-Trajanic date and yielding a radiocarbon determination of AD 1–130 (NZA 27005 cal 2 sigma). This was partly truncated at its western end by grave 1288, which lay on a somewhat different alignment and contained a burial dated by radiocarbon to AD 60–240 (NZA 27007 cal 2 sigma). Both graves were subsequently cut by grave 1264, which can tentatively be dated to the late 3rd–4th century by its shared orientation with the more securely dated graves 1370 and 1353. Over such periods of time it is reasonable to presume that wooden grave markers would decay—though these may nevertheless have been inscribed and painted in the same manner and to the same standard as their stone counterparts.

Mourning and feasts

The completion of the funerary rites was not the end of the obligations of the living to the deceased, for the contemporary sources record that it was normal practice in Roman Italy at least for mourners to visit the grave on several occasions throughout the year to commemorate the dead (Toynbee 1971, 50–4). Indeed, it was not unusual for individuals to leave money in their wills to be spent on such commemorations (Hopkins 1983, 233). These occasions took the form both of public festivals, the most important of which was the *parentalia*, a festival of the dead lasting from February 13th to 21st, and more private observances such as the funerary feast eaten on the day of the funeral and celebrations on the birthday of the deceased. These celebrations usually took the form of a meal eaten at the grave-side, a portion of which may have been set aside for the deceased and libations poured. Scenes of dining depicted on tombstones, such as Tombstone 1, may refer to such meals, and occasionally graves were constructed with holes or pipes through which food and drink could be physically poured to the deceased, such as an example from Caerleon with a lead pipe (Toynbee 1971, 61 and plate 14).

At the Wotton cemetery these commemorative meals may be the source of the pottery and animal bone in the cemetery soil and incorporated incidentally into graves during back-filling, as well as the fish remains which may derive from the consumption during these meals of *garum* sauce. The makeup of these assemblages is more varied than that found within the graves, featuring quantities of Severn Valley ware and Dorset Black Burnished ware, small amounts of imported fineware, and sherds of amphora, and is more typical of a 'domestic' assemblage appropriate to the preparation and consumption of food than of a funerary assemblage. The setting aside of areas for such observances at the grave-side may be one explanation for the open areas and gravelled surfaces recorded at several locations within the cemetery (Heighway 1980, 64; Rawes 1983, 192; Wills 2000, 226).

Another form of memorial may be represented by the vessel crushed beneath Tombstone 2, which presumably lay on the ground surface when the tombstone fell and may have been placed deliberately as an offering on or beside a grave. Clarke (1979, 185) noted other possible examples of such 'surface offerings' at Lankhills, including an occurrence where two flagons and a pile of three coins were placed on the ground surface around the slight mound left by the back-filling of a grave.

Cenotaphs, memorials and ritual deposits

Four features originally recorded as burials contained no skeletal material (1149, 1352, 1759, 1763). Bone preservation throughout the cemetery was quite poor, with almost half the skeletons less than 25% complete, and it is possible that some of these features may have been graves in which the bone had simply not survived—feature 1763 in particular was the size and shape of a child's grave and was filled by a sterile deposit of re-deposited clay containing only sherds of pottery that are probably residual, and it is possible that the fragile bones of its occupant had simply decayed. However, the others contained more complex deposits and it is possible that some or all of them were not intended as graves. An inverted flagon had been placed at the centre of rectangular pit 1149, and two flagons and some animal bone had been placed at one end of feature 1352, the other half of which was occupied by a wooden box, with two glass unguent bottles placed to one side of it. Whether feature 1352 was a burial is very much open to debate, as although the box may have contained the remains of a child it would still be necessary to explain why the bones of the individual decayed while those of the animal did not. Feature 1759 was the only one of this group of features with the dimensions of an adult grave, but it is unlikely that it formerly contained a body that has since decayed completely as the partial skeleton of a domestic fowl, which would be less robust and more susceptible to decay, was preserved within it. Also, the feature was located among a cluster of other graves which presumably experienced similar ground conditions and in which skeletons were preserved. The items placed in these features have the appearance of deliberate deposits, representing an act of some significance. To this group can probably be added pit 1306, a severely truncated feature within which was the base of a flagon.

These anomalous deposits cannot be explained satisfactorily by recourse to arguments based on the decay of the bone or truncation of the feature, and seem to be the product of deliberate practices carried out within the cemetery. Furthermore, they form a rather heterogeneous group and may require different interpretations, although their locations within the cemetery suggest that some association with the dead is a common link between them. Feature 1759 has the physical appearance of a grave, albeit with the body lacking, and may be a cenotaph. A custom existed in the Roman world of creating an empty grave for individuals whose body was not available for burial, or occasionally for those buried elsewhere (Toynbee 1971, 54), and this grave-shaped feature may be such a monument. If the body was not available, the placing within it of a domestic fowl, the sacred animal of Mercury in his role as guider of souls to the underworld would be particularly appropriate to such a 'lost' soul. If feature 1352 is also a cenotaph, the objects in it represent a particularly interesting group. The feature dates from the late 1st–early 2nd century AD, when cremation was still the dominant funerary rite, and contained two flagons, two unguent bottles and a deposit of mammal bone. The inclusion of melted fragments of unguent bottles in cremation burials 1209 and 1766 suggests that it was usual for these items to be deposited on the pyre after use, but the two examples in this feature are intact and unburnt, as is the mammal bone. It is possible that this assemblage represents the package of items necessary to carry out a cremation ceremony, and that they have been buried because the cremation could not take place for some reason, perhaps because the body was not available.

Pits 1149 and 1306 are less obviously grave-like in form, although the vessels placed within them are similar to flagons placed as ancillary vessels with contemporary cremations 1145 and 1243. It is possible that these deposits related in some way to the funeral process, representing some form of ritualised deposition of items rendered unclean by use in funerary rites or debris from subsequent commemorative feasts. Or else they may be memorials, the pot in pit 1149 perhaps having been inverted to make it a more appropriate offering for the deceased, or to represent the deceased symbolically. Alternatively, they may not have been associated with burials, but represent some form of ritual deposit placed in the cemetery to communicate with or to draw on the power of the dead or the chthonic deities. Indeed, a number of classical authors refer to the popular belief that witches frequented cemeteries and made use of corpses in their practices (Hope 2000, 121–2).

In a similar vein, McKinley (2000c, 42–3) has discussed a group of cremation burials from a number of late Iron Age and Roman period cemeteries in Britain and France that contain very small quantities of cremated bone and has questioned their identification as graves, suggesting that they may more accurately be viewed as memorials. However, the difference between these two concepts is clearly blurred by the token nature of most deposits of cremated remains in the Roman period.

Cremation burials 1227, 1768 and 1770, which contained only 1.5–17.5 g of burnt bone, may be examples of this practice at the Wotton cemetery.

Funerary rites for children

Children are commonly under-represented in Romano-British urban cemeteries (Philpott 1991, 98) and the Wotton cemetery is no exception. Only seven individuals under the age of 12 years were recorded at 120–122 London Road, with a further three aged 13–17 years, and there is evidence that the younger group were afforded different funerary rites than those used for adults.

Three of the four burials of children below the age of 12 years were placed in a crouched position rather than the supine posture that was the norm for adolescents and adults. This posture precluded the use of coffins or shrouds for these burials, and may also have other implications regarding the rites carried out at burial: if a supine posture was associated with funerary orations addressed to the deceased, the use of crouched postures for children may suggest that such speeches were not a part of their burial rites. As such speeches praised the life and achievements of the deceased, they may have been considered inappropriate to the burials of children. If the suggested association between the positions of the corpse's arms and the clothing in which the deceased was dressed for burial is correct, then the use of a crouched posture may indicate that children were not dressed for burial in the same way as adults.

Cremation burial 1266, which dated from the late 1st to early 2nd century, may provide evidence for the different treatment of children in the provision of grave goods. This burial, which contained the remains of two children aged 5–10 years and 10–15 years and was the only instance of the cremation of non-adults, contained a set of gaming pieces and dice, the only cremation burial provided with grave goods other than ceramic vessels (See Cool, Chapter 5 for discussion of gaming set). Taylor (2001, 125) has noted that grave goods are more commonly provided to accompany the burials of children, and it is possible that this was intended to placate the spirits of individuals who had died before their time: particularly if the gaming pieces buried with cremation burial 1266 were treasured possessions of one or both of the individuals buried therein. The provision of a stone cist for the burial of the perinatal individual in grave 1756 may similarly be associated with the need to quiet the spirit of the deceased, whether intended to provide a chamber for the spirit to inhabit or to contain a potentially troublesome spirit. Prone burial is another practice that has been interpreted as intended to contain an unquiet spirit, perhaps as a result of early death. There is some evidence that this practice was common in burials of children, as skeleton 1112 in grave 1143 was an individual aged 13–17 years buried in a prone posture, and two juvenile burials at 124–130 London

Road were buried prone, one of which was also decapitated.

BURIAL AND BELIEF

The funerary rites of the individuals buried in the excavated part of the Wotton cemetery were informed by the religious and superstitious beliefs of the people conducting the funerals, and are our best evidence for the beliefs of the population of the *colonia* regarding the fate awaiting the dead. However, the relationship between burial practice and religious belief is not a straightforward one. Practice does not necessarily imply belief, and may rather be associated with fashion, tradition or group identity, and it is axiomatic within the study of funerary archaeology that such practices may have more to do with the deeds of the living than the dead (Parker-Pearson 1999). It can never be proved that the individual within a particular grave, or those conducting the funeral, genuinely ascribed to the beliefs expressed in the ceremony, but it is reasonable to infer that these beliefs were current among the community at the time. It is intended here only to sketch in outline some of the beliefs indicated by the burial practices recorded in the excavation, although the evidence suggests that the beliefs of individuals varied considerably, albeit perhaps within a common overall cosmology.

Although most of the burials appear to be ostensibly very similar, details such as the posture of the body and the provision of grave goods were very variable, indicating that a wide range of belief and superstition was current among the community. The contemporary written and epigraphic sources are concerned largely with the upper echelons of society and are geographically biased toward the core provinces of Italy and the Mediterranean, but they record a wide range of beliefs with no dominant orthodoxy (Hopkins 1983, 226–35). The most common beliefs implied by the evidence from the excavation appear to have been associated with the survival of the individual after death, and a belief that the well-being of the dead could be affected by the actions of the living: hence the need to provide a place for them, accord them the proper funerary rites, and commemorate them through subsequent feasts and physical memorials. The provision of nourishment in the form of the food and drink held in the pots placed in the grave, and of items of footwear, indicate that the dead were believed to have some form of corporeal existence. Furthermore, the placing in some graves of personal items such as the gaming sets in cremation burial 1266 and the jewellery worn by a minority of individuals may suggest that individual identity was thought to be maintained in death, a suggestion strengthened by the provision of tombstones or other grave markers commemorating the deceased.

The provision of these things at the grave suggests that the dead were believed to remain at the place of burial, but it is possible that this sojourn at the grave was only brief. The footwear placed in a number of graves may imply that the dead undertook a journey to reach their final destination, and the victuals buried with them may have been intended to nourish them only for the period before this, or perhaps as supplies for the journey. There is also a possibility that some goods placed in the grave or consumed on the pyre were intended not for the dead person, but as offerings to the chthonic deities to ease the passage of the deceased to the underworld. The domestic fowl placed in graves 1374, 1505 and 1759, for example, may have been offerings to Mercury, who in Roman mythology guided the spirits of the dead to the underworld and whose sacred animal this was. Perhaps the clearest example of a grave good placed as such an offering is the coin placed in the hand of an individual buried at 124–130 London Road—presumably payment for Charon, the ferryman who conveyed the dead to the underworld across the River Styx.

There are, however, indications that at least some of the dead were to be feared, and that measures were required to prevent them from exerting a malevolent influence on the affairs of the living. The burial of six individuals face down in a prone position may have been intended to prevent them from wandering, or perhaps even to imprison them in the grave and deny them access to the underworld, and the motive behind the burial of a gaming set with the two young children in cremation burial 1266 (see Cool, Chapter 5) may have been to placate them by the provision of a familiar and treasured possession. Indeed, even the placing of the dead in a discrete cemetery beyond the limits of the city and defined by physical boundaries indicates a desire to maintain a physical separation from the world of the living (Esmonde Cleary 2000, 137–8).

It has been suggested that burials with graves oriented east-west, with the head to the west, may represent the remains of Christians, particularly if they dated from the later part of the Roman period and were interred in a coffin and without grave goods (Philpott 1991, 239). All five burials on this orientation lacked grave goods, and three were coffined, but as coffins were common and grave goods rare in the excavation as a whole they are in no way remarkable in this, and so cannot reasonably be identified as forming a discrete group with a distinct burial rite. Indeed, the attributes considered to be characteristic of Christian burial rites are in fact typical of most burials from Roman Britain in the 3rd and 4th centuries, regardless of any religious affiliations (Barber and Bowsher 2000, 321–2).

THE MASS GRAVE

The discovery of a mass grave of Roman date is almost unparalleled in British archaeology. The only record of potentially similar features are two pits discovered in the 1870s during the construction of York railway station (RCHME 1962, 79). Unfortunately no detailed record of these pits was made,

although they were described as measuring 9 m long by 4.5 to 6 m wide with a depth of 3 to 3.5 m, and contained a disordered jumble of skeletons 'thrown into them in large numbers without order or respect, the feet often higher than the head' (ibid.). This description would certainly be consistent with deposits comparable to that at London Road, but otherwise the lack of parallels from other sites inevitably hampers attempts to interpret the circumstances in which they were made.

The aspect of the mass grave that most singles it out from normative Romano-British burial practices is the overt lack of formality in the deposition of the bodies. It was usually considered important in the Roman world that the dead should be treated with respect and disposed of with the proper ritual. Failure to provide a suitable resting place or to complete the burial rites adequately could result in repercussions for both the living and the dead, and cautionary tales warned that spirits suffering this fate might not pass to the afterlife and could consequently haunt the living (Hope 2000, 106). The rituals surrounding burial were also thought necessary to remove the ritual pollution associated with contact with the dead, while emotional, familial or social connections with the deceased would have provided a motivation to dispose of them in a respectful and compassionate manner. At London Road, although the burials appear to be of individuals of fairly low status and are not well furnished with grave goods, there has nevertheless been some effort made to ensure that the dead were buried appropriately. However, these obligations toward the dead appear to have been suspended in the case of those individuals interred in the mass grave, and clearly any interpretation of this deposit must explain this.

It is known that mass graves, referred to as *puticuli*, existed at Rome for the disposal of the remains of those who were too poor to afford a proper burial, or who left no family or other associates who could take responsibility for the funeral, and it is possible that the pit at London Road, and those at York, represent a similar practice. Although it could be argued that Rome, with its much larger impoverished under-class, was a special case, and no examples of *puticuli* are recorded outside Rome. It would nevertheless have been necessary for urban communities such as that at Gloucester to have some mechanism for dealing with corpses for which no-one else took responsibility. Such a scenario might also explain the demographic profile of the individuals buried in the pit, with its emphasis on young adults, perhaps representing individuals drawn to the town by its economic and commercial opportunities and who died without having developed the local social connections which might otherwise have given them the possibility of being afforded a more 'normal' burial (J Pearce pers comm). It should be borne in mind, however, that the skeletal remains provide no evidence that the individuals buried in the mass grave represent a distinct section of the community that was poorer or of lower status than those buried in the discrete burials. They were no less well nourished or less healthy, and appear to have derived from a single population, exhibiting a similar range of pathological conditions and non-metric traits. The results of the analysis of oxygen and strontium isotopes also suggest that they had a similar range of geographical origins. If the mass grave does indeed represent the last resting place of the poor and indigent, this might also explain why it was dug in a marginal part of the cemetery, away from the more prestigious area on the road frontage. The pits at York were similarly described as being located 'on the outskirts' of the Railway Station cemetery, which may have been an area of lower status burial relative to the more prestigious Mount Cemetery (RCHME 1962, 79).

However, it could be questioned whether a community the size of the *colonia* would have had a large enough destitute population to fill the pit, unless it was left open for an extended period of time during which the deposit accumulated through the repeated deposition of further corpses. The latter scenario is not impossible, as pits with a similar function in 18th century Paris are known to have remained open for several months or even years (Ariès 1981, 56). There is, however, some evidence that the deposit formed over a much shorter length of time, and possibly represents a single event (see Chapters 2 and 3). The entangled nature of the remains suggests that at least some of the corpses were deposited together, perhaps dumped from a cart or wheelbarrow, rather than accumulating more gradually, and the absence of evidence for any of the remains having been exposed to sunlight or scavengers would suggest that the pit was not open for any lengthy period.

If the mass grave was buried in a single event rather than accumulating over a longer period of time, an alternative interpretation presents itself, in which the individuals buried in the pit were the victims of a catastrophic occurrence that resulted in the need to dispose of a large number of corpses with no opportunity for the normal formalities. As Loe *et al.* have discussed elsewhere in this report (Chapter 3) the most likely cause of this would be an epidemic, as the skeletons revealed no evidence for violent death and the mortality profile of the victims is most consistent with a random cross-section of the population struck down indiscriminately by some catastrophic event, which did not preferentially affect individuals according to age or sex.

The mass grave and the Antonine Plague

The ancient sources record a number of epidemics that effected the Roman empire (Cartwright and Biddiss 2004, 10–17). Pestilence appears to have been a periodic occurrence and occasionally had a direct impact on historical events, causing the deaths of several emperors, including Lucius Verus and Marcus Aurelius (ibid., 11–12). Although the disaster

that resulted in the deaths of the individuals buried in the mass grave need not be among the recorded epidemics, it is nevertheless a possibility worthy of consideration.

As no pathological evidence was detected on the skeletal remains that might help to establish the identity of the disease that may have caused these deaths, its possible identification with a historically documented epidemic must rely on the correlation of its date with those in the ancient sources. The grave contained a number of artefacts that help in establishing a date for the deposit. The pottery assemblage included the substantial parts of at least six South West Black Burnished ware jars, some of which displayed right-angled to slightly oblique burnished lattice indicative of a date during the later 2nd to 3rd century AD. Three brooches were also present, probably worn by victims at the time of burial, among which were a Wroxeter brooch, current from the middle of the 2nd century until at least the end of that century, and a knee brooch also datable to the later 2nd to early 3rd century. A hairpin found in the upper part of the back-fill was of Crummy Type 2, most common during the 2nd century. In addition to the artefactual dating evidence, samples from four skeletons were submitted for radiocarbon dating, but unfortunately three of these yielded insufficient collagen for analysis. The one successful sample, from skeleton 1630, produced a determination of AD 70–240 (NZA 27008 cal 2 sigma). All the dating evidence would thus be compatible with a date during the second half of the 2nd century or the early part of the 3rd century, although the predominantly 2nd century dates for the use of the Wroxeter brooch and hairpin may suggest that a date in the 3rd century is less likely.

Of the epidemics recorded in the contemporary sources, the only candidate consistent with the date of the mass grave is the Antonine Plague, also known as the Plague of Galen after the physician who reported it. This pestilence first appeared at the end of AD 165 or the beginning of AD 166 in Mesopotamia during the emperor Verus' Parthian campaign and quickly spread throughout the empire, reaching Rome within the year. The historian Ammianus Marcellinus records that the epidemic spread to Gaul and the Rhine (23.6.24; Gilliam 1961, 232), and there is no reason to suppose that Britain was spared. After the initial outbreak, it persisted for many years, with its final and perhaps most virulent outbreak not occurring until AD 189. Symptoms described by Galen were a high fever, inflammation of the mouth and throat, thirst, diarrhoea and skin eruption, from which modern scholars have been able to conclude that the plague was probably an outbreak of smallpox (Littman and Littman 1973, 252). This is a particularly acute disease, epidemics of which may infect 60–80% of the population and produce a fatality rate of about 10% (ibid., 254). Estimates of the effects of the plague on the population of the Roman world vary, some scholars believing it to have had a catastrophic impact on manpower that precipitated the eventual decline of the Empire, while others have claimed that the resultant excess mortality was no more than 1% (Greenburg 2003, 413). Dio Cassius reported that the outbreak in 189 caused as many as 2000 deaths each day in Rome alone, and although Gloucester had a much smaller population an outbreak here would certainly have caused an emergency severe enough to force the local authorities to resort to the sort of mass burial of victims that has been identified by the excavation.

The correlation of archaeological evidence with historically recorded events is always problematic, and the identification of the emergency that resulted in the mass grave with a historically recorded epidemic can only ever be a matter of speculation. Although there is some evidence that the deposit may have been created in a single event this is not certain and other interpretations may be equally valid, particularly the possibility that the pit was used for the disposal of the corpses of individuals too poor to afford a proper burial (see discussion above). The osteological evidence neither supports nor refutes the case for these individuals being the victims of an epidemic, or for the identification of any possible epidemic as smallpox (see Chapter 3). It is also entirely possible that the deposit represents the victims of an otherwise unknown and perhaps purely local outbreak. However, in view of the unusual nature of the deposit it is a question worth pursuing, and the weight of available evidence does not contradict the suggestion, offered tentatively here, that the individuals buried in the mass grave may have been struck down as a result of the Antonine Plague.

THE PEOPLE OF ROMAN GLOUCESTER

The structure of the population

The 64 inhumations, at least ten individuals from cremation burials, and 91 bodies from the mass grave represent by far the largest sample of human remains that has been excavated from the cemeteries of Roman Gloucester. As such they provide an excellent opportunity to investigate the structure and health of the individuals buried in the part of the cemetery investigated by the excavation, although it must be borne in mind that these individuals may have been of relatively low status and are not necessarily representative of the entire community. Of the 37 inhumation and cremation burials from the cemetery that could be assigned a biological sex 26 were male and 11 female, a striking imbalance between the sexes that represents a male to female ratio of 2.4:1. A note of caution in interpreting these figures is however suggested by the corresponding statistics from the adjacent excavation at 124–130 London Road, which yielded a more equal division between the sexes consisting of 23 males and 21

females, or a ratio of 1.1:1. This could be interpreted as implying that different areas of the cemetery were used by distinct groups within the community with differing balances between the sexes, perhaps representing families with differing traditions of burial based on an individual's gender, or in the case of the male dominated areas representing plots used by burial clubs or similar associations. Some support for this suggestion is provided by the distribution of the burials to which a sex could be attributed (Fig. 6.3). A group of four female burials at the eastern edge of the site is situated adjacent to a distinct cluster of female burials in Area 1 of the excavation at 124–130 London Road (Foundations Archaeology 2003, fig. 6). Meanwhile, the concentration of 3rd–4th century graves in the south-eastern part of the site, in which four of the five sexed burials are male, is close to an area of similarly late burials in Area 4 of the Foundations site that are also predominantly male (ibid.). Nevertheless, the overall imbalance still persists, as the combined figures from the two excavations produce an overall male to female ratio of 1.5:1 from a total of 87 sexed burials.

The under-representation of females is a commonly observed feature of Romano-British cemeteries. The eastern cemetery of London (1.7:1) (Barber and Bowsher 2000, 311) and Lankhills School, Winchester (1.6:1) (Clarke 1979, 123) have produced similar ratios to that recorded at Wotton, and the excavation at Trentholme Drive in the Mount cemetery, York produced an even greater disparity, with a ratio of 3.6:1 (Warwick 1968, 147). It is unlikely that these figures are fortuitous, the result of male and female burials being located in different parts of the cemetery, as if this were the case one would expect corresponding female-dominated areas to have been discovered. The conclusion would appear to be either that some females received different funerary rites which cannot be detected archaeologically or that the ratios observed in the excavated samples are a true reflection of the make-up of the population. The remains from the mass grave form a useful check on these figures, as these individuals are likely to represent a sample of the population that has not been selected according to any customs governing entitlement to burial in the cemetery, and may therefore provide a more representative cross-section of the population. This assemblage, perhaps surprisingly, exhibits a greater imbalance than that from the inhumations, with the 49 sexed individuals comprising 35 males and 14 females, or a male to female ratio of 2.5:1. It is possible that females lived more sheltered lives and were less exposed to infection, but the evidence from the mass grave certainly does not contradict the suggestion that the population of the *colonia* contained considerably more men than women. Wells (1982a, 135) has suggested that the imbalance between the sexes at Cirencester may have been due to the prevalence of retired soldiers, and although there is no reason to believe that this was the case at Cirencester it may nevertheless have been

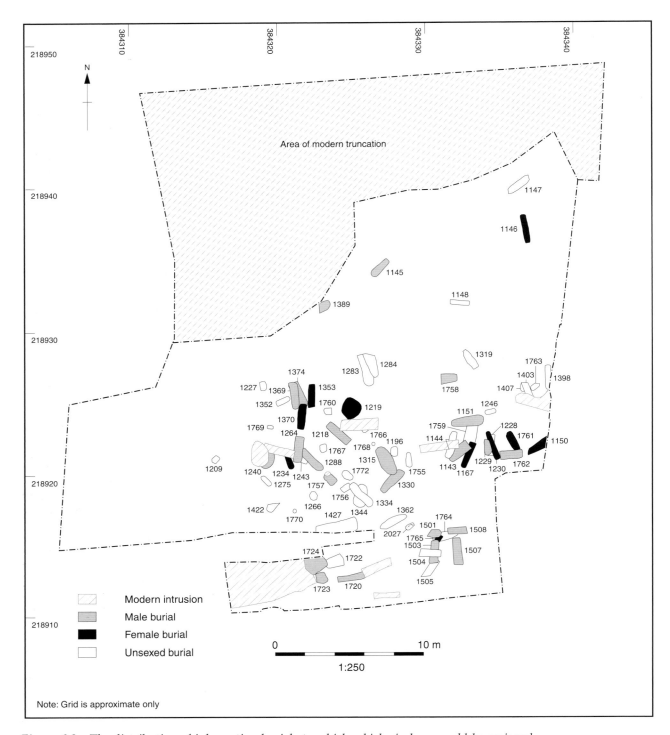

Figure 6.3   The distribution of inhumation burials to which a biological sex could be assigned.

a factor at Gloucester, since the *colonia* was originally founded as a settlement for veterans and may have continued to attract veteran settlement after its initial foundation (see below). However the general nature of the imbalance at numerous towns throughout Roman Britain may indicate that other factors were also responsible, and the infanticide of female babies must also be considered a possibility (see discussion below).

The age at death profile of the cemetery indicated that adult deaths were highest between the ages of 18 and 35 years, representing 36.5% of the individuals

142

from inhumation burials, with seven individuals (11.1%) living into the older age category, defined as over 45 years (see Chapter 3 for more detail). As with female burials, those of subadults are typically under-represented in cemeteries of the Roman period (Barber and Bowsher 2000, 311), and this was the case at 120–122 London Road, where only nine individuals (14.3%) were aged less than 18 years, and clearly this is not a true reflection of the age profile of the living population. A similar situation was recorded at 124–130 London Road, where 12 burials (16.2%) from the total of 74 excavated were subadults. Of the adults at 120–122 London Road, females appear to have been more likely to die before the age of 25 years, presumably as a result of the rigours of childbirth, and at the opposite end of the age range a greater proportion of males (21.7%) than females (9%) lived beyond 45 years. The age profile of the individuals in the mass grave has a striking peak in the 18–25 years age group, suggesting that the emergency responsible for this deposit struck down many individuals in their prime. As with the assemblage from the cemetery, males outnumber females in the older category.

Health

Overall, there was nothing remarkable about the population in general in terms of its health and physical attributes. An exception is perhaps the levels of non-specific infection which seem to be higher than in other Romano-British populations (see Chapter 3). Patterns of element involvement suggest that among the London Road population systemic disease, including infection, was prevalent.

Evidence for injuries sustained during life was found in the form of ante-mortem fractures observed on the bones of 16 individuals from the cemetery and mass grave, all of them male, representing 16.9% of all male individuals. There were no traumatic injuries recorded on female skeletons. The majority of these fractures are likely to have resulted from accidents rather than inter-personal violence, a trend that is also seen among other assemblages of this period (Roberts and Cox 2003, 157) and suggests that the towns of Roman Britain were generally not unruly places.

Status and society

The study of social complexity and individual status is a major concern of funerary archaeology, but the interpretation of cemetery evidence is fraught with difficulties. It is possible that funerary customs may serve to create an idealised image of society rather than reflecting reality. Also, it is difficult to attribute value to the grave goods or practices of past societies, and much of the symbolism used in the funerary rites may not now be understood (Parker Pearson 1999). Nevertheless it may be possible to draw some tentative conclusions regarding the population buried in the area of the cemetery investigated.

The most obvious expression of social status found within Roman cemeteries are the mausolea and other structures or enclosures that were used to mark the burials of the wealthy or powerful. No such structures were present within the area investigated at 120–122 London road, which is likely to be an area of the cemetery containing the graves of individuals of relatively low status. The only possible evidence for a more humble form of funerary monument was part of a gully (1358) that may have enclosed a burial. However, even this possibility could not be confirmed as the gully lay in an area of the site that had been badly effected by truncation, and could not be associated with a surviving grave. The only other burials that may have been marked out as being special or different by virtue of their construction were the graves of two children: the burial of a perinatal individual placed in a stone cist (1756), and the grave of a child aged 5–12 years, the upper part of which was back-filled with limestone rubble that may have formed a mound defining the grave (1772). If these different grave forms were intended to express status then it surely refers to the status of the family rather than that of the children themselves, but it is equally possible that the particular forms of these graves are associated with superstitions regarding the need to contain the spirits of the deceased rather than with displays of status.

Only a small proportion of the burials were provided with grave goods, and those items that are present are not of obvious material value. They are not made from valuable materials, associated in non-burial contexts with high status, or of exotic origin. This would suggest that grave goods and other archaeologically identifiable aspects of the burials were not generally used to express the status of the deceased in this part of the cemetery, perhaps due to the low status and relative poverty of those buried here. It is interesting in this respect that the child buried in grave 1246 was accompanied by an iron finger ring, which was traditionally worn as a sign of citizen status, while it has been suggested (see above) that the asymmetrical positioning of the arm of some of the burials may be associated with the wearing of a toga, a right exclusive to citizens. The presence of individuals with citizen status is not unexpected as the *colonia* was founded as a settlement of Roman citizens, and is not inconsistent with the suggestion that this was an area of low status burials as citizen status was of course no guarantee against poverty.

Some objects, especially items of clothing or jewellery such as the bracelet and ring worn by the individual in grave 1362 and the finger ring from burial 1505, may have been chosen for deposition in the grave because they were of personal significance to the deceased, or because of a fear that the deceased might be able to haunt items with which he or she had been closely associated in life. Other items are likely to have been deposited for reasons associated with beliefs regarding the fate and subsequent needs of the dead (see above).

There is some evidence that the status of individuals may have been related to age and sex. The youngest members of the population are noticeably absent from the cemetery: Only a single infant below the age of two years was present among an excavated population of 64 individuals, and only two more examples were found among the 74 from 124–130 London Road. The under-representation of this age group is common at Roman cemeteries (Philpott 1991, 98) and may indicate that children of this young age were not usually entitled to burial in the community's burial ground, perhaps because they were not considered to be full members of society (Philpott 1991, 101). Pliny (Nat Hist VII, 15, cited in Philpott 1991, 101) claimed that children did not gain a soul until the age of teething, and it is possible that until they were old enough to walk and talk children were not considered to be full people. Children between this age and about 12 years appear to have still been treated differently from adults as regards burial, with three out of four individuals from this age group buried in a crouched posture rather than the more normal supine position, implying that the people of the *colonia* recognised childhood as a distinct status. Childhood appears to have been considered to end at puberty, as the bodies of the three individuals in the 13–17 age group were buried according to the same practices as the majority of the adults, including one individual who was buried prone.

Although the women in the cemetery received the same burial rites as the men, their apparent under-representation within the population may have implications regarding the status of women at the *colonia*, particularly regarding the possible practice of female infanticide (see above). If infants were not regarded as full people, infanticide would have been an easy way of dealing with unwanted births, and it is possible that among the poorer members of society social and economic pressures associated with a requirement to provide a dowry for daughters resulted in the preferential selection of female births for this fate. A willingness to give up female children in this way might be associated with a reduced status for females in general, at least in those groups within the population for whom such a practice was economically necessary. No direct evidence for this practice would be expected, as the unwanted female births would have joined the rest of the infant deaths that were disposed of by some means that has left little archaeologically detectable trace.

The possible lower status of women among the part of the population buried here may contrast with the situation among the native population, and even with more high status sections of the *colonia*. The group of apparently high status late Iron Age burials at Birdlip are arranged around the central grave of an adult female, suggesting that women were able to hold high status within the native community (Staelens 1982). The programme of isotope analysis carried out as part of this project has demonstrated that some, and probably most, of the females buried

in the cemetery originated from Britain and are likely to derive from the native population. It is thus possible that we are seeing evidence for the loss of the traditional role of women within native society that Allason-Jones (1989b) has argued may have arisen from the break-down of tribal structure associated with the migration to urban centres.

The peopling of Roman Gloucester

The arrival at Gloucester of the Roman military in AD 49 occasioned the introduction into the region of a new population with alien practices. This is particularly true in the case of funerary practice, where the establishment of the fortresses, first at Kingholm and later at the city centre on the future site of the *colonia*, was accompanied by the establishment of the attendant cemetery and the introduction of the rite of cremation. This rite had not been practised by the local native population, whose funerary traditions appear to have comprised mainly of excarnation, albeit with some evidence for crouched burials (Moore 2006, 111). The earliest evidence for the burials of this new population are two cremation burials, and a further six excavated at 124–130 London Road, which are associated with pottery of pre-Flavian date, contemporary with the occupation of the Kingsholm fortress. These burials are all of adults, comprising two males and a female (where they could be sexed), and it is tempting to interpret the males as being soldiers garrisoned at the fortress. The presence of a female, if correctly identified, indicates that a non-military population was also associated with the fortress. Settlements of civilians often grew up beside military bases, providing service industries for the soldiery and even housing wives and families, although the latter were not officially recognised (Mattingly 2006, 170–6). The physical remains of such a settlement at so early a date have not been identified at Gloucester but the grave of this woman is evidence that civilians were not only present but were permitted to share the garrison's cemetery, indicating that the two communities were very closely connected. We cannot, however, know how substantial this civilian population was, or whether it originated from camp followers who had arrived with the army or from members of the local native population attracted by the economic and social opportunities afforded by the presence of the military.

After the army had moved on, the site of the city centre fortress was reused for the founding of a civilian settlement, although the precise date of neither of these events is known and there may have been some interlude before the town was established. The full name of the settlement, Colonia Nerva (or Nerviana) Glevensium (Wacher 1995, 150) indicates that it was specifically founded as a *colonia*, a settlement for retired soldiers. Research by Fulford (1999, 178) has indicated that veterans typically settled in the frontier regions in which they had served rather than returning to their homelands, and there is evidence that some of the burials at Wotton were of individuals with a military background. The adult male (1542) associated with possible belt fittings in the mass grave may have been a soldier as the wearing of belts is not normally associated with civilians. Two burials at 124–130 London Road associated with a brooch, buckle and belt plate, and a coin and spearhead are also likely to be soldiers, the latter having been interpreted by Cool (2003) as a possible auxiliary trooper. In addition, the tombstone of a veteran of the Twentieth Legion dated to the 2nd century or later (Hassall and Tomlin 1984) has been found at the Coppice Corner cemetery north of Kingsholm. It is therefore entirely likely that soldiers retiring from the British garrison continued to settle at Gloucester long after the initial settlement, perhaps due to a continued link, formal or otherwise, maintained between the *colonia* and the unit formerly based there.

Wacher (1995, 165) has somewhat harshly characterised the military origins of the people of Gloucester as producing 'a tightly knit community with rigid social strata according to army rank and years of service' with a population 'introverted and ultra-conservative', but this underestimates the contribution of the native population. The presence of individuals from the native community within the population of the *colonia* is suggested by the occurrence of crouched burials, and perhaps also by the early extended inhumations (see above). It is likely that these burials represent members of the local population who were integrated into the population of the *colonia*, but had not adopted Roman customs sufficiently to abandon their traditional burial practices. This suggestion has received support from the programme of isotope analysis (see Appendix 3), which indicated that crouched burial 1238 in grave 1240 was of local origin. During the late 1st and 2nd centuries when these inhumation burials were made the custom of inhumation had not yet been adopted as the main form of burial, and so the part of the population who buried their dead in this way would have clearly stood out from the rest of the community, who were practising cremation at this time.

The results of the isotope analysis, undertaken on a sample of individuals from both the cemetery and the mass grave, has demonstrated that the population had a range of origins, deriving both from the local area and also from elsewhere in the province of Britannia, as well as a small group probably from the Mediterranean area and two individuals from another, unidentified non-UK source (Appendix 3). The individuals from the Mediterranean area were clearly not restricted to military personnel as they include a female aged 18–25 years buried wearing a copper alloy bracelet and ring (1360, grave 1362). This group is presumably a small sample of the many government officials and traders and their families who settled, permanently or temporarily, at the *colonia*. The local origins of the majority of the population is only to be expected, but the presence of individuals from elsewhere in Britain, including two who may have come from the Pennines, suggests that Gloucester was sufficiently vibrant economically to attract settlers from beyond the immediate area. The implication of these results is that the population of the *colonia*, if not exactly cosmopolitan, was at least more varied than has been previously appreciated.

Appendices

APPENDIX 1: DENTAL HEALTH STATUS METHODOLOGY

Enamel hypoplasia

Enamel hypoplasia was scored for the buccal crown surfaces of permanent teeth. All formed crowns from all permanent maxillary and mandibular teeth were examined. Where present, defects were recorded by employing the definitions and guidelines set out by the *Fédération Dentaire Internationale* (FDI, 1982).

Dental caries

All developed and erupted teeth were examined for caries. This was diagnosed when there was clear evidence of loss of tooth substance (Hillson 2001). The severity of the lesion was classified according to the categories drawn by Brothwell (1981) and Kelley *et al.* (1991).

The number of teeth affected was counted instead of the number of mandibles/individuals affected. Many teeth were found loose and many mandibles fragmented. Presenting caries as a percentage of teeth affected was advantageous because it included isolated teeth and increased the sample size (Hillson 2001, 256). It also allowed obtaining frequencies according to tooth category (anterior dentition, posterior dentition). In addition, most mandibles or maxillae did not preserve all the teeth, and making inferences about prevalence of DC in an individual when teeth were missing would have been unreliable.

Although information was obtained from each surface and tooth, dental caries frequencies were pooled to overall rates according to tooth class (anterior, posterior) as recommended by Hillson (2001). Anterior teeth included incisors and canines, while posterior teeth included premolars and molars.

Ante-mortem tooth loss (AMTL)

Ante-mortem tooth loss was identified based on the degree of alveolar bone resorption. All the alveoli that could be observed were counted and any that had started to regenerate or that were completely regenerated were scored as having been lost before death. In the case of discrete burials where there is a number of teeth and the alveoli have not preserved, the rate of AMTL was scored according to the number of teeth present. Thus, if a discrete skeleton had 32 loose teeth present (the mandibular and maxilla portions very fragmented and poorly preserved), the prevalence of AMTL was still recorded as none out of 32.

Dental calculus

Calculus was scored as present or absent. When present, dental calculus was observed as slight, moderate or considerable following Brothwell (1981), although post-mortem manipulation (eg washing) may have affected the quantity that is present during analysis in the laboratory.

Periodontal disease

In archaeological material, examination of periodontitis is based on the distance between the cemento-enamel junction (CEJ) of the tooth and the alveolar crest for each tooth in the jaw. Recording of periodontal disease followed the schemes devised by Brothwell (1981). In general, lower degrees of advanced periodontitis tend to suggest a good standard of oral health.

Periapical cavities

The identification of a periapical cavity was diagnosed by the presence of a perforating fistula in a specific alveolar location. These lesions were distinguished from post-mortem damage by observing smooth, biological (healed) margins indicative of an ante-mortem condition (Roberts and Manchester 1995, 51).

Dental anomalies

Anomalies such as dental overcrowding, the presence of enamel pearls, congenital absence of teeth, and supernumerary dentition were also recorded for each of the skeletons when present.

147

APPENDIX 2: SUMMARY OF DISARTICULATED HUMAN BONE

Ctx/Sf	Context description	Bones present	MNI	Age	Sex
sf154	context 1333, backfill of 1334	Occipital bone	1	Adult	M
1020	Roman soil	1 fragment of cranial vault	1	Adult	
1024	Fill of modern pit 1023	Femur, humerus, fragments of long bones	1	Adult	
1025	Medieval soil	1 fragment of cranial vault and 1 lower left second premolar	1	Adult	
1090	backfill of grave 1757	1 fragment of tibia	1	Adult	
1105	Post-medieval garden soil	15 fragments including 1 fragment of ulna and 14 fragments of skull	1	Adult	
1106	Soil layer	Fragments of skull, humerus, ulna, metacarpal, femur, tibia, fibula, patella, tarsals (left and right calcaneous) and foot phalanx	1	Adult	
1113	Backfill of grave 1143	33 fragments including 6 cranial fragments including supraorbital margin and 26 long bone fragments including the right distal humerus	1	Adult	
1121	Fill of post-medieval ditch 1055	1 fragment of radius and one of ulna	1	Adult	
1132	Backfill of grave 1146	3 left maxillary teeth (left canine and premolars), 2 fragments of cranial vault, 1 fragment of humerus	1	Adult	
1158	Fill of post-medieval ditch 1055	1 fragment of cranial vault	1	Adult	
1175	Fill of post-medieval ditch 1725	1 fragment of occipital bone, including nuchal crest	1	Adult	
1182	Grave 1230	Parietal, occipital, left femur and right femur, left and right tibiae, left fibula, right ulna, right scapula, right radius, right os coxa, right calcaneous and two left calcanei	2	Adult male (and sub?)	
1254	Fill of modern pit 1255	1 fragment of distal humerus, distal ulna, rib, scapula and 4 unidentified fragments	1	Adult	
1247	Natural	1 fragment of tibia	1		
1265	Fill of Roman gully 1358	3 fragments of skull, 2 of scapula and 6 long bones fragments	1	Adult	
1269	Grave 1144	Right scapula, left os coxa, ribs, right medial cuneiform, left radius, left fibula, fibula, left MT3, frontal, parietal bones	1	Adult	
1282	Backfill of grave 1284	7 teeth including lower second molars, lower right third molar and lower left first molar, the latter with a carious lesion on the coronal (lingual) face. No other pathology apart from slight calculus on lower right premolars and slight periodontitis on lower molars, right MT3, right MT5, ribs, right ulna, right mandible and thoracic vertebra	1	Young adult	
1285	Backfill of grave 1288	6 teeth, left side: lower deciduous M2s, upper and lower M1 (roots open), unerupted 2nd molar and one unerupted canine. All from individual *c* 7 years. In addition fragments of radius, ulna, mandible with 2 unerupted incisors and one unerupted premolar, subadult skull fragments and some unidentified fragments. 2 fragments of femoral condyles probably belonged to an adult skeleton	1	Subadult and 1 adult?	
1312	Backfill of grave 1315	1 fragment of right distal humerus	1	Adult	
1341	Fill of grave 1344	1 thin skull fragment	1	?	
1361	Backfill of grave 1362	50 small (10–4 mm) fragments unidentified	1	?	
1365	Back fill of grave 1370	Skull bones: frontal, parietal, occipital, temporal bones, and left zygomatic, mandible, right humerus, left tibia, teeth present (n=11) with no pathology	1	Young Adult	

Ctx/Sf	Context description	Bones present	MNI	Age	Sex
1368	Grave 1369	Rib and right radius?	1	Adult	
1387	Backfill of grave 1388	1 fragment of rib and *c* 20 small bone fragments unidentified	1	?	
1397	Backfill of grave 1398	3 unidentified fragments	1	?	
1402	Backfill grave 1403	1 middle phalanx, vertebral body and 13 unidentified fragments, left femur, left tibia, left fibula, left ilium, sacrum, lumbar vertebra, hand phalanx	1	Adult	
1406	Backfill grave 1407	14 fragments of foot: 6 fragments of MTs, 8 phalanges (5 proximal, 1 intermediate and two distal)	1	Adult	
1409	Pit 1408	Metacarpal, rib, skull fragments, cremated tibia fragment, left ilium, right femur, left ulna, right humerus, right humerus, humerus, right calcaneous, hand phalanx, right femur, left femur, left femur, left tibia, right tibia, left tibia, left tibia, right tibia, right tibia, right ilium, lumbar vertebra, left fibula, 2 left petrous, right maxilla with M2, M1, P2 and P1 and on left LM1, LM2 and LM3, thoracic vertebra, left humerus, left humerus, radius, ulna, phalanx, left femoral head	3	Adult	
1411	Backfill of grave 1763	1 fragment distal tibia	1	Adult	
1413	Post-medieval ditch 1412	Left talus, right tibia, right ulna, sacrum, ilium, left and right parietals, right frontal, metacarpal	1	Adult	
1414	Post-medieval ditch 1412	Parietal, left humerus, right radius	1	Adult	
1416	Modern posthole 1415	Left ulna and one cervical vertebra	1	Adult	
1418	Modern posthole 1417	Skull fragments	1	Subadult	
1426	Grave 1427	Right radius, right ulna, hand proximal and intermediate phalanx	1	Adult	
1433	Fill of modern pit 1432	40 fragments labelled disarticulated, including 9 skull fragments, two teeth (upper right premolars), fragments of femur, tibia, left calcaneous and left talus, vertebra, ribs, fragments of long bones	1	Adult	
1435	Post-medieval ditch	1 fragment of cranial vault: an occipital with a nuchal crest	1	Adult	
1454	Grave 1501	Right femur, right femur, left femur, femur, femur, femur, left patella, left tibia, left ilium, left ulna, right radius, ulna, radius, metacarpal, metatarsal, phalanges and skull fragments	2	Adult	
1457	Backfill of grave 1502	13 skull fragments, 24 long bone fragments, 4 teeth (upper right premolars, upper left P2 and lower right M1), clavicle, ulna, patella, fibula, skull with right zygomatic, two left zygomatics, right temporal, axis, right navicular, right radius, right clavicle, right? Clavicle, right ulna, left scapula, femur, cervical vertebra, left mandible, left mandible, right mandible	2	Young Adult	F?
1465	Post-medieval ditch 1729	Left ulna	1	Adult	
1468	Grave 1504	Left scaphoid, metacarpal, cervical vertebra and femur fragments	1	Adult	
1480/sf319	Grave 1505	2 phalanges inside a finger ring	1	Adult	
1481	Fill of grave 1505	19 fragments of skull and long bones	1	Adult	
1536	Grave 1765	1 clavicle fragment	1	Adult	
1713	Grave 1723	Occipital	1	Adult	

APPENDIX 3: OXYGEN AND STRONTIUM ANALYSIS OF TOOTH ENAMEL

(NERC Isotope Geoscience Laboratory Report Series No.221)
by Carolyn Chenery

Introduction

This report presents $^{87}Sr/^{86}Sr$ and $\delta^{18}O$ oxygen isotope data for tooth enamel from permanent molars collected from 21 individuals buried in a Roman cemetery at London Road, Gloucester, Gloucestershire. The samples were provided by Oxford Archaeology and were analysed at the NERC Isotope Geoscience Laboratory at the British Geological Survey (NIGL/BGS) as part of the AHRC-funded project 'Diaspora Communities in Roman Britain' based at The University of Reading. The purpose of the work is to further our understanding of diversity in Roman Britain by assessing the proportion of individuals who:

(a) might be of local origin and those who can be defined as 'non local',

(b) to constrain the place of childhood origin for any 'non locals' and

(c) to assess any variations found against archaeological factors such as sex, burial type and artefacts.

Methodology

Tooth Sampling

At Oxford Archaeology, teeth were taken from 21 individuals, 10 from individual inhumations and 11 from the mass burial pit for oxygen and strontium analysis. See Table A3.1 for details of individuals and teeth sampled and Table A3.2 for grave and skeletal descriptions.

Photographs of each tooth (mesial, distal, buccal, lingual and occlusal orientations and internal views of slices for most teeth) were made prior to extraction of samples from the crown and are contained in the site archive.

Isotope Analysis

Each tooth was cut in half using a flexible diamond edged rotary dental saw. The half selected for analysis was cleaned ultrasonically for five minutes in high purity water and rinsed twice to remove loosely adhered material. A tungsten carbide dental burr was used to abrade off the enamel surface to a depth of > 100 microns. Secondary dentine was removed and discarded and the enamel and primary dentine were separated. The dentine was reserved for future potential carbon, nitrogen and background strontium analyses and the enamel was prepared for oxygen and strontium analysis as follows.

Table A3.1 Details of individuals and teeth samples.

Skeleton	Sex	Age	Teeth present	Tooth sampled
1103	F	Middle adult	26	M3 lower right
1127	?M	Young adult	2	M3 lower right
1131	F	Young adult	11	M3 lower right
1181	F	Middle adult	24	M2 lower right
1216	M	Mature adult	14	M3 lower left
1238	?M	Mature adult	14	M3 lower left
1328	M	Middle adult	18	M3 lower left
1340	IND	Old adult	8	M2 lower left
1360	IND	Young adult	15	M2 lower left
1364	?F	Young adult	19	M3 lower left
1518	?Male	Middle adult	23	M2 upper left
1520	Female	Young adult	28	M3 upper left
1539	Female	Middle adult	29	M3 lower right
1541	Male	Young adult	31	M3 lower left
1544	Male	Middle adult	29	M3 lower left
1546	ND	Mature adult	29	M3 lower right
1553	Male	Middle adult	30	M3 lower right
1560	Female	Young adult	26	M3 lower right
1561	Male	Young adult	30	M3 upper left
1565	Female	Young adult	27	M2 lower left
1596	Female	Middle adult	7	M2 upper right

Oxygen isotope analysis

Biogenic phosphate was converted to silver phosphate using the method of O'Neil *et al.* (1994) and is briefly summarised here. The core enamel samples were crushed to a fine powder and cleaned in hydrogen peroxide for 24 hours to remove organic material. The peroxide was evaporated to dryness and the sample dissolved in 2M HNO_3. The sample solutions were transferred to clean polypropylene test tubes and each sample was treated with 2M KOH followed by 2M HF to remove Ca from the solution by precipitation. The following day, the samples were centrifuged and the solution was added to beakers containing silver amine solution and silver phosphate precipitated, filtered, rinsed and dried.

Analytical measurement was by Continuous Flow Isotope Ratio Mass Spectrometry (CFIRMS) using the method of Venneman *et al.* (2002). The instrumentation is comprised of a TC/EA (thermo chemical elemental analyser) coupled to a Delta Plus XL isotope ratio mass spectrometer via a ConFlo III interface, all by Thermo Finnigan. All reported isotope ratios are expressed using the delta (δ) notation in parts per thousand (permil: ‰) relative to a standard:

$$\delta(‰) = ((R_{sample}/R_{standard}) - 1) \times 1000$$

The reference material NBS120C, calibrated against certified reference material NBS127 (assuming $\delta^{18}O$ of NBS127 = +20.3‰ versus SMOW), has an

150

Table A3.2   Grave and skeletal description.

Skeleton	Grave	Orientation	Posture	Grave furniture	Grave goods
Single Burials					
1103	1150	NE-SW	Prone, legs extended and parallel	None	None
1127	1145	SW-NE	Prone, extended. Lower parts of legs removed by later truncation	None	Ring-necked flagon
1131	1146	.N-S	Supine, legs extended with feet together	None	None
1181	1230	S-N	Prone, legs extended with feet together	None	None
1216	1218	SE-NW	Supine, legs extended with feet together	Fe nails	None
1238	1240	n/a	Crouched, lying on left side with the head to the east	None	None
1328	1330	NE-SW	Supine, legs extended and parallel	Coffin, Fe nails	None
1340	1344	SE-NW	Supine, legs extended and parallel	Coffin, Fe nails	Two hobnail shoes
1360	1362	SW-NE	Supine, Legs extended and parallel, left tibia displaced toward right leg	Coffin, Fe nails	Fe bracelet worn on left arm, Fe ring
1364	1370	N-S	Supine, legs extended	Coffin	None
Mass grave					
1518	1485	Pit E-W	Commingled human remains	None	A number of artefacts were found associated with the skeletons, including at least 3 pairs of hobnailed shoes, two copper alloy trumpet brooches, one copper alloy bracelet, two belt buckles and two finger rings. At least eight near-complete, though fragmented, vessels had been deposited in mass grave 1483 probably during the later 2nd century, although pottery recovered from upper fills was of later 3rd or 4th century date.
1520	1485	Pit E-W	Commingled human remains	None	
1539	1485	Pit E-W	Commingled human remains	None	
1541	1485	Pit E-W	Commingled human remains	None	
1544	1485	Pit E-W	Commingled human remains	None	
1546	1485	Pit E-W	Commingled human remains	None	
1553	1485	Pit E-W	Commingled human remains	None	
1560	1485	Pit E-W	Commingled human remains	None	
1561	1485	Pit E-W	Commingled human remains	None	
1565	1485	Pit E-W	Commingled human remains	None	
1596	1485	Pit E-W	Commingled human remains	None	

expected value of 21.70‰ (Chenery 2005). Each sample was analysed in triplicate. The internal mass spectrometry reproducibility for this set of analyses is $\pm$ 0.18‰ (1σ n=34). The batch reproducibility was 0.15‰ (n=6, 1σ). Drinking water values are calculated using Levinson's equation (Levinson *et al.*, 1987), $\delta^{18}O_{Drinking\ Water} = (\delta^{18}O_{Phosphate\ Oxygen} - 19.4)/0.46$, after correction for the difference between the average published values for NBS120C used at NIGL of $\delta^{18}O = 21.71 \pm 0.35‰$ (1σ) n=11

(Chenery 2005) and the value for NBS120B used by Levinson of $\delta^{18}O = 20.06 \pm 0.27‰$ (2σ).

Strontium isotope analysis

In a clean laboratory, the enamel samples were washed in acetone and cleaned twice, ultrasonically, in high purity water to remove dust and impurities. They were dried and weighed into pre-cleaned Teflon beakers. Each sample was mixed with ^{84}Sr tracer solution and then dissolved in Teflon distilled 16M HN0₃. The sample was then converted to Chloride and taken up in 2.5M HCl. Strontium was collected using conventional, Dowex® resin ion exchange methods.

The Sr isotope composition and concentrations were determined by Thermal Ionisation Mass spectroscopy (TIMS) using a ThermoFinningan Triton multi-collector mass spectrometer. Samples were run at *c* 5V using single Re filaments loaded using TaF following the method of Birck (1986). The international standard for ^{87}Sr/^{86}Sr, NBS987, gave a value of 0.710275 ± 0.000006 (1σ, n=12). All strontium ratios have been corrected to a value for the standard of 0.710250. Strontium procedural blanks provided a negligible contribution.

Results

Oxygen and strontium results are presented in Table A3.3 and Figure A3.1.

Oxygen isotopes

The enamel phosphate oxygen isotope ratios (δ^{18}Op) from this sample set present a broad scatter of results ranging from +17.05‰ to 19.18‰, with a range of calculated drinking water oxygen isotope ratios (δ^{18}Odw) of −8.15‰ to −3.51‰. These data split roughly into two groups; those who fall within the expected UK Adult range (δ^{18}O$_{enamel}$ 17.00‰ to 18.50‰, δ^{18}O$_{drinking\ water}$ -8.50‰ to -5.00‰), which was calculated from the 'Robust Mean' $\pm$ 2σ of δ^{18}O ratios of 363 individuals from the UK, and a second

group, with higher values than expected for the UK (see Fig. A3.1).

Statistical comparisons (F and t-tests) of oxygen isotopes of individuals from single graves with the mass burial pit show no significant difference in the two populations at the 95% level. Similarly comparison by sex also showed no significant difference at the 95% level.

Strontium isotopes

The strontium isotope ratios (^{87}Sr/^{86}Sr) cover a broad range of values from 0.70880 to 0.71347 (Fig. A3.1). The bulk of the ^{87}Sr/^{86}Sr values plot within the range of 0.7088 to 0.7106. Individuals in this group are compatible with a limited set of values obtained from plants and bottled waters from Jurassic and Triassic sediments ranging from 0.7081 to 0.7100 (Montgomery *et al.*, 2006 and Evans *et al.*, in press). Two individuals GLR1131 and GLR1364 have similar values (0.71141 and 0.71145) and these along with GLR1541 (0.712200) are compatible with values found in bottled water from Silurian mudrocks and Palaeozoic rocks in the Pennines. The very high values for GLR1561 and GLR 1518 (0.71345 and 0.71301) are compatible with Malvern and similar Precambrian volcanic rocks.

Strontium concentrations vary from 51 to 177ppm and fall within the typical UK range (Montgomery 2002).

Statistical comparisons (F and t Tests) of individuals from single graves with the mass burial pit show no significant difference in the two populations for strontium isotope ratios and strontium concentration

Table A3.3 Oxygen and strontium isotope results.

Sample	Burial	Sr ppm	87Sr/86Sr	Mean d^{18}O$_P$	Mean δ^{18}O $_{DW}$
GLR1103	Grave	114	0.709465	+18.44 ± 0.12	−5.12 ± 0.27
GLR1127	Grave	121	0.709694	+17.19 ± 0.13	−7.82 ± 0.29
GLR1131	Grave	133	0.711453	+17.09 ± 0.14	−8.05 ± 0.32
GLR1181	Grave	76	0.710599	+17.60 ± 0.15	−6.93 ± 0.32
GLR1216	Grave	93	0.709432	+19.18 ± 0.15	−3.51 ± 0.34
GLR1238	Grave	52	0.708937	+17.14 ± 0.05	−7.93 ± 0.11
GLR1328	Grave	57	0.710584	+17.97 ± 0.14	−6.13 ± 0.30
GLR1340	Grave	104	0.709606	+17.91 ± 0.15	−6.26 ± 0.34
GLR1360	Grave	133	0.709021	+19.01 ± 0.17	−3.88 ± 0.38
GLR1364	Grave	104	0.711405	+18.23 ± 0.10	−5.57 ± 0.22
GLR1518	Pit	72	0.713005	+17.91 ± 0.15	−6.27 ± 0.33
GLR1520	Pit	130	0.709732	+18.64 ± 0.07	−4.67 ± 0.15
GLR1539	Pit	66	0.708805	+17.50 ± 0.04	−7.16 ± 0.08
GLR1541	Pit	51	0.712200	+17.05 ± 0.08	−8.14 ± 0.19
GLR1544	Pit	102	0.709969	+18.18 ± 0.08	−5.69 ± 0.19
GLR1546	Pit	177	0.710889	+19.05 ± 0.06	−3.80 ± 0.14
GLR1553	Pit	84	0.709269	+17.44 ± 0.20	−7.28 ± 0.43
GLR1560	Pit	114	0.709486	+18.71 ± 0.21	−4.53 ± 0.46
GLR1561	Pit	67	0.713468	+18.70 ± 0.10	−4.54 ± 0.23
GLR1565	Pit	104	0.709773	+19.01 ± 0.14	−3.87 ± 0.31
GLR1596	Pit	105	0.709067	+17.71 ± 0.13	−6.71 ± 0.28

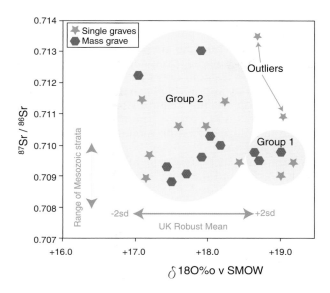

Figure A3.1 Plot of enamel strontium and oxygen isotope results.

at the 95% level. Similarly comparison by sex also showed no significant difference at the 95% level.

Discussion

Based on combined oxygen and strontium values, our sample set can be divided into two main groups (Fig. A3.1). The first group is quite diverse and has a wide range of $^{87}Sr/^{86}Sr$ values and $\delta^{18}O$ values that mirror the normal distribution of UK reference data (Montgomery 2002; Montgomery *et al.* 2006; Evans *et al.* in press; Darling *et al.* 2003). The second group have $\delta^{18}O$ values outside those of the UK robust mean values and they also have restricted $^{87}Sr/^{86}Sr$ values around 0.7094. Two points are not easily attributed to either group. They both have non-UK oxygen but more radiogenic Sr than is typical of the main group 2 samples.

Group 1

Group one is compatible with a relatively diverse UK derived population; there is a wide range of $^{87}Sr/^{86}Sr$ (0.7090 – 0.7135) values but most of these (0.7090 to 0.7099) can be derived within a 20 km distance from Gloucester. The most radiogenic value in this group (0.7135) is consistent with data obtained from mineral waters from the Precambrian of the nearby Malvern Hills (Montgomery *et al.* 2006) an area of Roman pottery and tile manufacture. The oxygen, however, suggested the origins of this group might be more widely dispersed throughout Britain as their oxygen covers the full range of UK values.

While the strontium and oxygen isotope values found in this group are consistent with lithologies and drinking water zones found within the UK, we

cannot rule out possible European origins from these results, specifically regions where the geology and oxygen combine to give the same range of values. However, the simplest interpretation is that they are from the UK.

The smaller Group 2

These samples have oxygen isotopes values that suggest a warmer climate of origin than can be found in the UK and the clustering of the Sr would suggest a common region or dietary origin. The strontium values are close to modern seawater (~0.709) and may possibly be caused by a diet high in marine components such as fish, shellfish and seaweed. Certain geological bedrocks can be ruled out, assuming they generate the overlying soil, Rb-rich granites, basalt terrains, pure limestone and chalk, and the majority of pre-Mesozoic silicate terrains.

The oxygen isotopes of this group exceed those expected for the UK, ranging from +18.65‰ to +19.18‰ ($\delta^{18}Odw$ −4.67 to −3.51). Exceptionally high values such as these might be expected along the extreme western or southern coastal Europe, northern Africa or in extremely arid locations. Very few values have been published for these areas; however, Darling (2003) records a range of −4.0 to −5.0 for the Outer Hebrides and small areas on the extreme westerly coast of Cornwall and Ireland, and Longinelli (2003) cites values of >−5.0 for the eastern Italian coast south of Brindisi.

Two other individuals with oxygen isotopic values that lie outside the UK range have higher strontium isotope values, suggesting that they came from somewhere different than group 2.

Conclusions

The isotope data do not correlate within any archaeological or osteological criteria, and in particular, there is no difference between the bodies in the mass grave and those in single graves, suggesting that they may well have come from the same population. This supports the interpretation based on the osteological evidence (see Chapter 3) that the individuals buried in the mass grave were victims of an epidemic that struck the population of Gloucester randomly, rather than a distinct group of people that were selected for mass burial on account of their place of origin, age, sex or social status.

The results of this study suggest that Gloucester was a town in which individuals from reasonably diverse areas of the UK lived and died. However, within this community the isotope data also identified a group whose origins lay in a region with a warmer climate than the UK. Additional archaeological or osteological information on the individuals analysed here would help to put these findings into context and may aid in further interpretations of the data presented here.

APPENDIX 4: DETAILED RECORDS OF CREMATIONS

Cremation burial 1196

Description: The skull was represented by the frontal, parietal and occipital bones only. The area of the external occipital protuberance was present. Very few rib and vertebra fragments were recovered as well as few fragments of the body of the ilium. Amongst the long bones, all were represented. The largest fragment measured 43 mm from a humerus.
MNI: Only the remains of 1 individual were identified.
Age: The dimensions of the skull and long bone fragments indicated an adult individual. The coronal and sagittal sutures were open.
Sex: Sex could not be determined due to the lack of the landmarks required for sex estimation.
Pathological lesions: Some pitting was present in the ectocranial surface of one parietal bone (2 g).
Colour and fracture pattern: The bones reflected the typical fissure pattern characteristic of green bones when burnt. The colour was predominantly white (177 g) and white with shades of blue and grey (76 g), with some fragments from the upper and lower limbs and even the skull predominantly grey (1 g) and blue (10 g). In summary, a homogeneous cremation fired at high combustion.
Animal Remains: A total of 20.8 g of burnt animal bone. Five fragments of calcined probable pig bone including cranial and long bone fragments were recovered from the cremation deposit itself. The backfill contained eleven fragments of burnt medium and large mammal long bone and 14 fragments of unburnt large mammal long bone, recovered from sieved residues and through hand collection. One indeterminate fragment was charred and the remaining burnt fragments were fully calcined. None of these fragments could be identified to species and some may be human.
Conclusion: One possibly adult individual.

CREMATION BURIAL 1196

BONE ELEMENT	WEIGHT (g)
CRANIAL VAULT (Neurocranium)	42.5
MANDIBLE	0.5
RIBS	4
VERTEBRAE	2
SHOULDER GIRDLE	0.5
PELVIS	4
UPPER LIMB BONES	37.5
LOWER LIMB BONES	51
FOOT BONES	0.5
LONG BONE UNIDENTIFIED (>4 mm)	37
UNIDENTIFIED FRAGMENTS	90
TOTAL WEIGHT	**269.5 g**

Cremation burial 1209

Description: Several skull bones were present including the frontal, parietal, occipital, temporal, maxilla, mandible and sphenoid bones. Landmarks include a portion of the left supraorbital margin, the nuchal crest and a gonion of the mandible. Dental fragment included roots and crowns, fragments possibly belonging to an upper first premolar, an upper second premolar and an upper molar. Both the shoulder and pelvic girdles were represented, followed by vertebrae (cervical), ribs and the long bones: humerus, radius, ulna, femur, tibia and fibula. The patella was also present. Hand bones included metacarpals and phalanges whilst foot bones included a talus, metatarsals and phalanges. The maximum fragment size was that of a tibia shaft measuring 59 mm.
MNI: Only the remains of 1 individual were identified.
Age: The dimensions of the skull and long bones clearly indicate an adult (>18 years) individual. The complete formation of the premolar roots provides a safe estimate of over 12 years of age. The lambdoid and coronal sutures are open.
Sex: The sex was difficult to determine and the result possibly reflected a male individual, although the traits are very limited. The supraorbital margin gave an ambiguous sex so the trait was intermediate. The posterior zygomatic arch provided a robusticity characteristic of a male individual. The nuchal crest was also ambiguous although it did tend to be rather more marked as in males. One hand phalanx subjectively showed probably typical male dimensions.
Colour and fracture pattern: The bones reflected the typical fissure pattern characteristic of green bones when burnt. The colour was predominantly white (94 g) and white with shades of blue and grey mainly (91 g), with some fragments from the upper and lower limbs and even the skull predominantly grey (18.5 g), brown (1 g) in a hand phalanx and one unidentified fragment, and finally black (0.5 g) for a proximal foot phalanx. In summary, a homogeneous cremation fired at high combustion. The remaining is trabecular bone and mostly the colour is unidentifiable.
Other observations: Five mandibular teeth (the first incisors, the second incisors and the left canine) were lost post-mortem. One unidentified bone fragment with corroded metal attached. Some slight (<1 mm) enthesophytes observed in the 30% that is present of the patella.
Animal remains: 11.9 g of burnt medium mammal sized animal bone including cranial fragments, long bone fragments and sheep sized rib blade fragments. Two fragments from a large mammal skull fragment (possibly human) and a pig phalanx from a juvenile animal were recovered from the cremation deposit (1202) and one indeterminate medium mammal sized fragment recovered from the fill of ancillary vessel 1199. The majority of the burnt animal bone was recovered from the backfill (1198).
Conclusion: An adult individual, probably male.

CREMATION BURIAL 1209

BONE ELEMENT	WEIGHT (g)
CRANIAL VAULT (Neurocranium)	49.5
FACIAL BONES (Splanchnocranium, excluding mandible)	1.5
MANDIBLE	1
TEETH	1
RIBS	6
VERTEBRAE	1
SHOULDER GIRDLE	1.5
PELVIS	1
UPPER LIMB BONES	29
LOWER LIMB BONES	39.5
HAND BONES	2.5
FOOT BONES	4
LONG BONE UNIDENTIFIED (>4 mm)	24
PATELLAE	2
UNIDENTIFIED FRAGMENTS	118
TOTAL WEIGHT	**281.5 g**

Cremation burial 1227

Description: This is a backfill context and only four fragments survive and range in size between 10 and 4 mm. While one fragment belongs to the skull fragment, the other three were not identified.
MNI: Only the remains of 1 individual were identified.
Age: Unknown.
Sex: Sex could not be determined due to the lack of the landmarks required for sex estimation.
Colour and fracture pattern: All the bones were white in colour indicating a cremation fired at high combustion.
Conclusion: One individual, age and sex unknown.

CREMATION BURIAL 1227

BONE ELEMENT	WEIGHT (g)
CRANIAL VAULT (Neurocranium)	0.5
UNIDENTIFIED FRAGMENTS	1
TOTAL WEIGHT	**1.5 g**

Cremation burial 1266

Description: The frontal, parietal, occipital and possibly the temporal bones have been identified. Some fragments include the different cranial sutures. An anterior fragment of the mandible was also present. Several dental remains were recovered including three roots and twelve crown fragments. These dental remains correspond to permanent upper second molars, an identified upper molar (root only), a lower second molar, one lower molar root and the lower left and right premolars. There was also an unidentified third molar and clearly an upper left third molar. There were only four small vertebral fragments, 1 fragment of clavicle, a shaft of either a metacarpal or a metatarsal and an

unidentified phalanx. The ribs were represented with 98 shaft fragments. The remaining bones corresponded to the humerus, radius, ulna, femur and tibia only. The maximum fragment was 38 mm long, probably belonging to a radius.
MNI: Two subadult individuals were identified, according to the dental age given by the teeth as well as by the different (and non-corresponding) dimensions of the bones.
Age: The dental remains clearly reveal two subadult individuals, one of whom died around 5 years of age (category 2–6 years) and another who died in the age range 6–12 years. In addition, long bone and rib fragments indicated two individuals of different dimensions. Excluding an upper and a lower molar unidentified with at least 3/4 of the root formed, the age was determined by the formation of the teeth as shown in the table below:

Permanent tooth	Location	Stage of formation (Moorrees et al. 1963)	Estimated age (Smith 1991 for lower teeth)
P1	Lower left and right	Cr1/2	4.1
P2	Lower left	Cr1/4	5.0
Molar	Upper	>R3/4	(unidentified molar)
Molar	Lower	>R3/4	(unidentified molar)
M2	Lower	Cr1/2	5.1–5.4 years
M2	Upper right and left	Cr1/2	Upper teeth (Ubelaker's 1989 chart = c 5 years)
M3	Upper left	Cr1/4-Cr1/2	11.3

In addition, the mandibular fragment revealed a socket for an erupted deciduous incisor and below it a socket for an unerupted permanent incisor with an estimated formation grade of R1/4 (Moorrees et al. 1963), which reveals an age-at-death range of 2–6 years. The teeth, therefore, indicate at least one individual between the ages of 2–6 years. Taking into account, the identified third molar with its stage of formation, there is clearly an older individual in the age range >6–12 years.
Finally, some trabecular bone from metaphysis with unfused epiphyses were identified.
Sex: Sex unknown.
Colour and fracture pattern: The bones reflected the typical fissure pattern characteristic of green bones when burnt. The colour was predominantly white (86.5 g) and white with shades of blue and grey (36 g), with some fragments from the upper and lower limbs, neurocranium and teeth dark blue (10 g) with some shades of grey. The remaining fragments, mainly trabecular bone fragments, were not classified into any colour category. In summary, a homogeneous cremation fired at high combustion.
Other observations: Some corroded metal adhered on two (1.5 g) cranial fragments.

Animal remains: A medium mammal long bone fragment and five indeterminate fragments were recovered from the backfill, and one medium mammal or bird long bone fragment from a soil sample. None of this material was burnt and it may all be residual in the soil matrix and not of funerary origin.

Conclusion: Two individuals with an age of 2–6 and >6–12 years respectively.

CREMATION BURIAL 1266

BONE ELEMENT	WEIGHT (g)
CRANIAL VAULT (Neurocranium)	32
MANDIBLE	0.5
TEETH	3
RIBS	8.5
VERTEBRAE	1
SHOULDER GIRDLE	0.5
UPPER LIMB BONES	12
LOWER LIMB BONES	3.5
HAND BONES or FOOT BONES	1
LONG BONE UNIDENTIFIED (>4 mm)	21.5
UNIDENTIFIED FRAGMENTS	59.5
TOTAL WEIGHT	**143 g**

Cremation burial 1766

Description: The most represented bones were those from the cranial vault and the long bones. Apart from the frontal, parietal and temporal (petrous part) bones, other cranial vaults such as the maxilla, sphenoid and a right zygomatic. A left condyle of a mandible was also identified, alongside a number of dental roots, one belonging to lower incisors, as well as upper and lower canines, upper and lower premolars and a lower molar. Fragments of clavicle, humerus, radius, ulna, femur and possibly fibula were represented. The largest fragment measured 47 mm and belonged to a clavicle. Cervical and thoracic vertebrae were identified. The remaining bone fragments were unidentified.

MNI: A minimum of only 1 individual was identified. There were no repeated bones and none from a different age.

Age: The size, dimensions and texture of the bones, especially the long bones, were representative of an adult (>18 years) individual. The dental roots belonging to premolars, canines and incisors were complete providing a safe minimum age of 15 years and over (upper premolars). Lambdoid and sagittal sutures were open.

Sex: Sex could not be determined due to the lack of the landmarks required for sex estimation.

Non-metric traits: The only trait available for observation was the multi-foramina in the zygomatic which was present.

Pathological lesions: No pathological lesions were observed, although pitting in palate was noted.

Colour and fracture pattern: Warping and transverse fracture pattern was observed in the bones indicating the body was fleshed or green when cremated. Most of the bones were white (111.5 g) or white with shades of other colours but mainly grey (12 g) and others blue (7 g) or grey (1 g) some of which are darker colours (eg some dental roots). This overall white colour indicates high and complete combustion of all the organic parts. Two fragments were black and one was dark blue amongst the unidentified fragments. One long bone shaft had a mix of blue and orange shades.

Animal remains: 86.8 g (166 fragments) of burnt animal bone including fragments from at least two pigs. The pigs were represented by cranial and tooth fragments, a left tibia, a left astragalus, a calcaneum, a left humerus, and two left ulnae. Epiphyseal fusion indicates that one of the pigs was under 30 months and one was over 12 months old at death. Further medium or large mammal sized scapula, long bone, tooth and indeterminate fragments may also be pig. It is not clear whether the pigs were burnt as complete carcasses or disarticulated joints and no butchery marks were identified.

Conclusion: A minimum of one individual, possibly adult.

CREMATION BURIAL 1766

BONE ELEMENT	WEIGHT (g)
CRANIAL VAULT (Neurocranium)	14
FACIAL BONES (Splanchnocranium, excluding mandible)	4.5
MANDIBLE	0.5
TEETH	2.5
RIBS	5
VERTEBRAE	2
SHOULDER GIRDLE	6
PELVIS	0.5
UPPER LIMB BONES	18
LOWER LIMB BONES	1
HAND BONES	0.5
LONG BONE UNIDENTIFIED (>4 mm)	21
UNIDENTIFIED FRAGMENTS	57
TOTAL WEIGHT	**132.5 g**

Cremation burial 1767

Description: Amongst the skull fragments, the frontal, parietal, occipital and temporal bones were present. Portions of the left and right orbits were identified. Maxilla and mandible were present. Dental fragments were recovered belonging to at least four premolars and five molars. Cervical, thoracic and lumbar vertebrae fragments were identified, as well as over 250 rib shaft fragments. Clavicles, scapulae, os coxae, humeri, radii, ulnae, femora, tibiae, fibulae, metacarpals, metatarsals and phalanges were also present. The longest fragment measured 58 mm and belonged to the shaft of a fibula. There were also numerous femora and tibiae shaft fragments that measured 55 mm in length.

MNI: Three mandibular condyles (preservation over 50%) were found. All of these three were identified as belonging to the right side of the mandible. Therefore, the MNI assuming all siding is correct (minimum two individuals) results in a total of three individuals in this assemblage. One comes from context (1062) and the other two from backfill context (1377). Moreover, two portions of two different axis vertebrae (the dens) were found in the same context (1377) and indicating at least two individuals within the same context.

Age: Through the size and dimensions of the bones none were clearly subadult. Therefore the three individuals were adult. Some of the sutures such as the lambdboid were open whilst portions of sagittal suture displayed minimal closure. The dental roots of molars were completely formed providing a safe minimum age of 12/15 years.

Sex: one clavicle, one humerus, two femora and one tibia fragments subjectively seemed to be of male dimensions. The size and robusticity of two mandibular fragments, belonging to two different individuals, also indicated possible male traits.

Pathological lesions: There were no signs of osteoarthritis in a lower right facet of vertebra, in two rib facets, in a mandibular condyle, nor in a superior right thoracic vertebrae facet. There was, however, clear periostitis in five shaft fragments of tibiae (2 g, 2/120 = 1.6%) and in two shaft fragments of fibula (1 g, 1/17.5 = 5.7%) characterised pitting and striae. It was difficult to establish whether the lesions were active or healed at the time of death. Pitting in palate was also noted. Slight enthesophytes in the spinous process of TV or LV were also recorded. Joint disease was present at the base of a proximal foot phalanx for ray 1 which had marked osteophytosis and deformity as well as pits that may be reflective of osteochondritis dissecans.

Colour and fracture pattern: The bones reflected the typical fissure pattern characteristic of green bones when burnt. The colour was predominantly white (251 g) and white with shades of blue and grey (830 g), with some fragments from the upper and lower limbs and even the skull predominantly blue (42 g), grey (22 g) and lastly brown (18 g). The rest are fragments of trabecular bone. In summary, a homogeneous cremation fired at high combustion.

Animal remains: Ten fragments (48.6 g) of cremated animal bone were recovered from the cremation deposit, comprising a possible cattle rib and a medium mammal sized long bone and cranial fragments, as well as an unburnt fish rib/process and an unburnt indeterminate fragment. The fill of ancillary vessel 1063 contained a medium mammal long bone fragment and three indeterminate bone fragments weighing a total of 8 g, all of which were unburnt.

Conclusion: A minimum of three adult individuals were identified, two possibly male. Periostitis was present in the lower limb bones.

CREMATION BURIAL 1767

BONE ELEMENT	WEIGHT (g)
CRANIAL VAULT (Neurocranium)	151
FACIAL BONES (Splanchnocranium, excluding mandible)	5.5
MANDIBLE	3.5
TEETH	5
RIBS	55
VERTEBRAE	23.5
SHOULDER GIRDLE	15
PELVIS	45
UPPER LIMB BONES	82
LOWER LIMB BONES	330
HAND BONES	3.5
FOOT BONES	20
LONG BONE UNIDENTIFIED (>4 mm)	115
UNIDENTIFIED FRAGMENTS	401.5
TOTAL WEIGHT	**1255.5 g**

Cremation burial 1768

Description: Only 73 fragments were found in this deposit. A few skull vault fragments and parts of humeri, radii and ulnae were identified in addition to a root of an upper canine. The rest was unidentified. The maximum fragment size was 28 mm measured on a portion of shaft of a radius.

MNI: Only the remains of 1 individual were identified.

Age: According to the dimensions and size of the bones, these were typical of an adult individual. The full formation of the canine root provided a safe minimum of 12 years of age.

Sex: Sex could not be determined due to the lack of the landmarks required for sex estimation.

Pathological lesions: No pathological lesions were observed, although two fragments of skull vault appeared to be abnormal, as if a 'bulge' in the endocranial lesions, perhaps similar to hyperostosis frontalis interna but the small remains (<2.5 g) and the lack of other parts limited this diagnosis.

Colour and fracture pattern: The bones reflected the typical fissure pattern characteristic of green bones when burnt. All the fragments were white in colour.

Animal remains: Five fragments (1.8 g) of burnt medium mammal sized long bone and indeterminate bone fragments were recovered from the cremation deposit in this burial.

Conclusion: A few fragments belonging possibly to one adult individual.

CREMATION BURIAL 1768

BONE ELEMENT	WEIGHT (g)
CRANIAL VAULT (Neurocranium)	6
TEETH	0.5
RIBS	0.5
UPPER LIMB BONES	3.5
LONG BONE UNIDENTIFIED (>4 mm)	5
UNIDENTIFIED FRAGMENTS	2
TOTAL WEIGHT	**17.5 g**

Cremation burial 1769

Description: Amongst the skull bones, only one fragment of maxilla and one of parietal, temporal and occipital were identified. The occipital bone presented a portion of the lambdoid suture whilst the maxilla presented three alveoli (incisors, canine) where the teeth had been lost post-mortem. Amongst the 29 dental fragments were a first and two second lower incisors, an upper canine, four upper molars including a second upper molar, and possibly two lower molars minimum. 47 rib shaft fragments were present and amongst the few vertebral fragments, the atlas vertebra was identified. With regard to long bones, the humerus, radius, ulna, femur, metacarpal, metatarsal and hand and foot phalanges were represented. The maximum size of a fragment was 44 mm measured on a shaft fragment of a radius.

MNI: Only the remains of 1 individual were identified.

Age: The dimensions and texture of the bones indicated an adult individual. More importantly, the full formation of the first and second molars indicated a minimum of 15 years of age. The observation of no dental wear (no dentine exposed, cusps unworn) in a portion of molar may indicate a young adult individual. The sagittal and lambdoid sutures were also open. This may tentatively indicate that this individual was not of old age, bearing also in mind that this individual was not edentulous.

Sex: Sex could not be determined due to the lack of the landmarks required for sex estimation.

Pathological lesions: Two skull vault fragments (one from occipital bone) have marked pitting in the ectocranial surface (1.5 g/26.5 g = 5.6%); two tibia fragments (8 g) with periostitis; one metacarpal shaft with active periostitis (0.5 g) and one unidentified shaft fragment with active periostitis too (0.5 g); one fragment unidentified (either skull or pelvis) with abnormal and high density pitting; one metatarsal fragment (1 g) also with periostitis; 14 long bone shaft fragments with active periostitis (8 g) and similar with one fragment of ilum body, same type of periosteal reaction, pitting and some striae. If we take all the long bone fragments including hand and foot bones, the percentage of fragments with periostitis with regard to weight is 21% (18/85.5). There seems to be a systemic infection in this skeleton. Finally only one joint surface was observed, the facet for dens articulation in atlas, but there were no degenerative changes.

Colour and fracture pattern: The bones reflected the typical fissure pattern characteristic of green bones when burnt. The colour was predominantly white (22 g) and white with shades of blue and grey (152 g), with some fragments from the upper and lower limbs and even the skull predominantly grey (15 g), blue (6 g) and lastly brown (1 g). In summary, a homogeneous cremation fired at high combustion.

Animal remains: Cremation burial 1769 contained the greatest quantity of burnt animal bone (325 fragments, 119 g). These fragments comprised pig skull, right radius and left tibia fragments, and further medium mammal sized cranial, vertebral, rib, long bone and indeterminate fragments which may also be pig. Fusion of the radius fragments indicates that the pig was between 12 and 42 months old at death. The burnt state of the bones negates analysis of osteometric data, but the bones were from a large animal, similar in size to that of a 40 month female wild boar held in the English Heritage reference collection (CfA 3289). The faunal pyre goods can be interpreted as a complete pig skeleton, and possibly a further bird pyre good.

Conclusion: The remains of one adult individual, likely to be younger than 45 years of age.

CREMATION BURIAL 1769

BONE ELEMENT	WEIGHT (g)
CRANIAL VAULT (Neurocranium)	27
TEETH	7
RIBS	3.5
VERTEBRAE	1
PELVIS	0.5
UPPER LIMB BONES	22
LOWER LIMB BONES	16
HAND BONES	1.5
FOOT BONES	1
LONG BONE UNIDENTIFIED (>4 mm)	45
UNIDENTIFIED FRAGMENTS	136.5
TOTAL WEIGHT	**261 g**

Cremation burial 1770

Description: Only a total of 23 fragments (8.5 g): 5 from the skull vault, 1 rib fragment, 1 humerus fragment, 1 radius fragment and the rest unidentified. The maximum fragment size was 39 mm from a long bone, perhaps humerus.

MNI: Only the remains of 1 individual were identified.

Age: All the bones seemed to indicate adult dimensions. Therefore the remains present here belonged most probably to an adult.

Sex: Sex could not be determined due to the lack of the landmarks required for sex estimation.

Pathological lesions: No pathological lesions were observed, although two long bone fragments may have had some bone remodelling but the striae present is unsure if it is due to post-mortem disturbances.

Colour and fracture pattern: The bones reflected the typical fissure pattern characteristic of green bones when burnt. All but two fragments (<0.5 g) which were dark blue, were white with shades of light grey.

Conclusion: One individual, possibly adult.

CREMATION BURIAL 1770

BONE ELEMENT	WEIGHT (g)
CRANIAL VAULT (Neurocranium)	1
RIBS	0.5
UPPER LIMB BONES	1
LONG BONE UNIDENTIFIED (>4 mm)	5
UNIDENTIFIED FRAGMENTS	1
TOTAL WEIGHT	**8.5 g**

APPENDIX 5: PHOTOMICROGRAPHS OF THE TOMBSTONES *by Kevin Hayward*

Photomicrograph of tombstone 1: *Martialis* (Plate A5.1)

Rock Type: Oosparite (Folk 1959; 1962)
Geological Source: Painswick Stone – Lower Jurassic (Aalenian), Painswick Hill, Gloucestershire GR SO 865 115
Note: Horny, angular ooid edges, spalled rims where the edges of the Ooids (round grains) fracture. Cement between grains coarse (poikilotopic).

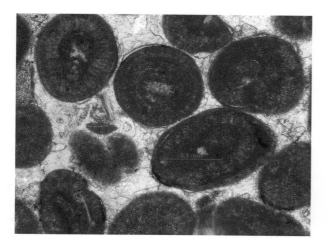

Plate A5.1 Photomicrograph of tombstone 1 (Field of view 2.4 mm plane polarised light).

Photomicrograph of tombstone 2: *Lucius Octavius Martialis* (Plate A5.2)

Rock Type: Oosparite (Folk 1959; 1962)
Geological Source: Painswick Stone – Lower Jurassic (Aalenian), Painswick Hill, Gloucestershire GR SO 865 115
Note: Horny, angular ooid edges, spalled rims where the edges of the Ooids (round grains) fracture. Cement between grains coarse (poikilotopic).

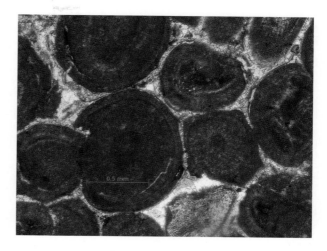

Plate A5.2 Photomicrograph of tombstone 2 (Field of view 2.4 mm plane polarised light).

Comparative photomicrograph of Painswick Stone (Plate A5.3)

Geological Source: Catsbrain Quarry, Painswick Stone – Lower Jurassic (Aalenian) Painswick Hill, Gloucestershire GR SO 865 115

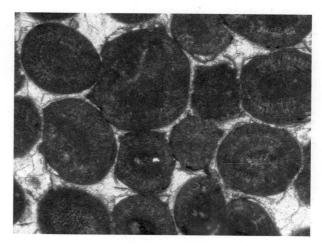

Plate A5.3 Comparative photomicrograph of Painswick Stone (Field of view 2.4 mm plane polarised light).

APPENDIX 6: THE PLEISTOCENE VERTIBRATE REMAINS *by Dr Danielle Schreve*

Introduction

An assemblage of vertebrate remains comprising the very fragmentary partial remains of a single adult hippopotamus (*Hippopotamus amphibius*), with additional material from a single individual each of probable bison (cf. *Bison priscus*) and elephant (Elephantidae sp.) were recovered during the excavation. The remains were found in sediments attributed to the Wotton hillock gravel cap, which had previously been mapped as forming part of the fourth terrace of the River Severn (eg Wills 1938; Worssam *et al.* 1989). They lay within a restricted area of a few square metres within the lower part of the gravel, and included a number of elements that were found in close association and may have been articulated, most notably a femoral shaft (sf 151, Plate A6.1), distal femoral condyle (sf 187) and tibia (sf 186).

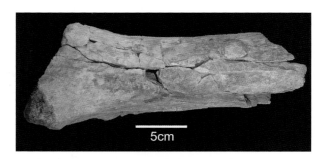

Plate A6.1   Partial femoral shaft of Hippopotamus amphibius.

Methodology

Although some specimens were cleaned prior to study, the faunal material was presented predominantly in field damp condition, with several specimens lifted in blocks of soil. Preservation of the material is extremely poor, both in terms of the overall surface condition and the high degree of fragmentation. This is particularly noticeable with elements of the dentition, especially canines and incisors, which are exceptionally comminuted and are represented by many hundreds of small fragments (Plate A6.2). None of the material extracted is complete and in some cases, the original surface of the bone has been completely destroyed, exposing the cancellous bone below. Virtually all the material is heavily crushed, although it is not possible to establish whether this is the result of past activities such as trampling by large mammals, sediment pressure or more recent factors such as damage by heavy machinery at the ground surface. A combination of old breaks and recent excavation damage is also apparent on most of the material. However some conjoining bone fragments were observed and it was therefore decided to

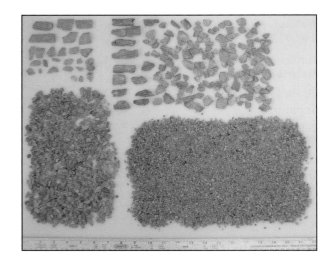

Plate A6.2   Comminuted upper canine of Hippopotamus amphibius.

undertake as much refitting and stabilisation work as possible during the analysis in order to maximise the amount of identifiable material. Although time-consuming, this approach proved extremely worthwhile by facilitating the identification of both dental and post-cranial remains that would otherwise have been impossible to recognise. The clay blocks were washed through a 500μn sieve in order to check for additional large bone or tooth material preserved within them and to recover microvertebrate and invertebrate remains. Again, the approach proved justified when a virtually complete molar of hippopotamus (sf 186, Plate A6.3) was recovered from inside one of the blocks, together with long bone fragments of probable hippopotamus tibia. No small vertebrates were noted in any of the residues. Measurements, where possible, were taken with electronic callipers according to the methodology of von den Driesch (1976).

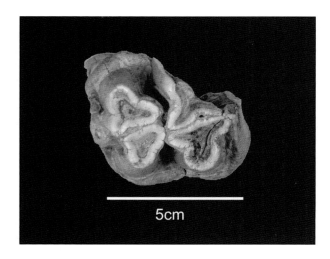

Plate A6.3   Virtually complete ?LM3 of Hippopotamus amphibius.

Species list

The list of identified species is given below, with Number of Identified Specimens (NISP) and Minimum Numbers of Individuals (MNI) in brackets.

PROBOSCIDEA
Elephantidae
Elephant undet., indeterminate elephant (NISP = 1; MNI = 1)

ARTIODACTLYA
Hippopotamidae
Hippopotamus cf. *amphibius* Linné, 1758, hippopotamus (NISP = 21; MNI = 1)

Bovidae
Bovini sp., large bovid, cf. *Bison priscus* Bojanus, 1827, bison (NISP = 4; MNI = 1)

Description of the finds

The most diagnostic elements within the assemblage are dental remains of hippopotamus, attributed to *Hippopotamus amphibius*, the extant African species. The anterior-projecting lower incisor tusks are large with a smooth surface and blunted points, whereas the upper incisors are much smaller. Refitting of specimen sf 1052, the very crushed ivory fragments of a left lower 1st incisor, allowed the blunted wear facet to be clearly discerned. The upper and lower canines consist of large, curving tusks, with fine grooves running lengthwise along their surface; in the largest modern adults, these may reach up to 700 mm overall (300 mm above the gum) (Skinner and Smithers 1990). The canines, like the incisors, grow continuously. They are triangular in section and are sharpened against each other, thereby creating a pronounced flat wear facet. The cheek teeth (premolars and molars) are also highly characteristic and readily identifiable. They are relatively low-crowned when compared to other herbivores, a reflection of the soft diet of the animals. Premolars have a single large cusp that rises to a rounded point, with a pronounced cingulum (ridge) and smaller accessory cusps near the base. The molars have four cusps, which rise to high peaks. Once in use, these form a highly recognisable, almost 'flower-like' pattern of wear. Three partial molars have been identified within the assemblage (sf 185, 186 and 194).

The postcranial remains of hippopotamus from the site consist of a partial atlas vertebra, one cervical vertebra (Plate A6.4), two partial thoracic vertebrae and other vertebral fragments. Major anterior elements such as the humeri and scapulae are apparently missing, although distal parts of the limbs are present in the form of a proximal right radius, a proximal left 2nd metacarpal and a first phalanx.

The only other animal identified to species level is a large bovid, identified on the basis of four postcranial elements: a distal humerus condylar fragment, an incomplete calcaneum, a femoral diaphysis fragment and a fragmentary proximal left

Plate A6.4   Reconstructed cervical vertebra of Hippopotamus amphibius.

tibia. Separation of the postcranial remains of aurochs (*Bos primigenius*) and Pleistocene bison (*Bison priscus*) is notoriously difficult (Gee 1993) but evaluation of the morphology of the specimens against recent and fossil comparative material suggested closer resemblance to the latter. Additional large long bone fragments (sf 151) have been tentatively attributed to an indeterminate elephant (Elephantidae sp.) on account of the compact and massive aspect of the material.

Taphonomy

From the remains recovered, it appears that a major part of the skull and dentition, with some vertebrae and postcranial elements, of a single adult hippopotamus was present at the site. Although these are in poor condition and demonstrate evidence of abrasion, the presence of associated remains provides a strong indication that they have not been transported a great distance since death. In particular, the presence of a mandibular process, fragments of mandibular ramus and isolated teeth suggests that a complete lower jaw with *in situ* dentition once occurred at the site. It is possible that more of the skeleton was initially present but only a few, incomplete postcranial elements have been identified. The majority of the postcranial skeleton may therefore have been destroyed previously or more widely scattered after disarticulation, beyond the limits of the site under investigation.

In addition to the high degree of fragmentation, most of the material is heavily iron-stained, from the post-depositional uptake of iron oxides, and bears evidence of moderate abrasion from transportation. A small number of specimens also show the fine tracery of acid etching left by roots. This indicates that either the decomposing carcass lay exposed on the land surface for a considerable period prior to its burial in the fluvial sediments, or that the bones became re-exposed at a later date, thereby allowing them to become root-damaged before being buried a second time. No evidence of carnivore, human or other modification, such as gnawmarks or cutmarks, was noted although the fragmentary state of the material may have obscured such evidence.

Evidence of local environment and climate from the vertebrate remains

Although the condition of the bones is poor, the different elements form a coherent assemblage that may credibly be interpreted as a single entity in terms of its palaeoecology. The modern hippopotamus *(H. amphibius)* is today restricted to sub-Saharan Africa although in historical times it extended from the Nile Valley into the Mediterranean. The smaller pygmy hippopotamus (*Choeropsis liberiensis*) of West Africa is not closely related to the Pleistocene species. In Britain, hippos were restricted to interglacial occurrences during the Pleistocene and were extremely widespread when present, extending as far north as North Yorkshire and as far west as south Wales during the Last Interglacial. As amphibious mammals they are found in close association with lakes or slow-flowing rivers sufficiently deep enough to allow total immersion, spending most of the day in the water and feeding nocturnally. Notable exceptions to immediate proximity to water are the numerous fossil records from Last Interglacial age cave sites (Marine Oxygen Isotope SubStage [MIS] 5e), particularly those from North Yorkshire such as Kirkdale Cave and Victoria Cave. At the latter site, the cave is located more than 2 km from and about 290 m above the floodplain of the River Ribble, the nearest source of water. It is assumed that the animals left the water at night to graze on the rich limestone herb flora (Stuart 1982a); even today hippos may travel substantial distances at night in search of food.

During the Last Interglacial, a period for which there are abundant palaeoenvironmental records available, hippopotamus apparently occurred during the climatic optimum of the interglacial (pollen zones II-early III) but not later in the stage (Stuart 1982b). There are no records of this animal from later parts of MIS 5, the early Devensian (Currant and Jacobi 2001). During MIS 5e mean summer temperatures were approximately 4° C warmer than in southern Britain today (Coope 2001). Temperate mixed-oak forest with *Quercus, Pinus, Corylus, Alnus* and *Carpinus* was widespread (eg Sparks and West 1970) but in many cases the floodplain vegetation was locally deforested and dominated by herbaceous vegetation such as plantain (*Plantago* sp.), the likely result of extensive grazing and trampling by large herbivores. At Barrington, Cambridgeshire, where hippopotamus remains were extremely abundant, the sediments had a notably high mineragenic content implying in-washing of soils from bare trampled ground, and the pollen spectra consisted of 90% herb pollen, implying clear modification of the vegetation by the megaherbivores (Gibbard and Stuart 1975). Bison are found in cold-climate and temperate

episodes alike and inhabit a wide range of environments at the present day, including both closed woodland and more open habitats.

The vertebrate assemblage from the site therefore suggests that the remains were laid down under temperate conditions with mean summer temperatures several degrees warmer than at present in proximity to a substantial body of water. In terms of the surrounding vegetation, a mosaic of environments with some regional temperate forest and locally open grassland is inferred.

Biostratigraphy and the date of the Wotton gravel cap

The utility of mammalian assemblages as indicators of relative age for Pleistocene sediments has been repeatedly demonstrated (eg Currant and Jacobi 2001; Schreve 2001; Stuart and Lister 2001). The vertebrate assemblage from the site, although small, is considered to be particularly age-diagnostic on account of the presence of hippopotamus. Rare early Middle Pleistocene ('Cromerian Complex') occurrences of an extinct hippopotamus (*Hippopotamus amtiquus = H. major*) are known from a number of sites in East Anglia, for example Norton Subcourse (Lewis *et al.* 2004). However, the modern species, *Hippopotamus amphibius*, is distinctive in that it makes only a single appearance in the British Pleistocene record, during the Last Interglacial. It is not known from any other late Middle Pleistocene or Late Pleistocene temperate episode (Schreve 2001) and is thus an excellent biostratigraphical indicator. The mammalian fauna of the Last Interglacial climatic optimum (the Joint Mitnor Cave Mammal Assemblage-Zone of Currant and Jacobi 2001), of which hippopotamus is the most characteristic component, has been dated on the basis of consistent radiometric dating of deposits clearly associated with this fauna to around 125 000 years BP. Uranium-series dating of speleothem sealing deposits containing a Hippopotamus assemblage at Victoria Cave has produced age-estimates of 120 ± 6 ka BP (Gascoyne *et al.* 1981) and these have since been corroborated at other Last Interglacial sites by further U-series age-estimates, for example 129–116 ka BP obtained from stalagmite fragments at Bacon Hole, Gower (Stringer *et al.* 1986). In the light of this the presence of hippopotamus would suggest that the deposits from 120–122 London Road contain material of Last Interglacial (MIS 5e) age, although this may have been reworked into younger deposits (see below).

A discrepancy therefore exists with the current age interpretation of the Wotton gravel spread, which has been mapped by the British Geological Survey as part of the fourth terrace of the River Severn sequence (Wills 1938), and the presence within it of remains *of H. amphibius*. The fourth terrace is underlain by sands and gravels of the Kidderminster Station Member, generally located 20–8 m above the modern River Severn (Maddy *et al.* 1995). Although no direct geochronological information is available the Kidderminster Station Member has been corre- lated with the Ailstone Member of the Avon Valley Formation (Maddy *et al.* 1991) and associated deposits at Strensham in Worcestershire (de Rouf- fignac, *et al.* 1995), both of which have been attributed to MIS 7–6 (*c* 245–128 000 years BP) on the basis of amino-acid geochronology (Maddy *et al.* 1995; Bowen 1999). This would suggest a substan- tially older age than the Last Interglacial. However, hippopotamus has not been recognised in any MIS 7 interglacial deposits despite the availability of numerous sites and many thousands of specimens (Schreve 2001). That observation strongly suggests that the current age interpretation for the Wotton gravel as fourth terrace is incorrect and should be re- examined.

The hippopotamus skeleton from London Road is clearly incomplete and has suffered substantial breakage and some abrasion, attesting to a degree of transportation after death. Nevertheless the presence of a hippopotamus mandible with teeth still *in situ* mitigates against transport over any substantial distance. A number of fan gravel deposits have been identified to the north of the location of the site (D. Maddy pers. comm. 21/4/06) and it is possible that the Wotton gravel represents a later fan gravel deposited on top of the Kidderminster Station gravel, similar to the deposition of the hippo- potamus-bearing Eynsham gravel on top of the

Summertown-Radley gravel in the Upper Thames (Bridgland 1994).

Deposits containing other reworked remains of Last Interglacial hippopotamus have been recognised nearby at the base of the Holt Heath Member in tributary valleys of the Severn, at Stourbridge in the Stour valley (Boulton 1917). However no actual Last Interglacial deposits have yet been identified in the Severn Valley itself, the closest being the New Inn Member at Cropthorne (Strickland in Jardine 1858) and Eckington Railway Cutting (Keen and Bridgland 1986) in the Avon valley. It is therefore likely that the hippopotamus came from now-vanished Last Inter- glacial deposits which were reworked during the early part of the ensuing Devensian cold stage (MIS 5d/b or MIS 4) when the fans would have been activated. Reworking of the hippopotamus and other faunal remains into an early last cold stage context would also fit well with the report of woolly rhinoceros (Coelodonta antiquitatis) bones found within sand and gravel deposits at a depth of 1.9 m on a plot of land adjacent to the site (Sermon 1996), as the presence of this animal would otherwise be palaeoecologically incompatible with hippopotamus. The megafaunal remains from 120–122 London Road are therefore of great significance in demonstrating the erstwhile presence of Last Interglacial deposits in this area and also in calling into question the published age of the Wotton gravel cap.

Bibliography

Adams, B J and Byrd, J E, 2006 Resolution of small-scale commingling: a case report from the Vietnam War, *Forensic Science International* **156**, 63–9

Allason-Jones, L, 1989a *Ear-rings in Roman Britain*, BAR Brit Ser **201**, Oxford

Allason-Jones, L, 1989b *Women in Roman Britain*, London

Anon, 1990 Verulamium, *Current Archaeology* **120**, 410–17

Ariès, P, 1981 *The Hour of Our Death*, New York

Atkins, M, 1987 *Found at Richard Cound: the Kingsholm dig*, Gloucester

Atkins, M and Garrod, A P (eds), 1987 Archaeology in Gloucester 1986, *Trans Bristol Gloucestershire Archaeol Soc* **105**, 233–41

Atkins, M and Garrod, A P (eds), 1988 Archaeology in Gloucester 1987, *Trans Bristol Gloucestershire Archaeol Soc* **106**, 209–18

Aufderheide, A C and Rodríguez-Martín, C, 1998 *The Cambridge Encyclopedia of Human Paleopathology*, Cambridge

Bailey, C J, 1967 An early Iron Age/Roman-British site at Pins Knoll. Litton Cheney. Final Report, *Proc Dorset Natural History and Archaeol Soc* **89**, 147–59

Barber, B and Bowsher, D, 2000 *The Eastern Cemetery of Roman London: excavations 1983–1990*, Museum of London Archaeology Service Monograph **4**

Barnes, E, 1994 Developmental defects of the axial skeleton in palaeopathology, Colorado

Bass, W M, 1987 *Human Osteology. Laboratory Field Manual* (3rd edition), Special Publication Number **2**, Missouri Archaeological Society, Columbia

Bateman, C and Williams, J, 2002 The South Gate Cemetery of Romans Gloucester: evidence from excavations off Parliament Street, 2001, *Glevensis* **35**, 25–8

Bauchhenss, G, 1988 *Corpus Signorum Imperii Romani. Deutschland III.1 Germania Inferior. Bonn und Umgebung. Militärische Grabdenmäler*, Bonn

Bayley, J and Butcher, S, 2004 *Roman brooches in Britain: a technological and typological study based on the Richborough collection*, RRCSAL **68**, London

Bello, S and Andrews, P, 2006 The intrinsic pattern of preservation of human skeletons and its influence on the interpretation of funerary behaviours, in R Gowland and C Knüsel, *Social Archaeology of Funerary Remains*, Oxford, 1–13

Bello, S M, Thomann, A, Signoli, M, Dutour, O and Andres, P, 2006 Age and sex bias in the reconstruction of past population structures, *American J Physical Anthropology* **129**, 24–38

Bennett, J, 1985 *Sea Mills: the Roman Town of Abonae. Excavations at Nazereth House 1972*, Bristol

Bermúdez de Castro, J M, 1989 Third molar agenesis in human prehistoric populations of the Canary Islands, *American J Physical Anthropology* **79**, 207–15

Berry, R C, and Berry, R J, 1967 Epigenetic variation in the human cranium, *Journal of Anatomy* **101**, 361–79

Biddle, M, 1967 Two Flavian burials from Grange Road, Winchester, *Antiquaries Journal* **47**, 224–50

Biddulph, E, 2005 Last orders: choosing pottery for funerals in Roman Essex, *Oxford J Archaeology* **24**, no. 1, 23–45

Biddulph, E, 2006 The Roman cemetery at Pepper Hill, Southfleet, Kent, *CTRL integrated site report series*, in CTRL digital archive, Archaeology Data Service, http://ads.ahds.ac.uk/catalogue/projArch/ctrl

Birck, J L, 1986 Precision K-Rb-Sr isotopic analysis - application to Rb-Sr chronology, *Chemical Geology* **56 (1–2)**, 72–83

Bland, R and Burnett, A, 1988 Normanby, Lincolnshire, in R Bland and A Burnett (eds), *The Normanby hoard and other Roman coin hoards*, Coin hoards from Roman Britain VIII, London, 114–215

Blockley, K, 1985 Marshfield: Ironmongers Piece Excavations 1982–3: an Iron Age and Romano-British settlement in the South Cotswolds, BAR Brit Ser **141**, Oxford

Boaz, R J and Behrensmeyer, A K, 1976 Hominid taphonomy: Transport of human skeletal parts in an artificial fluvial environment, *American J Physical Anthropology* **45**, 53–60

Bocquet-Appel, J and Masset, C, 1982 Farewell to paleodemography, *J Human Evolution* **11**, 321–33

Bodel, J, 2000 Dealing with the dead, in V M Hope and E Marshall (eds), *Death and Disease in the Ancient City*, London, 128–51

Booth, P, 2001 Late Roman cemeteries in Oxfordshire: a review, *Oxoniensia* **66**, 13–42

Booth, P, Crockett, A D, Fitzpatrick, A P, Powell, A B and Walker, K, forthcoming *The archaeology of the M6 Toll*, Oxford-Wessex Archaeol Joint Venture Monograph

Boppert, W, 1992 *Corpus Signorum Imperii Romani. Deutschland II.5 Germania Superior. Militärische Grabdenmäleraus Mainz und Umgebung*, Mainz

Boulton, W S, 1917 Mammalian remains in the glacial gravels at Stourbridge, *Proc Birmingham Natural History and Philosophical Society* **14**, 107–12

Bowen, D Q (ed.), 1999 *A revised correlation of Quaternary deposits in the British Isles*, Geological Society Special Report **23**, London

Boylston, A and Roberts, C, 1996 The Romano-British Cemetery at Kempston, Bedfordshire. Report on the Human Skeletal Remains, Unpublished report, University of Bradford

Boylston, A, Wiggins, R and Roberts, C, 1998 Material evidence. Human skeletal remains, in G Drinkall and M Foreman (eds), *The Anglo Saxon Cemetery at Castledyke South, Barton-On-Humber*, Sheffield Academic Reports **6**, Sheffield, 221–36

Boylston, A, Holst, M and Coughlan, J, 2000 Physical anthropology, in V Fiorato and C Knüsel (eds), *Blood Red Roses. The Archaeology of a Mass Grave from the Battle of Towton AD 1461*, Oxford, 45–59

Brickley, M and McKinley, J I, 2004 Guidelines to the Standards for Recording Human Remains, IFA Paper No **7**

Brickley, M, Mays, S and Ives, R, 2007 An Investigation of Skeletal Indicators of Vitamin D Deficiency in Adults: Effective Markers for Interpreting Past Living Conditions and Pollution Levels in 18th and 19th Century Birmingham, England, *American J Physical Anthropology* **132**, 67–79

Bridgland, D R, 1994 *Quaternary of the Thames*, Geological Conservation Review volume 7, London

Bronk Ramsey, C, 1995 Radiocarbon Calibration and Analysis of Stratigraphy: The OxCal Program, *Radiocarbon* **37**, 425–30

Bronk Ramsey, C, 1998 Probability and dating, *Radiocarbon* **40**, 461–74

Bronk Ramsey, C, 2001 Development of the radiocarbon calibration program, *Radiocarbon* **43**, 355–63

Bronk Ramsey, C, Higham, T F G, Owen, D C, Pike, A W G and Hedges, R E M, 2002 Radiocarbon dates from the Oxford AMS System; Datelist 31, *Archaeometry* **44(3)** Suppl. 1, 1–149

Bronk Ramsey, C, Higham, T, Bowles, A and Hedges, R, 2004a Improvements to the Pretreatment of Bone at Oxford, *Radiocarbon* **46**, 155–63

Bronk Ramsey, C, Higham , T and Leach, P, 2004b Towards High-oresicion AMS: Progress and Limitations, *Radiocarbon* **46**, 17–24

Brooks, S and Suchey, J M, 1990 Skeletal age determination based on the os pubis: a comparison of the Acsádi-Nemeskéri and Suchey-Brooks method, *Human Evolution* **5**, 227–38

Brothwell, D R, 1981 *Digging Up Bones*, Oxford

Brothwell, D and Zakrzewski, S, 2004 Metric and non-metric studies of archaeological human bone, in M Brickley and J McKinley (eds), *Guidelines to the Standards for Recording Human Remains*, IFA paper **7**, 28–33

Buckberry, J L and Chamberlain, A T, 2002 Age estimation from the auricular surface of the ilium: a revised method, *American J Physical Anthropology* **119**, 231–39

Buikstra, J E and Ubelaker, D H, 1994 *Standards for Data Collection from Human Skeletal Remains*, Arkansas Archaeological Survey Research Series No **44**

Cartwright, F F and Biddiss, M D, 2004 *Disease and History*, Stroud

Chamberlain, A, 2000 Problems and prospects in palaeodemography, in M Cox and S Mays (eds), *Human Osteology in Archaeology and Forensic Science*, Greenwich Medical Media, London, 101–15

CgMs, 2003 Archaeological Desk-based Assessment 118–120 London Road, Gloucester, Unpublished client report

Chenery, C A, 2005 The analysis of 18 O/ 16 O ratios of biogenic phosphates, NIGL Report Series No. **195**

Clarke, G, 1979 *The Roman Cemetery at Lankhills*, Winchester Studies **3**: Pre-Roman and Roman Winchester. Part II, Oxford

Clarke, S, 1996 Acculturation and continuity, in J Webster and N Cooper (eds), *Roman Imperialism: post-colonial perspectives*, Leicester University Monographs **3**, 71–84

Clough, S, 2003 Report on 56 *Skeletons, Disarticulated Remains and 18 Cremations from London Road, Gloucester*, The Rudyard Consultancy, unpublished report

Cohen, A and Serjeantson, D, 1996 *A Manual for the identification of Bird Bones from Archaeological Sites*, London

Collingwood, R G and Wright, R P, 1965 *Roman Inscriptions of Britain 1. Inscriptions on Stone*, Oxford

Conheeney, J, 2000 The inhumation burials, in B E Barber and D Bowsher, 277–96

Cook, S, 2004 *Archaeological Field Evaluation 118–120 London Road, Gloucester*, Unpublished client report

Cool, H E M, 1983 *A study of the Roman personal ornaments made of metal, excluding brooches, from southern Britain, unpubl*. PhD Thesis, Univ. Wales

Cool, H E M, 2003 The Metal Small Finds, in Foundations Archaeology 2003

Cool, H E M, 2004 *The Roman Cemetery at Brougham, Cumbria: Excavations 1966 and 1967*, Britannia Monograph **21**, London

Cool, H E M, 2006 *Eating and Drinking in Roman Britain*, Cambridge

Cool, H E M, forthcoming Finds from funerary contexts, in L Allason-Jones (ed.), *Artefacts in Roman Britain: Their Purpose and Use*, Cambridge

Cool, H E M, Lloyd-Morgan, G and Hooley, A D, 1995 *Finds from the Fortress*. Archaeology of York 17/10, York

Cool, H E M and Philo, C (eds.), 1998 *Roman Castleford Excavations 1974–85. Volume I: the small finds*. Yorkshire Archaeology **4**, Wakefield

Coope, G R, 2001 Biostratigraphical distinction of interglacial coleopteran assemblages from southern Britain attributed to Oxygen Isotope Stages 5e and 7, *Quaternary Science Reviews* **20**, 1717–22

Costa, R L Jr, 1980 Age, sex, and antemortem loss of teeth in prehistoric Eskimo samples from Point Hope and Kodiak Island, Alaska, *American J Physical Anthropology* **53**, 579–87

Cox, M, 2000 Ageing adults from the skeleton, in M Cox and S A Mays (eds), *Human Osteology in Archaeology and Forensic Science*, Greenwich Medical Media, London, 61–81

Crawford Adams, J, 1983 *Outline of Fractures* (8th ed.), New York

Crowfoot, E, 1981 Textile Impressions, in C S Green, M Paterson and L Biek, A Roman Coffin-Burial from the Crown Buildings Site, Dorchester: with particular reference to the head of well-preserved hair, *Proc Dorset Natural History and Archaeol Soc* **103**, 67–100

Crummy, N, 1983 *The Roman small finds from excavations in Colchester 1971–9*, Colchester Archaeological Report **2**, Colchester

Crummy, N, 1992 The Roman small finds from the Culver Street site, in P Crummy, *Excavations at Culver Street, the Gilberd School, and other sites in Colchester 1971–85*, Colchester Archaeology Report **6**, Colchester, 240–5

Crummy, N, Crummy, P and Crossan, C, 1993 *Excavations of Roman and later cemeteries, churches and monastic sites in Colchester, 1971–88*, Colchester Archaeological Trust

Crummy, P, Benfield, S, Crummy, N, Rigby, V and Shimmin, D, 2007 *Stanway*, Britannia Monograph **24**, London

Cunliffe, B, 1971 *Excavations at Fishbourne 1961–1969. Volume II: The Finds*, RRCSAL 27, Leeds

Currant, A P and Jacobi, R M, 2001 A formal mammalian biostratigraphy for the Late Pleistocene of Britain, *Quaternary Science Reviews* **20**, 1707–16

Darling, W G, Bath A H and Talbot, J C, 2003 The O & H stable isotopic composition of fresh waters in the British Isles. 2: Surface waters and ground water, *Hydrology and Earth System sciences* **7**(2), 183–95

de Rouffignac, C, Bowen, D Q, Coope, G R, Keen, D H, Lister, A L, Maddy, D, Robinson, J E, Sykes, G A and Walker, M J C, 1995 Late Middle Pleistocene interglacial deposits at Upper Strensham, Worcestershire, England, *Journal of Quaternary Science* **10**, 15–31

Dennehy, E, 2001 Children's burial ground, in *Archaeology Ireland* **15**, 20–3

Dias, G and Tayles, N, 1997 'Abscess cavity' – a misnomer, *International J Osteoarchaeology* **7**, 548–54

Dobney, K M, and Reilly, K, 1988 A method for recording archaeological animal bones: the use of diagnostic zones, *Circaea* **5**, 79–96

Down, A and Rule, M, 1971 *Chichester Excavations 1*, Chichester

Drancourt M, Roux V, Dang L V, Tran-Hung L, Castex D, Chenal Francisque V, Ogata H, Fournier P E, Crubezy E and Raoult D, 2004 Genotyping, Orientalis-like Yersinia pestis, and plague pandemics, *Emerg Infect Dis.* **10**, 1585–92

Driel-Murray, C van, 1999 And did those feet in ancient times … Feet and shoes as a material projection of the self, in P Baker (ed.), *TRAC 98*, Leicester, Oxford, 131–40

Duday, H, 2006 L'archéothanatologie ou l'archéologie de la mort (Archaeoethnoanatology or the Archaeology of Death), in R Gowland and C Knüsel (eds), *Social Archaeology of Funerary Remains*, Oxford, 30–56

Duncan-Jones, R P, 1996 The impact of the Antonine Plague, *J Roman Archaeol* **9**, 108–36

Duray, S M, 1996 Dental indicators of stress and reduced age at death in prehistoric native Americans, *American J Physical Anthropology* **99**, 275–86

Emery, G T, 1963 Dental pathology and archaeology, *Antiquity* **37**, 274–81

Erdal, Y S, 2006 A pre-Columbian case of congenital syphilis from Anatolia (Nicaea, 13th century AD), *International J Osteoarchaeology* **16**, 16–33

Esmonde Cleary, S, 2000 Putting the dead in their place: burial location in Roman Britain, in J Pearce *et al.*, 127–42

Evans, E and Maynard, D, 1997 Caerleon Lodge Hill cemetery: the Abbeyfield site 1992, *Britannia* **28**, 169–243

Evans, J A, Tatham, S, Chenery, S R and Chenery, C A, in press Anglo Saxon animal husbandry techniques revealed though isotope and chemical variations in cattle teeth, *Applied Geochemistry*

Farwell, D E and Molleson, T I, 1993 *Poundbury, vol. 2: The cemeteries*, Dorset Natural History and Archaeol Soc Monograph **11**

Fédération Dentaire Internationale (FDI), 1982 An epidemiological index of developmental defects of dental enamel (DDE Index), *International Dental Journal* **32**, 159–67

Finnegan, M, 1978 Non-metric variation of the infracranial skeleton, *Journal of Anatomy* **125**, 23–37

Fiorato, V, Boylston, A and Knüsel, C (eds), 2000 *Blood Red Roses. The Archaeology of a Mass Grave from the Battle of Towton AD 1461*, Oxford

Folk, R L, 1959 Practical petrographic classification of limestones, *American Association of Petroleum Geologists Bulletin*, v. **43**, 1–38

Folk, R L, 1962 Spectral subdivision of limestone types: Classification of carbonate Rocks, *American Association of Petroleum Geologists* Memoir **1**, 62–84

Foundations Archaeology, 2003 *124–130 London Road, Gloucester: Archaeological excavation report and post-excavation assessment*, http://www.foundations.co.uk/reports/gloucestershire/lrg.shtml

Frere, S S, 1991a *Britannia*, 3rd edition, London

Frere, S S, 1991b Roman Britain in 1990: sites explored, *Britannia* **22**, 256–308

Frere, S S, 1992 Roman Britain in 1991: sites explored, *Britannia* **23**, 222–92

Fulford, M, 1999 Veteran Settlement in 1st century Britain and the foundations of Gloucester and Lincoln, in H Hurst (ed.), 177–80

Fullbrook-Leggatt, L E W O, 1933 Glevum, *Trans Bristol Gloucestershire Archaeol Soc* **55**, 55–104

Galloway, A, 1999 *Broken Bones. Anthropological analysis of blunt force trauma*, Springfield

Garrod, P and Heighway, C, 1984 *Garrod's Gloucester: archaeological observations 1974–81*, Western Archaeological Trust, Gloucester

Gascoyne, M, Currant, A P and Lord, T, 1981 Ipswichian fauna of Victoria Cave and the marine palaeoclimatic record, *Nature* **294**, 652–4

Gee, H, 1993 The distinction between postcranial bones of *Bos primigenius* Bojanus, 1827 and *Bison priscus* Bojanus, 1827 from the British Pleistocene and the taxonomic status of *Bos* and *Bison*, *Journal of Quaternary Science* **8**, 79–92

Gejvall, N G, 1963 Cremations, in D Brothwell and E Higgs (eds), *Science in Archaeology*, London, 379–90

Genovés, S, 1962 Introducción al Diagnóstico de la Edad y del Sexo en Restos Óseos Prehistóricos, Universidad Nacional Autónoma de México, Mexico

Gibbard, P L and Stuart, A J, 1975 Flora and vertebrate fauna of the Barrington Beds, *Geological Magazine* 112, 493–501

Gilliam, J F, 1961 The Plague under Marcus Aurelius, *American Journal of Philology* 82(3), 225–51

Gloucester Archaeology, 1993 Archaeological Evaluation of Former Trent-Severn Depot, London Road, Gloucester, Unpublished client report

Gloucester Archaeology, 2002 Gloucester Archaeology Unit Annual Report, 2002, *Glevensis* 36, 55–63

Gowland, R, 2001 Playing dead: implications of mortuary evidence for the social construction of childhood in Roman Britain, in G Davies, A Gardner and K Lockyear (eds), *TRAC 2000: Proceedings of the Tenth Annual Theoretical Roman Archaeology Conference London 2000*, Oxford, 152–68

Grauer, A, 1991 Patterns of life and death: the palaeodemography of medieval York, in H Bush and M Zvelebil (eds), *Health in Past Societies. Biocultural Interpretations of Human Skeletal Remains in Archaeological Contexts*, BAR Int Ser 567, Oxford, 67–80

Grauer, A L and Roberts, C A, 1996 Paleoepidemiology, healing, and possible treatment of trauma in a medieval cemetery population of St. Helen-on-the-Walls, York, England, *American J Physical Anthropology* 100, 531–44

Greenburg, J, 2003 Plagued by doubt: reconsidering the impact of a mortality crisis in the 2nd c. AD, *J Roman Archaeology* 16, 413–25

Greep, S, 1998 The bone, antler and ivory artefacts, in H E M Cool and C Philo, 267–85

Haglund, W D and Sorg, M H (eds), 1997 *Forensic Taphonomy. The Postmortem Fate of Human Remains*, New York

Harman, M, Molleson, T and Price, J L, 1981 Burials, bodies and beheadings in Romano-British and Anglo-Saxon cemeteries, *Bull British Museum Nat Hist Geol* 35(5), 145–88

Hassall, M, 2000 Pre-Hadrianic Legionary Dispositions in Britain, in R J Brewer, *Roman Fortresses and their legions*, Soc Antiq And Nat Museum Wales, Cardiff, 51–67

Hassall, M and Hurst, H, 1999 Soldier and Civilian: a debate on the bank of the Severn, in H Hurst (ed.), 181–90

Hassall, M W C and Tomlin, R S O, 1984 Roman Britain in 1983: II. Inscriptions, *Britannia* 15, 333–56

Hauser, G and De Stefano, G F, 1989 *Epigenetic Variants of the Human Skull*, Schweizerbart, Stuttgart

Hayes, J, 1991 Second century grave of a wealthy citizen, *The Searcher* 71, 18–21

Heighway, C M, 1980 Roman cemeteries in Gloucester District, *Trans Bristol Gloucestershire Archaeol Soc* 98, 57–72

Henig, M, 1974 *A corpus of Roman engraved gemstones from British sites*, BAR 8, Oxford

Henig, M, 2004 *Corpus Signorum Imperii Romani. Great Britain I.9 Roman Sculpture from the North West Midlands*, British Academy, Oxford

Herbert, N M, 1988 *The Victoria County History of Gloucestershire, Volume IV: Gloucester City*

Hillson, S, 1996a *Mammal bones and Teeth. An Introductory Guide to Methods of Identification*, London

Hillson, S, 1996b *Dental Anthropology*, Cambridge

Hillson, S, 2001 Recording dental caries in archaeological human remains, *International J Osteoarchaeology* 11, 249–89

Hillson, S, Grigson, C and Bond, S, 1998 Dental defects of congenital syphilis, *American J Physical Anthropology* 107, 25–40

Holden, J L, Phakley, P P and Clement, J G, 1995 Scanning electron microscope observations of heat-treated human bone, *Forensic Science International* 74, 29–45

Hope, V M, 2000 Contempt and respect: the treatment of the corpse in ancient Rome, in V M Hope and E Marshall (eds), *Death and Disease in the Ancient City*, London, 104–27

Hopkins, K, 1983 *Death and Renewal*, Cambridge

Hurlburt, S, 2000 The taphonomy of cannibalism: a review of anthropogenic bone modification in the American Southwest, *International J Osteoarchaeology* 10, 4–26

Hurst, H, 1972 Excavations at Gloucester, 1968–71: first interim report, *Antiquaries Journal* 52, 24–69

Hurst, H, 1974 Excavations at Gloucester, 1971–1973: second interim report, *Antiquaries Journal* 54, 8–52

Hurst, H, 1985 *Kingsholm*, Gloucester Archaeological Reports Vol. 1

Hurst, H, 1988 Gloucester (*Glevum*), in G Webster (ed.), *Fortress into city*, London, 48–73

Hurst, H (ed.), 1999a *The Coloniae of Roman Britain*, Journal of Roman Archaeology Supplementary Series 36

Hurst, H, 1999b Topography and Identity in Glevum Colonia, in H Hurst (ed.), 113–35

Hurst, H, 2005 Roman Cirencester and Gloucester compared, *Oxford J Archaeology* 24(3), 293–305

Huskinson, J, 1994 *Corpus Signorum Imperii Romani. Great Britain I.8 Roman Sculpture from Eastern England*, British Academy, Oxford

Isaksen, L, Loe L and Saunders M, forthcoming, X-Bones: A new approach to recording skeletons in 3D, in G Earl (ed.), *Proceedings of the 2006 & 2007 Computer Applications and Quantitative Methods in Archaeology UK Conferences*, Southampton

Jacobi, F, Bramanti, B, Dresely, V and Alt, K W, 2006 *Why did they have to die? An Iron Age mass grave from Westerhausen, Germany*, Poster presented at the 16th Paleopathology Association European meeting 28th Aug–1st September 2006, Santorini, Greece

Jardine, W, 1858 *Memoirs of Hugh Edwin Strickland*, London

Jones, R, 1987 Burial Customs of Rome and the Provinces, in J Wacher (ed.), *The Roman World*, London and New York, 812–44

Jurmain, R D, 1999 *Stories from the Skeleton. Behavioural Reconstruction in Human Osteology*. Interpreting the Remains of the Past 1, Amsterdam

Kausmally, T, 2007 *East Smithfield Black Death Cemetery*, Centre for Human Bioarchaeology, Museum of London, http://www.museumoflondon.org.uk/English/Collections/OnlineResources/CHB/Database/Medieval+cemeteries/ESmithfieldBlackDeath.htm

Keen, D H and Bridgland, D R, 1986 An interglacial fauna from Avon No.3 Terrace at Eckington, Worcestershire, *Proc Geologists' Association* **97**, 303–7

Kelley, M A, Levesque, D R and Weidl, E, 1991 Contrasting patterns of dental disease in five early northern Chilean groups, in M A Kelley and C S Larsen (eds), *Advances in Dental Anthropology*, New York, 203–13

Kennedy, K A R, 1989 Skeletal markers of occupational stress, in Y M İşcan and K A R Kennedy (eds), *Reconstruction of Life From the Skeleton*, New York, 129–60

Key, C A, Aiello, L C and Molleson, T, 1994 Cranial suture closure and its implications for age estimation, *International J Osteoarchaeology* **4**, 193–207

King, T, Hillson, S and Humphrey, L T, 2002 A detailed study of enamel hypoplasia in a post-medieval adolescent of known age and sex, *Archives of Oral Biology* **47**, 29–39

Kooijmans, L P, 2005 *Bronze war, A collective burial at Wassenaar*, Amsterdam

Langsjoen, O, 1998 Diseases of the dentition, in A C Aufderheide and C Rodríguez-Martín, 393–412

Larsen, C S, 1997 *Bioarchaeology. Interpreting Behaviour from the Human Skeleton*, Cambridge Studies in Bioanthropology, Cambridge

Larsen, C S, Shavit, R and Griffin, M C, 1991 Dental caries evidence for dietary change: an archaeological context, in M A Kelley and C S Larsen (eds), *Advances in Dental Anthropology*, New York, 179–202

Lasker, G W, 1951 Genetic analysis of racial traits of the teeth, *Cold Spring Harbor Symposia on Quantitative Biology* **15**, 191–203

Lauwerier, R C G M, 1993 Bird remains in Roman graves, *Archaeofauna* **2**, 75–82

Levinson, A A, Luz, B and Kolodny, Y, 1987 Variations in oxygen isotopic compositions of human teeth and urinary stones, *Applied Geochemistry* **2**, 367–71

Lewis, M E, 2004 Endocranial lesions: their distribution and aetiology, *International J Osteoarchaeology* **14**, 82–97

Lewis, M and Roberts, C, 1997 Growing pains: the interpretation of stress indicators, *International J Osteoarchaeology* **7**, 581–6

Lewis, S G, Parfitt, S A, Preece, R C, Sinclair, J, Coope, G R, Field, M H, Maher, B A, Scaife, R G and Whittaker, J E, 2004 Age and palaeoenvironmental setting of the Pleistocene vertebrate fauna at Norton Subcourse, Norfolk, in D C Schreve (ed.), *The Quaternary Mammals of Southern and Eastern England*, Quaternary Research Association, London, 5–17

Littleton, J and Frohlich, B, 1993 Fish-eaters and farmers: dental pathology in the Arabian Gulf, *American J Physical Anthropology* **92**, 427–47

Littman, R J and Littman, M L, 1973 Galen and the Antonine Plague, *American J Philology* **94**, 243–55

Loe, L and Cox, M, 2005 Peri- and post mortem surface features on archaeological human bone: why they should not be ignored and a protocol for their identification and interpretation, in S R Zakrzewski and M Clegg (eds), *Proceedings of the fifth annual conference of the British Association for Biological Anthropology and Osteoarchaeology*, Oxford, 11–21

Mackreth, D F, 1995 Pre-Roman and Roman brooches, in K Blockley, M Blockley, P Blockley, S S Frere and S Stow, *Excavations in the Marlowe car park and surrounding areas*, Archaeology of Canterbury **V**, Canterbury, 955–82

Maddy, D, Green, C P, Lewis, S G and Bowen, D Q, 1995 Pleistocene geology of the Lower Severn Valley, UK, *Quaternary Science Reviews* **14**, 209–22

Maddy, D, Keen, D H, Bridgland, D R, Green, C P, 1991 A revised model for the Pleistocene development of the River Avon, Warwickshire, *J Geological Society of London* **148**, 473–84

Manning, W H, 1985 *Catalogue of Romano-British Iron Tools, Fittings and Weapons in the British Museum*, London

Manning, W H, 2000 The Fortresses of Legio XX, in R J Brewer (ed.), *Roman Fortresses and their Legions*, Soc Antiquaries of London and Nat Museum and Galleries of Wales, London

Maresh, M M, 1972 Measurements from roentgenograms, in R W McCammon, (ed.), *Human Growth and Development*, Springfield, IL, 157–200

Margerison, B J, 1997 A Comparison of the Palaeodemography of Catastrophic and Attritional Cemeteries, Unpublished Ph.D. thesis, University of Bradford

Margerison, B J, and Knüsel, C J, 2002 Paleodemographic comparison of a catastrophic and an attritional death assemblage, *American J Physical Anthropology* **119**, 134–43

Martin-Kilcher, S, 2000 *Mors immatura* in the Roman world—a mirror of society and tradition, in Pearce *et al.*, 63–77

Mattingly, D, 2006 An Imperial Possession: Britain in the Roman Empire, London

May, T, 1930 *Catalogue of the Roman Pottery in the Colchester and Essex Museum*, Cambridge

Mays, S A, 1993 Infanticide in Roman Britian, *Antiquity* **67**, 883–8

Mays, S, 1998 *The Archaeology of Human Bones*, London

Mays, S, 2000 The archaeology and history of infanticide, in J Sofaer-Derevenski (ed.), *Children and Material Culture*, London, 180–90

Mays, S, 2002 The relationship between molar wear and age in an early 19th century AD archaeological human skeletal series documented age at death, *J Archaeological Science* **29**, 861–71

McKern, T W, 1970 Estimation of skeletal age: from puberty to about 30 years of age, in T D Stewart (ed.), *Personal Identification in Mass Disasters*, National Museum of Natural History, Washington D.C., 41–56

McKinley, J I, 1993 Bone fragment size and weights of bone from modern British cremations and it implications for the interpretation of archaeological cremations, *International J Osteoarchaeology* **3**, 283–87

McKinley, J I, 1994 Bone fragment size in British cremation burials and its implications for pyre technology and ritual, *J Archaeological Science* **21**, 339–42

McKinley, J I, 1997 Cremated human bone from burial and cremation-related contexts, in A P Fitzpatrick, *Archaeological Excavations on the Route of the A27 Westhampnett Bypass, West Sussex, 1992. Volume 2: The Cemeteries*, Wessex Archaeology and the Highways Agency, Salisbury, 244–52

McKinley, J I, 2000a Cremation burials, in B Barber and D Bowsher (eds), 264–77

McKinley, J, 2000b The analysis of cremated bone, in M Cox and S Mays (eds), *Human osteology in archaeology and forensic science*, London, 403–21

McKinley, J, 2000c Phoenix rising: aspects of cremation in Roman Britain, in J Pearce *et al.* (eds), 38–44

McKinley, J, 2004 Compiling a skeletal inventory: disarticulated and co-mingled remains, in M Brickley and J McKinley (eds), 14–17

McKinley, J, forthcoming Ryknield Street, Wall (Site 12), in Booth *et al.* forthcoming

McKinley, J I and Roberts, C A, 1993 *Excavation and Post-Excavation Treatment of Cremated and Inhumed Human Remains*, IFA Technical Paper No 13, Birmingham

McWhirr, A, Viner, L and Wells, C, 1982 *Romano-British Cemeteries at Cirencester*, Cirencester Excavations Committee, Cirencester

Meindl, R S and Lovejoy, C O, 1985 Ectocranial suture closure: A revised method for the determination of skeletal age at death based on the lateral-anterior sutures, *American J Physical Anthropology* **68**, 29–45

Miles, A, 1962 Assessment of age of a population of Anglo-Saxons from their dentition, *Proc Royal Society of Medicine* **55**, 881–6

Miles, A E W, 2001 The Miles method of assessing age from tooth wear revisited, *J Archaeological Science* **28**, 973–82

Miles, D, Palmer, S, Smith, A and Jones, G P, 2007 *Iron Age and Roman settlement in the Upper Thames Valley*. Thames Valley Landscapes Monograph **26**, Oxford Archaeology

Millett, M, 1986 An early Roman cemetery from Alton, Hampshire, *Proc Hampshire Field Club and Archaeol Soc* **42**, 43–87

Millett, M, 1990 *The Romanization of Britain: an essay in archaeological interpretation*, Cambridge

Mills, J M, 1993 Hobnails, in D E Farwell and T L Molleson 1993

Molleson, T and Cox, M, 1993 *The Spitalfields Project Volume 2 – The Anthropology – The Middling Sort*, CBA Res Rep **86**, York

Montgomery, J, 2002 Lead and Strontium Isotope Compositions of Human Dental Tissues as an Indicator of Ancient Exposure and Population Dynamics, Unpublished PhD thesis, University of Bradford

Montgomery, J, Evans, J A and Wildman, G, 2006 87Sr/86Sr isotope composition of bottled British mineral waters for environmental and forensic purposes, *Applied Geochemistry* **21**, 1626–34

Moore, T, 2006 *Iron Age Societies in the Severn-Cotswolds: developing narratives of social and landscape change*, BAR Brit Ser **421**, Oxford

Moorrees, C F A, Fanning, E A and Hunt, E E Jr, 1963 Age variation of formation stages for ten permanent teeth, *J Dental Research* **42**, 1490–1502

Moyniham, P J, 1998 Update on the nomenclature of carbohydrates and their dental effects, *J Dentistry* **26**, 209–18

OA, 1992 *Fieldwork Manual*, (ed. D Wilkinson, first edition, August 1992)

O'Neil, J R, Roe, L J, Reinhard, E and Blake, R E, 1994 A rapid and precise method of oxygen isotope analysis of biogenic phosphate, *Israel J Earth Science* **43**, 203–12

Ortner, D J and Erikson, M F, 1997 Bone changes in the human skull probably resulting from scurvy in infancy and childhood, *International J Osteoarchaeology* **7**, 212–20

Ortner, D J and Putschar, W G J, 1981 *Identification of Pathological Conditions in Human Skeletal Populations*, Washington DC

Ostendorf Smith, M, 1997 Osteological indications of warfare in the Archaic period of the Western Tennessee Valley, in D L Martin and D W Frayer (eds), *Troubled Times. Violence and Warfare in the Past*, Amsterdam, 241–66

Parker Pearson, M, 1999 *The Archaeology of Death and Burial*, Stroud

Parkhouse, J and Evans, E, 1996 *Excavations at Cowbridge, South Glamorgan 1977–88*, BAR Brit Ser **245**, Oxford

Pearce, J, 1998 From death to deposition: the sequence of ritual in cremation burials of the Roman period, in C Forcey, J Hawthorne and R Witcher (eds), *TRAC 97: Proceedings of the seventh annual Theoretical Roman Archaeology Conference*, Oxford, 99–111

Pearce, J, 2001 Constructions of infancy—mortuary rituals for infants in the Roman provinces', in A Gardner *et al.* (eds.), *Proceedings of the 9th Theoretical Roman Archaeology Conference*, Oxford, 125–42

Pearce, J, Millett, M and Struck, M (eds), 2000 *Burial, Society and Context in the Roman World*, Oxford

Philpott, R, 1991 *Burial practices in Roman Britain*, BAR Brit Ser **219**, Oxford

Pindborg, J J, 1982 Aetiology of developmental enamel defects not related to fluorosis, *International Dental Journal* **32**, 123–34

Polfer, M, 2000 Reconstructing funerary rituals: the evidence of ustrina and related archaeological structures, in J Pearce, M Millett and M Struck (eds), 30–7

Pope, E J, O'Brian, M A and Smith, C, 2004 Identification of traumatic injury in burned cranial bone: an experimental approach, *Journal of Forensic Science* **49**(3), 431–40

Potter, T W, 1979 *Romans in north-west England*, Cumberland and Westmorland Antiquarian and Archaeological Society Research Series **1**, Kendal

Powell, K, forthcoming The metal finds, in P Booth *et al.* forthcoming

Powell, M L, 1985 The analysis of dental wear and caries for dietary reconstruction, in R I Jr Gilbert and J H Mielke (eds), *The Analysis of Prehistoric Diets*, New York, 307–38

Price, J and Cottam, S, 1998 *Romano-British glass vessels: a handbook*. CBA Practical Handbook in Archaeology **14**, York

Price, J and Cool, H E M, 1985 Glass (including glass from 72 Dean's Way), in H R Hurst, *Kingsholm*, Gloucester Archaeol. Rep. No. **1**, Cambridge, 41–54

Rawes, B, 1972 Roman pottery kilns at Gloucester, *Trans Bristol Gloucestershire Archaeol Soc* **91**, 18–59

Rawes, B 1983 (ed.), Archaeological Review No. 7 1982, *Trans Bristol Gloucestershire Archaeol Soc* **101**, 189–96

Rawes, B (ed.), 1991 Archaeological Review No. 15 1990, *Trans Bristol Gloucestershire Archaeol Soc* **109**, 223–38

Rawes, B (ed.), 1992 Archaeological Review No. 16 1991, *Trans Bristol Gloucestershire Archaeol Soc* **110**, 219-224

Rawes, B (ed.), 1993 Archaeological Review No. 17 1992, *Trans Bristol Gloucestershire Archaeol Soc* **111**, 215–35

Rawes, J A and Wills, J (eds), 1998 Archaeological Review No. 22 1997, *Trans Bristol Gloucestershire Archaeol Soc* **116**, 191–212

RCHME, 1962 *An inventory of the historical monuments in the city of York: Volume 1: Ebvracvm*, London

Reece, R, 1962 The Oakley Cottage Romano-British Cemetery, Cirencester, *Trans Bristol Gloucestershire Archaeol Soc* **81**, 51–73

Reece, R 1999 Colonia in context: Glevum and the civitas Dobunnorum, in H Hurst (ed.), 73–85

Reimer, P J, Baillie, M G L, Bard, E, Bayliss, A, Beck, J W, Bertrand, C J H, Blackwell, P G, Buck, C E, Burr, G S, Cutler, K B, Damon, P E, Edwards, R L, Fairbanks, R G, Friedrich, M, Guilderson, T P, Hogg, A G, Hughen, K A, Kromer, B, McCormac, G, Manning, S, Bronk Ramsey, C, Reimer, R W, Remmele, S, Southon, J R, Stuiver, M, Talamo, S, Taylor, F W, van der Plicht, J and Weyhenmeyer, C E, 2004 IntCal04 Terrestrial radiocarbon age calibration, 0–26 Cal Kyr BP, *Radiocarbon*, **46**, 1029–58

Resnick, D and Niwayama, G, 1995 Osteomyelitis, septic arthritis, and soft tissue infection: mechanisms and situations, in D Resnick, *Diagnosis of Bone and Joint Disorders*, 3rd ed. vol. 4, London, 2325–418

Richmond, I A, 1946 The four coloniae of Roman Britain, *Archaeol J* **103**, 57–84

Rhodes, M, 1980 Leather Footwear, in D M Jones, *Excavations at Billingsgate Buildings 'Triangle', Lower Thames Street, 1974*, London and Middlesex Archaeol Soc Special Paper No. **4**, 99–128

Roberts, C A, 1989 The human remains from 76 Kingsholm, Gloucester, Unpublished report, Calvin Wells Laboratory, University of Bradford, Bradford

Roberts, C, 1991 Trauma and treatment in the British Isles in the historic period: a design for multidisciplinary research, in D J Ortner and A C Aufderheide (eds), *Human Palaeopathology: Current Synthesis and Future Options*, Smithsonian Inst. Press, Washington, D.C., 225–40

Roberts, C A and Manchester, K, 1995 *The archaeology of disease*, 2nd edition, New York

Roberts, C and Cox, M, 2003 *Health and disease in Britain from prehistory to the present day*, Stroud

Roberts, C and Connell, B, 2004 Guidance on recording palaeopathology, in M Brickley and J I McKinley (eds), 34–9

Rogers, J and Waldron, T, 1995 *A Field Guide to Joint Disease in Archaeology*, Chichester

Rogers, J, Rogers, J, Watt, I and Dieppe, P, 1981 Arthritis in Saxon and Medieval skeletons, *British Medical Journal* **283**, 1668

Rosten, J, 2007 Identities in life and death in Roman Britain: the case of Baldock, in B Croxford, N Ray, R Roth and N White (eds), *TRAC 2006: Proceedings of the Sixteenth Annual Theoretical Roman Archaeology Conference*, Oxford, 172–82

Rousham, E K and Humphrey, L T, 2002 The dynamics of child survival, in H Macbeth and P Collinson (eds), *Human Population Dynamics: Cross-Disciplinary Perspectives*, 14th Biological Society Symposium Series, Cambridge, 124–40

Rowbotham, F W, 1978 The River Severn in Gloucester, *Glevensis* **12**, 4–10

Rudder, S, 1779 *A New History of Gloucester*, Cirencester

Sauer, E W, 2005 Inscriptions from Alchester: Vespasian's base of the Second Augustan Legio, *Britannia* **36**, 101–33

Saville, A, 1990 Hazelton North. *The Excavation of a Neolithic Long Cairn of the Cotswold-Severn Group*, English Heritage Archaeol Rep **13**, London

Scheuer, L and Black, S, 2000 *Developmental Juvenile Osteology*, London

Schmid, E, 1972 *Atlas of Animal Bones*, Amsterdam

Schreve, D C, 2001 Differentiation of the British late Middle Pleistocene interglacials: the evidence from mammalian biostratigraphy, *Quaternary Science Reviews* **20**, 1693–1705

Scott, E, 1991 Animal and infant burials in Romano-British villas: a revitalisation movement, in P Garwood, D Jennings, R Skeates and J Toms (eds), *Sacred and profane: proceedings of a conference on archaeology, ritual and religion, Oxford 1989*, OUCA Monograph **32**, Oxford, 115–21

Seeley, F, 1995 Roman doorbells, *Roman Finds Group Newsletter* **IX**, 5–6

Sermon, R, 1995 *Gloucester Archaeology Annual Report, 1995* http://www.gloucester.gov.uk/Content.aspx?cindex=149andcitem=6749andurn=1009

Sermon, R, 1996 *Gloucester Archaeology Annual Report, 1996* http://www.glos-city.gov.uk/Content.aspx?urn=1010

Sermon, R, 2003 Gloucester Archaeology Unit Annual Report 2002, *Glevensis* **36**, 55–63

Shennan, S, 1997 *Quantifying Archaeology*, Second edition, Edinburgh

Shipman, P, Foster, G, and Schoeninger, M, 1984 Burnt bones and teeth: an experimental study of colour, morphology, crystal structure and shrinkage, *J Archaeological Science* **11**, 307–25

Signoli *et al.*, 2004 Discovery of a mass grave of Napoleonic period in Lithuania (1812, Vilnius), *Comptes Rendus Palevol* **3**, Issue 3, 219–27

Sjøvold, T, 1984 A report on the heritability of some cranial measurements and non-metric traits, in G N van Vark and W W Howells (eds), *Multivariate Statistics in Physical Anthropology*, Dordrecht, The Netherlands, 223–46

Skinner, J D and Smithers, R H N, 1990 *The Mammals of the Southern African Subregion (New Edition)*, Pretoria

Skinner, M and Goodman, A H, 1992 Anthropological uses of developmental defects of enamel, in M A Katzenberg and S R Saunders (eds), *Skeletal Biology of Past Peoples: Research Methods*, New York, 153–74

Smith, B H, 1991 Standards of human tooth formation and dental age assessment, in M A Kelley and C S Larsen (eds), *Advances in Dental Anthropology*, New York, 143–68

Smith, P and Kahila, G, 1992 Identification of infanticide in archaeological sites: a case study from the late Roman—early Byzantine periods at Ashkelon, Israel, *J Archaeological Science* **19**, 667–75

Sparks, B W and West, R G, 1970 Late Pleistocene deposits at Wretton, Norfolk. 1. Ipswichian interglacial deposits, *Philosophical Transactions of the Royal Society of London* B258, 1–30

Spry, N, 1971 The Northgate Turnpike, *Journal of Gloucestershire Society for Industrial Archaeology*, 1–58

Staelens, Y, 1982 The Birdlip Cemetery, *Trans Bristol Gloucestershire Archaeol Soc* **100**, 20–31

Stead, I M and Rigby, V, 1989 *Verulamium. The King Harry Lane site*, English Heritage Archaeol Rep **12**

Steckel, R H, 1995 Stature and the standard of living, *Journal of Economic Literature* **33**, 1903–40

Stewart, T D, 1979 *Essentials of Forensic Anthropology*, Springfield

Stirland, A J, 1998 Musculoskeletal evidence for activity: problems of evaluation, *International J Osteoarchaeology* **8**, 341–62

Stringer, C B, Currant, A P, Schwarcz, H P and Collcutt, S N, 1986 Age of Pleistocene faunas from Bacon Hole, Wales, *Nature* **320**, 59–62

Stuart, A J, 1982a *Pleistocene vertebrates of the British Isles*, London

Stuart, A J, 1982b The occurrence of Hippopotamus in the British Pleistocene, *Quartärpaläontologie* **6**, 209–18

Stuart, A J and Lister, A M, 2001 The mammalian faunas of Pakefield/Kessingland and Corton, Suffolk, UK: evidence for a new temperate episode in the British early Middle Pleistocene, *Quaternary Science Reviews* **20**, 1677–92

Stuart-Macadam, P, 1985 Porotic hyperostosis: representative of a childhood condition, *American J Physical Anthropology* **66**, 391–8

Stuart-Macadam, P, 1991 Amaemia in Roman Britain: Poundbury camp, in H Bush and M Zvelebil (eds), *Health in Past Societies. Biocultural Interpretations of Human Skeletal Remains in Archaeological Contexts*, BAR Int Ser **567**, Oxford, 101–13

Stuiver, M and Kra, R S, 1986 Editorial comment, *Radiocarbon*, **28**(2B), ii

Stuiver, M and Polach, H A, 1977 Reporting of C^{14} data, *Radiocarbon*, **19**, 355–63

Sutherland, T, 2000 Recording the grave, in V Fiorato *et al.*, 36–44

Swift, E, 2000 *Regionality in Dress Accessories in the late Roman West*, Mongraphie Instrumentum **11**. Millau.

Sykes, N J, 2001 The Norman Conquest: a zooarchaeological perspective, unpublished Ph.D. thesis, University of Southampton

Sykes, N J, forthcoming The Rabbit, in T P O'Connor and N J Sykes (eds), *The Extinct and Introduced Fauna of Britain*

Tacitus, Annals of Tacitus: 'Annals' 1.1–54 Books 1–6 (Cambridge Classical Texts and Commentaries), Cambridge

Tatham, S, 2004 Aspects of health and population diversity in 10th–12th century Northern Europe, Unpublished Ph.D. thesis, University of Leicester

Taylor, A, 2001 *Burial Practice in Early England*, Stroud

Thomas, A, Holbrook, N and Bateman, C, 2003 *Later Prehistoric and Romano-British Burial and Settlement at Hucclecote, Gloucestershire*, Bristol and Gloucestershire Archaeol Rep **2**

Thomas, M, Gilbert, P, Bandelt, H-J, Hofreiter, M and Barnes, I, 2005 Assessing ancient DNA studies, *Trends in Ecology and Evolution* **20**, 541–3

Timby, J R, 1990 Severn Valley wares: a reassessment, *Britannia* **21**, 243–52

Timby, J R, 1991 The Berkeley Street kiln, Gloucester, *J Roman Pottery Studies* **4**, 19–31

Timby, J R, 1999 Pottery supply to Gloucester *colonia*, in H Hurst (ed.), 33–44

Timby, J R, forthcoming The pottery (from London Road). Publication report prepared for Foundations Archaeology (2004)

Tomlin, R S O and Hassall, M W C, 2005 Roman Britain in 2005. II. Inscriptions, *Britannia* **36**, 473–97

Toynbee, J M C, 1971 *Death and Burial in the Roman World*, Baltimore and London

Trinkhaus, E, 1985 Cannibalism and burial at Krapina, *J Human Evolution* **14**, 203–16

Trotter, M, 1970 Estimation of stature from intact long limb bones, in T D Stewart (ed.), *Personal Identification in Mass Disasters. [Report of a Seminar Held in Washington, D.C., 9–11 December 1968, by Arrangement Between the Support Services of the Department of the Army and the Smithsonian Institution]*, National Museum of Natural History, Washington D.C, 71–83

Trotter, M and Gleser, G C, 1952 Estimation of stature from long bones of American Whites and Negroes, *American J Physical Anthropology* **10**, 463–514

Trotter, M and Gleser, G C, 1958 A re-evaluation of estimation based on measurements of stature taken during life and long bones after death, *American J Physical Anthropology* **16**, 79–123

Tyrell, A, 2000 Skeletal non-metric traits and the assessment of inter- and intra-population diversity: past problems and future potential, in M Cox and S Mays (eds), *Human Osteology in Archaeology and Forensic Science*, London, 289–306

Ubelaker, D H, 1989 *Human Skeletal Remains. Excavation, Analysis, Interpretation*, 2nd edn, Taraxacum, Washington

Vennemann, T W, Fricke, H C, Blake, R E, O'Neil, J R and Coleman, A, 2002, Oxygen isotope analysis of phosphates: a comparison of techniques for analysis of Ag3PO4, *Chemical Geology* **185**, 321–36

Villa, P and Mahieu E, 1991 Breakage patterns of human long bones, *J Human Evolution* **21**, 27–48

von den Driesch, A, 1976 *A Guide to the Measurement of Animal Bones from Archaeological Sites*, Peabody Museum Bulletin **1**, Harvard

Wacher, J, 1995 *The Towns of Roman Britain, 2nd edition*, London

Waldron, H A and Cox, M, 1989 Occupational arthropathy: evidence from the past, *British Journal of Industrial Medicine* **46**, 420–22

Waldron, T, 1994 *Counting the Dead. The Epidemiology of Skeletal Populations*, Chichester

Waldron, T, 1998 A note on the estimation of height from long-bone measurements, *International J Osteoarchaeology* **8**, 75–7

Walker, P L, 1997 Wife beating, boxing and broken noses: skeletal evidence for the cultural patterning of violence, in D W Frayer and D C Martin (eds), *Troubled Times: Osteological and Archaeological Evidence of Violence*, Amsterdam, 145–79

Walker, P L, Dean, G and Shapiro, P, 1991 Estimating age from tooth wear in archaeological populations, in M A Kelley and C S Larsen (eds), *Advances in Dental Anthropology*, New York, 169–78

Warwick, R, 1968 The skeletal remains, in L P Wenham, 111–216

Webster, G, 1993 *The Roman invasion of Britain*, London

Wells, C, 1982a The human burials. South of the Fosse Way, in A McWhirr *et al.*, 135–96

Wells, C, 1982b The human burials. North of the Fosse Way, in A McWhirr *et al.*, 197–202

Wenham, L P, 1968 *The Romano-British Cemetery at Trentholme Drive, York*, HMSO, London

Wheeler, H, 1985 The racecourse cemetery, *Derbyshire Archaeol J* **105**, 222–80

Whimster, R, 1981 Burial Practices in Iron Age Britain, BAR Brit Ser **90**, Oxford

White, T D, 1992 *Prehistoric Cannibalism At Mancos 5MTUMR-2346*, Oxford

White, T D, 2003 *Human Osteology*, London

White, T D and Folkens, P A, 1991 *Human Osteology*, New York

Whiting, W, 1925 The Roman cemetery at Ospringe. Description of the finds continued, *Archaeologia Cantiana* **37**, 83–96

Wigg, A, 1993 Zu Funktion und Deutung der Aschengruben, in M Struck (ed.) *Römerzeitliche Gräber als Quellen zur Religion, Bevölkerungsstruktur und Sozialgeschichte*, Johannes Gutenberg Institut für Vor- und Frühgeschichte, Mainz

Wills, J (ed.), 2000 Archaeological Review No. 24 1999, *Trans Bristol Gloucestershire Archaeol Soc* **118**, 213–34

Wills, L J, 1938 The Pleistocene development of the Severn from Bridgenorth to the sea, *Quarterly Journal of the Geological Society of London* **94**, 161–242

Wols, H D and Baker, J E, 2004 Dental health of elderly confederate veterans: evidence from the Texas State cemetery, *American J Physical Anthropology* **124**, 59–72

Worley, F, forthcoming a. Taken to the Grave: An Archaeozoological Approach Assessing the Role of Animals as Crematory Offerings in First Millennium AD Britain

Worley, F, forthcoming b. Cremated animal bone, in P Booth *et al.* forthcoming

Worssam, B C, Ellison, R A and Moorlock, B S P, 1989 *Geology of the Country Around Tewkesbury*, Memoir of the British Geological Survey, Sheet 216 (England and Wales), London

Wright, R, 2003 Collecting Metric Data from Four Human Long Bones for an Experimental Commingling Study, Unpublished draft manuscript

Index

175

crouched . . . 12, 21, 125, 130, 135, 144–5
decapitated . . . 131, 133
distribution of . . . 21, 126
prone . . . 12, 16, 18, 21, 24–5, 81, 84, 86–7, 95, 101, 130–5, 138–9, 151
supine . . . 21–3, 132
urned . . . 19, 121
Burnt . . . 19, 73, 78, 121, 128, 130, 154–8
animal bone . . . 121, 154, 156
bone grave assemblages . . . 121
bones . . . 9, 73–4, 119–21, 138

C
Catherine's Church . . . 5, 129–30
Cattle . . . 119–21
Cemetery
population . . . 62–3, 65, 71
urban . . . 123, 125–7, 130, 132, 135
Wotton . . . 4–7, 123–30, 134–6, 138
Cenotaph . . . 25–6, 120, 134, 137
Children . . . 19, 29, 59, 68, 79, 107–8, 111, 138, 143–4
burials of . . . 20, 138
Cinerary urns . . . 5, 6, 11–2, 19, 21, 72, 96–9, 105, 115, 122, 129–30
Cirencester . . . 6, 32, 34, 46–7, 51, 53–7, 62–3, 65, 71, 121, 132, 141
Cist . . . 24, 94, 133–4
Claudio-Neronian . . . 99, 116–8, 136
Clavicle . . . 40, 54–6, 63–4, 68, 149, 155–7
Coffin . . . 5, 7, 13, 24–5, 85–93, 95, 115–6, 132–4, 138–9, 151
nails . . . 8, 88
Coins . . . 5–7, 86, 103, 130, 132, 137, 139, 145
Colchester . . . 1, 108, 117, 125
Collagen . . . 28, 73
Colonia Nerva . . . 4, 144
Congenital syphilis . . . 45, 48, 71
Consumption . . . 43, 122, 128–9, 136–7
Containers, organic . . . 24, 73–4
Copper alloy . . . 13, 26, 110, 112–4, 134
Counters . . . 105–10
bone . . . 105–7
Cranial . . . 30, 33, 41, 52, 63, 96–7, 154, 156
vault . . . 50, 52, 60–2, 154–8
fragment of . . . 148–9
Cremated bone . . . 8, 19, 28, 72–4, 76, 78–9, 115, 119, 127–9, 137
deposits of . . . 73, 128–9
samples . . . 28
Cremation . . . 5–9, 19, 72–3, 75, 78, 81, 96, 119, 122, 126, 128, 136–8, 144, 154–5
burial deposits . . . 119
burials . . . 5, 6, 9, 10, 12, 19–21, 73–7, 85, 96–7, 99, 102–6, 108–10, 115–6, 120–5, 127–30, 137–9, 141, 154–8
urned . . . 6–9, 12, 19, 73, 79, 96–7, 99, 100, 103, 105, 120, 129
deposit . . . 8, 19, 96–8, 121, 129, 154, 157
process . . . 72–3, 79, 121
Crest, nuchal . . . 76, 148–9, 154
Cribra orbitalia . . . 46, 52–4, 62–3, 81, 86–90, 94–5
Crossbones . . . 31–2, 36–7, 70, 31–2, 37, 70
application of . . . 31, 36

Limb bones 51, 70
  lower 30, 32, 37, 54, 59, 63, 68, 70, 72–3, 154–8
  upper 37–8, 54, 63, 75, 154–8
London Road 1, 5–9, 28–9, 32, 34, 51, 53–7, 69, 71–2, 77–9, 102–4,
                                                    121–36, 138–9, 141, 143–5, 162–3
Long bones 29, 30, 36, 40, 65, 74–9, 84, 96–7, 121, 149, 154–8
  fragments of 75, 78, 96–7, 148–9, 154, 156–8, 160
  sized 97, 157

M
Male
  adolescent 21, 56, 60, 65, 132
  adult 13, 24, 51, 53, 56–7, 59, 65–6, 114, 145, 148
Mandibles 35, 37, 45, 50, 75, 147
Mastoid foramen 34–5, 42
Maxilla 45, 74, 154, 156, 158
Medieval 7, 8, 26, 99, 118, 120
  assemblage 119–20
Metacarpals 36, 51, 55–6, 61, 65, 75, 88, 90, 148–9, 154–6, 158, 161
Metatarsals 51, 59, 61–3, 75–6, 78, 86, 149, 155–6, 158
Molars 45, 48, 50–1, 75, 147–8, 155–8, 161
  lower 148, 155–6
  third 45, 48, 75, 155
Mourners 78–9, 127, 131, 134, 136

N
Nails 13, 24, 84, 86–90, 95, 97, 115–6, 133, 135
  Fe 151
Native population 123, 125, 144–5
Necrosis 59, 60
Neronian 9, 12, 99, 100
Neurocranium 154–8

O
OA (Osteoarthritis)
  see osteoarthritis
Occipital bone 39, 40, 50, 52, 56, 73, 77, 86, 148–9, 154–6, 158
Offerings 128–9, 139
Orbits 52–4, 73–4
Osteoarthritis 8, 54, 57–60, 63, 65, 68–70, 77, 84, 86–92, 94–5, 157
  rib 86, 88, 95
Osteomyelitis 45, 50–1, 62, 67, 70, 88
Osteophytosis 57, 59, 77, 84, 87–8, 91–2, 94
Oxidised ware 101
Oxygen isotopes 150, 152–3

P
Painswick Hill 116, 159
Painswick Stone 159
Patella 75, 148–9, 154
Pelvis 15, 18, 21–3, 30, 32, 40, 60, 74–5, 84–9, 92–3, 95–7, 120, 131, 154–6, 158
Periodontal disease 44–5, 47, 147
Periodontitis 42, 45, 47–50, 68, 84, 86, 88–9, 96, 148
  Musculo-skeletal markers 81, 86–8, 90, 95
Periostitis 50–2, 59, 61–2, 65, 67–8, 71, 76–7, 86, 88, 157–8
  active 83, 87, 89, 91–3, 158
  healed 83–92, 94–5
Phalanges 36, 65, 75, 88, 91, 149, 154, 156
Phalanx, hand 88, 149, 154
Pigs 97, 119–22, 128, 156, 158

W